[英 汉 对 照]

西方学术经典文库

神圣者的观念

THE IDEA OF THE HOLY

[德] 鲁道夫·奥托 著

丁建波 译

九州出版社
JIUZHOUPRESS

图书在版编目(CIP)数据

神圣者的观念:英汉对照/(德)奥托著;丁建波译.
北京:九州出版社,2007.4
(西方学术经典文库)
ISBN 978-7-80195-571-5

Ⅰ.神… Ⅱ.①奥…②丁… Ⅲ.宗教哲学—英、汉
Ⅳ.B920

中国版本图书馆 CIP 数据核字(2007)第 048754 号

神圣者的观念

作　　者	[德]鲁道夫·奥托　著　　丁建波　译
责任编辑	周红斌
出版发行	九州出版社
地　　址	北京市西城区阜外大街甲 35 号
邮政编码	100037
网　　址	www.jiuzhoupress.com
电子信箱	jiuzhou@jiuzhoupress.com
印　　刷	九洲财鑫印刷有限公司
开　　本	630×970mm　1/16
印　　张	27.25
字　　数	290 千字
版　　次	2007 年 4 月第 1 版
印　　次	2007 年 4 月第 1 次印刷
书　　号	ISBN　978-7-80195-571-5/C·122
定　　价	56.00 元

出版说明

在西方学术思想的发展流变中，出现过很多影响深远的经典著作，这些著作穿越时空，为人们长久研读，有的甚至影响了整个人类文明的发展进程。这套《西方学术经典文库》（英汉对照本），精选了其中最有代表性的一些名著，计划达到一百部，将陆续分批出版直至全部完成。

《西方学术经典文库》由多位专家学者指导分类选目，内容涵盖哲学、文学、宗教学、政治学、经济学、社会学、人类学、心理学、法学、历史学等类，注重权威性、学术性和影响性，收录了不同国家、不同时代、不同流派的诸多名著。

《西方学术经典文库》中译本译自英文原著或其他文种的英文译本，以英汉对照的形式出版，读者可以参照原文对作品有更加客观的理解，更好地把握西方学术思想的精髓。

为加以区别，原文中的英文注释，注释号用①、②……形式表示；中文译者注释则以〔1〕、〔2〕……形式表示。至于英译本中出现的原文页码和特殊索引等问题，中文译者在“译者后记”中将予以解释、说明。另外，在英文原著中，有一些表示着重意义的斜体或大写等字体，考虑到读者可以在对照英文阅读中看到，因此在中译文中，没有照样标出，还望读者理解。

九州出版社

The Idea Of The Holy
By *Rudolf Otto*
English Translation
By *John W. Harvey*

本书根据　Oxford University Press 1964 年版本译出

CONTENTS

目　录

CHAPTER I

The Rational And The Non-Rational

It is essential to every theistic conception of God, and most of all to the Christian, that it designates and precisely characterizes deity by the attributes spirit, reason, purpose, good will, supreme power, unity, selfhood. The nature of God is thus thought of by analogy with our human nature of reason and personality; only, whereas in ourselves we are aware of this as qualified by restriction and limitation, as applied to God the attributes we use are 'completed', i. e. thought as absolute and unqualified. Now all these attributes constitute clear and definite *concepts*: they can be grasped by the intellect; they can be analysed by thought; they even admit of definition. An object that can thus be thought conceptually may be termed *rational*. The nature of deity described in the attributes above mentioned is, then, a rational nature; and a religion which recognizes and maintains such a view of God is in so far a 'rational' religion. Only on such terms is *belief* possible in contrast to mere *feeling*. And of Christianity at least it is false that 'feeling is all, the name but sound and smoke';[①]—where 'name' stands for conception or thought. Rather we count this the very mark and criterion of a religion's high rank and superior value—that it should have no lack of *conceptions* about God; that it should admit knowledge—the knowledge that comes by faith—of the transcendent in terms of conceptual thought, whether those already mentioned or others which continue and develop them. Christianity not only possesses such conceptions but

① Goethe, *Faust*.

第一章　理性与非理性

对于任何一种有神论的神的观念，尤其是对于基督教的上帝观念来说，用精神、理性、目的、善良意志、最高权能、统一、自性等特性来标示和精确地描述神性，都是至关重要的。这样，对神之本质的思考就来自于人的与神相类似的理性与人格的本质，只不过，我们都很清楚，这些特性在被用于人自身时是有所限定的；而在被用于上帝时，则是完备的，也就是说，是绝对的，毫无限制的。现在，所有的特性都可以形成清晰明确的概念：这些概念能被理智把握，能被思想分析，甚至能被定义。一种能这样用概念思考把握的对象就可以被称做理性的。那么，用上述特性所描述的神性本质就是一种理性本质，而用这种观点来认识和对待上帝的宗教就是理性的宗教。只有以这些理性概念为基础的信仰，才能够与纯粹的情感相抗衡。至少对基督教来说，说“情感就是一切，名号只是虚声”①是错误的——在这里“名号”指的是概念和思想。在更大程度上，我们把理性概念视作一种宗教的较高层次、较大价值的标志和尺度，这种宗教不会缺乏关于上帝的观念，它会以概念思维的形式承认那些无论是已经提到过的还是继承和发展的关于超越者的知识——也就是通过信仰得到的知识。基督教不仅拥有这些概念，而且在拥有这些概念方面

① 歌德《浮士德》。

possesses them in unique clarity and abundance, and this is, though not the sole or even the chief, yet a very real sign of its superiority over religions of other forms and at other levels. This must be asserted at the outset and with the most positive emphasis.

But, when this is granted, we have to be on our guard against an error which would lead to a wrong and one-sided interpretation of religion. This is the view that the essence of deity can be given completely and exhaustively in such 'rational' attributions as have been referred to above and in others like them. It is not an unnatural misconception. We are prompted to it by the traditional language of edification, with its characteristic phraseology and ideas; by the learned treatment of religious themes in sermon and theological instruction; and further even by our Holy Scriptures themselves. In all these cases the 'rational' element occupies the foreground, and often nothing else seems to be present at all. But this is after all to be expected. All language, in so far as it consists of words, purports to convey ideas or concepts;—that is what language means;—and the more clearly and unequivocally it does so, the better the language. And hence expositions of religious truth in language inevitably tend to stress the 'rational' attributes of God.

But though the above mistake is thus a natural one enough, it is none the less seriously misleading. For so far are these 'rational' attributes from exhausting the idea of deity, that they in fact imply a nonrational or supra-rational Subject of which they are predicates. They are 'essential' (and not merely 'accidental') attributes of that subject, but they are also, it is important to notice, *synthetic* essential attributes. That is to say, we have to predicate them of a subject which they qualify, but which in its deeper essence is not, nor indeed can be, comprehended in them; which rather requires comprehension of a quite different kind. Yet, though it eludes the conceptual way of understanding, it must be in some way or other within our grasp, else absolutely nothing could be asserted of it. And even mysticism, in speaking of it as

表现出其独有的清晰与丰富,就此而言——尽管不是唯一的或者甚至不是主要的,但这正是基督教优于其他形式的以及处于不同层面的宗教的真正标志。这是在一开始就必须正面加以确认的。

但是,尽管承认这一点,我们也必须提防下面一种误解,它会把我们引向对宗教的错误的和片面的理解。这种观点就是:神的本性能够通过上述的或在别处提到的"理性的"性质被完备地彻底地表达出来,这并不是一种不合情理的误解。通过传统的训导语言和它特有的术语与观念,通过对在传道和神学教诲中出现的奇迹问题的专业处理,甚至通过《圣经》的经文本身,我们都很容易陷入上述错误。在这些情形中,"理性的"因素非常突出,而其他因素则丝毫没有显露出来,不过这也在意料之中。一切语言——只要它是由词汇构成的——都声称以传达观念或者概念为业,而这正是语言的意义所在;一种语言在概念与观念的表达上越是清晰明确,这种语言就越好。因此,通过语言来阐释宗教真理,就不可避免地要倾向于强调上帝的是"理性"的性质。

尽管上述错误是再自然不过的了,但是,它仍不失为严重的误导。由于这些"理性的"性质根本不能穷尽神性观念,它们事实上意味着一种非理性或者超理性的主体,而这些性质就是这一主体的诸多属性。它们是那一主体的"根本的"(而不仅仅是"偶然的")性质,但是必须注意的是,它们也是一些假想的根本性质。也就是说,我们不得不借助它们来界定那个由它们修饰的主体,但是那一主体的更深的本质却不是、事实上也不能通过它们来领会,而更要靠一种完全不同的领会。然而,尽管这一主体总是躲避着概念式的理解方式,但它必然会以某种方式为我们所把握,否则,我们对它就绝对没有任何可说的了。即便是神秘主义——

τὸ ἄρρητον, the ineffable, does not really mean to imply that absolutely nothing can be asserted of the object of the religious consciousness; otherwise, mysticism could exist only in unbroken silence, whereas what has generally been a characteristic of the mystics is their copious eloquence.

Here for the first time we come up against the contrast between rationalism and profounder religion, and with this contrast and its signs we shall be repeatedly concerned in what follows. We have here in fact the first and most distinctive mark of rationalism, with which all the rest are bound up. It is not that which is commonly asserted, that rationalism is the denial, and its opposite the affirmation, of the miraculous. That is manifestly a wrong or at least a very superficial distinction. For the traditional theory of the miraculous as the occasional breach in the causal nexus in nature by a Being who himself instituted and must therefore be master of it—this theory is itself as massively 'rational' as it is possible to be. Rationalists have often enough acquiesced in the possibility of the miraculous in this sense; they have even themselves contributed to frame a theory of it;—whereas anti-rationalists have been often indifferent to the whole controversy about miracles. The difference between rationalism and its opposite is to be found elsewhere. It resolves itself rather into a peculiar difference of *quality* in the mental attitude and emotional content of the religious life itself. All depends upon this: in our idea of God is the non-rational overborne, even perhaps wholly excluded, by the rational? Or conversely, does the non-rational itself preponderate over the rational? Looking at the matter thus, we see that the common dictum, that orthodoxy itself has been the mother of rationalism, is in some measure well founded. It is not simply that orthodoxy was preoccupied with doctrine and the framing of dogma, for these have been no less a concern of the wildest mystics. It is rather that orthodoxy found in the construction of dogma and doctrine no way to do justice to the non-rational aspect of its subject. So far from keeping the non-rational element in religion alive in the heart of the religious

当它把这一主体当作不可言说之物来谈论时——也并不是真的意味着宗教意识的对象就是真的绝对不可言说,不然,神秘主义就只能存在于沉寂之中,然而,神秘主义者的一个总的特征就是他们的滔滔雄辩。

在这里,我们首次遭遇到理性主义与更深刻的宗教之间的冲突,而且在下面我们还要反复提及这种冲突及其表现。事实上,我们在这里即应获得了理性主义的最主要的也是最显著的特征,而它的其他特征都是与此紧密联系在一起的。它并不是人们通常所确认的理性主义否定奇迹,而宗教则相反,是对奇迹的肯定。这很显然是一种错误的或者至少是十分肤浅的区别。传统的奇迹理论将奇迹视为自然的因果链条的偶然断裂,而这一因果链条及其断裂都是由一个存在者创立并控制的——这一理论本身就不能再是非常"理性的"了。理性主义者们一贯默认这种意义上的奇迹,甚至自己也对建构这种理论作出了贡献,而与之相反,反理性主义者们则往往对有关奇迹的整个争论持漠不关心的态度。理性主义与其对立面之间的区别要到其他地方去找寻。这种区别甚至将自己与宗教生活中的精神态度与情感内容的质的区别缠绕在一起。所有这些都取决于这一点:在我们关于上帝的观念中,是非理性主义被理性主义压服甚至是被完全地排斥呢,或者相反,是非理性主义胜过了理性主义呢?如此看来,我们便发现,那种把正统观念视为理性主义之根的普通格言在一定意义上是颇有根据的。这不单是因为正统派专注于教义与教条的建构,还因为这些还牵涉到那些最狂热的神秘主义者。原因更在于正统派在建构教条与教义时,找不到能够公正地对待主体的非理性方面的途径。由于远未做到将宗教中的非理性因素活生生地保留在宗教体验

experience, orthodox Christianity manifestly failed to recognize its value, and by this failure gave to the idea of God a one-sidedly intellectualistic and rationalistic interpretation.

This bias to rationalization still prevails, not only in theology but in the science of comparative religion in general, and from top to bottom of it. The modern students of mythology, and those who pursue research into the religion of ' primitive man ' and attempt to reconstruct the ' bases ' or ' sources ' of religion, are all victims to it. Men do not, of course, in these cases employ those lofty ' rational ' concepts which we took as our point of departure; but they tend to take these concepts and their gradual ' evolution ' as setting the main problem of their inquiry, and fashion ideas and notions of lower value, which they regard as paving the way for them. It is always in terms of concepts and ideas that the subject is pursued, ' natural ' ones, moreover, such as have a place in the general sphere of man's ideational life, and are not specifically ' religious '. And then with a resolution and cunning which one can hardly help admiring, men shut their eyes to that which is quite unique in the religious experience, even in its most primitive manifestations. But it is rather a matter for astonishment than for admiration! For if there be any single domain of human experience that presents us with something unmistakably specific and unique, peculiar to itself, assuredly it is that of the religious life. In truth the enemy has often a keener vision in this matter than either the champion of religion or the neutral and professedly impartial theorist. For the adversaries on their side know very well that the entire ' pother about mysticism ' has nothing to do with ' reason ' and ' rationality '.

And so it is salutary that we should be incited to notice that religion is not exclusively contained and exhaustively comprised in any series of ' rational ' assertions; and it is well worth while to attempt to bring the relation of the different ' moments ' of religion to one another clearly before the mind,

的核心,正统的基督教显然没有认识到非理性的价值,并且由于这种错误,他们赋予上帝观念以片面的理智主义的和理性主义的解释。

这种理性化的倾向不仅仍然主宰着神学,而且也完全主宰着一般的比较宗教学的研究。那些神话学的现代研究者们,以及那些将研究深入到“原始人”的宗教中并力图重新建构起宗教的“基础”和“源泉”的人,都是这种理性化倾向的受害者。当然了,在这些研究中,人们并没有采用我们引为出发点的神圣的“理性的”概念,但是他们倾向于使用这些概念以及概念的逐步“进化”来设定他们所探究的主要问题、制定一些具有较低价值的观念与看法,并以此来拓展道路。人们总是以“自然的”概念或者观念的形式来述诸该主题,这些概念或者观念都存在于人们的观念生活的一般范围之中,而且并不是十分“宗教的”。然后,通过一种让人不得不羡慕的坚定和狡黠,人们断然无视那些在宗教体验中非常独特的东西,即便它们是最原始的信仰形式。但是这一点与其说让人欣羡,不如说让人震惊!因为,如果有一个关于人类经验的独特领域,它能为我们展示出尤其对于其自身来说是毫无疑问的特别而独具的东西,那么,这无疑就是宗教生活。事实上,无论是比起宗教的斗士还是中立的、保持着职业的不偏不倚的理论家,宗教的敌人对这一问题的见解都更加敏锐。从他们的立场出发,反对者非常清楚,所有的“关于神秘主义的争吵”都与“理智”和“理性”毫不相干。

因此,对我们有利的一点就是,我们应当被激励着去注意,宗教并不是由一系列“理性的”断言所独断地彻底地构成的。同时,努力把不同的宗教“要素”之间的关系清晰地揭示出来,从而使宗

so that its nature may become more manifest.

This attempt we are now to make with respect to the quite distinctive category of the holy or sacred.

教的本质更加清晰明白,也是一件值得去做的事情。

目前我们所要致力于其中的,就是“神圣”这一十分特殊的范畴。

CHAPTER II

' Numen' And The ' Numinous'

' Holiness'—' the holy'—is a category of interpretation and valuation peculiar to the sphere of religion. It is, indeed, applied by transference to another sphere—that of ethics—but it is not itself derived from this. While it is complex, it contains a quite specific element or ' moment', which sets it apart from ' the rational' in the meaning we gave to that word above, and which remains inexpressible—an ἄρρητον or *ineffabile*—in the sense that it compltely cludes apprehension in terms of concepts. The same thing is true (to take a quite different region of experience) of the category of the beautiful.

Now these statements would be untrue from the outset if ' the holy' were merely what is meant by the word, not only in common parlance, but in philosophical, and generally even in theological usage. The fact is we have come to use the words ' holy', ' sacred' (*heilig*) in an entirely derivative sense, quite different from that which they originally bore. We generally take ' holy' as meaning ' completely good'; it is the absolute moral attribute, denoting the consummation of moral goodness. In this sense Kant calls the will which remains unwaveringly obedient to the moral law from the motive of duty a ' holy' will; here clearly we have simply the *perfectly moral* will. In the same way we may speak of the holiness or sanctity of duty or law, meaning merely that they are imperative upon conduct and universally obligatory.

But this common usage of the term is inaccurate. It is true that all this moral significance is contained in the word ' holy', but it includes in addition—as even we cannot but feel—a clear overplus of meaning, and this it is now our taskto isolate. Nor is this merely a

第二章 “神秘”与“神秘者”

“神圣”即“神圣者”，是宗教领域中一个特有的解释与评价范畴。事实上，它也被转用于其他的领域，如伦理学，但它本身却不是从这一领域中来的。尽管它有些复杂，但是，这一范畴却包含着十分独特的因素或者“要素”，这种因素或“要素”不同于上述我们给予“理性”这一词的含义，并且由于无法使用概念来把握，它也是不可言说的。关于美的范畴（就一个完全不同的经验领域来说）也是如此。

如果“神圣”一词不仅在普通的用法上，而且在哲学甚至是神学的用法上仅仅是其字面意思，那么，上述说法从一开始就是完全错误的。事实上，我们只是在完全派生的意义上使用 holy、sacred（*heilig*）等词的，这种含义与其本义相去甚远。通常我们用“神圣”来表示“完全的善”，这是一种绝对的道德性质，指的是道德至善。在这一意义上，康德将那种出于责任的动机而坚决服从道德律的意志称为“神圣”意志。很显然，这里我们所得到的仅仅是完全道德的意志。用同样的方式，我们还可以谈论责任或者法律的神圣性，但是这也仅仅意味着它们在行动上的必要性和普遍的强制性。

但是，对“神圣”一词的这种普通用法是不正确的。的确，所有的道德含义都包含在“神圣”一词之中，但是除此之外，它还包含着（即便是我们只能感觉到）一种明显的额外含义，而当下我们

later or acquired meaning; rather, 'holy', or at least the equivalent words in Latin and Greek, in Semitic and other ancient languages, denoted first and foremost *only* this overplus: if the ethical element was present at all, at any rate it was not original and never constituted the whole meaning of the word. Any one who uses it today does undoubtedly always feel 'the morally good' to be implied in 'holy'; and accordingly in our inquiry into that element which is separate and peculiar to the idea of the holy it will be useful, at least for the temporary purpose of the investigation, to invent a special term to stand for 'the holy' *minus* its moral factor or 'moment', and, as we can now add, minus its 'rational' aspect altogether.

It will be our endeavour to suggest this unnamed Something to the reader as far as we may, so that he may himself feel it. There is no religion in which it does not live as the real innermost core, and without it no religion would be worthy of the name. It is pre-eminently a living force in the Semitic religions, and of these again in none has it such vigour as in that of the Bible. Here, too, it has a name of its own, viz. the Hebrew *qãdôsh*, to which the Greek *ἅγιος* and the Latin *sanctus*, and, more accurately still, *sacer*, are the corresponding terms. It is not, of course, disputed that these terms in all three languages connote, as part of their meaning, *good*, *absolute goodness*, when, that is, the notion has ripened and reached the highest stage in its development. And we then use the word 'holy' to translate them. But this 'holy' then represents the gradual shaping and filling in with ethical meaning, or what we shall call the 'schematization', of what was a unique original feeling-response, which can be in itself ethically neutral and claims consideration in its own right. And when this moment or element first emerges and begins

的任务就是将这一额外含义分离出来。这种含义绝不是后来才获得的,相反,“神圣”一词或者至少是拉丁语、希腊语、闪米特语以及其他古代语言中的同等的词汇,它的首先或者最主要的意义,都仅仅是这一额外含义:即便其中都包含有伦理的因素,但是无论如何这些伦理因素都绝不是原初的,而且绝对不能构成该词的全部含义。今天任何一个使用该词的人,无疑都会感受到包含在“神圣”一词中的“道德的善”。因此,在我们探究神圣观念的独特因素时,创造一个专门的术语来代表“神圣”,剔除其中的道德因素,同时(就像我们能够加上一样)一块儿去除其中“理性的”方面,这将是有所裨益的——至少就我们当下的研究目的来说是这样的。

我们将尽我们所能向读者暗示这种尚未命名的东西,以便读者能自己感受到它。任何一种宗教的最核心处都有这种东西存在,如果没有它,宗教也就不成其为宗教了。在闪米特人的宗教中,它是一种卓越的活生生的力量,而这种力量在任何一种宗教中,都不及在《圣经》中那样具有活力。同样,在《圣经》中,这种东西已经拥有了自己的名字,这就是希伯来语的 *qādôsh*,希腊语的 *ἅγιος*,拉丁语的 *sanctus*(更确切地说,应当是 *sacer*),都是与之相当的词。当然,无可争议的是,当这一概念逐渐成熟起来并达到它发展的最高阶段时,上述三种语言中的这些词汇也都把善、至善作为部分的含义包含在自身之中。那么我们就用“神圣”一词来翻译它们。不过这个“神圣”在那时所代表的是逐渐成形和逐渐充实的伦理含义,或者是那种我们应当称之为“图式化”的做法,即对于一种独特的原初性的情感反应的图式化处理——这种情感反应可以只是纯伦理性的并要求只从它本身的权力来考虑。

its long development, all those expressions (*qādôsh*, *ἅγιος*, *sacer*, &c.) mean beyond all question something quite other than 'the good'. This is universally agreed by contemporary criticism, which rightly explains the rendering of *qādôsh* by 'good' as a mistranslation and unwarranted 'rationalization' or 'moralization' of the term.

Accordingly, it is worth while, as we have said, to find a word to stand for this element in isolation, this 'extra' in the meaning of 'holy' above and beyond the meaning of goodness. By means of a special term we shall the better be able, first, to keep the meaning clearly apart and distinct, and second, to apprehend and classify connectedly whatever subordinate forms or stages of development it may show. For this purpose I adopt a word coined from the Latin *numen*. Omen has given us 'ominous', and there is no reason why from *numen* we should not similarly form a word 'numinous'. I shall speak, then, of a unique 'numinous' category of value and of a definitely 'numinous' state of mind, which is always found wherever the category is applied. This mental state is perfectly *sui generis* and irreducible to any other; and therefore, like every absolutely primary and elementary datum, while it admits of being discussed, it cannot be strictly defined. There is only one way to help another to an understanding of it. He must be guided and led on by consideration and discussion of the matter through the ways of his own mind, until he reach the point at which 'the numinous' in him perforce begins to stir, to start into life and into consciousness. We can co-operate in this process by bringing before his notice all that can be found in other regions of the mind, already known and familiar, to resemble, or again to afford some special contrast to, the particular experience we wish to elucidate. Then we must add: 'This X of ours is not precisely *this* experience, but akin to this one and the opposite ofthat other. Cannot you now realize for yourself

当这种要素或因素出现并开始其漫长的发展时，所有这些词汇（*qādôsh*，*ἅγιος*，*sacer*，*& c.*）都毫无疑问地意味着与“善”大不相同的东西。这种观点已经为当代批评界所普遍认同，正是当代批评界正确地揭示了以“善”来译 *qādôsh* 是一种误译，是对这一术语的没有根据的“理性化处理”或者“道德化处理”。

相应地，正如我们所说过的，找一个语词来指称这种分离出来的因素，即上述“神圣”含义之外的并且超出了善的含义的那个“额外”部分，是十分有意义的。凭借这一特殊词汇，首先，我们就可以更好地把那层含义更清晰明确地标示出来；其次，我们也将更好地从联系的方面去理解、区分它随后显示出来的发展中的次生形式或阶段。为了这个目的，我采用了一个借助于拉丁文的 *numen* 而创制的词汇。既然 Omen（预兆）可以产生 ominous（有预兆的），那么就没有任何理由说，我们不可以从 *numen* 相似地造出一个 numinous。那么，我就需要说一说独特的“神秘的”价值范畴的与明确的“神秘的”心态——这种心态在使用该范畴的地方都可以发现。这种心态完全自成一类（*suigeneris*），不能简化为其他类，因此，就像每一个绝对重要和基本的公理一样，它们允许讨论，却不能被严格地界定。帮助他人理解这种心态的途径只有一条：他必须通过自己的心灵对这种心态加以考虑和探讨，从而得到引导，直到这种“神秘者”在他的生活和意识中不由自主地生发出来。在这个过程中，我们可以相互配合，即让他注意在他心灵的其他地方所能找到的所有那些已经了解并且熟悉的东西，来类比或者再次专门对比那些我们意欲阐明的特殊经验。然后我们还要作如下补充：“我们的这个 X 并不恰好就是这种经验，但却类似于这个经验而

what it is?' In other words our X cannot, strictly speaking, be taught, it can only be evoked, awakened in the mind; as everything that comes 'of the spirit' must be awakened.

与别的经验相冲突。难道到现在你还认识不到它是什么吗?”换言之,我们的这个 X 严格地说来是不能教的,它只能在心中被激起与唤醒,就像任何一种东西,只要“出自精神”,那就必须被唤醒。

CHAPTER III

The Elements In The 'Numinous'

Creature-Feeling

The reader is invited to direct his mind to a moment of deeply-felt religious experience, as little as possible qualified by other forms of consciousness. Whoever cannot do this, whoever knows no such moments in his experience, is requested to read no farther; for it is not easy to discuss questions of religious psychology with one who can recollect the emotions of his adolescence, the discomforts of indigestion, or, say, social feelings, but cannot recall any intrinsically religious feelings. We do not blame such an one, when he tries for himself to advance as far as he can with the help of such principles of explanation as he knows, interpreting 'aesthetics' in terms of sensuous pleasure, and 'religion' as a function of the gregarious instinct and social standards, or as something more primitive still. But the artist, who for his part has an intimate personal knowledge of the distinctive element in the aesthetic experience, will decline his theories with thanks, and the religious man will reject them even more uncompromisingly.

Next, in the probing and analysis of such states of the soul as that of solemn worship, it will be well if regard be paid to what is unique in them rather than to what they have in common with other similar states. To be *rapt* in worship is one thing; to be morally *uplifted* by the contemplation of a good deed is another; and it is not to their common features, but to those elements of emotional content peculiar to the first that we would have attention directed as precisely as possible. As Christians we undoubtedly here first meet with feelings familiar enough in a weaker form in other departments of experience, such

第三章 “神秘者”的诸因素

被造感

首先,我们请读者以一种宗教体验的瞬间深刻感受来导引自己的心灵,尽量不用别的意识形式来描摹这种经验。谁做不到这一点,对自己体验中的这种瞬间一无所知,那就不要再继续读下去了。因为对于那些能够回想起儿时的情绪、因消化不良引起的不适,或者说,能记起社会性的情感却丝毫都记不起内在的宗教情感的人,是很难与他讨论有关宗教心理的问题的。当一个人试图借助于他所知道的解释原理——如以感官愉悦来解释“美学”、以社交本能和社会标准或者更加原始的某种东西来解释“宗教”——来尽可能地自我提升时,我们是不会责怪他的。不过,那些对审美体验中的独特元素了如指掌的艺术家们会婉言谢绝他的解释,而宗教信徒则会更加坚定地拒斥之。

其次,在探究和分析诸如庄严崇拜这样的心灵状态时,我们应该把注意力集中在这种心态所独有的东西上,而不要集中在那些与类似心态所共有的东西上。沉迷于崇拜是一回事,通过冥思善行而得到道德上的鼓舞是另一回事。我们所要尽可能认真关注的不是它们共有的特点,而是那些为前者所独具的情感因素。作为基督徒,无疑我们在这里首先遇到了一些以较弱的形式存在于其

as feelings of gratitude, trust, love, reliance, humble submission, and dedication. But this does not by any means exhaust the content of religious worship. Not in any of these have we got the special features of the quite unique and incomparable experience of solemn worship. In what does this consist?

Schleiermacher has the credit of isolating a very important element in such an experience. This is the 'feeling of dependence'. But this important discovery of Schleiermacher is open to criticism in more than one respect.

In the first place, the feeling or emotion which he really has in mind in this phrase is in its specific quality not a 'feeling of dependence' in the 'natural' sense of the word. As such, other domains of life and other regions of experience than the religious occasion the feeling, as a sense of personal insufficiency and impotence, a consciousness of being determined by circumstances and environment. The feeling of which Schleiermacher wrote has an undeniable analogy with these states of mind: they serve as an indication to it, and its nature may be elucidated by them, so that, by following the direction in which they point, the feeling itself may be spontaneously felt. But the feeling is at the same time also qualitatively different from such analogous states of mind. Schleiermacher himself, in a way, recognizes this by distinguishing the feeling of pious or religious dependence from all other feelings of dependence. His mistake is in making the distinction merely that between 'absolute' and 'relative' dependence, and therefore a difference of degree and not of intrinsic quality. What he overlooks is that, in giving the feeling the name 'feeling of dependence' at all, we are really employing what is no more than a very close analogy. Anyone who compares and contrasts the two states of mind introspectively will find out, I think, what I mean. It cannot be expressed by means of anything else, just because it is so primary and elementary a datum in our psychical life, and

他体验领域中的非常熟悉的感情，诸如感激之情、信任之情、喜爱之情、信赖之情、谦卑驯顺以及奉献之情等。但是，这些并没有穷尽宗教崇拜的内涵。在上面所述的各种情感因素中，我们都找不到庄严崇拜的那种独一无二的同时又是无与伦比的经验的特征。这些特征会存在于什么地方呢？

施莱尔马赫因从这种体验中分离出一个非常重要的因素而声名卓著。这个重要因素就是"依赖感"。但是施氏的这一重要发现还有很多方面值得商榷。

首先，在他心中，"依赖感"这一术语中所包含的感觉或者情感是就其特殊意义而言的，并不是该词的"自然"意义。这种情感更多地从其他生活领域和其他体验领域中而不是从宗教生活经验中产生出来，诸如人对欠缺与无能为力的感觉，即对受制于条件与环境的感觉等。施莱尔马赫笔下的"依赖感"与这些心态有着无法否定的相似性：这些心态对"依赖感"起着一种指示作用，而"依赖感"的本质能被这些心态所阐明，因此，遵循这些心态的指向，这种情感能够被自发地感受到。然而，这种情感同时又与这些类似的心态有着质的差异。施莱尔马赫自己也多少认识到了这一点，这从他把虔敬感或者宗教依赖感从其他所有的依赖感中区分出来就可以看到。他的错误在于，他对二者仅做了"绝对的"和"相对的"依赖感的区分，由此认为二者只是度的差别，而不是内在的质的不同。他所忽视的是，在给这种感受完全命名为"依赖感"时，我们真正采用的正是这种非常接近的相似性。我认为，任何一个通过内省来比较这两种心态的人都会明白我的意思。这种感受不能用任何别的东西所表达，因为它是我们精神生活中最原始和最基本的东西，因此，只能通过它自身来加以界定。如果我举一个非

therefore only definable through itself. It may perhaps help him if I cite a well-known example, in which the precise 'moment' or element of religious feeling of which we are speaking is most actively present. When Abraham ventures to plead with God for the men of Sodom, he says (Gen. xviii. 27): 'Behold now, I have taken upon me to speak unto the Lord, which am but dust and ashes.' There you have a selfconfessed 'feeling of dependence', which is yet at the same time far more than, and something other than, *merely* a feeling of dependence. Desiring to give it a name of its own, I propose to call it 'creature-consciousness' or creature-feeling. It is the emotion of a creature, submerged and overwhelmed by its own nothingness in contrast to that which is supreme above all creatures.

It is easily seen that, once again, this phrase, whatever it is, is not a *conceptual* explanation of the matter. All that this new term, 'creature-feeling', can express, is the note of submergence into nothingness before an overpowering, absolute might of some kind; whereas everything turns upon the *character* of this overpowering might, a character which cannot be expressed verbally, and can only be suggested indirectly through the tone and content of a man's feeling-response to it. And this response must be directly experienced in oneself to be understood.

We have now to note a second defect in the formulation of Schleiermacher's principle. The religious category discovered by him, by whose means he professes to determine the real content of the religious emotion, is merely a category of *self*-valuation, in the sense of self-depreciation. According to him the religious emotion would be directly and primarily a sort of *self*-consciousness, a feeling concerning oneself in a special, determined relation, viz. one's dependence. Thus, according to Schleiermacher, I can only come upon the very fact of God as the result of an inference, that is, by reasoning to a cause beyond myself to account for my 'feeling of dependence'. But this is entirely opposed to the psychological facts of the case. Rather, the 'creature-feeling' is itself a first subjective

常有名的例子,或许会对施莱尔马赫有所帮助——这一例子中,我们所谈论的那种宗教感受的“要素”或者因素非常明显。当亚伯拉罕冒昧地向上帝请求宽恕所多玛时,他说:“我虽然是灰尘,还敢对主说话。”(《创世纪》第18章27节)在这里,你可以看到一种自认的“依赖感”,但是同时又远不止于或者根本就不仅仅是一种依赖感。由于渴望着给它一个属于自己的名字,我建议称之为“被造物意识”或者“被造感”。这是一个被造物的感受——与那个高踞于万物之上的造物主相比,被造物完全被自己的虚无感所遮蔽与压制着。

人们很容易再次发现,这个术语(不管它是什么)并不是要对事情作概念上的解释。“被造感”这一新术语所能表达的所有含义,就是对于面对着某种极端强大的绝对力量所产生的没入虚无之中的感受的阐释。而每一事物都仰赖于这一超强力量的特性,这种特性是难于言传的,而只能通过人们对此作出的感觉反应的语调和内容得到间接的暗示。只有亲身体验,才能够有所领悟。

现在我们来指出施莱尔马赫的原理阐释的第二个缺陷。这个由他找到的宗教范畴——他声称要由此确定宗教情感的真实内容——只不过是一种自我贬损意义上的自我评价。在他看来,宗教情感直接地并且主要地是一种自我意识,是一种处身于一个特殊的、确定的关系中,即人们有所依赖的状态下的感受。那么,依施莱尔马赫所言,只是作为一种推论的结果,也就是说,通过论证一个在我之外的原因来解释我的“依赖感”,我才能发现上帝的真实存在,但是这是与心理事实完全相左的。事实上,“被造感”本身只是另外一个情感因素的第一主观伴生物及效果,这种感受因素投射出来成为“被造感”,而它本身

concomitant and effect of another feeling-element, which casts it like a shadow, but which in itself indubitably has immediate and primary reference to an object outside the self. ①

Now this object is just what we have already spoken of as 'the numinous'. For the 'creature-feeling' and the sense of dependence to arise in the mind the 'numen' must be experienced as present, a *numen praesens*, as is in the case of Abraham. There must be felt a something 'numinous', something bearing the character of a 'numen', to which the mind turns spontaneously; or (which is the same thing in other words) these feelings can only arise in the mind as accompanying emotions when the category of 'the numinous' is called into play.

The numinous is thus felt as objective and outside the self. We have now to inquire more closely into its nature and the modes of its manifestation.

---

① This is so manifestly borne out by experience that it must be about the first thing to force itself upon the notice of psychologists analysing the facts of religion. There is a certain naïveté in the following passage from William James's *Varicties of Religious Experience* (p. 58), where, alluding to the origin of the Grecian representations of the gods, he says: 'As regards the origin of the Greek gods, we need not at present seek an opinion. But the whole array of our instances leads to a conclusion something like this: It is as if there were in the human consciousness *a sense of reality*, *a feeling of objective presence*, *a perception* of what we may call "*something there*", more deep and more general than any of the special and particular "senses" by which the current psychology supposes existent realities to be originally revealed.' (The italics are James's own.) James is debarred by his empiricist and pragmatist standpoint from coming to a recognition of faculties of knowledge and potentialities of thought in the spirit itself, and he is therefore obliged to have recourse to somewhat singular and mysterious hypotheses to explain this fact. But he grasps the fact itself clearly enough and is sufficient of a realist not to explain it away. But this 'feeling of reality', the feeling of a 'numinous' *object* objectively given, must be posited as a primary immediate datum of consciousness, and the 'feeling of dependence' is then a consequence, following very closely upon it, viz. a depreciation of the *subject* in his own eyes. The latter presupposes the former.

却不容置疑地立即并且首先牵涉到某个外在于自我的对象。①

这个对象就是我们已经谈论过的“神秘者”。由于在心中产生了“被造感”和依赖感,“神秘者”就必定像在亚伯拉罕那个例子中一样,是一种被体验为一种现时的东西。在这里,必然会感受到某种“神秘的”东西,即那种承载了“神秘者”的特征的、心灵会自发地向其转化的东西。或者换言之,只有当“神秘的”范畴“出场”时,这些感受(“被造感”和依赖感)才会作为一种伴随性的情感在心灵中呈现出来。

神秘者便由此方式被感受为客观的和外在于自我的。我们现在就要进一步探究它的性质和表现形式。

---

① 这一经由经验而产生出来的东西如此明显,以致它必然成为分析宗教事实的心理学家注意的首要对象。下面一段话摘自威廉·詹姆士的《宗教体验的种类》一书第58页,天真地谈到了希腊诸神的起源,他说:“关于希腊诸神的起源,我们无须马上找到一个答案。但是我们全部的实例都导向这样一个结论:似乎在人们的意识中有一种关于实在的感受,一种关于客观存在的感受,一种关于我们可以称之为‘有某物在’的知觉,这种感知要比任何别的特殊的‘感觉’更深刻更普遍得多——当代心理学就是用这种特殊的‘感觉’将存在的实在设定为最初的被揭示者。”(重点是詹姆士所加)詹姆士囿于其经验主义和实用主义的立场认识不到包含在精神中的知识的能力和思想的潜力,因此,他不得不求助于一些多少有点奇异神秘的假说来解释这一事实。但是他非常清楚地抓住了这一事实本身,而且作为一个地道的实在论者,并不为之作辩解。然而,这种“对于实在的感受”,即对于一种被客观地给予的关于“神秘的”对象的感受,必须被假定为一种原初的、直接的意识材料,这样,“依赖感”就是紧随其后的结果,也就是说,在当事人自己看来是对主体的一种贬抑。后者是以前者为前提的。

CHAPTER IV

‘Mysterium Tremendum’

The Analysis of ‘Tremendum’

We said above that the nature of the numinous can only be suggested by means of the special way in which it is reflected in the mind in terms of feeling. ‘Its nature is such that it grips or stirs the human mind with this and that determinate affective state.’ We have now to attempt to give a further indication of these determinate states. We must once again endeavour, by adducing feelings akin to them for the purpose of analogy or contrast, and by the use of metaphor and symbolic expressions, to make the states of mind we are investigating ring out, as it were, of themselves.

Let us consider the deepest and most fundamental element in all strong and sincerely felt religious emotion. Faith unto salvation, trust, love—all these are there. But over and above these is an element which may also on occasion, quite apart from them, profoundly affect us and occupy the mind with a wellnigh bewildering strength. Let us follow it up with every effort of sympathy and imaginative intuition wherever it is to be found, in the lives of those around us, in sudden, strong ebullitions of personal piety and the frames of mind such ebullitions evince, in the fixed and ordered solemnities of rites and liturgies, and again in the atmosphere that clings to old religious monuments and buildings, to temples and to churches. If we do so we shall find we are dealing with something for which there is only one appropriate expression, ‘*mysterium tremendum*’. The feeling of it may at times come sweeping like a gentle tide, pervading the mind with a tran-

第四章 “令人畏惧的神秘”

对“畏惧”的分析

我们上面说了,“神秘者”的本质只能通过一种特殊的方式来加以暗示,在这种方式中,“神秘者”以感受的形式被反映到心灵中。“它的本质是这样的:它以这种或那种确定的感受状态来影响或者激发人们的心灵。”我们现在应当对这些确定的状态作更进一步的标示。我们必须通过援引那些与这种状态类似的感受来做类比或对比,并且通过隐喻和象征的表达方式,再次努力使我们正在探究的这些心态以其本来的面貌浮现出来。

让我们来考虑一下那些被强烈地、诚挚地感受到的宗教情感中的最深层、最基本的因素。对得救的信仰、对信赖的信仰、对爱的信仰都存在于此。但是,除了这些因素之外,还有一个因素,它偶尔与这些因素完全无关,却会深刻地影响我们,并以一种几乎令人混乱的力量占据人的心灵。让我们尽量利用同情与想象性的直觉,在它出现的每一个地方——在我们周围的那些生命中,在个人虔敬的突然强烈爆发以及由此展示出的心灵结构中,在宗教仪式的井然有序的庄严肃穆中,以及在附着于古老的宗教遗迹和建筑物如寺庙、教堂等的氛围中——去追寻这种因素。倘若我们这样做,我们就会发现,我们是在和这样一个东西打交道,对它只有一个恰当的表述,就是令人畏惧的神秘。对它的感受有时如同微波掠过,心中充盈着最深挚的崇敬

quil mood of deepest worship. It may pass over into a more set and lasting attitude of the soul, continuing, as it were, thrillingly vibrant and resonant, until at last it dies away and the soul resumes its 'profane', non-religious mood of everyday experience. It may burst in sudden eruption up from the depths of the soul with spasms and convulsions, or lead to the strangest excitements, to intoxicated frenzy, to transport, and to ecstasy. It has its wild and demonic forms and can sink to an almost grisly horror and shuddering. It has its crude, barbaric antecedents and early manifestations, and again it may be developed into something beautiful and pure and glorious. It may become the hushed, trembling, and speechless humility of the creature in the presence of—whom or what? In the presence of that which is a *mystery* inexpressible and above all creatures.

It is again evident at once that here too our attempted formulation by means of a concept is once more a merely negative one. Conceptually *mysterium* denotes merely that which is hidden and esoteric, that which is beyond conception or understanding, extraordinary and unfamiliar. The term does not define the object more positively in its qualitative character. But though what is enunciated in the word is negative, what is meant is something absolutely and intensely positive. This pure positive we can experience in feelings, feelings which our discussion can help to make clear to us, in so far as it arouses them actually in our hearts.

1. *The Element of Awefulness*

To get light upon the positive '*quale*' of the object of these feelings, we must analyse more closely our phrase *mysterium tremendum*, and we will begin first with the adjective.

Tremor is in itself merely the perfectly familiar and 'natural' emotion of *fear*. But here the term is taken, aptly enough but still only by analogy, to denote a quite specific kind of emotional response, wholly distinct from that of being afraid, though it so far resembles it

带来的宁静。随后,它会转化为一种更加稳定和持久的心态,像它过去一向的样子,以持续地轻颤和回荡,直到最后渐渐消逝,而心灵重又回到“世俗的”、非宗教的日常经验中。它会从灵魂深处与抽搐和惊厥一同爆发出来,或者引发最奇特的激动,变为极度狂乱,变为惊喜,变为迷狂。它有着野性的、魔鬼的种种形式并能够沉入几乎是令人震惊的恐惧与战栗之中。它有着粗野的、凶残的远古形式和早期表现,此外,它又会发展成为某种美丽的、纯洁的、荣耀的东西。它可以变成被造物面对着“不知道是谁或者是什么”时的一种静寂、战栗与无言的谦卑。这种谦卑是被造物在面对某种不可言说的、高踞于万物之上的神秘者时所产生的。

很清楚,我们在这里通过一种概念而尝试的公式化不过再次是一种否定的东西。概念化的神秘仅仅意味着隐匿的神秘难解的东西,意味着超出了概念或者理解力的东西,这种东西是异乎寻常的、陌生的。这个术语还没有从其质的特征方面更加肯定地界定这一对象。然而,尽管这一语词所明确阐述的是否定的东西,但是它的意指却是绝对肯定的。我们能够在感受中体验到这种纯粹肯定的东西,这种感受是我们的讨论可以帮助弄清的,只要这种纯粹肯定的东西能在我们心中把这些感受实际地激发出来。

1.**敬畏的因素**

为了揭示这些感受对象的这种肯定的“可感性”,我们必须更加仔细地分析令人畏惧的神秘这一短语,我们首先从修饰词开始。

Tremor 本身不过是那种人们非常熟悉的、“自然的”恐惧感。但是,在这里,这个词被很贴切地却仍然只是近似地用来指称一种很特别的情感反应,这种情感反应完全不同于害怕,尽管它非

that the analogy of fear may be used to throw light upon its nature. There are in some languages special expressions which denote, either exclusively or in the first instance, this 'fear' that is more than fear proper. The Hebrew *hiqdīsh* (hallow) is an example. To 'keep a thing holy in the heart' means to mark it off by a feeling of peculiar dread, not to be mistaken for any ordinary dread, that is, to appraise it by the category of the numinous. But the Old Testament throughout is rich in parallel expressions for this feeling. Specially noticeable is the '*ēmāh* of Yahweh ('fear of God'), which Yahweh can pour forth, dispatching almost like a daemon, and which seizes upon a man with paralysing effect. It is closely related to the δεῖμα *πανικόν* of the Greeks. Compare Exod. xxiii. 27: 'I will send my fear before thee, and will destroy all the people to whom thou shalt come . . . '; also Job ix. 34; xiii. 21 ('let not his fear terrify me'; 'let not thy dread make me afraid'). Here we have a terror fraught with an inward shuddering such as not even the most menacing and overpowering created thing can instil. It has something spectral in it.

In the Greek language we have a corresponding term in *σεβαστός*. The early Christians could clearly feel that the title *σεβαστός* (*augustus*) was one that could not fittingly be given to any creature, not even to the emperor. They felt that to call a man *σεβαστός* was to give a human being a name proper only to the *numen*, to rank him by the category proper only to the *numen*, and that it therefore amounted to a kind of idolatry. Of modern languages English has the words 'awe', 'aweful', which in their deeper and most special sense approximate closely to our meaning. The phrase, 'he stood aghast', is also suggestive in this connexion. On the other hand, German has no native-grown expression of its own forthe higher and riper form of the emotion we are considering, unless

常类似于害怕,以致可以用这种近似的害怕来揭示它的本质。在一些语言中,有一些特殊的表达方式,它们所表明的,仅仅是或者首先是这种超出狭义的害怕的"畏惧"。希伯来语的 *hiqdīsh*(敬畏)就是一个例证。要"在心中保持一件事物的神圣"就意味着要以一种特殊的畏惧之情(不可错当做任何普通的惧怕)去把它隔离开来,用"神秘"这个范畴去评价它。在《旧约》中自始至终都充满了这种类似的表达方式。其中尤其要特别注意的是 *émäh* of Yahweh(对上帝的畏惧)这一表述方式,这种恐惧能够由耶和华就像魔鬼般迅速地倾泻出来,其力量足以让人动弹不得。这种畏惧与希腊语的 *δεϊμα πανικόν* 紧密相关。比较一下《出埃及记》(第 23 章第 27 节):"凡你所到的地方,我要使那里的众民在你面前惊骇,扰乱……";亦见《约伯记》第 9 章第 34 节、第 13 章第 21 节("勿使你的惊惶威吓我";"勿使你的恐惧让我害怕")。在这里,我们看到的是任何一种极具威胁性的、最强大的被造物也无法激起的、充满了内在的战栗的恐惧。这种恐惧内部包含有某种魔力。

在希腊语里,我们可以找到一个相应的术语,这就是 *σεβ αστ σs*。早期的基督徒非常清楚,*σεβαστós*(*augustus*)这一个称谓不适用于任何一个被造物,甚至不可给予帝王。他们认为,称一个人为 *σεβαστós*,就是把一个只适用于神秘者(*numen*)的名字给予了凡人,就是用这个只适用于神秘者的范畴将他提升到一种类似于偶像的地位上来了。在现代语言中,英语有两个词,awe 和 aweful(敬畏和敬畏的),在其最深层和最特殊的意义上与我们所讲的"畏惧"相近。"他惊呆了"这个表述也能暗示出这种联系。另一方面,德语则没有自己本土的词汇来表达我们所谈论的这种较高级、较成熟的感受,只有

it be in a word like *erschauern*, which does suggest it fairly well. It is far otherwise with its cruder and more debased phases, where such terms as *grausen* and *Schauer*, and the more popular and telling *gruseln* ('grue'), *gräsen*, and *grässlich* ('grisly'), very clearly designate the numinous element. In my examination of Wundt's Animism I suggested the term *Scheu* (dread); but the special 'numinous' quality (making it 'awe' rather than 'dread' in the ordinary sense) would then, of course, have to be denoted by inverted commas. 'Religious dread' (or 'awe') would perhaps be a better designation. Its antecedent stage is 'daemonic dread' (cf. the horror of Pan) with its queer perversion, a sort of abortive offshoot, the 'dread of ghosts'. It first begins to stir in the feeling of 'something uncanny', 'eerie', or 'weird'. It is this feeling which, emerging in the mind of primeval man, forms the starting-point for the entire religious development in history. 'Daemons' and 'gods' alike spring from this root, and all the products of 'mythological apperception' or 'fantasy' are nothing but different modes in which it has been objectified. And all ostensible explanations of the origin of religion in terms of animism or magic or folk-psychology are doomed from the outset to wander astray and miss the real goal of their inquiry, unless they recognize this fact of our nature—primary, unique, underivable from anything else—to be the basic factor and the basic impulse underlying the entire process of religious evolution. ①

---

① Cf. my papers in *Theologische Rundschau*, 1910, vol. i, on 'Myth and Religion in Wundt's *Völkerpsychologie*', and in *Deutsche Literaturzeitung*, 1910, No. 38. I find in more recent investigations, especially those of R. R. Marett and N. Söderblom, a very welcome confirmation of the positions I there maintained. It is true that neither of them calls attention quite as precisely as, in this matter, psychologists need to do, to the unique character of the religious 'awe' and its qualitative distinction from all 'natural' feelings. But Marett more particularly comes within a hair's breadth of what I take to be the truth about the matter. Cf. his *Threshold of Religion* (London, 1909), and N. Söderblom's Das Werden des *Gottesglaubens* (Leipzig, 1915), also my review of the latter in *Theol. Literaiurzeitung*, Jan. 1915.

erschauern（战栗）一词还算合适。除此之外，在德语的更原始、更低级的词汇中，有一些词语，诸如 *grausen*、*Schauer* 以及更加流行、更具影响的 *gruseln*（战栗），*gräsen* 和 *grässlich*（恐怖的），也非常清楚地指出了这种"神秘"的因素。在考察冯特的泛神论时，我曾经提出了一个词 *Scheu*（畏惧），但是那种特殊的"神秘的"性质——它引起"敬畏"而非一般意义上的"畏惧"——当然还不得不反过来理解。也许"宗教之畏"（或者"敬畏"）是更好的名称。这一表达方式的早期阶段是"对魔鬼的畏惧"（比较：对潘神的恐慌），它有一种奇怪的曲解，即早已废止的"对鬼魅的畏惧"。这种畏惧最初是从对某种"离奇的"、"可怕的"或者"怪诞的"东西引起的。正是这种出现在原始人心中的畏惧之情，形成了历史上整个宗教发展的出发点。"魔鬼"与"神灵"同样地从这一根基上产生出来，而"神话领悟"或者"幻想"的所有产物，都无非是被对象化了的这种畏惧的不同形式。一切依据泛灵论、魔法或者大众心理学对宗教的肤浅解释都注定了从一开始就误入歧途，从而迷失了他们所追究的真实目标，除非他们认识到我们的本性这一事实——起初的、唯一的、非派生的——是蛰伏在整个宗教发展过程下面的基本因素和基本冲动。①

① 参见我发表在《神学评论》1910 年第 1 卷上的《冯特〈大众心理学〉中的神话与宗教》一文，以及《德国文学报》1910 年第 38 期上的论文。在最近的研究中，尤其是在马雷特（R. R. Marett）和索德布罗姆（N. Söderblom）的研究中，我发现了对我所坚持立场的非常值得欢迎的肯定。的确，他们两人在这件事上，都没有像心理学家应当做的那样，重视宗教"敬畏"的独特性质以及它与一切"自然"感受的本质区别。不过马雷特与我在该问题上所持的观点更加接近。参见他的《宗教入门》（伦敦，1909）、索德布罗姆的《上帝信仰的产生》（莱比锡，1915），以及我对于后者的看法（载于 1915 年 1 月的《神学评论》与《德国文学报》）。

Not only is the saying of Luther, that the natural man cannot fear God perfectly, correct from the standpoint of psychology, but we ought to go farther and add that the natural man is quite unable even to 'shudder' (*grauen*) or feel horror in the real sense of the word. For 'shuddering' is something more than 'natural', ordinary fear. It implies that the mysterious is already beginning to loom before the mind, to touch the feelings. It implies the first application of a category of valuation which has no place in the everyday natural world of ordinary experience, and is only possible to a being in whom has been awakened a mental predisposition, unique in kind and different in a definite way from any 'natural' faculty. And this newly-revealed capacity, even in the crude and violent manifestations which are all it at first evinces, bears witness to a completely new function of experience and standard of valuation, only belonging to the spirit of man.

Before going on to consider the elements which unfold as the '*tremendum*' develops, let us give a little further consideration to the first crude, primitive forms in which this 'numinous dread' or *awe* shows itself. It is the mark which really characterizes the so-called 'religion of primitive man', and there it appears as 'daemonic dread'. This crudely naïve and primordial emotional disturbance, and the fantastic images to which it gives rise, are later overborne and ousted by more highly developed forms of the numinous emotion, with all its mysteriously impelling power. But even when this has long attained its higher and purer mode of expression it is possible for the primitive types of excitation that were formerly a part of it to break out in the soul in all their original naïveté and so to be experienced afresh. That this is so is shown by the potent attraction again and again exercised by the element of horror and 'shudder' in ghost stories, even among persons of high all-round education. It is a remarkable fact that the physical reaction to which this unique 'dread' of the uncanny gives rise is also unique, and is not found in the case of any 'natural' fear or terror. We say: 'my blood ran icy cold', and 'my flesh crept'. The 'cold blood' feeling may be a

路德说:“自然人是不可能完全惧怕上帝的。”这句话不仅在心理学的立场上是正确的,而且我们还要进一步补充,即自然人甚至完全不可能“战栗”(*grauen*)或者在这个词的真实含义上感受到惊惧。因为“战栗”远甚于“自然的”、通常的惊惧,它意味着神秘的东西已经开始隐隐出现在心灵之中,并触发了感觉。它暗示着一种评价范畴的最初运用,这种评价范畴在日常经验的自然世界中是没有任何地位的,只是对这种人有可能:在他心中,一种独特的、不同于任何一种确定的“自然”能力的精神癖好已经被唤醒,而这种新近才被揭示出来的能力,即便是在其最开始表现出来的一切原始粗犷的形式中,也证明了只为人的精神所具有的全新的经验功能和评价标准。

在继续考察那些在“畏惧”的发展中展现出来的要素之前,让我们先约略考察一下这种“神秘的畏惧”或者敬畏用以表现其自身的那些最粗糙的、原始的形式。这种畏惧是所谓的“原始人的宗教”的真正标志,它表现为“对魔鬼的畏惧”。这种极为简单原始的情感骚动以及由它引发的怪诞意向后来被这种“神秘”感受——包括它所有的神秘的驱动力——的更高发展形式所压制和强迫。但是尽管这种畏惧在获得了特殊的更高更纯的表现形式很久之后,那种先前曾经是其一个方面的原始激情类型仍有可能以其原初的质朴形式在心灵中爆发出来,并被再次体验到。这一点可通过包含在鬼怪故事中的令人恐惧与“战栗”的因素所一再引发的强烈吸引力表现出来,即便在受过全面高等教育的人中也是如此。一个值得注意的事实是,由这种独特的神秘“畏惧”所引发的生理反应也是独特的,在任何“自然的”害怕和惊恐中都找不到。我们说:“我的血液变得冰凉”,“我感到毛骨悚然”。这里,“血液变凉”的感

symptom of ordinary, natural fear, but there is something non-natural or supernatural about the symptom of 'creeping flesh'. And any one who is capable of more precise introspection must recognize that the distinction between such a 'dread' and natural fear is not simply one of degree and intensity. The awe or 'dread' *may* indeed be so overwhelmingly great that it seems to penetrate to the very marrow, making the man's hair bristle and his limbs quake. But it may also steal upon him almost unobserved as the gentlest of agitations, a mere fleeting shadow passing across his mood. It has therefore nothing to do with intensity, and no natural fear passes over into it merely by being intensified. I may be beyond all measure afraid and terrified without there being even a trace of the feeling of uncanniness in my emotion.

We should see the facts more clearly if psychology in general would make a more decisive endeavour to examine and classify the feelings and emotions according to their qualitative differences. But the far too rough division of elementary feelings in general into pleasures and pains is still an obstacle to this. In point of fact 'pleasures' no more than other feelings are differentiated merely by degrees of intensity: they show very definite and specific differences. It makes a specific difference to the condition of mind whether the soul is merely in a state of pleasure, or joy, or aesthetic rapture, or moral exaltation, or finally in the religious bliss that may come in worship. Such states certainly show resemblances one to another, and on that account can legitimately be brought under a common class-concept ('pleasure'), which serves to cut them off from other psychical functions, generically different. But this class-concept, so far from turning the various subordinate species into merely different degrees of the same thing, can do nothing at all to throw light upon the essence of each several state of mind which it includes.

Though the numinous emotion in its completest development shows a world of difference from the mere 'daemonic dread', yet not even at the highest level does it belie its pedigree or kindred. Even when the worship of 'daemons' has long since reached the higher level of worship of 'gods', these gods still retain as *numina* something of the 'ghost' in the

觉可能是一种普通的、自然的害怕表征，但是，“毛骨悚然”的感觉则意味着有某种非自然的或者超自然的东西。任何一个能做精确的内省的人，都一定能够认识到，这种“畏惧”与自然的害怕之间的差别绝不仅仅是程度上与强度上的。这种敬畏或者“畏惧”或许确实是无比巨大，以致能渗透到骨髓之中，使人发根直立、四肢震颤；但它也可能像最轻微的焦虑丝毫不引人注意地悄悄笼罩住他，如同一片阴影掠过他的心田。因此，这种“畏惧”与强度无关，任何自然的害怕都不能仅仅通过被强化而转变成它。我可能感到极度害怕，却丝毫没有神秘的感觉。

如果一般心理学能够更加努力地按照它们质的不同来对感觉与情绪加以检验分类，那么，我们将会更清晰地看到这些事实。然而，过于粗疏地将基本情感大致区分为愉悦与痛苦，这仍然是我们见到上述事实的一个障碍。实际上，“愉悦”同其他情感一样，都只是通过强度来区分的：它们显示出十分明确而具体的不同。无论心灵仅仅处于一种愉悦状态，还是快乐、审美的迷醉、道德的兴奋，或者最后由崇拜而产生的宗教至福，都有着具体的差别。这些心态的确显得相互类似，因此，它们可以被合法地归结到一个普遍的类概念（“愉悦”）名下，这个类概念所起的作用，就是把它们以类的差别从其他生理功能中区分出来。但是这个类概念由于远未做到把各种从属种类单纯转换为同一事物的不同等级，因此，它完全不能说明它所包含的每种心态的本质。

尽管最完满的神秘感受展现了一个不同于单纯的“对魔鬼的畏惧”的世界，但是，即使是在最高的水准上，它也没有遮掩自身的起源或关系，甚至当“魔鬼”崇拜早就已经演化为“神灵”崇拜的更高水平时，这些神灵在它们给那些崇拜者造成的感受中依然保持着

impress they make on the feelings of the worshipper, viz. the peculiar quality of the 'uncanny' and 'aweful', which survives with the quality of exaltedness and sublimity or is symbolized by means of it. And this element, softened though it is, does not disappear even on the highest level of all, where the worship of God is at its purest. Its disappearance would be indeed an essential loss. The 'shudder' re-appears in a form ennobled beyond measure where the soul, held speechless, trembles inwardly to the farthest fibre of its being. It invades the mind mightily in Christian worship with the words: 'Holy, holy, holy'; it breaks forth from the hymn of Tersteegen:

God Himself is present:
Heart, be stilled before Him,
Prostrate inwardly adore Him.

The 'shudder' has here lost its crazy and bewildering note, but not the ineffable something that holds the mind. It has become a mystical awe, and sets free as its accompaniment, reflected in self-consciousness, that 'creature-feeling' that has already been described as the feeling of personal nothingness and submergence before the awe-inspiring object directly experienced.

The referring of this feeling numinous *tremor* to its object in the numen brings into relief a property of the latter which plays an important part in our Holy Scriptures, and which has been the occasion of many difficulties, both to commentators and to theologians, from its puzzling and baffling nature. This is the *ὀργή* (*orgé*), the Wrath of Yahweh, which recurs in the New Testament as *ὀργή θεοῦ*, and which is clearly analogous to the idea occurring in many religions of a mysterious *ira deorum*. To pass through the Indian Pantheon

"鬼魅"所具有的某种神秘性,这也就是这种"神秘"和"敬畏"的特殊性质,这种性质是与崇高、高尚的性质一道存活下来的,或者是通过这种性质表现出来的。这种因素,尽管已被弱化了,但它甚至在其最高水准上——在这里,对上帝的崇拜是其最纯粹的形式——都没有消失。它的消失将确实是一种根本的损失。在无言的灵魂向着它所具有的最深远的品质秘密地颤抖的地方,这种"战栗"以一种无比崇高的形式再现出来。它伴随着"圣哉,圣哉,圣哉"的话语强有力地侵入到基督教的崇拜之中,并从特尔斯特根的赞美诗中迸发出来:

上帝本身出现了:

在他面前,心灵悄无声息,

唯有在内心匍匐赞美。

在这里,"战栗"已经失去了它的疯狂与迷乱的含义,但是依然葆有着那种控制心灵的无法言说的东西。它已经变成了一种神秘的的敬畏,并把反映在自我意识中的"被造感"作为它的附属物释放出来——这种"被造感"就是前面已经描述过的、在直接经验到的激发敬畏感的对象面前所产生的那种个人的一无所是、卑微渺小的感觉。

从这种神秘的战栗的感受与其处于神秘中的对象的关系中生发出后者的一种特性,这种特性在我们的《圣经》中起着重要作用;同时,又由于其扑朔迷离的性质,无论是对于评论者还是对神学家,它都成了许多困难的诱因。这就是 *ὀργή*(*orgé*),也就是耶和华的愤怒,它在《新约》中以 *ὀργήθεοῦ* 的形式出现,并且很明显地类似于许多种宗教中的那种神秘的 *ira deorum*(神的愤怒)的观念。只要浏览一下印度的万神殿,就会发现,那里的神祇几

of gods is to find deities who seem to be made up altogether out of such an ὀργή; and even the higher Indian gods of grace and pardon have frequently, beside their merciful, their 'wrath' form. But as regards the 'wrath of Yahweh', the strange features about it have for long been a matter for constant remark. In the first place, it is patent from many passages of the Old Testament that this 'wrath' has no concern whatever with moral qualities. There is something very baffling in the way in which it 'is kindled' and manifested. It is, as has been well said, 'like a hidden force of nature', like stored-up electricity, discharging itself upon anyone who comes too near. It is 'incalculable' and 'arbitrary'. Anyone who is accustomed to think of deity only by its rational attributes must see in this 'wrath' mere caprice and wilful passion. But such a view would have been emphatically rejected by the religious men of the Old Covenant, for to them the Wrath of God, so far from being a diminution of His Godhead, appears as a natural expression of it, an element of 'holiness' itself, and a quite indispensable one. And in this they are entirely right. This *ὀργή* is nothing but the *tremendum* itself, apprehended and expressed by the aid of a naïve analogy from the domain of natural experience, in this case from the ordinary passional life of men. But naïve as it may be, the analogy is most disconcertingly apt and striking; so much so that it will always retain its value and for us no less than for the men of old be an inevitable way of expressing one element in the religious emotion. It cannot be doubted that, despite the protest of Schleiermacher and Ritschl, Christianity also has something to teach of the 'wrath of God'.

It will be again at once apparent that in the use of this word we are not concerned with a genuine intellectual 'concept', but only with a sort of illustrative substitute for a concept. 'Wrath' here is the 'ideogram' of a unique emotional moment in religious experience, a moment whose

乎全都是由这种 ὀργή（愤怒）造成的，甚至那些有更高层次的仁爱和宽恕的印度神，除了它们宽恕的一面外，常常还有其“发怒”的形态，但是就“耶和华的愤怒”而言，关于它的这种奇异特征很久以来就是一个被不断谈论的问题。首先，从《旧约》的许多段落来看，很明显，这种“愤怒”与道德性质没有任何关系。在其被“点燃”与被显示的方式中有着某种非常令人困惑的东西。有人说得好，它“有如隐藏的自然力”，有如储存起来的电力，会在任何一个离它太近的人身上释放出自己。它是“不可预料的”，又是“专横跋扈的”。任何一个只是习惯于从神的理性性质来看待神的人，都必须在这种“愤怒”中看到任性与固执的情绪。但是这种看法会遭到信奉《旧约》教徒的坚决反对，因为在他们看来，上帝的愤怒远非对上帝神性的削弱，而是这种神性的自然表达，它就是这种“神性”本身的一种因素，而且是一种必不可少的因素。在这一点上，他们是完全正确的。这种 ὀργή（愤怒）不是别的，就是畏惧自身，它借助于自然经验领域的简单类比来加以领悟和表述，在这里，它所借助的是人们的日常情感生活。尽管这个类比可能显得简单了点，但是毫无疑问，它是最贴切最引人注目的，因此，它总是保持着它的价值，并且，无论对于我们还是对于古人来说，它都是用来表达宗教情感的一种因素的必然方式。不容置疑，尽管施莱尔马赫和利奇尔存有异议，基督教关于“上帝的愤怒”的看法也能给人以某种启迪。

这立即又很明显，当我们使用“愤怒”这个词时，我们所关注的并不是一个真正智性的“概念”，而仅仅是对一个概念的解说性的替代。“愤怒”在这里是对宗教体验中的独特感受因素的“表意符号”，这种因素所具有的独一无二的威慑力和激发敬

singularly *daunting* and awe-inspiring character must be gravely disturbing to those persons who will recognize nothing in the divine nature but goodness, gentleness, love, and a sort of confidential intimacy, in a word, only those aspects of God which turn towards the world of men.

This *ὀργή* is thus quite wrongly spoken of as 'natural' wrath: rather it is an entirely non-or super-natural, i. e. numinous, quality. The rationalization process takes place when it begins to be filled in with elements derived from the moral reason: righteousness in requital, and punishment for moral transgression. But it should be noted that the idea of the wrath of God in the Bible is always a synthesis, in which the original is combined with the later meaning that has come to fill it in. Something supra-rational throbs and gleams, palpable and visible, in the 'wrath of God', prompting to a sense of 'terror' that no 'natural' anger can arouse.

Beside the 'wrath' or 'anger' of Yahweh stands the related expression 'jealousy of Yahweh'. The state of mind denoted by the phrase 'being jealous *for* Yahweh' is also a numinous state of mind, in which features of the *tremendum* pass over into the man who has experience of it.

2. *The element of 'Overpoweringness'* ('*majestas*')

We have been attempting to unfold the implications of that aspect of the *mysterium tremendum* indicated by the adjective, and the result so far may be summarized in two words, constituting, as before, what may be called an 'ideogram', rather than a concept proper, viz. 'absolute unapproachability'.

It will be felt at once that there is yet a further element which must be added, that, namely, of 'might', 'power', 'absolute overpoweringness'. We will take to represent this the term *majestas*, majesty—the more readily because anyone with a feeling for language must detect a last faint trace

畏的性质严重地扰乱那样一些人:他们在神性中只看到了善、温柔、爱以及一种极度信赖的亲密,简而言之,他们只是看到了上帝转入人的世界的那些方面,此外则一无所见。

因此,这个 ὀργή(愤怒)被十分错误地当做“自然的”愤怒来谈论,实际上,它具有一种完全的非自然或者超自然的性质,即神秘的性质。当这种性质被那些来自道德理性的因素——报复的正当性与对道德败坏的惩戒——所填充时,这种理性化的过程就发生了。但是应当指出,在《圣经》中,“上帝的愤怒”这一观念总是综合的,其中,最初的含义与后来填充进来的含义是结合在一起的。在“上帝的愤怒”中,显然有某种超理性的东西在跳动和闪耀,它所引起的“恐惧”感是任何“自然的”愤怒所不能引发的。

与“耶和华的愤怒”相毗邻的,还有一个相关的表述,即“耶和华的嫉妒”。通过“为耶和华而嫉妒”这一短语所标示出来的心态也是一种“神秘的”心态,在其中,畏惧的诸特征转移到了体验它的那个人心中。

2.“不可抗拒”(“威严”)的因素

我们一直试图展示令人畏惧的神秘的限定词所标示出的那个方面的含义,其结果可以被概括为两个词,来构建出一个比前面所提到的“表意符号”更加合适的概念,即“绝对不可接近性”。

人们立刻会感到,这里还必须加上一个进一步的因素,这也就是“权力”、“强力”、“绝对不可抗拒”的因素。我们想用 *majestas* 即威严一词来代表这一因素,因为任何一个有语言感受力的人都必然能很容易地发现持续附着在这个词上的神秘

of the numinous still clinging to the word. The *tremendum* may then be rendered more adequately *tremenda majestas*, or ' aweful majesty'. This second element of majesty may continue to be vividly preserved, where the first, that of unapproachability, recedes and dies away, as may be seen, for example, in mysticism. It is especially in relation to this element of majesty or absolute overpoweringness that the creature-consciousness, of which we have already spoken, comes upon the scene, as a sort of shadow or subjective reflection of it. Thus, in contrast to ' the overpowering' of which we are conscious as an object over against the self, there is the feeling of one's own submergence, of being but 'dust and ashes' and nothingness. And this forms the numinous raw material for the feeling of religious humility. ①

Here we must revert once again to Schleiermacher's expression for what we call ' creature-feeling', viz. the ' feeling of dependence'. We found fault with this phrase before on the ground that Schleiermacher thereby takes as basis and point of departure what is merely a secondary effect; that he sets out to teach a consciousness of the religious *object* only by way of an inference from the shadow it casts upon *self*-consciousness. We have now a further criticism to bring against it, and it is this. By 'feeling of dependence' Schleiermacher means consciousness of *being conditioned* (as effect by cause), and so he develops the implications of this logically enough in his sections upon Creation and Preservation. On the side of the deity the correlate to ' dependence' would thus be ' causality', i. e. God's character as all-causing and all-conditioning. But a sense of this does not enter at all into that immediate and first-hand religious emotion which we have in the moment of worship, and which we can recover in a measure for analysis; it belongs on the contrary decidedly to

① Cf. R. R. Marett, 'The Birth of Humility', *in The Threshold of Religion*, 2nd ed., 1914. [Tr.]

的微弱痕迹。这样，畏惧就可以更充分地被译为令人畏惧的威严。如同在神秘主义中所能看到的那样，在第一种因素即“不可接近性”逐渐消退的地方，第二种因素却继续生动地保存下来。正是在与这种威严因素或者绝对不可抗拒因素的联系中，我们前面所谈论过的被造意识作为它的投影或者主观反映浮现出来。这样，当我们与这种“不可抗拒的”因素——我们是把它作为与自我相对立的对象来观照的——相对照时，便会有这种自我卑微感，以及自己不过是“灰尘”与虚无的感觉。这正是形成宗教谦卑感的“神秘的”原始材料。[1]

这里，我们必须再次回到施莱尔马赫的“依赖感”——我们称之为“被造感”。我们以前发现施莱尔马赫使用这一术语的错误的理由在于：他把一种仅仅是次要的影响当做了基础与出发点；他仅仅是从宗教对象投射到自我意识上的投影的推论的形式出发，去宣扬对于宗教对象的意识。现在我们对此要作更进一步的批评，如下所述。由于施莱尔马赫的“依赖感”指的是受限制的意识（如同结果受制于原因），因此，他在其“创造与保持”这一部分中，非常符合逻辑地阐述了其诸多含义。在神这一方面，与“依赖”相关的应当是“因果性”，也就是说，上帝的性质就是引起一切和规定一切。但是，这种感觉根本没有进入直接的、原始的宗教感受中，这种宗教感受是我们在宗教崇拜中获得的，并且为了分析我们可以部分地重现；相反，它无疑属于上帝观念的理性的一面。

---

〔1〕 参见 R. R. 马雷特《宗教入门》中的“谦卑的诞生”（第二版，1914 年）。

the *rational* side of the idea of God; its implications admit of precise conceptual determination; and it springs from quite a distinct source. The difference between the 'feeling of dependence' of Schleiermacher and that which finds typical utterance in the words of Abraham already cited might be expressed as that between the consciousness of *createdness* ①and the consciousness of *creaturehood*②. In the one case you have the creature as the work of the divine creative act; in the other, impotence and general nothingness as against overpowering might, dust and ashes as against 'majesty'. In the one case you have the fact of having been created; in the other, the status of the creature. And as soon as speculative thought has come to concern itself with this latter type of consciousness—as soon as it has come to analyse this 'majesty'—we are introduced to a set of ideas quite different from those of creation or preservation. We come upon the ideas, first, of the annihilation of self, and then, as its complement, of the transcendent as the sole and entire reality. These are the characteristic notes of mysticism in all its forms, however otherwise various in content. For one of the chiefest and most general features of mysticism is just this *self-depreciation* (so plainly parallel to the case of Abraham), the estimation of the self, of the personal 'I', as something not perfectly or essentially real, or even as mere nullity, a self-depreciation which comes to demand its own fulfilment in practice in rejecting the delusion of selfhood, and so makes for the annihilation of the self. And on the other hand mysticism leads to a valuation of the transcendent object of its reference as that which through plenitude of being stands supreme and absolute, so that the finite self contrasted with it becomes conscious even in its nullity that 'I am naught, Thou art all'. There is no thought in this of any causal relation between God, the creator, and the self, the creature. The point from which speculation starts is not a 'consciousness of absolute dependence'—of myself as result and effect of a divine cause—for that would in point of fact lead to insistence upon the

① *Geschaftenheit.*

② *Geschöflichkeit.*

它的含义容许精确的概念化界定，而且它产生于一个截然不同的来源。施莱尔马赫的“依赖感”与以上引述的亚伯拉罕的话语中的典型表达的区别，可以表示为被造意识①与被造物身份意识②之间的区别。在一种情形中，你所拥有的是作为神的创造性活动的一件作品的被造物；而在另一种情形中，你所拥有的则是面对不可抗拒的强力的无能为力与一无所是，是面对“威严”的灰与尘。在一种情形中，你所拥有的是已经被创造出来的事实；而在另一种情形中，你所拥有的，是被造物的身份。一旦纯粹推理的思想以后来的这种意识类型来关注自身——一旦它开始分析这种“威严”时，我们就会被引到与创造或保持完全不同的一套观念上去。首先我们遇到的是自我泯灭的观念，其次是——作为上述观念的补充——作为唯一的完全的实在的卓越的观念。这些是一切形式的神秘主义的典型特征，尽管它们在内容上各不相同。因为神秘主义的最主要的、最一般的特征之一就是这种自我贬抑（与亚伯拉罕的情形完全相同），即把自我、人格“我”看做某种不完善的、根本不真实的东西，甚至仅仅是一种虚无——这种自我贬抑在拒斥自我欺骗的实践中追求自我的实现，并因此走向自我的泯灭。另一方面，神秘主义导致了对与之相关的那个超越对象的一个评价，即它是那种通过存在的完满而体现出来的最高与绝对，以致有限的自我在与之对比时，即便是在自己的虚无中也能意识到“我不过是零，您却是一切”。在这种意识中，根本想不到上帝（造物主）与自我（被造物）之间的任何因果联系。这一思路的出发点并不是“绝对的依赖意识”，即对神是原因我是结果的意识，因为那会在实际上导致对自我实在性的强调；这种推论是从对于远非我自己的某种力量的绝对优越性或至高无上

① 被造意识

② 被造物身份意识

reality of the self; it starts from a consciousness of the absolute superiority or supremacy of a power other than myself, and it is only as it falls back upon ontological terms to achieve its end—terms generally borrowed from natural science—that that element of the *tremendm*, originally apprehended as ' plenitude of power' , becomes transmuted into ' plenitude of being' .

This leads again to the mention of mysticism. No mere inquiry into the genesis of a thing can throw any light upon its essential nature, and it is hence immaterial to us how mysticism historically arose. But essentially mysticism is the stressing to a very high degree, indeed the overstressing, of the non-rational or supra-rational elements in religion; and it is only intelligible when so understood. The various phases and factors of the non-rational may receive varying emphasis, and the type of mysticism will differ according as some or others fall into the background. What we have been analysing, however, is a feature that recurs in all forms of mysticism everywhere, and it is nothing but the ' creature-consciousness' stressed to the utmost and to excess, the expression meaning, if we may repeat the contrast already made, not ' feeling of our createdness' but ' feeling of our creaturehood' , that is, the consciousness of the littleness of every creature in face of that which is above all creatures.

A characteristic common to all types of mysticism is the *Identification*, in different degrees of completeness, of the personal self with the transcendent Reality. This identification has a source of its own, with which we are not here concerned, and springs from ' moments' of religious experience which would require separate treatment. ' Identification' alone, however, is not enough for mysticism; it must be Identification with the Something that is at once absolutely supreme in power and reality and wholly non-rational. And it is among the mystics that we most encounter this element

性的意识开始的，而且，只是在这种思考转而求助于本体论的术语——这些术语总是从自然科学中借来的——来实现其目的时，那个最初被理解为“力量的完满”的“畏惧”因素才被转化为“存在的完满”。

这又重新把我们领回到神秘主义的话题上来了。仅仅探究一个事物的起源，是很难解释它的本质特性的，因此，对我们来说，神秘主义是如何在历史上产生的并不重要。重要的是，神秘主义对宗教中的非理性的者超理性的因素作了很高的，确切地说是无以复加的强调；而且，只有这样看待神秘主义，它才是易于理解的。非理性的不同阶段与不同因素会受到不同的重视，而神秘主义的类型也由于这些不同阶段或者因素所进入的背景而各不相同。但是，我们一直在分析的，是在所有的神秘主义中都一再出现的特征，它不是别的，正是那种被强调到无以复加程度的“被造物意识”。如果我们再重复一下已经做出的对比，那么，这一术语的含义就不是“我们的被造感”，而是“我们的被造物身份感”，也就是每一个被造物在面对那个高踞于万物之上者时所产生的那种卑微渺小感。

所有类型的神秘主义的一个共同的特征，就是这种带有超常的实在性的个性自我在不同完整程度上的认同。这种认同有其自身的来源——此处不再提及，并且是从宗教经验的诸多“要素”中产生出来的，对这些要素需要单独处理。然而，对于神秘主义来说，仅有“认同”是不够的；它必须是带有对某种东西的认同，这种东西在力量、实在性以及全部的非理性中同时是绝对的至高无上。正是在神秘主义者中，我们更多地遇到这种宗教意识的要素。雷西雅克在他的《论神秘意识的诸因素》(巴

of religious consciousness. Récéjac has noticed this in his *Essai sur les fondements de la connaissance mystique* (Paris, 1897). He writes (p. 90):

Le mysticisme commence par la crainte, par le sentiment d'une *domination* universelle, *invincible* et devient plus tard un désir d'union avec ce qui domine ainsi.

And some very clear examples of this taken from the religious experience of the present day are to be found in W. James (*op. cit.*, p. 66):

The perfect stillness of the night was thrilled by a more solemn silence. The darkness held a presence that was all the more felt because it was not seen. I could not any more have doubted that *He* was there than that I was. Indeed, I felt myself to be, if possible, the less real of the two.

This example is particularly instructive as to the relation of mysticism to the 'feelings of identification', for the experience here recounted was on the point of passing into it. ①

3. *The Element of 'Energy' or Urgency*

There is, finally, a third element comprised in those of *tremendum* and *majestas*, awefulness and majesty, and this I venture to call the 'urgency' or 'energy' of the numinous object. It is particularly vividly perceptible in the *ὀργή* or 'wrath'; and it everywhere clothes itself in symbolical expressions—vitality, passion, emotional temper, will, force, movement, ② excitement, activity, impetus. These features are typical and recur again and again from the daemonic level up to the idea of the 'living' God. We have here the factor

---

① Compare too the experience on p. 70: '... What I felt on these occasions was a temporary loss of my own identity'.

② The 'mobilitas Dei' of Lactantius.

黎,1897)中已经注意到这一点了。他写道(第90页):

神秘主义起源于一种恐惧,一种对于某个万能的、不可战胜的力量的感受。后来,它变为一种想与这种力量结合的愿望。

在W.詹姆士的著作中,可以找到一些取材于当前宗教经验的非常清晰的例子(《宗教体验的类别》第66页):

夜晚那完美的宁静因为某种更加肃穆的寂寥而让人感到毛骨悚然。黑暗引起不可见而更加让人感到它的存在。我丝毫不再怀疑他(神)的存在远甚于我的存在。事实上,如果两种存在都是可能的话,我感到我自己的存在更加缺乏真实性。

这个例子对于理解神秘主义与"认同感"的关系特别具有启发性,因为这里所描述的经验正是要进入认同之中。[1]

3."活力"或者催促因素

最后,在敬畏与威严中还包含着第三种因素,对此我斗胆称之为这一神秘对象的"催促"或者"活力"因素。这一因素在"愤怒"(*ὀργή*)中尤为生动可感;而且它还到处以象征性的形式来装饰自己,诸如生机、激情、情绪、意志、力量、活动[2]、激越、行动、动力等。从魔鬼观层面到"活的"上帝观念,这些特征都表现得很典型并且再三出现。在这里,我们得到的是这样一个

① 比较在第70页上的经验描写:"……我在这些场合所感受到的,是自我身份的一种临时丧失"。

② 拉克坦修斯的"活动的神"。

that has everywhere more than any other prompted the fiercest opposition to the 'philosophic' God of mere rational speculation, who can be put into a definition. And for their part the philosophers have condemned these expressions of the energy of the numen, whenever they are brought on to the scene, as sheer anthropomorphism. In so far as their opponents have for the most part themselves failed to recognize that the terms they have borrowed from the sphere of human conative and affective life have merely value as analogies, the philosophers are right to condemn them. But they are wrong, in so far as, this error notwithstanding, these terms stood for a genuine aspect of the divine nature—its non-rational aspect—a due consciousness of which served to protect religion itself from being 'rationalized' away.

For wherever men have been contending for the 'living' God or for voluntarism, there, we may be sure, have been non-rationalists fighting rationalists and rationalism. It was so with Luther in his controversy with Erasmus; and Luther's *omnipotentia Dei* in his *De Servo Arbitrio* is nothing but the union of 'majesty'—in the sense of absolute supremacy—with this 'energy', in the sense of a force that knows not stint nor stay, which is urgent, active, compelling, and alive. In mysticism, too, this element of 'energy' is a very living and vigorous factor, at any rate in the 'voluntaristic' mysticism, the mysticism of love, where it is very forcibly seen in that 'consuming fire' of love whose burning strength the mystic can hardly bear, but begs that the heat that has scorched him may be mitigated, lest he be himself destroyed by it. And in this urgency and pressure the mystic's 'love' claims a perceptible kinship with the *ὀργή* itself, the scorching and consuming wrath of God; it is the same 'energy', only differently directed. 'Love', says one of the mystics, 'is nothing else than quenched wrath.'

The element of 'energy' reappears in Fichte's speculations

因素,它在一切地方都比其他任何因素更多地引起了针对那种仅仅是理性沉思的、能够被加以界定的、“哲学式的”上帝的最激烈的反对态度。在哲学家这一方面,无论神秘的力量在何处出现,哲学家们将其表现形式都斥之为纯粹的拟人说。只要哲学家的反对者们自己在最大程度上没有认识到他们从人类意向性和感受型生活领域中借来的术语仅有类比的价值,那么,哲学家们的贬斥就是正确的。然而这些哲学家们错了,尽管有些失误,这些术语在一定程度上代表了神性本质的真实方面——其非理性方面,这是确保了宗教本身不被“理性化”化掉的一个恰当的意识。

因为无论在哪里,只要有人为“活的”上帝或者唯意志论而斗争,我们都可以确定,那里就一定有非理性主义者同理性主义者以及理性主义的斗争。路德与伊拉斯谟的论战就是如此,而且路德的万能的神(*omnipotentia Dei* in his *De Servo Arbitrio*)正是绝对的至高无上意义上的“威严”与不加节制、变动不居的力量意义上的“活力”这二者的结合,这种“活力”是急切的、能动的、强制性的和生机盎然的。在神秘主义中,这种“活力”因素也是非常活跃、非常有力的因素,无论如何在“唯意志论的”神秘主义及关于爱的神秘主义中就是如此。在这种神秘主义中,“活力”因素可以在爱的“烈焰”中被非常清楚地发现,它的燃烧力是神秘主义者难以承受的,他只能祈求那种炙烤着他的灼热能够平息下来,以免他因此被自己摧毁。在这种催促和压力下,神秘主义者的“爱”声称与 ὀργή 即上帝的灼热而强烈的愤怒有明显的亲缘关系;它是同一种“活力”,只不过被引向了不同的方向。某个神秘主义者说:“爱不过是熄灭了的愤怒。”

在费希特关于绝对性的沉思中,这种“活力”因素以巨大的、

on the Absolute as the gigantic, never-resting, active worldstress, and in Schopenhauer's daemonic 'Will'. At the same time both these writers are guilty of the same error that is already found in myth; they transfer 'natural' attributes, which ought only to be used as 'ideograms' for what is itself properly beyond utterance, to the non-rational as real qualifications of it, and they mistake symbolic expressions of feelings for adequate concepts upon which a 'scientific' structure of knowledge may be based.

In Goethe, as we shall see later, the same element of energy is emphasized in a quite unique way in his strange descriptions of the experience he calls 'daemonic'.

永不停息的、活跃的世界压力的形式重现，在叔本华那里，则表现为魔鬼般的"意志"。同时，这两位作家都犯了神话中已经发现过的同样的错误，他们把那种只应当被用做"表意符号"——用来指称那种它自身无法准确表述的东西——的"自然的"性质看成是非理性的真正性质，并且他们把情感的象征性表达方式错当成了"科学的"知识结构得以确立其上的充足概念。

在哥德那里，如我们后面将会看到的，在他称之为"魔鬼般的"经历的奇特描述中，这个同样的活力因素以一种独特的方式被强调。

CHAPTER V
The Analysis Of ‘ Mysterium’

Ein begriffeher Gott ist Kein Gott

‘ A God comprehended is no God. ’

(TERSTEEGEN.)

We gave to the object to which the numinous consciousness is directed the name *mysterium tremendum*, and we then set ourselves first to determine the meaning of the adjective *tremendum*—which we found to be itself only justified by analogy—because it is more easily analysed than the substantive idea *mysterium*. We have now to turn to this, and try, as best we may, by hint and suggestion, to get to a clearer apprehension of what it implies.

4. *The ‘ Wholly Other’*

It might be thought that the adjective itself gives an explanation of the substantive; but this is not so. It is not merely analytical; it is a synthetic attribute to it; i. e. *tremendum* adds something not necessarily inherent in *mysterium*. It is true that the reactions in consciousness that correspond to the one readily and spontaneously overflow into those that correspond to the other; in fact, anyone sensitive to the use of words would commonly feel that the idea of ‘ mystery’ (*mysterium*) is so closely bound up with its synthetic qualifying attribute ‘ aweful’ (*tremendum*) that one can hardly say the former without catching an echo of the latter, ‘ mystery’

第五章 对“神秘”的分析

“一个被理解的上帝绝不是上帝。”

（特尔斯特根）

我们把那种神秘的意识被引向的对象命名为令人畏惧的神秘物，然后我们首先确定“令人畏惧的”作为形容词的含义——我们发现这种含义仅仅是通过类比而得到确认的——因为它比“神秘”这样一个实质性概念更容易分析。现在我们就转向这一观念，并且尽我们所能，通过暗示的方式，力图对它所意味着的东西获得更加清晰的理解。

4.“完全的他者”

人们也许会认为：一个词的形容词部分本身就给出了它的名词部分的释义，但事实并非如此。一个词不仅是分析性的，它还有综合性，也就是说，“畏惧”一词加上了并不必然内在于“神秘”中的东西。的确，在意识中，符合于一种事物的反应会很容易、很自然地过渡到符合于另一事物的反应中；事实上，任何一个对词汇的使用敏感的人，都会同样地感到“神秘”这一观念是如此紧密地与它的综合性的限定性质“敬畏”联系在一起，以致几乎没有人能在说到前者时不从后者得到回应；对我们来说，“神秘”本身几乎

almost of itself becoming 'aweful mystery' to us. But the passage from the one idea to the other need not by any means be always so easy. The elements of meaning implied in 'awefulness' and 'mysteriousness' are in themselves definitely different. The latter may so far preponderate in the religious consciousness, may stant out so vividly, that in comparison with it the former almost sinks out of sight; a case which again could be clearly exemplified from some forms of mysticism. Occasionally, on the other hand, the reverse happens, and the *tremendum* may in turn occupy the mind without the *mysterium*.

This latter, then, needs special consideration on its own account. We need an expression for the mental reaction peculiar to it; and here, too, only one word seems appropriate, though, as it is strictly applicable only to a 'natural' state of mind, it has here meaning only by analogy: it is the word 'stupor'. *Stupor* is plainly a different thing from *tremor*; it signifies blank wonder, an astonishment that strikes us dumb, amazement absolute.① Taken, indeed, in its purely natural sense, *mysterium* would first mean merely a secret or a mystery in the sense of that which is alien to us, uncomprehended and unexplained; and so far *mysterium* is itself merely an ideogram, an analogical notion taken from the natural sphere, illustrating, but incapable of exhaustively rendering, our

① Compare also *obstupefacere*. Still more exact equivalents are the Greek *θάμβος* and *θαμβεῖν*. The sound θ α μ β (*thamb*) excellently depicts this state of mind of blank, staring wonder. And the difference between the moments of *stupor* and *tremor* is very finely suggested by the passage, Mark x. 32 (*cf. infra*, p. 158). On the other hand, what was said above of the facility and rapidity with which the two moments merge and blend is also markedly true of *θάμβος*, which then becomes a classical term for the (ennobled) awe of the numinous in general. So Mark xvi. 5 is rightly translated by Luther 'und sie entsetzten sich', and by the English Authorized Version 'and they were affrighted'.

就是“令人敬畏的神秘”。但是,从一个观念过渡到另一个观念并不总是如此容易,隐含在“畏惧”与“神秘”中的意义的因素本身是完全不同的。在宗教意识中,后者远远地超出了前者,它是如此生动地表现出来,以致前者在与之对比中几乎淡出了视野;这一情形可以再次从几种神秘主义中得到清晰的例证。另一方面,相反的情形也偶尔发生,“畏惧”会在没有“神秘”的情况下逐渐占据心灵。

因此,后一观念需要特别的关注。我们需要一个术语来指称这种只对它发生的精神反应,而且这里也仅有一个词显得合适,尽管它只能被严格地应用于“自然的”心灵状态,在这里,它仅仅通过类比获得了其含义,这就是“瞠目结舌”一词。瞠目结舌和畏惧明显不是同一种东西;它意味着茫然的惊奇,一种令我们哑口无言的惊吓,一种绝对的震惊。[1] 确实,就其纯粹的自然含义来说,神秘首先仅仅意味着一个秘密或者一个神秘之物,这种秘密或者神秘之物在一定意义上是与我们相背离的,是无法理解和不可解释的;而且迄今为止,神秘本身不过是一个表意符号,即一个取自自然领域的类比概念,说明着但是却不能彻底地表达我

---

① 还要与 *obstupefacere* 比较。更加准确的同义词是希腊语的 *θάμβος* 和 *θαμβεῖν*,*θάμβ* 的发音(*thamb*)极好地描述了这种茫然的、目瞪口呆的心理状态。瞠目结舌与畏惧之间的差别还通过《马可福音》第 10 章第 32 节(参见下文第 158 页——此处指英文原版,以下同)得到了很好的表明。另一方面,上面所谈到的两种因素可以出现并混合在一起的便利与快捷对于 *θάμβος* 也同样适用,因此,*θάμβος* 变成了用来表示包含在神秘中的(被尊奉的)畏惧的经典术语。因此,《马可福音》第 16 章第 5 节被路德正确地译为“und sie entsetzten sich”(他们深感惊愕),而据权威的英文版本则是“他们感到害怕”。

real meaning. Taken in the religious sense, that which is 'mysterious' is—to give it perhaps the most striking expression—the 'wholly other' (*θάτερν* *anyad*, *alienum*), that which is quite beyond the sphere of the usual, the intelligible, and the familiar, which therefore falls quite outside the limits of the 'canny', and is contrasted with it, filling the mind with blank wonder and astonishment.

This is already to be observed on the lowest and earliest level of the religion of primitive man, where the numinous consciousness is but an inchoate stirring of the feelings. What is really characteristic of this stage is *not*—as the theory of Animism would have us believe—that men are here concerned with curious entities, called 'souls' or 'spirits', which happen to be invisible. Representations of spirits and similar conceptions are rather one and all early modes of 'rationalizing' a precedent experience, to which they are subsidiary. They are attempts in some way or other, it little matters how, to guess the riddle it propounds, and their effect is at the same time always to weaken and deaden the experience itself. They are the source from which springs, not religion, but the rationalization of religion, which often ends by constructing such a massive structure of theory and such a plausible fabric of interpretation, that the 'mystery' is frankly excluded. ①Both imaginative 'myth', when developed into a system, and intellectualist Scholasticism, when worked out to its completion, are methods by which the fundamental fact of religious experience is, as it were, simply rolled out so thin and flat as to be finally eliminated altogether.

Even on the lowest level of religious development the essential characteristic is therefore to be sought elsewhere than in the appearance of 'spirit' representations. It lies rather, we repeat,

① A spirit or soul that has been conceived and comprehended no longer prompts to 'shuddering', as is proved by Spiritualism. But it thereby ceases to be of interest for the psychology of religion.

们的真实意图。从宗教的意义上来看,所谓"神秘的"就是——姑且给其一个或许是最显著的表达用语——"完全的他者"(*θάτερν anyad, alienum*),它完全超出了日常的、可理解的和熟悉的领域,并因此完全落在"审慎"的界限之外与之相对立,使心灵充满了迷茫的惊奇与惊愕。

这一情况在原始人的最低、最早阶段的宗教上——在这种神秘的意识还只是处于感觉的萌动期的地方就已经被发现了。这一阶段的真正特征不是像泛灵论要我们相信的那样,人们在这里关注的是那些被称做"灵魂"或者"精神"——那种似乎碰巧无法看见的奇怪实体。精神的表现与类似的概念都只是对先前体验的"理性化"的所有早期形式,对这些先前体验来说,它们是从属的。它们努力以这样或那样的方式——方式本身并不重要,去猜测这种先前体验提出的谜,而它们努力的结果同时又总是弱化和僵化这种体验自身。它们不是宗教,而是宗教的理性化发生的源泉,这一源泉常常因建构起一个庞大的理论体系和言之凿凿的解释框架而告终,结果"神秘"被完全地排斥出去。[①] 发展成为一个系统的虚构的"神话"与达到其完善阶段的知性论的经院哲学都是方法,透过这两种方法,宗教体验的基本事实就好像被简单地铺展开来,如此浅薄,如此单调,以致最终被完全消灭掉了。

即便在宗教发展的最低阶段,宗教体验的本质特征也不是在"精神"表现的表象中,而是在其他地方被追寻的。再重复一遍,

① 正如唯灵论所证明的那样,一种被构想和理解的精神或者灵魂不再能引发"战栗",但它也因此不再被宗教心理学感兴趣。

in a peculiar 'moment' of consciousness, to wit, the *stupor* before something 'wholly other', whether such an other be named 'spirit' or 'daemon' or 'deva', or be left without any name. Nor does it make any difference in this respect whether, to interpret and preserve their apprehension of this 'other', men coin original imagery of their own or adapt imaginations drawn from the world of legend, the fabrications of fancy apart from and prior to any stirrings of daemonic dread.

In accordance with laws of which we shall have to speak again later, this feeling or consciousness of the 'wholly other' will attach itself to, or sometimes be indirectly aroused by means of, objects which are already puzzling upon the 'natural' plane, or are of a surprising or astounding character; such as extraordinary phenomena or astonishing occurrences or things in inanimate nature, in the animal world, or among men. But here once more we are dealing with a case of association between things specifically different—the 'numinous' and the 'natural' moments of consciousness—and not merely with the gradual enhancement of one of them—the 'natural'—till it becomes the other. As in the case of 'natural fear' and 'daemonic dread' already considered, so here the transition from natural to daemonic amazement is not a mere matter of degree. But it is only with the latter that the complementary expression *mysterium* perfectly harmonizes, as will be felt perhaps more clearly in the case of the adjectival form 'mysterious'. No one says, strictly and in earnest, of a piece of clockwork that is beyond his grasp, or of a science that he cannot understand: "That is 'mysterious' to me."

It might be objected that the mysterious is something which is and remains absolutely and invariably beyond our understanding, whereas that which merely eludes our understanding for a time but is perfectly intelligible in principle should be called, not a 'mystery', but merely a 'problem'.

这一特征宁愿存在于意识的一种特殊“要素”之中，即在某种“完全的他者”之前的那种瞠目结舌，不管这种“完全的他者”被命名为“精神”“恶魔”“天神”，还是处于无名的状态中。无论人们是根据自身来创造出原初的肖像，还是采用出自传奇世界的想象——这种想象力的编造物远离于并且优先于任何因对魔鬼的恐慌而产生的骚动——去解释和保持他们对这种“他者”的理解，在这一方面都没有任何差别。

与那些我们后面将会再次谈到的法则相一致，这种对于“完全的他者”的感觉或意识会将自身附着于一些对象上，或者有时由于这些对象而被间接地引起，这些对象在“自然的”层面上就已经令人困惑不解，或者具有让人惊异或震惊的性质。例如在无机界、动物界以及人类之中发生的那些超常现象、引人震惊的事件或者事物。但是，我们在这里要再次论及的是迥然相异的两个事物之间的结合——意识的“神秘的”和“自然的”因素的结合，而不仅仅是谈论二者之一的“自然”因素的逐渐提升，直至它变成别的东西。就像在前面已经谈过的“自然的惧怕”与“对魔鬼的畏惧”的情形中一样，在这里，从自然的惊奇到魔鬼的惊愕的转换也不只是一个程度的问题。但是，神秘这一补充的表达方式只是与后者才完全相称，这一点在“神秘的”这一形容词的形式中或许可以感受得更清楚一些。对于一件超出他所能把握的机械装置或者他所不能理解的科学，没有人会严格地、认真地说：“那对于我来说是‘神秘’的。”

也许有人会反驳说，神秘是而且一直是绝对地、始终不变地超出了我们理解的某种东西，而那种只是暂时地躲避我们的理解但是在理论上是完全可以理解的东西，应当只被称做“问题”，

But this is by no means an adequate account of the matter. The truly 'mysterious' object is beyond our apprehension and comprehension, not only because our knowledge has certain irremovable limits, but because in it we come upon something inherently 'wholly other', whose kind and character are incommensurable with our own, and before which we therefore recoil in a wonder that strikes us chill and numb. ①

This may be made still clearer by a consideration of that degraded offshoot and travesty of the genuine 'numinous' dread or awe, the fear of ghosts. Let us try to analyse this experience. We have already specified the peculiar feelingelement of 'dread' aroused by the ghost as that of 'grue', grisly horror. ②Now this 'grue' obviously contributes something to the attraction which ghost-stories exercise, in so far, namely, as the relaxation of tension ensuing upon our release from it relieves the mind in a pleasant and agreeable way. So far, however, it is not really the ghost itself that gives us pleasure, but the fact that we are rid of it. But obviously this is quite insufficient to explain the ensnaring attraction of the ghost-story. The ghost's real attraction rather consists in this, that of itself and in an uncommon degree it entices the imagination, awakening strong interest and curiosity; it is the weird thing itself that allures the fancy. But it does this, not because it is 'something long and white'

---

① In *Confessions*, ii. 9. I, Augustine very strikingly suggests this stiffening, benumbing element of the 'wholly other' and its contrast to the rational aspect of the numen; the *dissimile* and the *simile*:

'Quid est illud, quod interlucet mihi et percutit cor meum sine laesione? Et inhorresco et inardesco. *Inhorresco*, in quantum *dissimilis* ei sum. Inardesco, in quantum similis ei sum.'

('What is that which gleams through me and smites my heart without wounding it? I am both a-shudder and a-glow. A-shudder, in so far as I am unlike it, a-glow in so far as I am like it.')

② *gruseln, gräsen.*

而不是“神秘”。但是,这绝不是对此问题的充分说明。真正“神秘的”对象是超出了我们的领会和理解的,这不仅因为我们的知识确实具有不可克服的局限,而且因为在其中,我们碰到了某种内在的“完全的他者”,这种“完全的他者”的种类和特性与我们的是不能比较的,因此,我们在它面前,只有退缩到那种让我们呆若木鸡的惊愕之中。①

通过对真正“神秘的”畏惧或者敬畏的退化了的分支与戏仿——对鬼魅的恐惧的思考,上述情形会显得更加清晰。让我们来试着分析一下这种经验。我们已经把有鬼魅引起的“畏惧”的特殊感受因素界定为“胆战心惊”、极端的恐惧。② 只要这种因惊恐而产生的紧张在得到缓解时能以一种两人愉悦的方式使心灵得到放松,那么,这种“胆战心惊”很显然对鬼怪故事的吸引力作出了贡献。然而,就此而言,给予我们愉悦的,并不真是鬼怪本身,而是我们要摆脱它的这一事实。但是,显然这一点并不足以解释鬼怪故事那种极具诱惑性的吸引力。鬼怪的真正吸引力与其说在于它自身,不如说在于它能在非同寻常的程度上诱发想象、唤醒强烈的兴趣与好奇;它就是诱发想象力的那种神秘之物本身。但是它这样做,并不是因为它是“某种又长又白的东西”

---

① 在《忏悔录》(ii.9.1)中,奥古斯丁非常鲜明地提出“完全的他者”所具有的令人僵硬麻木的因素以及它与“神秘”的理性方面的对比,相异与相同:

“那种穿透我并且重重地击打我的心房而又不伤害它的东西是什么?我既害怕得浑身战栗,又兴奋得浑身发烫。我战栗,是因为我不像它,我兴奋,是因为我像它。”(“Quid est illud, quod interlucet mihi et percutit cor meum sine lacsione? Et inhorresco et inardesco. Inhorresco, in quantum dissimilis ei sum. Inardesco, in quantum similis ei sum.”)

② 恐惧

(as someone once defined a ghost), nor yet through any of the positive and conceptual attributes which fancies about ghosts have invented, but because it is a thing that 'doesn't really exist at all', the 'wholly other', something which has no place in our scheme of reality but belongs to an absolutely different one, and which at the same time arouses an irrepressible interest in the mind.

But that which is perceptibly true in the fear of ghosts, which is, after all, only a caricature of the genuine thing, is in a far stronger sense true of the 'daemonic' experience itself, of which the fear of ghosts is a mere off-shoot. And while, following this main line of development, this element in the numinous consciousness, the feeling of the 'wholly other', is heightened and clarified, its higher modes of manifestation come into being, which set the numinous object in contrast not only to everything wonted and familiar (i. e. in the end, to nature in general), thereby turning it into the 'supernatural', but finally to the world itself, and thereby exalt it to the 'supramundane', that which is above the whole worldorder.

In mysticism we have in the 'beyond' (ἐπέκεινα) again the strongest stressing and over-stressing of those non-rational elements which are already inherent in all religion. Mysticism continues to its extreme point this contrasting of the numinous object (the numen), as the 'wholly other', with ordinary experience. Not content with contrasting it with all that is of nature or this world, mysticism concludes by contrasting it with Being itself and all that 'is', and finally actually calls it 'that which is nothing'. By this 'nothing' is meant not only that of which nothing can be predicated, but that which is absolutely and intrinsically other than and opposite of everything that is and can be thought. But while exaggerating to the point of paradox this *negation* and contrast—the

(就像有人曾经描述的鬼魅的样子),也不是通过关于鬼魅的想象所发明出来的任何肯定的、概念化的性质,而是因为它是"根本就不存在"的东西,是"完全的他者",是在我们的现实图景中无任何立锥之地但是却属于一种绝对不同的、同时在我们心灵中引发遏制不住的兴趣的某种东西。

但是,在对鬼怪的惧怕中感觉真实的,是"魔鬼"体验本身的更加强烈的真实感,毕竟,鬼怪只是真实事物的外在描摹,而对鬼怪的惧怕仅仅是魔鬼体验的一个分支。并且,遵循着这一发展主线,当神秘意识中的这种因素,即对于"完全的他者"的感受,得到提升和澄清时,它的更高的表现形式就产生出来了,这些表现形式不仅把这个神秘的对象与每一种熟悉的事物相对立(也就是最终与自然相对立),并因此将其转变为"超自然",而且最后还与世界本身相对立,并因此将其推崇到"超现世"的高度即高踞于整个世界秩序之上。

在神秘主义中,我们再次在"彼岸"(ἐπέκεινα)的观念中发现对于已经包含在所有宗教中的非理性因素的最强有力的、超级的强调。神秘主义继续将作为"完全的他者"的神秘对象(神秘者)与日常经验的对立推向极致。不满足于神秘对象与一切具有自然性质或者此岸性质的东西相对立,神秘主义通过让这种神秘对象与存在本身以及所有的"存在者"相对立,总结并最终声称它就是那种"虚无"。这时的"虚无"所指的,不仅是无法断言的某种东西,而且包括那种绝对地本质地不同于以及相反于所有现存的和能够被想到的事物。不过,当把这种否定性与对立性夸大到自相矛盾的地步

only means open to conceptual thought to apprehend the *mysterium*—mysticism at the same time retains the *positive quality* of the 'wholly other' as a very living factor in its overbrimming religious emotion.

But what is true of the strange 'nothingness' of our mystics holds good equally of the *sūnyam* and the *sūnyatā*, the 'void' and 'emptiness' of the Buddhist mystics. This aspiration for the 'void' and for becoming void, no less than the aspiration of our western mystics for 'nothing' and for becoming nothing, must seem a kind of lunacy to anyone who has no inner sympathy for the esoteric language and ideograms of mysticism, and lacks the matrix from which these come necessarily to birth. To such an one Buddhism itself will be simply a morbid sort of pessimism. But in fact the 'void' of the eastern, like the 'nothing' of the western, mystic is a numinous ideogram of the 'wholly other'.

These terms 'supernatural' and 'transcendent'① give the appearance of positive attributes, and, as applied to the mysterious, they appear to divest the *mysterium* of its originally negative meaning and to turn it into an affirmation. On the side of conceptual thought this is nothing more than appearance, for it is obvious that the two terms in question are merely negative and exclusive attributes with reference to 'nature' and the world or cosmos respectively. But on the side of the feeling-content it is otherwise; that is in very truth positive in the highest degree, though here too, as before, it cannot be rendered explicit in conceptual terms. It is through this positive feeling-content that the concepts of the 'transcendent' and 'supernatural' become forthwith designations for a unique 'wholly other' reality and quality, something of whose special character we can *feel*, without being able to give it clear conceptual expression.

---

① literally, supramundane: *überweltlich*.

时——这是概念性思维领会神秘的唯一方式——神秘主义同时又把这个"完全的他者"的肯定性质作为一种非常活跃的因素保留在它的充沛的宗教感受中。

不过我们的神秘主义者的那种奇怪的"虚无"的含义与佛教神秘主义者的"空"、"空无"(the *sūnyam* and the *sūnyatā*)基本相当。这种对"空"与变成空无的渴望正如我们西方神秘主义者对于"虚无"以及对于变成虚无的渴望,对于任何一个对神秘主义的奥秘语言与表意符号毫无内在同情的人,以及对于那些缺乏与生俱来的基质的人来说,这就像是一种精神错乱。对这样的人来说,佛教本身仅仅是一种病态的悲观主义。但是事实上,东方的"空"就像西方的神秘主义的"虚无",是"完全的他者"的神秘的表意符号。

"超自然的"与"超越的"[①]这些术语表现出肯定的性质,一旦被用于神秘的事物时,它们就显示出要剥去神秘一词原有的否定性的含义,并要将之转变成为一种肯定。从概念性思维的方面来看,这只不过是外观而已,因为很显然,被讨论的这两个术语仅仅分别是关于"自然"和世界或者宇宙的否定的、排外的性质。但是从感受内容的方面来看则是另一回事;感受的内容的确是最高程度的肯定,尽管在这里,如同在前面一样,它不能以概念性的术语被清晰地表达出来。正是通过这种肯定的感受内容,"超自然的"和"超越的"这两个概念立刻成为用来指称某个独特的"完全的他者"的实体与性质的标示——某种我们可以感受到它的特殊性质,但却不能给以清晰的概念表达的东西。

---

① 字面意思是"超现世的":*überwelilich*。

CHAPTER VI

5. The Element Of Fascination

The qualitative *content* of the numinous experience, to which ' the mysterious' stands as *form*, is in one of its aspects the element of daunting ' awefulness' and ' majesty', which has already been dealt with in detail; but it is clear that it has at the same time another aspect, in which it shows itself as something uniquely attractive and *fascinating*.

These two qualities, the daunting and the fascinating, now combine in a strange harmony of contrasts, and the resultant dual character of the numinous consciousness, to which the entire religious development bears witness, at any rate from the level of the ' daemonic dread' onwards, is at once the strangest and most noteworthy phenomenon in the whole history of religion. The daemonic-divine object may appear to the mind an object of horror and dread, but at the same time it is no less something that allures with a potent charm, and the creature, who trembles before it, utterly cowed and cast down, has always at the same time the impulse to turn to it, nay even to make it somehow his own. The ' mystery' is for him not merely something to be wondered at but something that entrances him; and beside that in it which bewilders and confounds, he feels a something that captivates and transports him with a strange ravishment, rising often enough to the pitch of dizzy intoxication; it is the Dionysiacelement in the numen.

The ideas and concepts which are the parallels or ' schemata' on the rational side of this non-rational element of ' fascination' are love, mercy, pity, comfort; these are all ' natural' elements of the

第六章

5.沉迷的因素

神秘经验的质的内容——“神秘”是作为它的形式——是存在于前面已经详细讨论过的令人畏缩的“敬畏”和“威严”因素的诸多方面之一;但是很清楚,这种经验同时具有其他的方面,在其中它将自身显示为独具吸引力和迷醉性质的某种东西。

这两种性质,即令人畏缩和引人迷醉的性质以一种奇特的对立统一的方式结合起来了,而作为结果的这个神秘意识的二元性质——至少从先前“对魔鬼的畏惧”的层面上整个宗教发展都可以为之证明——立刻成为整个宗教历史中最奇特的和最值得关注的现象。这种魔-神对象可以在心灵中显现为一种令人惊恐畏惧的对象,但是,它又可以是能产生强大魅力的某种东西,而那些被造物,那些在它面前战战兢兢、恐惧万分而又沮丧不安的人,同时又总是不由自主地转向它,不仅如此,他甚至还要将它变成他自己的东西。对他来说,“神秘”不仅是某种令他惊愕的东西,而且也是进入他内心深处的某种东西;紧邻着那种让他深感迷乱困惑的东西,他还感受到某种吸引他并引他获得奇特的销魂的感觉,这种感觉常常上升到一种让人头晕目眩、极度迷狂的程度;这就是神秘中的狄奥尼索斯因素。

“沉迷”的非理性因素的理性方面的类比与“图解”的观念和概念是爱、仁慈、怜悯以及慰藉;它们都是普通精神生活的“自然

common psychical life, only they are here thought as absolute and in completeness. But important as these are for the experience of religious bliss or felicity, they do not by any means exhaust it. It is just the same as with the opposite experience of religious infelicity—the experience of the ὀργή or 'wrath' of God:—both alike contain fundamentally non-rational elements. Bliss or beatitude is more, far more, than the mere natural feeling of being comforted, of reliance, of the joy of love, however these may be heightened and enhanced. Just as 'wrath', taken in a purely rational or a purely ethical sense, does not exhaust that profound element of *awefulness* which is locked in the mystery of deity, so neither does 'graciousness' exhaust the profound element of *wonderfulness* and rapture which lies in the mysterious beatific experience of deity. The term 'grace' may indeed be taken as its aptest designation, but then only in the sense in which it is really applied in the language of the mystics, and in which not only the 'gracious intent' but 'something more' is meant by the word. This 'something more' has its antecedent phases very far back in the history of religions.

It may well be possible, it is even probable, that in the first stage of its development the religious consciousness started with only one of its poles—the 'daunting' aspect of the numen —and so at first took shape only as 'daemonic dread'. But if this did not point to something beyond itself, if it were not but one 'moment' of a completer experience, pressing up gradually into consciousness, then no transition would be possible to the feelings of positive self-surrender to the numen. The only type of worship that could result from this 'dread' alone would be that of ἀπαιτεῖσθαι and ἀποτρέπειν, taking the form of expiation and propitiation, the averting or the appeasement of the 'wrath' of the numen. It can never explain how it is that 'the numinous' is the object of search and desire and yearning, and that too for its own sake and not only for the sake of the aid and backing that men expect from it in the natural sphere. It can never explain how this takes place, not only in the forms of 'rational' religious

的"因素,只是在这里它们才被当作绝对的和完满之物被思考。尽管这些观念对于表达宗教福佑与宗教幸福的经验是重要的,它们却绝没有穷尽这种经验。作为其反面即不幸的宗教经验——那种对上帝的"愤怒"(the ὀργή)的经验——也同样如此:两者都在根本上包含着非理性的因素。福佑或者至福远甚于被慰藉、信任以及爱的愉悦等自然感受,无论这些自然感受得到了怎样的提升与加强。就像在纯粹理性与纯粹伦理意义上的"愤怒"没有穷尽那被禁闭在神性的神秘之中的敬畏的深刻因素一样,"仁慈"也同样没有穷尽存在于神的神秘赐福的体验中的惊奇与狂喜的深刻因素。"恩典"这一术语也许的确是这种极乐经验最贴切的表达,但是另一方面,只有在它被真正应用于神秘主义者的语言中它才有此意义,并且在神秘主义者的语言中,这一词汇不仅意味着"恩典意图",还指"更多的东西"。这种"更多的东西"在宗教史的初期就有其表现了。

情况有可能,甚至很可能是这样的:在宗教意识发展的最初阶段,它只是从其一端——神秘的"令人畏惧的"方面——开始,并且最初只是形成"对魔鬼的恐惧"。但是,如果这一因素不指向超越自身的某种东西,如果它只不过是逐渐强化到意识中去的较为完满的经验的一个"因素"而已,那么,就不可能发生向神秘者主动臣服这一感受的转化了。单单因为这种"畏惧"而产生的唯一的崇拜形式,是采取赎罪与和解形式的 ἀπαιτεῖσθαι 和 ἀποτρέπειν,是对神秘者的"愤怒"的转移与平息。它永远无法解释为什么"神秘"是人们追求、向往与渴望的对象,为什么人们不只是要在自然领域中期望从它那里得到帮助与依靠,而是为了"神秘"本身而追求"神秘"。它也永远无法解释为什么这种情况不仅发生在"理性的"宗教崇拜的

worship, but in those queer 'sacramental' observances and rituals and procedures of communion in which the human being seeks to get the numen into his possession.

Religious practice may manifest itself in those normal and easily intelligible forms which occupy so prominent a place in the history of religion, such forms as propitiation, petition, sacrifice, thanksgiving, &c. But besides these there is a series of strange proceedings which are constantly attracting greater and greater attention, and in which it is claimed that we may recognize, besides mere religion in general, the particular roots of mysticism. I refer to those numerous curious modes of behaviour and fantastic forms of mediation, by means of which the primitive religious man attempts to master 'the mysterious', and to fill himself and even to identify himself with it. These modes of behaviour fall apart into two classes. On the one hand the 'magical' identification of the self with the numen proceeds by means of various transactions, at once magical and devotional in character—by formula, ordination, adjuration, consecration, exorcism, &c.: on the other hand are the 'shamanistic' ways of procedure, possession, indwelling, self-fulfilment in exaltation and ecstasy. All these have, indeed, their starting-points simply in magic, and their intention at first was certainly simply to appropriate the prodigious force of the numen for the natural ends of man. But the process does not rest there. Possession of and by the numen becomes an end in itself; it begins to be sought for its own sake; and the wildest and most artificial methods of asceticism are put into practice to attain it. In a word, the *vita religiosa* begins; and to remain in these strange and bizarre states of numinous possession becomes a good in itself, even a way of salvation, wholly different from the profane goods pursued by means of magic. Here, too, commences the process of development by which the experience is matured and purified, till finally it reaches its consummation in the sublimest and purest states of the 'life within the Spirit' and in the noblest mysticism. Widely various as these

形式中，而且发生在那些古怪的“圣典的”惯例和仪式以及交往程序中——在这些活动中，人类力图把神秘据为己有。

宗教实践可以将自身表现在那些正常的、易于理解的形式中，这些形式，诸如和解、祈祷、献祭、感恩等，在宗教史上占据了显著的位置。但是除了这些，还有一系列正在不断地引起人们越来越大的注意的奇怪程序，据说我们在其中除了可以认识一般的宗教以外，还能认识到神秘主义的特殊的根源。我指的是那些众多的古怪行为方式和异想天开的冥想形式，凭借这些形式，原始宗教信徒试图去把握“神秘”，并且力图充实自身，甚至想以“神秘”来界定自身。这些行为模式分解为两类：一种是自我与神秘的“魔法”认同，即通过各种各样同时具有魔法和祷告性质的转换行为，诸如宗教仪式、神职授任、恳请祷告、献祭以及驱魔等等，使自我认同于“神秘”。另一种是“萨满教的”方式，即在兴奋和迷醉中与“神秘”融为一体。的确，这些形式完全可以在魔法中找到其起点，而且它们的最初意图肯定只是为了人类的自然目标去占有神秘者的巨大力量，但是这一进程到此为止。占有神秘或者被神秘占有变成了目的本身；神秘开始因为自身的缘故而被探求；为了最终获得神秘，最疯狂的、最做作的禁欲主义的方法被施行起来。一句话，宗教史开始了；而驻留在这些奇异的反常的神秘占有状态之中变成了它自身的目的，甚至成了一种拯救的方式，完全不同于靠着魔法手段所追求的世俗的目的。这里也开始了一个发展过程，通过它，宗教经验得到了成熟与净化，直到最终，它在“生活在圣灵之中”这种最庄严的最纯净的状态中以及最高贵的神秘主义中达到了它的圆满。尽管这些状态本身各不相同，但

states are in themselves, yet they have this element in common, that in them the *mysterium* is experienced in its essential, positive, and specific character, as something that bestows upon man a beatitude beyond compare, but one whose real nature he can neither proclaim in speech nor conceive in thought, but may know only by a direct and living experience. It is a bliss which embraces all those blessings that are indicated or suggested in positive fashion by any 'doctrine of salvation', and it quickens all of them through and through; but these do not exhaust it. Rather by its allpervading, penetrating glow it makes of these very blessings more than the intellect can conceive in them or affirm of them. It gives the peace that passes understanding, and of which the tongue can only stammer brokenly. Only from afar, by metaphors and analogies, do we come to apprehend what it is in itself, and even so our notion is but inadequate and confused.

'Eye hath not seen, nor ear heard, neither have entered into the heart of man, the things which God hath prepared for them that love him.' Who does not feel the exalted sound of these words and the 'Dionysiac' element of transport and fervour in them? It is instructive that in such phrases as these, in which consciousness would fain put its highest consummation into words, 'all images fall away' and the mind turns from them to grasp expressions that are purely negative. And it is still more instructive that in reading and hearing such words their merely negative character simply is not noticed; that we can let whole chains of such negations enrapture, even intoxicate us, and that entire hymns—and deeply impressive hymns—have been composed, in which there is really nothing positive at all! All this teaches us the independence of the positive content of this experience from the implications of its overt conceptual expression, and how it can be firmly grasped, thoroughly understood, and profoundly appreciated, purely in, with, and from the feeling itself.

Mere love, mere trust, for all the glory and happiness they

是，它们却有一个共同的因素，这就是，在这些状态中神秘在其根本的、肯定的和特殊的性质中被体验给予人类以无与伦比的祝福的某种东西，但是这种东西的真实性质既不能为言辞所宣讲，也不能以思维来构想，而只能通过直接的、活生生的经验来认识。这是一种福佑，它包含了通过“拯救的信条”以肯定的形式指明或者暗示了的所有祝福，而且它还全面地激活了这些祝福；但是，这些祝福并没有穷尽它。相反，它以其遍照一切的闪耀的光芒，把这些祝福变成了远非理智所能构想和断言的东西。它给予超越理解的宁静，而语言对此几乎无法顺畅地表达。只有从远处以隐喻和类比的方式，我们才能理解它本身是什么，而且即便如此，我们的观念依然是不充分的和困惑的。

“眼睛看不到，耳朵听不到，两者都未进入人的心中，这就是上帝为爱他的众生所准备的东西。”谁会感受不到这些话语的兴奋的声音和其中包含的狂喜与热情的“狄奥尼索斯”因素呢？富有启发意义的是，在上述语句中——意识很乐意于将其最高的完满交付语言，“所有的意象都消失了”，心灵离开它们，转而抓住了纯粹否定的表达。更具启发意义的是，在阅读和聆听这些话语时，它们的那些否定的性质几乎不被注意到；由此我们可以让这种否定之链的全部环节把我们带入到狂喜和迷醉之中，而那全部的圣歌——那些具有深刻感染力的圣歌——已被谱写完成，其中，的确丝毫不存在肯定的东西！所有这些告诉我们，这种经验的肯定性的内容是独立于它的公开的概念化表述的含义，以及它是怎样纯粹在感受中、与感受一同以及从感受本身出发而被紧紧地抓住，彻底地理解和深刻地欣赏的。

单是爱，单是信任，尽管它们能带来荣耀与幸福，但是却没

bring, do not explain to us that moment of rapture that breathes in our tenderest and most heart-felt hymns of salvation, as also in such eschatological hymns of longing as that Rhyme of St. Bernard in which the very verses seem to dance.

Urbs Sion unica, mansio mystica, condita coelo,
Nunc tibi gaudeo, nunc tibi lugeo, tristor, anhelo,
Te, quia corpore non queo, pectore saepe penetro;
Sed caro terrea, terraque carnea, mox cado retro.
Nemo retexere, nemoque promere sustinet ore,
Quo tua moenia, quo capitolia plena nitore.
Id queo dicere, quo modo tangere pollice coelum,
Ut mare currere, sicut in aere figere telum.
Opprimit omne cor ille tuus decor, O Sion, O Pax.
Urbs sine tempore, nulla potest fore laus tibi mendax.
O nova mansio, te pia concio, gens pia munit,
Provehit, excitat, auget, identitat, efficit, unit.'①

① 'O Sion, thou city sole and single, mystic mansion hidden away in the heavens, now I rejoice in thee, now I moan for thee and mourn and yearn for thee; thee often I pass through in the heart, as I cannot in the body, but being but earthly flesh and fleshly earth soon I fall back. None can disclose or utter in speech what plenary radiance fills thy walls and thy citadels. I can as little tell of it as I can touch the skies with my finger, or run upon the sea or make a dart stand still in the air. This thy splendour overwhelms every heart, O Sion, O Peace! O timeless City, no praise can belie thee. O new dwelling-place, thee the concourse and people of the faithful erects and exalts, inspires and increases, joins to itself, and makes complete and one.'

有向我们解释那种流露在我们最温柔、最深情的拯救的圣歌中的狂喜因素,就像流露在圣伯纳德的渴望末日的圣歌中的狂喜一样——在这些圣歌中,这些诗篇就像是在翩翩起舞。

Urbs Sion unica, mansio mystica, condita coelo,
Nunc tibi gaudeo, nunc tibi lugeo, tristor, anhelo,
Te, quia corpore non queo, pectore saepe penetro;
Sed caro terrea, terraque carnea, mox cado retro.
Nemo retexere, nemoque promere sustinet ore,
Quo tua moenia, quo capitolia plena nitore.
Id queo dicere, quo modo tangere pollice coclum,
Ut mare currere, sicut in aere figere telum.
Opprimit omne cor ille tuus decor, O Sion, O Pax.
Urbs sine tempore, nulla potest fore laus tibi mendax.
O nova mansio, te pia concio, gens pia munit,
Provehit, excitat, auget, identitat, efficit, unit. '①

① 啊,锡安,你这独一无二的圣城!远远地隐身于天堂的神秘居所;现在我为你欢欣,为你呜咽,为你悲伤,也为你渴望;我常常在我的心中,而不能在我的身体中将你穿越,但是生命那俗走的肉身与肉身的俗走很快又让我跌回。没人能用言辞来揭示或者表述你城堡与墙壁是多么得辉煌灿烂。就像我不能以手触天,以脚行海,或者让一支标枪停留在空气中一样,我对你的城堡同样无法言说。你的显赫征服了每一个心灵,啊,锡安,啊,安宁!啊,永恒的圣城,没有任何赞美能够配得上你。啊,崭新的家园,你是群众聚集的场所,信徒们建立你,赞美你,唤醒你,扩大你,你也加入自身之中,使自己变得完美无缺。

This is where the living 'something more' of the *fascinans*, the element of fascination, is to be found. It lives no less in those tense extollings of the blessing of salvation, which recur in all religions of salvation, and stand in such remarkable contrast to the relatively meagre and frequently childish import of that which is revealed in them by concept or by image. Everywhere salvation is something whose meaning is often very little apparent, is even wholly obscure, to the 'natural' man; on the contrary, so *far as he understands it*, he tends to find it highly tedious and uninteresting, sometimes downright distasteful and repugnant to his nature, as he would, for instance, find the beatific vision of God in our own doctrine of salvation, or the *henōsis* of 'God all in all' among the mystics. 'So far as he understands', be it noted; but then he does not understand it in the least. Because he lacks the inward teaching of the Spirit, he must needs confound what is offered him as an expression for the experience of salvation — a mere ideogram of what is felt, whose import it hints at by analogy—with 'natural' concepts, as though it were itself just such an one. And so he 'wanders ever farther from the goal'.

It is not only in the religious feeling of longing that the moment of fascination is a living factor. It is already alive and present in the moment of 'solemnity', both in the gathered concentration and humble submergence of private devotion, when the mind is exalted to the holy, and in the common worship of the congregation, where this is practised with earnestness and deep sincerity, as, it is to be feared, is with us a thing rather desired than realized. It is this and nothing else that in the solemn moment can fill the soul so full and keep it so inexpressibly tranquil. Schleiermacher's assertion① is perhaps true of it, as of

① *Glaubenslehre*, § 5.

这正是可以找到那种活生生的“更多的东西”(*fascinans*)即沉迷的因素的地方。它存在于那些颂扬拯救的赞美的状态中,在所有有关拯救的宗教中得到重现,并且如此显著地不同于那些相对贫乏的、通常是幼稚的领悟,即以概念与想象来领悟被揭示的东西。无论在哪里,对于“自然的”人来说,拯救是那种意义通常不是十分明显,甚至完全模糊的某种东西;相反,只要他理解了这种意义,他就会发现它非常得单调乏味,有时候是完全讨厌的,并与其本性相悖,例如,他会在我们自己的拯救的信条中发现上帝的赐福形象,或者在神秘主义者中发现“上帝无所不在”的“唯我独尊地位”(*henōsis*)。注意这个“只要他理解”,但是另一方面他丝毫都不理解拯救的意义。因为他缺乏圣灵内在的教导,他偏要把其中提供给他作为拯救经验的表达形式的东西——这不过是被感受到的东西的表意符号,其含义是通过类比来暗示的——与“自然的”概念混淆,就好像经验本身就是这样一种概念。因此,他就“越发远离了目标”。

并不仅仅是在宗教的渴望感中,沉迷的因素才是一种活生生的因素。在“庄严”的因素中,它已经活跃并出现了,既出现在私人礼拜的全神贯注与卑微虔诚中——此时他的心灵已经被提升到了神圣的高度,又出现在圣会的共同崇拜中——在此这些仪式是伴着郑重其事与深刻的诚挚来施行的,就像在诚惶诚恐中与我们相伴的事物,与其说是我们认识到的,不如说是我们所渴望的。正是这种在庄严因素中的沉迷因素才能够如此充溢地充实我们的灵魂,并将它保持在无法言表的宁静状态之中。施莱尔马赫对它的断言或许是对的,[①]就像

① 见《教义》(*Glaubenslehre*)第5节。

the numinous consciousness in general, viz. that it cannot really occur alone on its own account, or except combined and penetrated with rational elements. But, if this be admitted, it is upon other grounds than those adduced by Schleiermacher; while, on the other hand, it may occupy a more or less predominant place and lead to states of calm (ἡσυχία) as well as of transport, in which it *almost* of itself wholly fills the soul. But in all the manifold forms in which it is aroused in us, whether in eschatological promise of the coming kingdom of God and the transcendent bliss of Paradise, or in the guise of an entry into that beatific reality that is 'above the world'; whether it come first in expectancy or pre-intimation or in a present experience ('When I but *have* Thee, I ask no question of heaven and earth'); in all these forms, outwardly diverse but inwardly akin, it appears as a strange and mighty propulsion towards an ideal good known only to religion and in its nature fundamentally non-rational, which the mind knows of in yearning and presentiment, recognizing it for what it is behind the obscure and inadequate symbols which are its only expression. And this shows that above and beyond our rational being lies hidden the ultimate and highest part of our nature, which can find no satisfaction in the mere allaying of the needs of our sensuous, psychical, or intellectual impulses and cravings. The mystics called it the basis or ground of the soul.

We saw that in the case of the element of the mysterious the 'wholly other' led on to the supernatural and transcendent and that above these appeared the 'beyond' (ἐπέκεινα) of mysticism, through the nonrational side of religion being raised to its highest power and stressed to excess. It is the same in the case of the element of 'fascination'; here, too, is possible a transition into mysticism. At its highest point of stress the fascinating becomes the 'overabounding', 'exuberant', ①the mystical 'moment' which exactly corresponds upon this

① *das Überschwen gliche.*

他对一般的神秘意识的看法一样,也就是说,沉迷的因素除非结合并深入到理性因素之中,它不能真正地独立出现。但是,如果承认这一点,那是在别的基础上,而不是施莱尔马赫引证的基础上。然而,另一方面,它会占据某种较为突出的位置并导致平静(ἡσυχία)与狂喜的心态,在这种心态中,它本身几乎就整个地充满了灵魂。但是,在我们心中被激起的所有的各色形式中,无论是在上帝之国即将到来的末世论的承诺中以及超验的天国的至福中,还是在凭借着某个入口进入到“世界之上”的赐福的实在中;无论它最初是在期望或者预告中到来,还是在当下体验中到来(“只要我拥有您,我就不再询问天国和尘世”);在所有这些表面上看来各不相同却内在类同的形式中,它都呈现为一种奇特有力的推动力,这种推动力指向一种只为宗教所理解而且在其本性上是一种根本的非理性的理想的目的,这种目的是心灵在向往与预感中把握到的,心灵将它看做那种隐藏在模糊贫乏的象征符号背后的东西——这些象征符号是它仅有的表现形式。这表明,在我们的理性存在之上与之外,存在着我们的天性中隐藏着的最后与最高的部分,这些部分并不能通过单纯地减少我们感官的、精神的、理智的以及欲望的需要来得到满足。神秘主义者将其称为灵魂的基础或根基。

我们已经看到,在神秘的因素这一例子中,“完全的他者”持续地导致超自然和超验的东西,并且在其上面,通过宗教存在的非理性方面上升到它的最高力量并得到极度的强调,神秘主义的“彼岸”(ἐπέκεινα)就显示出来。在“沉迷”的因素这一例子中也同样如此;在这里,向神秘主义的转化也是有可能的。在其强调的最高点,沉迷变成了“激情奔放”、“过度热情”,[1]变成神秘的

① 过度热情(*das Überschwωen gliche*)。

line to the ἐπέκεινα upon the other line of approach, and which is to be understood accordingly. But while this feeling of the 'over-abounding' is specially characteristic of mysticism, a trace of it survives in all truly felt states of religious beatitude, however restrained and kept within measure by other factors. This is seen most clearly from the psychology of those great experiences—of grace, conversion, second birth—in which the religious experience appears in its pure intrinsic nature and in heightened activity, so as to be more clearly grasped than in the less typical form of piety instilled by education. The hard core of such experiences in their Christian form consists of the redemption from guilt and bondage to sin, and we shall have presently to see that this also does not occur without a participation of nonrational elements. But leaving this out of account, what we have here to point out is the unutterableness of what has been yet genuinely experienced, and how such an experience may pass into blissful excitement, rapture, and exaltation verging often on the bizarre and the abnormal. ①This is vouched for by the autobiographical testimony of the 'converted' from St. Paul onward. William James has collected a great number of these, without, however, himself noticing the nonrational element that thrills in them.

Thus, one writes

... For the moment nothing but an ineffable joy and exaltation remained. It is impossible fully to describe the experience. It was like the effect of some great orchestra, when all the separate notes

① This may be found fatal to the attempt to construct a 'religion within the limits of pure reason', or 'of humanity'; but, none the less, the matter is as we have described it, as far as concerns the psychological inquiry into religion, which asks, not what it is within the aforementioned limits, but what it is in its own essential nature. And for that matter this proceeding of constructing a 'humanity' prior to and apart from the most central and potent of human capacities is like nothing so much as the attempt to frame a standard idea of the human body after having previously cut off the head.

"因素",这种因素准确地对应着一条通向"彼岸"的道路,也对应着靠近的另一条道路,对此应当相应地理解。但是,尽管这种"过度激情"是神秘主义的独有特征,无论它怎样被其他因素限制和保持在一定的范围内,它的踪迹总是隐现在所有真正被感受到的宗教福佑之中。这一点可以非常清楚地从关于那些经验,诸如恩赐、转变、再生等的心理学中看到,在其中,宗教经验以其纯粹的内在性质和高度的活跃性表现出来,这样,比起在通过教育逐渐灌输的虔诚的不太典型的形式中,它可以被更清晰地把握到。处于基督教形式中的这种经验的核心,是由负疚到原罪的救赎构成的,而我们很快就会看到,没有非理性因素的参与,这也是不会发生的。如果不考虑这一点,我们在这里必须指出的,是那种被真正体验到的不可言说之物,以及这种经验是怎样转化成为那种常常濒临奇异和反常的赐福的刺激、狂喜以及得意洋洋的。① 这一点已经从圣保罗以来的关于"信仰转换"的传记材料中得到证明。威廉·詹姆士收集了很多这方面的资料,然而,他本人却没有注意到在其中闪动的非理性的因素。

有一人写道:

……此时只有一种无法表达的快乐与激动。要充分描述这种经验是不可能的,那种效果就像某些管弦乐队的演奏一样:所有

---

① 对于想要构建一种"在纯粹理性范围内的宗教"或者"在人性范围内的宗教"的意图来说,这一点或许是至关重要的;但是,正如我们已经描述过的,当牵涉到宗教中的心理学研究时,这一点依然是决定性的,因为这一研究所追问的,不是在上述限度内宗教是什么,而是在其自身的本质特性中宗教是什么。对这件事来说,这种先于并且离开人的能力的最核心、最具潜力的部分去构建一种"人性"的行动,不啻于先把人的脑袋砍掉然后再来构建一种关于人体的标准观念的企图。

have melted into one swelling harmony, that leaves the listener conscious of nothing save that his soul is being wafted upwards and almost bursting with its own emotion. (*Varieties of Religious Experience*, p. 66.)

And another:

... The more I seek words to express this intimate intercourse, the more I feel the impossibility of describing the thing by any of our usual images. (Ibid., p. 68.)

And almost with the precision of dogma, a third (Jonathan Edwards) indicates the qualitative difference of the experience of beatitude from other 'rational' joy:

The conceptions which the saints have of the loveliness of God and that kind of delight which they experience in it are quite peculiar and entirely different from anything which a natural man can possess or of which he can form any proper notion. (Ibid., p. 229.)

Cf. also pp. 192, 225; and the testimony of Jacob Boehme given on p. 417. Also this of Boehme:

But I can neither write nor tell of what sort of Exaltation the triumphing in the Spirit is. It can be compared with nought, but that when in the midst of death life is born, and it is like the resurrection of the dead.

With the mystics these experiences pass up wholly into the 'overabounding'. 'O that I could tell you what the heart feels, how it burns and is consumed inwardly! Only, I find no words to express it. I can but say: Might but one little drop of what I feel fall into Hell, Hell would be transformed into a Paradise.' So says St. Catherine of Genoa; and all the multitude of her spiritual kindred testify to the same effect.

What we Christians know as the experiences of grace and the second birth have their parallels also in the religions of high spiritual rank beyond the borders of Christianity. Such are the breaking out of

单个的乐音都化作和谐的旋律，听音乐的人只感到自己的心灵正飘然上升并差不多为心灵自身的充沛的感受所迸裂。（《宗教体验的类别》第 66 页）

另一人写道：

……我越是寻求用词语来表达这种亲密的交流，我就越是感到不可能用任何我们通常的意象来描述这种东西。（同上，第 68 页）

而第三个人（乔纳森·爱德华兹）近乎于以一种教条的精确，指出了这种赐福体验与其他“理性的”愉悦的质的区别：

信徒用以表达上帝之爱的那些概念，以及他们在这种爱中所体验到的那种喜悦，是全然不同于一个自然人所能拥有或所能构成恰当观念的任何东西的。（同上，第 299 页）

同时也请参阅第 192 页、225 页，以及第 417 页上雅各布·伯麦的声明。还有伯麦的这段话：

我既写不出也说不出那种包含在圣灵之中的喜悦是怎样一种兴奋。可以把它与无相比较，但它却是生命在死亡之中诞生时的无，同时它又像死者的复活。

按照神秘主义者的观点，这些经验完全上升到了“过度热情”。“啊，让我告诉你我内心的感受吧，它在怎样地燃烧和怎样地在内部消耗啊！只是啊，我找不到表达它的语词。我只能说：只需要有哪怕只是一丁点我所感受到的权能落入地狱，地狱就会转变成为天堂。”热那亚的圣凯瑟琳如是说；而她所有的精神上的类似感受都证实了相同的结果。

我们基督徒所知道的作为救赎和重生的体验，在基督教之外的那些高精神等级的宗教中也有类似的表现。诸如摆脱拯救的

the saving 'Bodhi', the opening of the 'heavenly eye', the *ñāna*, by *Iśvaras prasāda*, which is victorious over the darkness of nescience and shines out in an experience with which no other can be measured. And in all these the entirely non-rational and specific element in the beatific experience is immediately noticeable. The qualitative character of it varies widely in all these cases, and is again in them all very different from its parallels in Christianity; still in all it is very similar in intensity, and in all it is a 'salvation' and an absolute 'fascination', which in contrast to all that admits of 'natural' expression or comparison is deeply imbued with the 'over-abounding' ('exuberant') nature of the numen.

And this is also entirely true of the rapture of Nirvana, which is only in appearance a cold and negative state. It is only conceptually that 'Nirvana' is a negation; it is felt in consciousness as in the strongest degree positive; it exercises a 'fascination' by which its votaries are as much carried away as are the Hindu or the Christian by the corresponding objects of their worship. I recall vividly a conversation I had with a Buddhist monk. He had been putting before me methodically and pertinaciously the arguments for the Buddhist 'theology of negation', the doctrine of Anātman and 'entire emptiness'. When he had made an end, I asked him, what then Nirvana itself is; and after a long pause came at last the single answer, low and restrained: 'Bliss—unspeakable'. And the hushed restraint of that answer, the solemnity of his voice, demeanour, and gesture, made more clear what was meant than the words themselves.

And so we maintain, on the one hand, following the *via eminentiae et causalitatis*, that the divine is indeed the highest, strongest, best, loveliest, and dearest that man can think of; but we assert on the other, following the *via negationis*, that God is not *merely* the

"顿悟"(Bodhi),"天眼"开启,由"自在净"所生的慧见(the *fñāna*, by *Išvaras prasāda*)——它战胜无明的黑暗,并在一种不能度量的经验中照射出来。而在所有这些中,那种包含在赐福体验中的完全非理性的、独特的因素立刻就是可注意到的。在所有这些情形中,它的质的特性变化很大,而且在这些情形中,它再次与基督教中的类似表现完全不同;但在所有形式中,它在强度上非常近似,而且在所有形式中,它都是"拯救"和绝对的"沉迷",与包含着"自然的"表达或者比较的所有东西不同,它强烈地充满了"神秘"的"过度热情"的性质。

这一点也完全适用于"涅槃"的狂喜,"涅槃"只是在表面上处于冷漠和否定的状态。只是在概念的意义上,"涅槃"才是一种否定;在意识中它被感受为处于最强烈程度的肯定之中;它通过运用一种"沉迷",可以将其信徒席卷而去,就像印度教徒或者基督教徒被他们崇拜的相应对象席卷而去一样。我清楚地回想起我和一个佛教僧人的对话。他在我面前有系统地执著地阐发着佛教的"否定式神学"的观点,即"无我"(*Anātman*)与"空"的教义。当他讲完之后,我问他,到底什么是"涅槃";他沉吟半晌,然后以低沉而压抑的声音给出了一个简明的回答:"不可言说的极乐。"他回答问题时的静谧压抑,他的声音、举止、姿态的庄重,比那些话语本身更清晰地表达出了他的意思。

因此,一方面,按照"杰出与原因的方法"(*via eminentiae et causalitatis*),我们坚信,神性的确是人所能想象的最高、最强、最好、最可爱和最可亲的东西;但是另一方面,按照"否定的方法"(*via negationis*),我

ground and superlative of all that can be thought; He is in Himself a subject on His own account and in Himself.

*　*　*　*　*

In the adjective *δεινός* the Greek language possesses a word peculiarly difficult to translate, and standing for an idea peculiarly difficult to grasp in all its strange variations. And if we ask whence this difficulty arises, the answer is plain; it is because *δεινός* is simply the numinous (mostly of course at a lower level, in an arrested form, attenuated by rhetorical or poetic usage). Consequently *δεινός* is the equivalent of *dirus* and *tremendus*. It may mean evil or imposing, potent and strange, queer and marvellous, horrifying and fascinating, divine and daemonic, and a source of 'energy'. Sophocles means to awaken the feeling of 'numinous awe' through the whole gamut of its phases at the contemplation of man, the creature of marvel, in the choric song of the *Antigone*:

πολλὰ τὰ δεινά, κοὐδὲν ἀνθρώπου δεινότερον πέλει.

This line defies translation, just because our language has no term that can isolate distinctly and gather into one word the total numinous impression a thing may make on the mind. The nearest that German can get to it is in the expression *das Ungeheuere* (monstrous), while in English 'weird' is perhaps the closest rendering possible. The mood and attitude represented in the foregoing verse might then be fairly well rendered by such a translation as:

Much there is that is weird; but nought is weirder than man.

The German *ungeheuer* is not by derivation simply 'huge', in quantity

们断言,上帝不仅仅是能够被思考的基础和顶点;上帝本身就是一个自给自足的主体。

*　*　*　*　*

δεινός 是一个希腊语的形容词,它很难翻译,代表某种在其所有的奇特变化中很难把握到的观念。而一旦我们询问困难从何产生,回答却非常简单:因为 *δεινός* 就是“神秘”(当然主要是处于较低水平的、存在于一种被压抑的形势中的、被修辞的或者诗歌的用法所削弱了的“神秘”)。结果,*δεινός* 就成了“可怕”(*dirus*)和“畏惧”的同义词,它可以指邪恶的或者壮丽的、有力的和奇异的、古怪的和绝妙的、惊骇的和沉迷的、神性的和魔怪的以及某种“能量”之源。在《安提戈涅》的合唱歌曲:

πολλὰ τὰ δεινά,κοὐδέν ἀνθρώπον δεινότερον πέλει. 中,索福克勒斯在凝思人这一神迹的造物时,试图通过它的各阶段的全部音阶来唤醒对“神秘的敬畏”的感觉。这一行歌词是不能被翻译的,就是因为在我们的语言中还没有这样一个术语,能够把某个事物在心灵上形成的整个“神秘的”印象清楚地区分出来并且集中到一个词汇之中。与它最接近的一个德语的表达是 *das Ungeheuere*(异常的、可怕的),而英语的“weird”一词可能是最相近的一个翻译。那么,表现在上述歌词中的语气和态度或许可以通过下面的翻译得到相当好的表达:

世界上神奇的事情不少,但是没有比人更神奇的了。德语的 *ungeheuer* 并不单单是指质的或者量的“巨大”;这种意思,在通常含义上,其实是对真实观念理性化化解释;它是那种并不可怕的

or quality;—this, its common meaning, is in fact a rationalizing interpretation of the real idea; it is that which is not *geheuer*, i. e. approximately, the *uncanny*—in a word, the numinous. And it is just this element of the uncanny in man that Sophocles has in mind. If this, its fundamental meaning, be really and thoroughly felt in consciousness, then the word could be taken as a fairly exact expression for the numinous in its aspects of mystery, awefulness, majesty, augustness, and 'energy'; nay, even the aspect of fascination is dimly felt in it.

The variations of meaning in the German word *ungeheuer* can be well illustrated from Goethe.① He, too, uses the word first to denote the huge in size—what is too vast for our faculty of space-perception, such as the immeasurable vault of the night sky. In other passages the word retains its original non-rational colour more markedly; it comes to mean the uncanny, the fearful, the dauntingly 'other' and incomprehensible, that which arouses in us *stupor* and *θάμβος*; and finally, in the wonderful words of Faust which I have putat the beginning of this book, it becomes an almost exact synonym for our 'numinous' under all its aspects.

Das Schaudern ist der Menschheit bestes Teil.
Wie auch die Welt ihm das Gefe hl verteuere,
Ergriffen fühlt er tief das Ungeheuere.②

---

① Cf. *Wilhelm Meisters Wanderjahre*, Bk. I, ch. 10; *Wahlverwandtschaften*, 2. 15; *Dichtung und Wahrheit*, 2. 9: 4. 20.

② Awe is the best of man: howe'er the world's
Misprizing of the feeling would prevent us,
Deeply we feel, once gripped, the weird Portentous.
(Goethe, *Fausi*, Second Part, Act 1, Sc. v.)

(*geheuer*)东西,也即是近似于"离奇"的东西,一句话,它就是"神秘"。那种存在于索福克勒斯心中的,就是这种人们之中的离奇的因素。如果就其根本含义而言,这种因素在意识中被真正地、彻底地感受到,那么,*ungeheuer* 这个词就可以被看做是对神秘的神奇、敬畏、权威、威严以及"活力"的非常准确的表达;不仅如此,甚至沉迷的方面也可以在其中被隐约地感到。

包含在德语词汇 *ungeheuer* 中的多种含义可以从歌德那里得到很好的说明。[①] 歌德也是首次使用这个词去指尺寸上的巨大,即那种对于人的空间知觉能力来说过于庞大的东西,例如不可衡量的夜空的穹顶。在另外一些篇章中,这一词汇更显著地保留了它原初的非理性色彩;它进而去指离奇的、可怕的、令人畏缩的"他者"和不能理解的东西——那种在我们内心深处引起"惊愕"和"惊奇"(*θάμβος*)的东西;最后,在我在本书一开始就引用的《浮士德》的美妙文字中,它在各个方面都变成了我们的"神秘"一词的、几乎是精确的同义词。

Das Schaudern ist der Menschheit bestes Teil.
Wie auch die Welt ihm das Gefühl verteuere,
Ergriffen fühlt er tief das Ungeheuere. [②]

① 参见《威廉·迈斯特的漫游年代》第 1 卷第 10 章;《亲和力》(*Wahlverwandtschaften*)第 2 章第 15 节;《诗与真》第 2 章第 9 节、第 4 章第 20 节。

② 敬畏是人性中的最好部分,
无论世人对这种感受怎样阻挠我们,
禀有它,我们就会深刻感受到离奇的预兆。
(歌德《浮士德》第 2 部第 1 幕第 5 场)

CHAPTER VII

Analogies And Associated Feelings

In order to give an adequate account of this second aspect of the numinous, we were led to add to its original designation as *mysterium tremendum* that it at the same time exercises a supreme 'fascination'. And this its dual character, as at once an object of boundless awe and boundless wonder, quelling and yet entrancing the soul, constitutes the proper *positive* content of the *mysterium* as it manifests itself in conscious feeling. No attempt of ours to describe this harmony of contrasts in the import of the *mysterium* can really succeed; but it may perhaps be adumbrated, as it were from a distance, by taking an analogy from a region belonging not to religion but to aesthetics. In the category and feeling of the *sublime* we have a counterpart to it, though it is true it is but a pale reflexion, and moreover involves difficulties of analysis all its own. The analogies between the consciousness of the sublime and of the numinous may be easily grasped. ① To begin with, 'the sublime', like 'the numinous', is in Kantian language an idea or concept 'that cannot be unfolded' or explicated (*unauswickelbar*). Certainly we can tabulate some general 'rational' signs that uniformly recur as soon as we call an object sublime; as, for instance, that it must approach, or threaten to overpass, the

① We are often prone to resort to this familiar feeling-content to fill out the negative concept 'transcendent', explaining frankly God's 'transcendence' by His 'sublimity'. As a figurative analogical description this is perfectly allowable, but it would be an error if we meant it literally and in earnest. Religious feelings are not the same as aesthetic feelings, and 'the sublime' is as definitely an aesthetic term as 'the beautiful', however widely different may be the facts denoted by the words.

第七章　类比和联想感受

为了充分说明神秘的第二个方面,我们不得不给它最初的意指即“神秘的畏惧”加上了它同时产生的极度的“沉迷”。正是这种二元的性质——即同时作为无比敬畏与无比惊愕的对象,既压制着灵魂又刺激着灵魂——当神秘在有意识的感受中表现自身时,形成了神秘固有的肯定的内容。任何想要描述这种在对立中的和谐在神秘中的重要性的意图都不能真正成功;但是它或许能够被勾画出来,因为它来自较远的领域,是通过取材于美学而非宗教领域的类比而得来的。在崇高这一范畴与感受中,我们找到了它的一个副本,尽管它的确只是一个苍白的反应,而且在其本身还包含着许多分析的困难。处于崇高意识与神秘意识之间的类似应该比较容易把握。① 首先,正如“神秘”一样,在康德哲学的话语中,“崇高”也是一种“不能展开”或者“不可阐明”(*unauswickelbar*)的观念或者概念。确实,我们可以列出当我们把某一对象称为崇高时所一再出现的某些一般的“理性”标记;例如,

① 我们常常倾向于用这种熟悉的感受内容去填充“超越的”这一否定性概念,径直用上帝的“崇高”来解释上帝的“超越性”。作为一种形象的类比的描写,这是完全允许的,但是如果我们在字面上去说明并且真诚地相信,那么这就是一个错误。宗教感受不等同于美学感受,而“崇高”与“美丽”一样,确然是一个美学的术语,无论这些词汇所指称的事实有多么大的不同。

bounds of our understanding by some 'dynamic' or 'mathematic' greatness, by potent manifestations of force or magnitude in spatial extent. But these are obviously only conditions of, not the essence of, the impression of sublimity. A thing does not become sublime merely by being great. The concept itself remains unexplicated; it has in it something mysterious, and in this it is like that of the numinous. A second point of resemblance is that the sublime exhibits the same peculiar dual character as the numinous; it is at once daunting, and yet again singularly attracting, in its impress upon the mind. It humbles and at the same time exalts us, circumscribes and extends us beyond ourselves, on the one hand releasing in us a feeling analogous to fear, and on the other rejoicing us. So the idea of the sublime is closely similar to that of the numinous, and is well adapted to excite it and to be excited by it, while each tends to pass over into the other.

The Law of the Association of Feelings

As these expressions 'excite' and 'pass over' will later assume importance, and as the latter in particular is hedged about with misconceptions which are prominent in the modern doctrines of Evolution and give rise to quite erroneous conclusions, we will enter at once upon a closer consideration of them.

It is a well-known and fundamental psychological law that ideas 'attract' one another, and that one will excite another and call it into consciousness, if it resembles it. An entirely similar law holds good with regard to feelings. A feeling, no less than an idea, can arouse its like in the mind; and the presence of the one in my consciousness may be the occasion for my entertaining the other at the same time. Further, just

崇高的对象必定会以某种“力学的”或者“数学的”巨大,即以力量的强劲表现和空间范围的无比巨大,来接近或者似有可能超出我们理解的界限。但是这些显然只是崇高发生影响的条件,而不是本质,一个事物不会仅仅因为巨大而变得崇高。崇高这一概念本身尚未被阐明;在它里面有某种神秘的东西,就此而言,它就像是包含在神秘中的那种东西。第二点类似是,崇高也像神秘一样,展现出了同样特别的二元性质:在它施加给心灵的影响中,既是令人畏缩的,同时又再次表现出异乎寻常的吸引力。它让我们自感卑微,同时又让我们自感崇高,既限制我们,又将我们扩张到我们自身之外,一方面让我们产生出类似恐惧的感受,另一方面,又让我们感到快乐愉悦。因此,崇高的观念酷似神秘观念,而且它完全适用于引起神秘的感受或者被神秘的感受引起,与此同时,二者又倾向于向对方过渡。

感受联想律

鉴于“激发”、“转化”这些词语在后面呈现出的重要性,特别是鉴于后者,即“转化”被各种误解所围困,这些误解在现代进化论中很显著并且导致了十分错误的结论,我们要立即着手对它们进行更进一步的思考。

一个人所共知的、基本的心理学规则是观念之间相互“吸引”,只要彼此相似,一种观念就可以激发另一种观念,并将其召唤到意识中去。在感觉中,也存在完全类似的规则。一种感觉,就像一种观念,可以在心灵中引起与之类似的感觉;一种感觉出现在我的意识中时,或许正是我同时接受另一种感觉的时机。更进一

as in the case of ideas the law of reproduction by similarity leads to a mistaken substitution of ideas, so that I come to entertain an idea *x*, when *y* would have been the appropriate one, so we may be led to a corresponding substitution of feelings, and I may react with a feeling *x* to an impression to which the feeling *y* would normally correspond. Finally, I can pass from one feeling to another by an imperceptibly gradual transition, the one feeling *x* dying away little by little, while the other, *y*, excited together with it, increases and strengthens in a corresponding degree. But it is important here to recognize the true account of the phenomenon. What passes over—undergoes transition—is not the feeling itself. It is not that the actual feeling gradually changes in quality or 'evolves', i. e. transmutes itself into a quite different one, but rather that *I* pass over or make the transition from one feeling to another as my circumstances change, by the gradual decrease of the one and increase of the other. A transition of the actual feeling into another would be a real 'transmutation', and would be a psychological counterpart to the alchemist's production of gold by the transmutation of metals.

And yet it is this transmutation that is assumed by the modern 'Evolutionism'—more properly to be called 'Transmutationism'—by the introduction of the equivocal phrase, 'gradually evolve' (i. e. from a thing of a certain quality to something qualitatively different), or the no less equivocal words 'Epigenesis', 'Heterogony', ① and their like. In this way, they would have us believe, the feeling, e. g. of moral obligation, 'evolves' or develops. At first, so it is said, all that exists is the simple constraint of uniform custom, as seen in

① Neither Heterogony nor Epigenesis is genuine Evolution. They are rather just what the biologists call *generatio eauivoca*, and therefore mereformation of an aggregate by addition and accumulation.

步地讲，正如在观念的情况下通过类似而得到繁殖与再生的规则会导致观念的错误取代，因此，当我准备接受观念X时，观念Y或许才是那个合适的，所以，我们会被引导到某种感觉的相关取代上，即我对某种影响回应一种感觉反应X，但是对它来说，感觉Y才是通常应有的反应。最后，通过觉察不到的渐进的转变，我可以从一种感觉过渡到另一种感觉，即一种感觉X一点一滴地逐渐消逝，而与之一道被激起的另一种感觉Y则以相应的程度逐渐增大变强了。不过，这里重要的是，要认清这一现象的真正原因。那种转变了的或者经受了转换的，并不是感觉自身，并不是实际的感受逐渐在质上把自身转变或者“进化”为——也就是把自身改变为一个完全不同的东西，实际上是当我的环境发生了改变时，通过逐渐削弱一种感觉并增强另一种感觉，我转变了或者造成了一种感觉向另一种感觉的转变。从实际感受向另一感受的转变将是一种真正的“嬗变”，就像是炼金术士通过使一般金属的质变来生产黄金那样的心理学上的对应物。

然而，现代“进化论”（它更应当被称做“嬗变论”）所主张的正是这种嬗变，它引进了某种模棱两可的词汇：“渐进说”（也就是说，从一种具有确定的质的事物转变为某种不同质的事物），或者同样含义模糊的词：“渐成说”、“形变说”①之类的概念。通过这种方式，他们想要我们相信，感觉，如对于道德义务的感觉，可以“进化”或者发展。首先，如其所述，所有存在的只是相同习俗的

---

① 无论是“形变”还是“渐成”都不是真正的进化。相反，它们是生物学家称之为同类繁殖（*gneratio couivoca*）的东西，因此，它们只是因为增加和积累所形成的集合体。

the community of the clan. Then, out of that, it is said, ' arises' the idea of a universally obligatory ' ought'. How the idea can do so is not disclosed. Now such a theory misses the fact that in moral obligation we have something *qualitatively* quite different from constraint by custom. The finer and more penetrating psychological analysis that can apprehend differences in quality is rudely ignored and in consequence the whole problem is misconceived. Or, if something of the essential difference is felt, it is covered up and glozed over by the phrase ' gradually evolve', and the one thing is made to turn into the other *par la durée*, much as milk grows sour from standing. But ' ought' is a primary and unique meaning, as little derivable from another as blue from bitter, and there are not ' transmutations' in the psychological any more than in the physical world. The idea ' ought' is only ' evolvable' out of the spirit of man itself, and then in the sense of being ' arousable', because it is already potentially implanted in him. Were it not so, no ' evolution' could effect an introduction for it.

The evolutionists may be quite correct in reconstructing the kind of historical process that took place, viz. the gradual and successive entry upon the scene of different ' moments' of feeling – consciousness in historical sequence, and the order of entry itself may have been correctly discovered. But the explanation of this process is quite different from that which they intend; it is, namely, the law of the excitation and arousing of feelings and ideas according to the measure of their resemblance. There is in point of fact a very strong analogy between constraint by custom and constraint by moral obligation, as both are constraints upon conduct. Consequently the former can *arouse* the latter in the mind if it —the latter—was already potentially planted there; the feeling of ' ought'

简单约束，正如人们在氏族团体中所看到的那样。然后，从这种约束中“产生出”一种具有普遍强制性的观念“应当”。这一观念何以有如此的普遍强制性在此处并未被揭示出来。这一理论忽略了这样一个事实，这就是，在道德义务中，我们拥有某种在质上大大不同于被习俗约束的东西。由于那种能够理解质的差别的更加精细的、更加敏锐的心理学分析被粗暴地忽略了，结果整个问题被误解了，或者，如果有某种本质区别的东西被感受到了，它也会被“渐进”一词所掩盖和遮蔽，而一事物被逐渐(*par la durée*)转变为另一事物，就好像牛奶因搁置而变酸一样。但是“应当”是一种首要的、独特的含义，就像从苦中不能生出蓝一样，是很难从其他的含义中推衍出来的，而且如同在物理世界中一样，在心理世界中也不存在什么“嬗变”。“应当”的观念只是从人的精神本身之中“进化”出来的，然后处于一种“可被引发的”意义上，因为它早就已经潜在地被植入到他的精神之中了。如果不是这样，那么，任何“进化”都不可能起到引发“应当”的观念的作用。

进化论者在重建那种已经发生了的历史进程方面应当说是非常正确的，即按照历史顺序重构那种确立在不同的感觉—意识因素的场景之上的渐进的、连续的入场，而这一入场本身的顺序可能已经被正确地发现了。但是，对这一过程的解释却大不同于他们原先所打算的；也就是说，他们所打算的是那种根据其相似程度而激发和引起感觉与观念的规律。事实上，被习俗约束与被道德义务约束之间存在着强大的类似性，因为二者都是对行为的约束。因此，前者就可以在心灵中引发后者——假如后者早已被潜在地植入在那里

may start into consciousness at the presence of the other feeling, and the man may gradually effect a transition to it from that other. But what we are concerned with is the *replacement* of the one by the other, and not the *transmutation* of the one into the other.

Now it is just the same with the feeling of the numinous as with that of moral obligation. It too is not to be derived from any other feeling, and is in this sense 'unevolvable'. It is a content of feeling that is qualitatively *sui generis*, yet at the same time one that has numerous analogies with others, and therefore it and they may reciprocally excite or stimulate one another and cause one another to appear in the mind. Instead of framing 'epigenetic' and other fabrications of the course the evolution of religion has taken, it is our task to inquire into these 'stimuli' or 'excitations', these elements that cause the numinous feeling to appear in consciousness, to intimate by virtue of what analogies they came to be able to do so, and so to discover the series or chain of these stimuli by whose operation the numinous feeling was awakened in us.

Such a power of stimulation characterizes the feeling of the sublime, in accordance with the law we found, and through the analogies it bears to the numinous feeling. But this is indubitably a stimulus that only makes its appearance late in the excitation-series, and it is probable that the feeling of the sublime is itself first aroused and disengaged by the precedent religious feeling—not from itself, but from the rational spirit of man and its *a priori* capacity.

Schematization

The 'association of ideas' does not simply cause the idea *y* to reappear in consciousness with the given idea *x* occasionally only, it also sets up under certain circumstances lasting com-

了;“应当”的感觉也能在其他的感觉出场时进入到意识之中,而人则可以逐渐地实现从别的感觉向“应当”的转变。但是我们所关注的是以彼代此的置换,而不是由此到彼的嬗变。

现在,无论是对于神秘感,还是对于道德责任感,这都是一样的。神秘感也不是得自任何别的感觉,它处于一种“非进化的”意义之上。它是一种感觉的内容,即是质上的自生(*sui generis*),但是同时又与别的感觉有着很多的类似,因此它与那些感觉能够在心中相互激发,相互引起,并促使对方显现在心灵之中。我们的任务不是去勾勒出宗教进化进程所采取的“渐进的”或者别的什么结构,而是要去探究这些“刺激”或者“激动”,即这些促使神秘感出现在意识之中的因素,揭示出这些因素依靠了什么样的类推才能够做到这些,并且由此去发现神秘因素在我们心中被唤醒的这些刺激的系列或者链条。

这样一种刺激的力量刻画出了崇高感的特征,与我们所发现的规则相一致,并且通过类比,它转化为神秘感。但是这无疑是后来在刺激丛中才将自身显示出来的一种刺激物,而且很有可能,崇高感首先是由自身引起并由先在的宗教感受所解放的——不是从其自身,而是从人的理性精神和他的先天(*a priori*)能力中解放出来的。

图示化

假定有一个观念 X,“观念的联想”并不只是简单地引起观念 Y 在意识中偶然再现;在一定条件下,它也要在二者之间建立持

binations and connexions between the two. And this is no less true of the association of feelings. Accordingly we see religious feeling in permanent connexion with other feelings which are conjoined to it in accordance with this principle of association. It is, indeed, more accurate to say 'conjoined' than really 'connected', for such mere conjunctions or chance connexions according to laws of purely external analogy are to be distinguished from necessary connexions according to principles of true inward affinity and cohesion. An instance of a connexion of this latter kind—an example, indeed, of an inner *a priori* principle—is (following the theory of Kant) the connexion of the category of causality with its temporal 'schema', the temporal sequence of two successive events, which by being brought into connexion with the category of causality is *known* and recognized as a causal relation of the two. In this case analogy between the two—the category and the schema—has also a place, but it is not chance external resemblance but essential correspondence, and the fact that the two belong together is here a necessity of our reason. On the basis of such a necessity the temporal sequence 'schematizes' the category.

Now the relation of the rational to the non-rational element in the idea of the holy or sacred is just such a one of 'schematization', and the non-rational numinous fact, schematized by the rational concepts we have suggested above, yields us the complex category of 'holy' itself, richly charged and complete and in its fullest meaning. And that the schematism is a genuine one, and not a mere combination of analogies, may be distinctly seen from the fact that it does not fall to pieces, and cannot be cut out as the development of the consciousness of religious truth proceeds onwards and upwards, but is only recognized with greater definiteness and certainty. And it is for the same reason inherently probable that there is more, too, in the combination of 'the holy' with 'the sublime' than a mere association of feelings; and perhaps we may say that, while as a matter of historical genesis such an association was the means whereby this combination was awakened in the mind and the occasion for it, yet the inward and lasting character of the connexion in all the higher religions does prove that 'the sublime' too is an authentic 'schema' of 'the holy'.

久的联合与联系。感受联想也是如此。因此,我们看到宗教感与别的感觉处于持久的联系之中,这些别的感觉正式基于这种联想的规则与它结合起来的。的确,说“结合”要比真实地表述为“连接”更加准确,因为这种基于纯粹外部相似律的单纯联合或偶然连接,与基于真正内在亲和力和凝聚力原则的必然联系是不同的。后一种联系的一个例子,的确,一个具有内在先天原则的例子就是——按照康德的理论——带有时间“图示”的因果性范畴的联系,这种时间图示是指两个相继事物在时间上的顺序,即这种靠着因果性范畴而被置于联系之中的两个事物被看做或者认知为两者之间的因果联系。在这一例子中,范畴与图示之间的类似也有了一席之地,但这不是偶然的外在相似,而是本质的对应,而二者相互从属的事实在此是我们理性的必然。在这种必然性的基础上,时间顺序把范畴“图示化”了。

神圣观念中的理性因素与非理性因素的关系就是这样一种“图示化”的联系,我们上面所提到过的那种被理性概念图示化了的非理性的神秘事实,使我们产生了“神圣”这一本身非常复杂的范畴,富有情感,非常完美,而且具有丰富的含义。这种图示化结合是一种真正的而非仅仅是类比的结合,这可以从这一事实中清楚地看到:它不会分裂成碎片,也不能随着宗教真理意识向上与向前的发展而被剪切掉,而只会以更大的明确性与确定性被认识到。由于同样的固有的理由,很有可能,“神圣”与“崇高”之间有着比诸感觉的单纯联合更多的结合;或许我们可以这样说,作为一种有历史起源的东西,这种联系是这一结合在心灵中被唤醒所凭借的手段和诱因,然而,存在于一切较高级的宗教中的这种联系的内在的持久的性质确实证明了“崇高”也是对“神圣”的一种可信的“图解”。

The intimate interpenetration of the non-rational with the rational elements of the religious consciousness, like the interweaving of warp and woof in a fabric, may be elucidated by taking another familiar case, in which a universal human feeling, that of personal affection, is similarly interpenetrated by a likewise thoroughly non-rational and separate element, namely, the sex instinct. It goes without saying that this latter lies just on the opposite side of 'reason' to the numinous consciousness; for, while this is 'above all reason', the sex impulse is below it, an element in our instinctive life. 'The numinous' infuses the rational from above, 'the sexual' presses up from beneath, quite wholesomely and normally out of the nature which the human being shares with the general animal world, into the higher realm of the specifically 'humane'. But though the two things I am comparing are thus manifestly opposite extremes, they have a closely corresponding relation to that which lies between them, viz. the reason. For the quite special domain of the 'erotic' is only brought into existence as the reproductive instinct passes up out of the merely instinctive life, penetrates the higher humane life of mind and feeling, and infuses wishes, cravings, and longings in personal liking, friendship, and love, in song and poetry and imaginative creation in general. Whatever falls within the sphere of the erotic is therefore always a composite product, made up of two factors: the one something that occurs also in the general sphere of human behaviour as such, as friendship and liking, the feeling of companionship, the mood of poetic inspiration or joyful exaltation, and the like; and the other an infusion of a quite special kind, which is not to be classed with these, and of which no one can have any inkling, let alone understand it, who has not learnt from the actual inward experience of *erōs* or love. Another point in which the 'erotic' is analogous to the 'holy' is in having in the main no means of linguistic expression but terms drawn from other fields of mental life, which only cease to be

宗教意识的理性因素与非理性因素固有的相互渗透,就像一件纺织品中相互交织在一起的经线与纬线一样,可以通过另一种熟悉的情形来加以说明,在这种情形中,一种普遍的人类情感,即个人的爱情,也被一种同样彻底非理性的、独立的因素,即性的本能所类似地渗透着。不用说,后者[1]正好存在于与神秘意识相对的、"理性"的对立面;因为,如果说神秘是"在所有理性之上"的,性冲动就是在"理性"之下的,是我们本能生命中的一个因素。"神秘"从上面灌输理性,"性感"从下面逼迫理性,从而使人非常健康地、正常地走出人类与一般的动物世界共享的自然界,进入更高的特别的"人道的"领域。尽管我正在比较的这两种事物是如此明显地极端对立,但是,它们与那个处于它们二者之间的东西——理性,却有着一种密切的对应关系。因为只有生殖本能超出了单纯的本能生命,渗透到更富有人性的心灵和情感生活,并且在个人爱好、友谊、爱情、歌曲、诗以及一般的想象性的创造中灌输希望、渴望和渴求时,"性爱"这个十分特别的领域才被引入到存在之中。因此,凡是进入到性爱领域中的总是由两种因素构成的混合物:一种是同样发生在一般人类行为领域中的某种东西,诸如友谊、爱好、友情、诗意灵感状态以及极度的快乐等;另一种则是某种非常特殊的东西的浸注,它没有被归入上述各类,人们对它也一无所知,更谈不上理解了,此处的人还没有从其实际的内在经验中懂得性爱(*erōs*)或者爱情。"性爱"与"神圣"的另一个相似点在于,当事人基本上找不到语言表达的手段,而只能借助于精神生活的其他领域中的一些术语——只有在意识

〔1〕 即性本能。

'innocuous' (i. e. only become genuinely 'erotic' terms) when it is realized that the lover, like the orator, bard, or singer, expresses himself not so much by the actual words he uses as by the accent, tone, and imitative gesture which reinforce them.

The phrase 'he loves me' is verbally identical, whether it is said by a child of its father or by a girl of her lover. But in the second case a 'love' is meant which is at the same time 'something more' (*viz. sexual* love), and something more not only in quantity but in quality. So, too, the phrase 'We ought to fear, love, and trust him'① is verbally identical, whether it refers to the relation of child to father or to that of man to God. But again in the second case these ideas are infused with a meaning of which none but the religiousminded man can have any comprehension or indeed any inkling, whose presence makes, e. g. the 'fear of God' 'something more' than any fear of a man qualitatively not merely quantitatively, though retaining the essence of the most genuine reverence felt by the child for its father. And Suso means in the same way to distinguish 'love' and 'love of God', when he says:

There was never a string so dulcet-toned but ceased to sound if stretched to a withered frame; a heart poor in love can no more understand speech rich in love than a German can an Italian. ②

There is another kind of experience in which we may find an example of the way in which rational elements in our feeling-consciousness may be thus penetrated by quite non-rational ones, and an example even more proximate to the complex feeling of the holy than that just described—'erotic'

① Luther's amplification of the First Commandment.

② Works, ed. Denifle, p. 309.

到恋爱者就像演说家、游吟诗人与歌手一样，与其说是用实际的话语，不如说是用强化言辞的口音、语调及模仿姿态来表达自己，这时，这些借用的术语才不再是“无伤大雅的”了，即真正地变成“性爱的”术语了。

无论是一个孩子说到他的父亲，还是一个姑娘说到她的情人，“他爱我”这句话在字面上是一样的。但是，在第二种情形中，“爱”还意味着“某种更多的东西”（亦即性爱）和某种不仅在量上而且在质上更多的东西。因此，同样，“我们应当惧怕、热爱和信赖他”[①]这句话，无论指的是孩子对父亲的关系，还是人对上帝的关系，在字面上都是一样的。然而，还是在第二种情形中，这些观念浸透着一种只有具有宗教情怀的人才能够得到的某些理解或者确切地说是某些暗示的含义，这种含义的出现，使得例如“对上帝的惧怕”比对某一个人的惧怕不仅在量上而且在质上多了“更多的某种东西”，尽管它保留了孩子对于父亲所感受到的最真实的尊敬的本质。而苏索以同样的方式区分了“爱”与“对上帝之爱”，他写道：

琴弦若绷在朽坏的琴身上，便再也发不出悦耳的音调；一个心灵缺少爱的人不再能懂得爱的丰富的言辞，正如法国人不理解意大利人一样。[②]

还有另外一种经验，从中我们可以找到在我们感觉—意识中的理性因素可能被完全非理性因素所渗透的方式的例子，以及比起刚刚描述过的“性爱”经验，更加接近于神圣的复杂感受的例

① 见路德对“第一诫”的详述。

② 见《著作选》，德尼弗尔编辑，第309页。

experience;—in so far as the non-rational element is, like the numinous feeling but unlike the sexual impulse, at the same time *supra*rational. I refer to the state of mind induced in us by a song set to music. The verbal text of the song expresses feelings that are ‘natural’, homesickness perhaps, or confidence in time of danger, hope for a future good, or joy in a present possession—all concrete elements in our ’natural human lot, and capable of being described in conceptual terms. But it is otherwise with the music, purely as music. It releases a blissful rejoicing in us, and we are conscious of a glimmering, billowy agitation occupying our minds, without being able to express or explain in concepts what it really is that moves us so deeply. And to say that the music is mournful or exultant, that it incites or restrains, is merely to use signs by analogy, choosing them for their resemblance to the matter in hand out of other regions of our mental life; and at any rate we cannot say what the object or ground of this mourning or exulting may be. Music, in short, arouses in us an experience and vibrations of mood that are quite specific in kind and must simply be called ‘musical’; but the rise and fall and manifold variations of this experience exhibit-though again only in part—definite, if fugitive, analogies and correspondences with our ordinary non-musical emotional states, and so can call these into consciousness and blend with them. If this happens, the specific ‘music-consciousness’ is thereby ‘schematized’ and rationalized, and the resultant complex mood is, as it were, a fabric, in which the general human feelings and emotional states constitute the warp, and the non-rational music-feelings the woof. The song in its entirety is therefore music ‘rationalized’.

Now here is illustrated the contrast between the legitimate and the illegitimate processes of ‘rationalization’. For, if the song may be called music ‘rationalized’ in the legitimate

子;就这种非理性因素而言,它类似于神秘感而不同于性冲动,它同时又是超理性的。我指的是那种由配上了音乐的歌词所引起的心态。歌曲的歌词内容表达了那种“自然的”感受,它可能是对家乡的思念,或者危险时刻的信心,或者是对未来美好的希望,或者是对当下拥有的快乐——这些全都是我们“自然的”人的命运的具体因素,而且能够以概念性的语词来加以描述。但是另一方面它又伴有音乐——纯粹作为音乐的音乐。它在我们心中释放出极大的欢乐,而我们则意识到一种微微发光的、汹涌澎湃的激动占据了我们的心灵,却无法用概念来表达或者解释那种如此深刻地感动我们的究竟是什么。说音乐是悲哀的或者欢快的、激越的或者压抑的,都只是使用通过类比给出的符号——我们只是因为它们类似于我们正在讨论的这个出自我们精神生活的其他领域的东西而选择它们;但是无论如何我们也无法说出这种令人悲伤的或者令人欢欣鼓舞的对象或基础会是什么。简而言之,音乐在我们心中某种体验与情绪的波动,其性质十分独特,只能被称为“音乐性的”;但是这种体验的起伏与多种变化显示出——尽管只是部分地——它与我们日常的非音乐情感状态的确定的(即便是易逝的)相似的对应,并因此才能将这些非音乐情感状态召集到意识之中并与之相混合。如果这种情况发生,那么,这种特殊的“音乐意识”就会因此被“图示化”和理性化,而作为结果的复杂的情感,就宛如一幅纺织品,其中,一般的人类感受和情绪状态是经线,而非理性的音乐感受则是纬线。因此,作为一个整体的歌曲就是“理性化了的”音乐。

现在,这里已经表明了合理的“理性化”过程与不合理的“理性化”过程之间的对比。因为,假如歌曲可以被称为合理的“理性

sense, in programme-music we have a musical 'rationalism' in the bad sense. Programme-music, that is to say, misinterprets and perverts the idea of music by its implication that the inner content of music is not—as in fact it is—something unique and mysterious, but just the incidental experiences—joy and grief, expansion and repression—familiar to the human heart. And in its attempt to make of musical tones a language to recount the fortunes of men programmemusic abolishes the autonomy of music, and is deceived by a mere resemblance into employing as a means what is an end and substantive content in its own right. It is just the same mistake as when the 'august' aspect of the numinous is allowed to evaporate into the 'morally good', instead of merely being 'schematized' by it, or as when we let 'the holy' be identified with 'the perfectly good' will. And not only programme-music is at fault here. The 'music-drama' of Wagner, by attempting a thoroughgoing unification of the musical and the dramatic, commits the same offence against both the non-rational spirit of the former and the autonomy of either. We can only succeed in very partial and fragmentary fashion in 'schematizing' the non-rational factor in music by means of the familiar incidents of human experience. And the reason is just this, that the real content of music is not drawn from the ordinary human emotions at all, and that it is in no way merely a second language, alongside the usual one, by which these emotions find expression. Musical feeling is rather (like numinous feeling) something 'wholly other', which, while it affords analogies and here and there will run parallel to the ordinary emotions of life, cannot be made to coincide with them by a detailed point-to-point correspondence. It is, of course, from those places where the correspondence holds that the spell of a composed song arises by a blending of verbal and musical expression. But the very fact that we attribute to it a spell, an enchantment, points in itself to that 'woof' in the fabric of music of which we spoke, the woof of the unconceived and non-rational.①

① This is the point of view from which to estimate both the excellent and the inadequate features of E. Hanslick's book, *Vom Musikalisch-Schönen*.

化”音乐，那么，在标题音乐中，我们就会发现坏的音乐“理性主义”。也就是说，标题音乐通过暗示曲解或者歪曲了音乐的观念，即音乐的内在的内容不是——实际上是——某种独特的神秘的东西，而只是人心中所熟悉的偶然经验，如快乐与悲伤，舒展与压抑。当标题音乐试图把乐音作为一种语言来叙述人的命运时，它废止了音乐的独立性，并被一种单纯的类似所欺骗，将对其本身来说是目的和真实内容的东西用作了手段。当神秘的“威严”方面被允许升华到“道德上的善”，而不是仅仅被它“图示化”，或者当我们让“神圣”被“至善的”意志所等同时，我们所犯的是同样的错误。不仅仅标题音乐在此犯错误，瓦格纳的“音乐剧”由于试图把音乐性与戏剧性彻底地统一起来，犯下了既侵犯了前者的非理性精神又侵犯了二者的独立性的同样的错误。在用人类经验的熟悉事件作为手段对音乐中的非理性因素加以“图示化”上，我们自能取得非常有限的成功。原因就在于，音乐的真正内容根本就不是取自普通的人类情感，也绝不仅仅是与通常语言比肩而立的、普通人类情感得以找到表达方式的第二种语言。相反，音乐感受（就像神秘感受一样）是某种“万全的他者”，尽管它提供了类比并到处与生活的普通感受相平行，但是不能通过详细的一一对应与普通感受完全一致。当然了，正是从那些对应之处，通过文字与音乐表达方式的融合，一首谱好的歌曲的魅力才生发出来。但是我们将歌曲归结为魅力、陶醉这一事实本身就指向了前面我们已经讲过的音乐结构的“纬线”，即那条无法构思的非理性的纬线。①

---

① 这也是用来评价 E. 汉斯立克的书《论音乐的美》（*Vom Musikalisch-Schönen*）的优劣的观点。

But we must beware of confounding in any way the non-rational of music and the non-rational of the numinous itself, as Schopenhauer, for example, does. Each is something in its own right, independently of the other. We shall discuss later whether, and how far, the former may become a means of expression for the latter.

但是我们必须小心，以免像叔本华那样，混淆了音乐的非理性与神秘的非理性。这两种非理性各依自身的性质，相互独立。后面我们将会讨论，前者是否可能以及在多大程度上能够成为后者的一种表达手段。

CHAPTER VIII

The Holy As A Category Of Value

Sin and Atonement

We have already met that strange and profound mental reaction to the numinous which we proposed to call 'creature-feeling' or creature-consciousness, with its concomitant feelings of submergence and prostration and of the diminution of the self into nothingness; bearing always in mind that these expressions do not hit with precision, but merely hint at what is really meant,[①] inasmuch as this 'diminution of the self', & c., is something very different from the littleness, weakness, or dependence of which we may become aware under other conditions than that of numinous feeling. And we had to notice that this experience marks a definite depreciation or disvaluation of the self in respect, so to speak, of its reality and very existence. We have now to put alongside of this another sort of self-disvaluation, which has long been a matter of common observation, and only needs to be suggested in order to be recognized. 'I am a man of *unclean* lips and dwell among a people of unclean lips.' 'Depart from me, for I am a *sinful* man, O Lord.' So say respectively Isaiah and Peter, when the numinous reality encounters them as a present fact of consciousness. In both cases this self-depreciating feeling-response is marked by an immediate, almost instinctive, spontaneity. It is not based on deliberation,

---

① Cf. Hugo of St. Victor's words: 'Sumpta sunt vocabula, ut intellegi aliquatenus posset quod comprehendi non poterat'. ('These words were chosen, that that which could not be comprehended might yet in some measure be understood.')

第八章　作为一种价值范畴的神圣

罪与赎罪

我们已经遇到了对神秘的奇特而又深刻的精神反应，即我们建议称做“被造感”或者造物意识，以及与它伴生的卑微感、跪拜感和将自我贬损到虚无的感觉；必须记住，这些表达方式并没有精确地命中目标，而只是暗示了那种被真正意指的东西，[①]因为这种“自我贬损”是非常不同于微小、柔弱或者在非神秘感的条件下我们能够认识到的可以依赖的某种东西。而我们不得不注意的是，这种经验标志着对于受尊敬的自我，也就是说，对于自我的真实与真实的存在的轻视与贬抑。现在我们还有提出与上述情况并列的另一种自我贬抑，它早就已为人们普遍观察到了，因此只需被提出来以便加以认识。“我是一个嘴巴不洁的人，居住在一个嘴巴不洁的人群中。”“主啊，请远离我，因为我是一个罪人。”这是以赛亚和彼得在神秘的实在作为意识的当下事实与他们相遇时分别说的话。在这两种情形中，这种自我贬抑的感受—反应是通过一种直接的、几乎是本能的自发性标志出来的。

① 参见圣维克多的雨果的这句话：“人们选择了这些虽然不可能被领会但在某种程度上仍可被理解的语词。”

nor does it follow any rule, but breaks, as it were, palpitant from the soul—like a direct reflex movement at the stimulation of the numinous. It does not spring from the consciousness of some committed transgression, but rather is an immediate datum given with the feeling of the numen: it proceeds to 'disvalue' together with the self the tribe to which the person belongs, and indeed, together with that, all existence in general. Now it is to-day pretty generally agreed that, all this being the case, these outbursts of feeling are not simply, and probably at first not at all, *moral* depreciations, but belong to a quite special category of valuation and appraisement. The feeling is beyond question not that of the transgression of the moral law, however evident it may be that such a transgression, where it has occurred, will involve it as a consequence: it is the feeling of absolute 'profaneness'.

But what is this? Again something which the 'natural' man cannot, as such, know or even imagine. He, only, who is 'in the Spirit' knows and feels what this 'profaneness' is; but to such an one it comes with piercing acuteness, and is accompanied by the most uncompromising judgement of self-depreciation, a judgement passed, not upon his character, because of individual 'profane' actions of his, but upon his own very existence as creature before that which is supreme above all creatures. And at the same moment he passes upon the numen a judgement of *appreciation* of a unique kind by the category diametrically contrary to 'the profane', the category 'holy', which is proper to the numen alone, but to it in an absolute degree; he says: '*Tu solus sanctus*'. This '*sanctus*' is not merely 'perfect' or 'beautiful' or 'sublime' or 'good', though, being like these concepts also a *value*, objective and ultimate, it has a definite, perceptible analogy with them. It is the positive *numinous* value or worth, and to it corresponds on the side of the creature a numinous *disvalue* or 'unworth'.

In every highly-developed religion the appreciation of moral

它不是建立在深思熟虑的基础上,也不遵循任何规则,而是好像从灵魂中迸发出的战抖——就像在神秘的刺激下的直接反应活动。它不是起源于某些犯罪意识,而是一种伴随着神秘感一道产生出来的东西:它在“贬抑”个人的同时,还“贬抑”他所属的部落,此外,还“贬抑”所有的一般存在。今天,人们普遍同意,在所有这些情形中,这些感受的迸发不单单是——或许最初根本就不是——道德的贬抑,而属于一种十分特殊的评价范畴。这种感受无疑不是那种违背了道德法则的感受,尽管很显然它可能就是这样一种违背,它出现在哪里,就会有一种结果伴随而来:这是那种绝对的“亵渎”的感觉。

但是,这究竟是什么呢?这又是“自然人”所同样不能认识甚至不能想象的东西。他——只有“处于圣灵中的”人,才能知道或者感受到“亵渎”是什么;但是对这种人来说,“亵渎”感来势凶猛,并且伴随着自我贬抑的最坚定的评判,这种评判并不因为他的个人的“亵渎”行为而针对他的人格而做出,而是针对他自己那个作为面对着高踞于万物之上的造物主的造物的存在而做出的。与此同时,他以一种直接对立于“亵渎”这一范畴的“神圣”范畴来给神秘一个独特的赞美的评判,只有“神圣”这一个范畴是适用于神秘的,但却是在绝对的程度上适合神圣;他说:“您是唯一的神圣者(*Tu solus sanctus*)。”这里的“神圣”不只是“完美”、“美丽”、“崇高”或者“善”,尽管就像这些概念一样,它也是一种客观的终极的价值,因此,它与这些概念有着明确的、显而易见的类似性。它是肯定性的神秘价值,而与之相对应的,在被造物一侧,则是一种神秘的“无价值”。

在各种高度发展的宗教中,对道德义务与道德责任的欣赏,

obligation and duty, ranking as a claim of the deity upon man, has been developed side by side with the religious feeling itself. None the less a profoundly humble and heartfelt recognition of 'the holy' may occur in particular experiences without being always or definitely charged or infused with the sense of moral demands. The 'holy' will then be recognized as that which commands our respect, as that whose real value is to be acknowledged inwardly. It is not that the awe of holiness is itself simply 'fear' in face of what is absolutely overpowering, before which there is no alternative to blind, awe-struck obedience. '*Tu solus sanctus*' is rather a paean of *praise*, which, so far from being merely a faltering confession of the divine supremacy, recognizes and extols a value, precious beyond all conceiving. The object of such praise is not simply absolute might, making its claims and compelling their fulfilment, but a might that has at the same time the supremest *right* to make the highest claim to service, and receives praise because it is in an absolute sense worthy to be praised. 'Thou art *worthy* to receive praise and honour and power' (Rev. iv. II).

When once it has been grasped that *qādôsh* or *sanctus* is not originally a *moral* category at all, the most obvious rendering of the words is 'transcendent' ('supramundane', *überweltlich*). The one-sided character of this rendering to which we had to take exception has been supplemented by the more detailed exposition of the numinous and its implications. But its most essential defect remains to be noted: 'transcendent' is a purely ontological attribute and not an attribute of *value*; it denotes a character that can, if need be, abash us, but cannot inspire us with *respect*. It might once again, therefore, be an advantage to introduce another term to underline this side of the numinous, and the words *augustus* and *σεμνός* suggest themselves for the purpose. *Augustus*, 'august', no less than *σεμνός*, is really appropriate only to numinous objects—to rulers only as offspring or descendants of gods. Then, while *σεβαστός* indicates the *being* of the numen, *σεμνός* or *augustus*

作为神对人的一种要求,随着宗教感受本身的发展而逐渐发展起来。尽管并不总是或者不明确地被道德律令意识所包含或者浸透,对神圣的一种深刻的谦卑与刻骨铭心的认识依然会在特殊的体验中产生出来。因此,神圣就会被认作那种要求我们尊敬的东西,即其真正的价值是要被内在地承认的。对神圣的敬畏本身并不仅仅是面对这绝对的至高无上者而产生的"害怕",即在面对绝对的至高无上者时除了盲目的、敬畏的服从,别无其他选择。"您是唯一的神圣者"(*To solus sanctus*)更是一句赞美的颂歌,它远非只是对神的至高无上的支支吾吾的告白,而是认识和赞扬了一种超乎想象的珍贵的价值。这种赞扬的对象不仅仅是绝对的权能,只是一味地提出自己的要求并强迫其实现,而是那种同时拥有最高的权力对服务作出最高的要求并得到赞美的权能,因为它是在一种绝对值得的意义上被赞美的。"你是值得荣耀、尊贵与权柄的"(《圣经·启示录》第4章第11节)

一旦抓住了这一点,即 *qādôsh* 和 *sanctus* 最初根本不是一种道德范畴,那么对这些词最明显的翻译就是"超验的"(远离尘世的 *überweltlich*)。我们所反对的这一翻译的片面特征已经由对神秘及其含义更加详尽的说明所弥补了,但是它最本质的缺陷依然有待指出:"超验的"是一个纯粹本体论的性质,而不是价值性质;它表示的这种性质,如果需要,就会羞辱我们,却不会以尊重来激励我们。因此,引入另一个术语来突出神秘的这一方面再次显示出其优势,而 *augustus* 和 *σεμνός* 显示出自身正当此任。*augustus* 和 *august* 同 *σεμνός* 一样,都是真正只适合于神秘对象的,即只适合于作为神的子孙后裔的统治者。那么,如果说 *σεβαστός* 指的是神秘的存在, *σεμνός* 和 *augustus* 指

would refer rather to its supreme worth or *value*, its illustriousness. There will, then, in fact be two values to distinguish in the numen; its 'fascination' (*fascinans*) will be that element in it whereby it is of *subjective* value (= beatitude) to man; but it is 'august' (*augustum*) in so far as it is recognized as possessing in itself *objective* value that claims our homage.

Mere 'unlawfulness' only becomes 'sin', 'impiety', 'sacrilege', when the character of *numinous unworthiness* or *disvalue* goes on to be transferred to and centred in *moral* delinquency. And only when the mind feels it as 'sin' does the transgression of law become a matter of such dreadful gravity for the conscience, a catastrophe that leads it to despair of its own power. The meaning of 'sin' is not understood by the 'natural', nor even by the merely moral, man; and the theory of certain dogmatists, that the demand of morality as such urged man on to an inner collapse and then obliged him to look round for some deliverance, is palpably incorrect. There are serious-minded men of sincere moral endeavour who cannot understand what such a 'deliverance' or 'redemption' may be, and dismiss it with a shrug of the shoulders. They are aware that they are erring and imperfect men, but they know and put into practice the methods of self-discipline, and so labour onward upon their way with sturdy resolution. The morally robust older rationalism was lacking neither in a sincere and respectful recognition of the moral law nor in honest endeavour to conform to it. It knew well and sternly condemned what was 'wrong', and the aim of its exhortations and instruction was that men should realize better and take more in earnest the facts of moral right and wrong. But no 'downfall' or 'collapse' and no 'need of redemption' came within its scheme, because the objection brought against it by its opponents was in fact just; rationalism lacked understanding of what 'sin' is①. Mere morality is not the soil from which

① Cf. the testimony of Theodore Parker—certainly a man of far from crude emental development—as to his own experience, given by W. James, *Varieties*, p. 81:

的就是神秘的最高价值,即它的光辉。这样,神秘中就事实上包含着两种不同的价值;“沉迷”因素是其中之一,并因此它对于人具有主观的价值(=至福);但是就它被认作是在其本身中拥有了要求人们尊敬的客观价值而言,它又具有“威严”因素。

只有当神秘的无价值与神秘的轻视的特征继续被转变并集中在道德的行为不端中,单纯的“不合法”才变成“罪”、“不敬”以及“亵渎”,并且只有当心灵将其感受为“罪”时,对法规的违犯才成为一件如此可怕的堕落,即导致良心对其自身的力量感到绝望的大灾难。“罪”的含义不能为“自然的”人所理解,甚至不能为纯粹道德的人所理解;而某些独断论者的理论,即认为道德的上述要求会将人逼迫到内在的崩溃并迫使他去寻找某种释放,这显然是错误的。那些在道德努力上非常诚挚并认真的人,不能理解这种“释放”或者“赎罪”会是什么东西,他们只是耸耸肩头就把它打发掉了。他们知道,他们是会犯错的不完美的人,但是他们知道自我约束的方法并将其付诸实施,在自己的道路上,他们以坚定的决心奋力前行。那些在道德上充满活力的老的理性主义者既不缺乏对道德法则的诚挚的、充满敬意的认识,也不缺乏诚实努力地去遵守。老理性主义清楚地知道并严厉地谴责“错误的”行为,它的训诫与教导的目的是,人们应当更好地认识道德上的对与错的事实,并且诚挚地从中吸取更多的东西。但是,在这种理性主义的框架中,却没有“堕落”、“坍塌”,也没有“救赎的需要”,因为它的反对者们所提出的异议事实上是公正的;理性主义对于“罪”是什么缺乏了解。①单纯

① 比较西奥多·帕克就他自己的经验所作的证言——他绝对不是一个精神发展不成熟的人。见W.詹姆士《宗教体验的类别》第81页:

grows either the need of 'redemption' and deliverance or the need for that other unique good which is likewise altogether and specifically numinous in character, 'covering', and 'atonement'. There would perhaps be less disputing as to the warrant and value of these latter in Christian doctrine if dogmatic theology itself had not transferred them from their mystical sphere into that of rational ethics and attenuated them into moral concepts. They were thus taken from a sphere where they have an authentic and necessary place to one where their validity is most disputable.

We meet the 'moment' of 'covering' in specially clear form in the religion of Yahweh, in its rites and the emotion they excite; but it is contained also, though more obscurely, in many other religions. It comprises, first, a manifestation of the numinous awe, viz. the feeling that the 'profane' creature cannot forthwith approach the numen, but has need of a covering or shield against the ὀργή of the numen. Such a 'covering' is then a 'consecration', i. e. a procedure that renders the approacher himself 'numinous', frees him from his 'profane' being, and fits him for intercourse with the numen. The means of 'consecration', however—'means of grace' in the proper sense—are derived from, or conferred and appointed by, the numen itself, which bestows something of its own quality to make man capable of communion with it. And this act is something very different from the

---

'They (sc. the heathen of classical antiquity) were conscious of wrath, of cruelty, avarice, drunkenness, lust, sloth, cowardice, and other actual vices, and struggled and got rid of the deformities; but they were not conscious of "enmity against God" and didn't sit down and whine and groan against non-existent evil. I have done wrong things enough in my life, and do them now: I miss the mark, draw bow, and try again. But... I know there is much "health in me"; and in my body, even now, there dwelleth many a good thing, spite of consumption and Saint Paul.'

If there is nothing crude about such a statement, it is at any rate *superficial*. The depths of the non-rational consciousness must be stirred to find with Anselm 'quanti ponderis sit peccatum'.

的道德既不是“救赎”和释放得以产生的土壤，也不是另一种独特的善得以产生的土壤，这种独特的善在性质上完全地、非常特殊地类似于神秘，即“荫庇”与“赎罪”。如果教条主义的理论不把“救赎”与“释放”等概念从神秘主义的领域中移植到理性的伦理学领域，并把它们弱化为道德概念，那么，关于后面这些概念在基督教教义中的根据与价值的争论就会少一些。由此，这些概念被从一个它们享有可信的、应有地位的领域带到了一个它们的合法性受到最大争议的领域。

在耶和华的宗教中，在它的各种仪式以及这些仪式所激发的感受中，我们看到了处于非常清楚的形式中的“荫庇”的“要素”；但是它也存在于其他的宗教中，尽管更加模糊。首先，这种要素包含着神秘畏惧的表现，即“世俗的”被造物不能立即接近神秘，但是需要一种庇护或遮掩以对抗神秘的愤怒（ὀργή）的那种感觉。这种“荫庇”因此而成为一种“神圣化”，也就是一种过程，通过它，使接近者本身变得“神秘”了，将他从他的“世俗的”存在中解放出来，并使他宜于与神秘交流。然而，这种“神圣化”的方式，在适当的意义上就是“恩典的方式”，它来自于神秘者本身，

“他们（即远古不信教的人）意识到了愤怒、残暴、贪婪、酗酒、好色、疏懒、怯懦以及其他一些现实的邪恶，他们与它们抗争并摆脱了它们；但他们却没有意识到‘对上帝的敌意’，并没有坐下来哀诉、呻吟，反对非存在的邪恶。我在我的生活中做了很多错事，并且现在还在做这样的错事：我并没有命中目标，故又抽箭再试。但……我知道，我内心有很多“健康的东西”；甚至现在，我的身体中也有许多好的东西，尽管有肺病与圣·保罗。”

虽然这段话并不粗鲁，那无论如何也是肤浅的。从安瑟姆的“quanti ponderis sit peccatum”（“罪恶是何等沉重”）这句话中，可以看到深层的非理性意识。

'annulment of mistrust', the phrase in which Ritschl seeks to rationalize these relations between God and man.

'Atonement', following our view, is a 'sheltering' or 'covering', but a profounder form of it. It springs directly from the idea of numinous value or worth and numinous disvalue or unworth as soon as these have been developed. Mere awe, mere need of shelter from the *tremendum*, has here been elevated to the feeling that man in his 'profaneness' is not *worthy* to stand in the presence of the holy one, and that his own entire personal unworthiness might defile even holiness itself. This is obviously the case in the vision of the call of Isaiah; and the same note recurs, less emphatically but quite unmistakably, in the story of the centurion of Capernaum (Luke vii. 1 – 10), and his words: 'I am not worthy that thou shouldest enter under my roof'. Here we have both the light thrill of awe before the *tremendum* of the numen and also, and more especially, the feeling of this unique disvalue or unworth of the profane confronted by the numen, which suggests to the man that even holiness itself may be tainted and tarnished by his presence.

Here, then, comes in the felt necessity and longing for 'atonement', and all the more strongly when the close presence of the numen, intercourse with it, and enduring possession of it, becomes an object of craving, is even desired as the *summum bonum*. It amounts to a longing to transcend this sundering unworthiness, given with the self's existence as 'creature' and profane natural being. It is an element in the religious consciousness, which, so far from vanishing in the measure in which religion is deepened and heightened, grows on the contrary continually stronger and more marked. Belonging,

或者是有神秘者本身赐予与分派的,神秘者将自身性质中的某种东西赋予人,使人能够与之交流。这种行为完全不同于“猜疑的终止”,这一术语是利奇尔找到用以对理性化人与上帝的关系的。

按照我们的观点,“救赎”也是一种“庇护”或“荫庇”,只不过程度更深一些。当神秘的价值与神秘的无价值的概念一开始发展起来,“救赎”的概念就直接从中生发出来。纯粹的畏惧,纯粹的挡住畏惧的需要,在此已经被升华为一种感受,即处于自己的“世俗的”状态中的人是不值得站在神圣者面前的,而且他自己整个的个人的无价值甚至会亵渎神圣本身。这一点很明显地出现在以赛亚的呼喊的幻象中;而同样的含义,尽管强调较少但是明白无误地重现在迦百农的百夫长的故事中(见《圣经·路加福音》第7章第1-10节),他说:“主呵,你不要劳动。因何到我舍下,我不敢当。”在此,我们不仅看到了在神秘的恐惧面前的那种轻微的畏惧的颤抖,而且尤其是发现了当世俗的人与神圣相遇时的这种独特的轻视或者无价值的感受,这种感受甚至向人暗示,就连神圣本身也因俗人的到场而受到玷污和失色。

因此,人们才感受到“救赎”的必要与渴望,而且,当接近神圣、与之交流、持续地占有它变成了渴望的对象时,所有的更加强烈的“救赎”的渴望甚至被当做至善来追求。只要自我是作为“被造物”以及世俗的自然物而存在着,这种救赎就汇集成为一种对超越这种分裂着的无价值的渴望。这是宗教意识中的一种因素,这种因素远未消失在宗教被深化与提升的手段中,相反,却不断地变得更为有力和更加显著了。由于完全属于宗教的非理性方

as it does, wholly to the non-rational side of religion, it may remain latent while, in the course of religious evolution, the rational side at first unfolds and assumes vigorous and definite form; it may retire for a time behind other elements and apparently die away, but only to return more powerfully and insistently than before. And again it may grow to be the sole, one-sided, exclusive interest, a cry that drowns all other notes, so that the religious consciousness is distorted and disfigured; as may readily happen where through long periods of time the rational aspects of religion have been fostered unduly and at the cost of the non-rational.

The special character of this consciousness of need for atonement may perhaps be brought home more clearly by an analogy from our 'natural' emotional life; but at the same time it is important that the religious feeling we are considering should itself be kept distinct from its analogue, as the two are frequently confounded. The analogy is with the feeling arising from moral transgression. There, too, we practise a kind of self-depreciation which is clear and familiar and perfectly intelligible to us, when we esteem ourselves *guilty* of a bad action and the action itself as morally evil. The evil of the action *weighs upon us* and deprives us of ourself-respect. We *accuse* ourselves and *remorse* sets in. But alongside this self-depreciation stands a second one, which while it may have reference to the same action as the other yet avails itself of definitely different categories. The same perverse action that before weighed upon us now *pollutes* us; we do not accuse ourselves, we are defiled in our own eyes. And the characteristic form of emotional reaction is no longer remorse but *loathing*. The man feels a need, to express which he has recourse to images of *washing* and cleansing. The two kinds of self-depreciation proceed on parallel lines and may relate to the same action; but none the less it is obvious that they are, inwardly and in their essence, determinately different. Now the second of them has a plain analogy with the need for 'atonement', and so can fairly be drawn upon for its elucidation; while at the same time it is

面,“救赎”在宗教的进化过程中可以保持潜在的状态,理性方面首先显示出来,并且采取了有力的明确的形式;“救赎”可以暂时退隐到其他因素后面并明显地消隐下来,但这只是为了比以前更加有力、更加坚决地回来。它会再次成长为单一的、片面的、排他的兴趣,成为一种淹没其他一切意见的呼喊,以致宗教意识遭到扭曲与损害;在漫长的岁月中,宗教的理性方面以牺牲非理性为代价而得以不适当的培养的地方,非常容易发生上述情况。

通过一个我们“自然的”感受生活的类比,这种救赎的需要意识的特殊性质能够得到更加清楚的认识;但是同时,我们所正在讨论的宗教感受必须将自身与其类比区分开来,这是很重要的,因为而且经常被混淆。这种类比就是从道德违规中生发出来的感受。在道德违规中,如果我们认定自己对某一种坏的行为负有罪责,而且坏的行为本身在道德上是邪恶的,那么,我们也能体验到这样一种自我贬抑,这种自我贬抑对我们来说是清晰的,熟悉的,是完全可以理解的。这种行为的邪恶压迫着我们,并剥夺了我们的自尊,我们谴责自己并且开始懊悔。而伴随着这种自我贬义,还有另外一种,这种自我贬抑像另一种一样,参照着同一种行为而将自身界定为决然不同的范畴。那种先前压在我们身上的不正当行为现在则玷污我们;我们不再谴责自己,而是感到自身的污秽。这种情感反应的特有形式不再是懊悔,而是厌恶。人感受到某种需要,为了表达这种需要,他求助于想象来洗刷和洁净自身的污点。这两种自我贬抑并行不悖并可以联系到同一种行为,但是依然非常明显,它们在内在本质上是截然不同的东西。现在第二种自我贬抑与“救赎”的需要之间有了一种清楚的类似,因此可以非常清楚地被用来对其加以阐明;然而同

yet nothing more than an analogy from another sphere, viz. that of morality.

No religion has brought the mystery of the need for atonement or expiation to so complete, so profound, or so powerful expression as Christianity. And in this, too, it shows its superiority over others. It is a more perfect religion and more perfectly religion than they, in so far as what is potential in religion in general becomes in Christianity a pure actuality. And the distrust and suspicion which so widely obtains with regard to this mystery is only to be explained from the general custom—for which our theoretical cult of homiletics, liturgy, and catechism is largely responsible—of taking into account only the rational side of religion. Yet this atonement mystery is a 'moment' which no Christian teaching that purports to represent the religious experience of the Christian and biblical tradition can afford to surrender. The teacher will have to make explicit, by an analysis of the Christian religious experience, how the 'very numen', by imparting itself to the worshipper, becomes itself the means of 'atonement'. And in this regard it does not matter so very much what the decisions of the commentators are as to what, if anything, St. Paul or St. Peter wrote on the subject of expiation and atonement, or whether, indeed, there is any 'scriptural authority' for the thing at all. Were there in scripture no word written about it, it might still be written to-day from our own experience. But it would indeed be extraordinary if it had not long ago been written of. For the God of the New Testament is not less holy than the God of the Old Testament, but more holy. The interval between the creature and Him is not diminished but made absolute; the unworthiness of the profane in contrast to Him is not extenuated but enhanced. That God none the less admits access to Himself and intimacy with Himself is not a mere matter of course; it is a grace beyond our power to apprehend, a prodigious paradox. To take this paradox out of Christianity is to make it shallow and superficial beyond recognition. But if this is so, the intuitions concerning, and the need felt for, 'covering'

时,它不过是来自另一领域,即道德领域的类比而已。

没有哪种宗教像基督教这样,给救赎需要或者赎罪需要的神秘性以如此全面、如此深刻、如此有力的表达,在这一方面,基督教也显示了它比其他宗教的优越性。它是一种更加完美的宗教,而且,在一般宗教中还是潜在的东西而在基督教中变成了纯粹的实在这一点上,基督教比其他宗教更加完美。对于这种神秘人们普遍持有的不信任和怀疑,只能以一般的习惯,即我们只是考虑到了宗教的理性方面的习惯来解释——我们的布道、礼拜和教义问答的理论崇拜对此要负很大的责任。然而,这种救赎神秘是一种“因素”,这种“因素”是任何旨在表现基督徒的宗教体验与圣经传统的基督教的教诲所不能放弃的。通过分析这种基督徒的宗教体验,教诲者将不得不解释清楚,“这种神秘”是怎样通过将自身透露给那些崇拜者,从而将自己变成“救赎”的工具的。在这一点上,对于圣保罗或者圣彼得关于赎罪与救赎写了些什么——如果有什么(区别)的话,或者无论在这件事情上到底有没有“经文权威”,评论者有什么样的论断并不是十分重要。即便在经文中对它只字不提,它也可以从我们自己的经验中在今天被书写出来。但是如果它不是在很久以前就已经被记录过,那就真的很反常了。因为《新约》的上帝并不比《旧约》的上帝更少神圣,而是更加神圣。被造物与上帝之间的距离不是被缩小了,而是变得绝对了;与上帝相对的世俗的人的无价值感不是被减轻了,而是被增强了。上帝依然允许我们接近他、亲近他,但这绝不是纯粹应当如此;这是一种超越我们理解力的恩典,一个巨大的悖论。将这种悖论从基督教中消除掉会将它变得无比浅薄、面目全非,但是如果那样,对于“荫庇”和“救赎”的直觉和关于“荫庇”与“救赎”

and 'atonement' result immediately. And the divinely appointed means of God's self-revelation, where experienced and appraised as such—'the Word', 'the Spirit', 'the Person of Christ',—become that to which the man 'flees', in which he finds refuge, and in which he 'hides' himself, in order that, consecrated and cleansed of his 'profaneness' thereby, he may come into the presence of Holiness itself.

That these ideas are viewed with a certain distrust may be traced to two causes. One is, that what is a specifically religious element is distortingly moralized. If we start from mere morality and in relation to a God understood as being the personification of the moral order endowed with love, then all these things are wholly inapplicable and a source of genuine difficulty. But we are concerned with *religious* (not merely moral) intuitions, and it is impossible to dispute how right or wrong they are with a man whose interest is wholly in morality and not in religion, and who is therefore quite incapable of appreciating them. Whoever, on the other hand, penetrates to the unique centre of the religious experience, so that it starts awake in his own consciousness, finds that the truth of these intuitions is experienced directly, as soon as he penetrates into their depths.

The other ground of distrust is that usually in our theological systems an attempt is made to develop conceptual *theories* of these ideas, which are all pure intuitions, emotional rather than conceptual in character. They are thus made objects of speculation, and the final outcome is the quasimathematical 'doctrine of imputation' and its drastic ascription to the credit of the 'sinner' of the 'merit' of Christ, not to mention the learned inquiry whether this transaction involves an 'analytic' or a 'synthetic' judgement of God.

* * * * *

Let us look back once more from the point we have reached over the course our inquiry has so far taken. As the sub-title of this book suggests, we were to investigate the non-rational element in the idea of the divine. The words 'non-rational' and 'irrational' are to-day used almost at random. The non-rational is sought

的需要立刻就作为结果出现了。那些被神圣地指定的上帝自我显示的手段——在我们体验到和赞美那些“圣言”、“圣灵”、“基督本人”的地方——变成为人所“逃离”的目标、追寻的避难所、“隐藏”自己的地方,以便由此来洗刷和净化人的“世俗性”,并因此使他能够来到神圣自身面前。

这些观念被人们怀着不信任的态度看待,原因可能是以下两个:一个原因是,那种独特的宗教因素被歪曲地道德化了。如果我们从纯粹的道德出发,并且在涉及上帝时,把他理解为赋予爱的道德秩序的化身,那么,所有这些东西就完全不适用,都成了真正困难的源泉。但是我们所关注的是宗教的(而不仅仅是道德的)直觉,而且,与一个兴趣完全在道德上而不在宗教上、因而完全无法理解直觉的人辩论直觉的对错,这是不可能的。另一方面,无论谁能够渗透到这种宗教经验的独特中心,由此它就会在他自己的意识中被唤醒,谁就会发现,一旦他渗透到这些直觉的深处,这些直觉的真理就会被直接地体验到。

不信任的另一个原因在于,通常在我们的神学系统中,人们力图将那些性质上是纯粹直觉的、情感的而非概念的观念发展成概念性的理论。这些直觉感受的观念成了思维的对象,而最终的结果是准数学的“归因原则”及其激烈的归因,即将基督的“美德”归因于“罪人”的信任,而不提及这种处理包含着对上帝的“分析”判断还是“综合”判断的学术探究。

* * * * * * *

让我们从目前所达到的高度来再次回顾一下我们的探究迄今为止所采取的路线。正如本书的副标题所指出的,我们所要研究的是神性观念中的非理性因素。今天,“非理性”与“无理性”的使用

over the most widely different regions, and writers generally shirk the trouble of putting down precisely what they intend by the term, giving it often the most multifarious meanings or applying it with such vague generality that it admits of the most diverse interpretations. Pure fact in contrast to law, the empirical in contrast to reason, the contingent in contrast to the necessary, the psychological in contrast to transcendental fact, that which is known a *posteriori* in contrast to that which is determinable *a priori*; power, will, and arbitrary choice in contrast to reason, knowledge, and determination by value; impulse, instinct, and the obscure forces of the subconscious in contrast to insight, reflection, and intelligible plan; mystical depths and stirrings in the soul, surmise, presentiment, intuition, prophecy, and finally the 'occult' powers also; or, in general, the uneasy stress and universal fermentation of the time, with its groping after the thing never yet heard or seen in poetry or the plastic arts—all these and more may claim the names 'non-rational', 'irrational', and according to circumstances are extolled or condemned as modern 'irrationalism'. Whoever makes use of the word 'non-rational' to-day ought to say what he actually means by it. This we did in our introductory chapter. We began with the 'rational' in the idea of God and the divine, meaning by the term that in it which is clearly to be grasped by our power of conceiving, and enters the domain of familiar and definable conceptions. We went on to maintain that beneath this sphere of clarity and lucidity lies a hidden depth, inaccessible to our conceptual thought, which we in so far call the 'non-rational'.

The meaning of the two contrasted terms may be made plainer by an illustration. A deep joy may fill our minds without any clear realization upon our part of its source and the object to which it refers, though some such objective reference there must always be. But as attention is directed to it the obscure object becomes clearly identified in precise conceptual terms. Such an object cannot, then, be called,

几乎是任意的。人们从最广阔的不同领域去追寻非理性,作家们总是避开准确地记下这些术语本身含义的麻烦,而经常给予它最多样化的含义,或者在非常模糊的含义上使用它,因此非理性包含了最多种多样的解释。与法则相对的纯粹事实,与理性相对的经验,与必然性相对的偶然性,与超验事实相对的心理事实,与先天决定物相对的后天决定物;与理性、知识及价值决定相对的强力、意志和武断选择;与洞见、反思及可理解的计划相对的冲动、本能和下意识的模糊力量;灵魂中的神秘深度与骚动、猜度、预感、直觉、预言,最后还有“超自然的”力量;或者,一般而言,那种不安的压力与时代的普遍的骚动,以及对那些在诗与造型艺术中未曾见闻过的事物的探索——所有这些以及更多的东西都可以冠以“非理性”或者“无理性”之名,并在不同的情形可以被称颂为或者谴责为现代“非理性主义”。今天,无论谁使用“非理性”一词,都应当说明他实际所指的是什么东西,这就是我们在导论部分所做的工作。我们是从上帝或者神性观念的“理性”部分开始的,通过这一术语,我们来指那些可为我们的构思能力明晰把握的,而且进入到了我们熟悉的、可以定义的概念领域中的东西。我们进而主张,在这一清晰明朗的领域之下,存在着一个隐秘的深层领域,是我们的概念性思维所无法接近的,我们在这个意义上称之为“非理性”。

“理性”与“非理性”这两个相互对立的术语的含义能够通过一个说明变得更加明了。一种深沉的快乐可以充满我们的心灵,而我们对它的来源以及它所指涉的对象却没有任何清晰的认识,尽管总是会存在着某种对象的关联,但是当注意力被引向它时,这一模糊的对象在精确的概念术语中得到了清晰的确认。于是,

in our sense of the word, 'non-rational'. But it is quite otherwise with religious 'bliss' and its essentially numinous aspect, the *fascinans*. Not the most concentrated attention can elucidate the object to which this state of mind refers, bringing it out of the impenetrable obscurity of feeling into the domain of the conceptual understanding. It remains purely a felt experience, only to be indicated symbolically by 'ideograms'. That is what we mean by saying it is non-rational.

And the same is true of all the moments of the numinous experience. The consciousness of a 'wholly other' evades precise formulation in words, and we have to employ symbolic phrases which seem sometimes sheer paradox, that is, irrational, not merely non-rational, in import. So with religious awe and reverence. In ordinary fear and in moral reverence I can indicate in conceptual terms what it is that I fear or revere; injury, e. g., or ruin in the one case, heroism or strength of character in the other. But the object of *religious* awe or reverence—the *tremendum* and *augustum*, cannot be fully determined conceptually: it is non-rational, as is the beauty of a musical composition, which no less eludes complete conceptual analysis.

Confronted by the fact of the non-rational thus interpreted we cannot be satisfied with a mere bare statement, which would open the door to all the vague and arbitrary phraseology of an emotionalist irrationalism. We are bound to try, by means of the most precise and unambiguous symbolic and figurative terms that we can find, to discriminate the different elements of the experience so far as we can in a way that can claim general validity.

这样一个对象就不能在我们的意义上被称做“非理性”。但是,宗教的“福佑”及其基本的神秘方面——“沉迷”,却完全是另一回事。即使是最集中的注意力也不能说明这种心态所指涉的对象,并将其从无法穿透的感受的模糊性中带到概念性理解的领域中去。它完全保持为一种被感受到的经验,只能由“表意符号”加以象征性地指称,这就是我们称之为非理性的含义。

神秘经验的所有要素也同样如此。对于“完全的他者”的意识规避着以文字的形式作出的精确的表达,我们不得不采用一些有时显得全然矛盾的象征性语词,也就是说,在重要性上,显得无理性,而不仅仅是非理性。宗教的畏惧与敬仰也是如此。在普通的害怕和道德的敬仰中,我可以以概念性的术语指出我所害怕或者敬仰的是什么,例如,在一种情形下,我害怕受到伤害或者毁灭,在另一种情形下,我敬仰英雄主义与人格力量。但是,宗教畏惧或者宗教敬仰的对象却不能被完全概念地界定:它是非理性的,就像一件音乐作品的美一样,同样躲避着完全概念的分析。

由于遇到了被如此解释的非理性的事实,我们不能满足于一种纯粹直白的陈述,这种陈述会向那些易受感动的人的非理性主义的所有模糊专断的措辞打开大门。我们一定要努力通过我们所能找到的最准确无误的象征和比喻的术语,尽我们所能,以一种可称做普遍有效性的方式,把这种经验中的不同因素区分开来。

CHAPTER IX

Means Of Expression Of The Numinous

I. *Direct Means*

It may serve to make the essential nature of the numinous consciousness clearer if we call to mind the manner in which it expresses itself outwardly, and how it spreads and is transmitted from mind to mind. There is, of course, no 'transmission' of it in the proper sense of the word; it cannot be 'taught', it must be 'awakened' from the spirit. And this could not justly be asserted, as it often is, of religion as a whole and in general, for in religion there *is* very much that *can* be taught—that is, handed down in concepts and passed on in school instruction. What is incapable of being so handed down is this numinous basis and background to religion, which can only be induced, incited, and aroused. This is least of all possible by mere verbal phrase or external symbol; rather we must have recourse to the way all other moods and feelings are transmitted, to a penetrative imaginative sympathy with what passes in the other person's mind. More of the experience lives in reverent attitude and gesture, in tone and voice and demeanour, expressing its momentousness, and in the solemn devotional assembly of a congregation at prayer, than in all the phrases and negative nomenclature which we have found to designate it. Indeed, these never give a positive suggestion of the object to which the religious consciousness refers; they are only of assistance in so far as they profess to indicate *an* object, which they at the same time contrast with another, at once distinct from and

第九章　表达神秘的各种方式

1.直接的方式

如果我们回想一下神秘意识外在地将自身表达出来的方式，以及它怎样展开并从一个心灵传输到另一个心灵，这或许有助于使神秘意识的本质特征更加清楚一些。当然，就“传输”一词的本来意义而言，不存在神秘意识的“传输”；神秘意识是不能“被教给”的，它只能从精神中加以“唤醒”。对于作为整体和一般的宗教来说，这一说法实际上并不确然如此，因为在宗教中，的确有着许多能够被教给的东西，也就是以概念和学校教育的方式流传下来的东西。那种不能以此种方式流传下来的是宗教的神秘基础与背景，它们只能被诱导、被激发和被唤醒。单靠口头词汇或者外在的符号是很难做到这一点的；相反，我们必须求助于所有其他的情绪与感受得以传输的那种方式，求助于洞悉他人心灵的渗透性的想象的同情。大多数体验存活于虔敬的态度与姿态中，存活于语调、声音与行为举止中，表现着它的重要性，还存活于庄严虔敬的祈祷的圣会中，而不是存活于我们已经找到的用来指称这些体验的所有表达方式与否定性的术语中。的确，这些表达方式从来没有给予宗教意识所指涉的对象以肯定的指示；对于它们表示出的要去指示的某个对象，它们只具有辅助作用，同时，这种方式又使这一对象与另一对象相对立，是一个有别于、低于另一个，

inferior to it, e. g. 'the invisible', 'the eternal' (non-temporal), 'the supernatural', 'the transcendent'. Or they are simply ideograms for the unique content of feeling, ideograms to understand which a man must already have had the experience himself. Far the best means are actual 'holy' situations or their representation in description. If a man does not *feel* what the numinous is, when he reads the sixth chapter of Isaiah, then no 'preaching, singing, telling', in Luther's phrase, can avail him. Little of it can usually be noticed in theory and dogma, or even in exhortation, unless it is actually *heard*. Indeed no element in religion needs so much as this the *viva vox*, transmission by living fellowship and the inspiration of personal contact. ①

But the mere word, even when it comes as a living voice, is powerless without the 'spirit in the heart' of the hearer to move him to apprehension. And this spirit, this inborn capacity to receive and understand, is the essential thing. If that is there, very often only a very small incitement, a very remote stimulus, is needed to arouse the numinous consciousness. It is indeed astonishing to see how small a stimulus suffices—and that too coming sometimes only in clumsy and bewildered guise—to raise the spirit of itself to the strongest pitch of the most definitely religious excitement. But where the wind of the spirit blows, there the mere 'rational' terms themselves are indued with power to arouse the feeling of the 'non-rational', and become adequate to tune the mood at once to the right tone. Here 'schematization' starts at once and needs no prompting. He who 'in the spirit' reads the

---

① Suso says of the transmission of the mystical experience: 'One thing there may be known; unlike as it is, when a man heareth himself a dulcet instrument of strings sweetly sounding, compared to whoso but heareth tell thereof, even so are the words which are received in the purity of grace and flow forth out of a living heart by a living mouth unlike to those same words if they are beheld upon the dead parchment.... For there they grow cold, I know not how, and wither away like roses that have been plucked. For the lovely melody that above all toucheth the heart is then quenched to silence; and in the waste places of the withered heart are they then received.'

例如“不可见的”、“永恒的(无时间性的)”、“超自然的”、“超验的”。或者,它们仅仅是那种感受的独特内容的表意符号,一个人要理解这种表意符号,他本人必须已经具有了这种体验。最好的表达方式就是实际的“神圣”境遇或者对这种境遇的描述。如果一个人在读了《以赛亚书》第6章后并没有感受到神秘是什么,那么,任何“说教、唱诗、讲解”(路德语)都不能帮助他。通常在理论和教义中,甚至在讲道词中,神秘很难被人们注意到,除非它被实际地听到。的确,在宗教中,没有哪个因素需要如此多的“口头表述”,即通过生活中的伙伴关系以及个人交往的灵感来传输。①

但是仅仅是词汇,即使它是以一种活生生的声音出现,如果听众缺乏“心中的灵性”来推动他去理解,那也是无力的。这种灵性,这种天生的接收和理解的能力,是一种根本性的东西。如果具有了这种能力,那么通常只需要非常微小的刺激物、非常微弱的刺激,就可以引发神秘的意识。看到这么小的一点刺激就足以把这种灵性本身提高到最确定的宗教刺激的最强程度,而这些刺激有时只是在一种笨拙的、令人迷惑的外观下出现,这真是非常令人吃惊。但是哪里有这种灵性之风吹拂,那里纯粹“理性的”术语本身就被赋予了力量,来引发“非理性”的感受,并足以把心境立刻调整到适当的位置。这里,“图示化”过

① 苏索对这种神秘体验的传递是这样说的:“有一点是可以知道的,一个人亲自聆听一曲美妙音乐的演奏,与那种由别人向他转述该音乐的演奏,是大不相同的。即使同样的话,如果我们是从一个有灵魂的活人嘴里听到的,也和从死板的羊皮纸上见到的大不相同……因为它们变冷了并且像连根拔起的玫瑰花那样枯萎了,尽管我不知道这些是如何发生的。因为那最先触动心灵的动人旋律这时已归于沉寂,然后才被接纳到枯萎心灵的荒凉之地。”

written word lives in the numinous, though he may have neither notion of it nor name for it, nay, though he may be unable to analyse any feeling of his own and so make explicit to himself the nature of that numinous strand running through the religious experience.

2. *Indirect Means*

For the rest, the methods by which the numinous feeling is presented and evoked are indirect; i. e. they consist in those means by which we express kindred and similar feelings belonging to the 'natural' sphere. We have already become acquainted with these feelings, and we shall recognize them at once if we consider what are the means of expression which religion has employed in all ages and in every land.

One of the most primitive of these—which is later more and more felt to be inadequate, until it is finally altogether discarded as 'unworthy'—is quite naturally the 'fearful' and horrible, and even at times the revolting and the loathsome. Inasmuch as the corresponding feelings are closely analogous to that of the *tremendum*, their outlets and means of expression may become indirect modes of expressing the specific 'numinous awe' that cannot be expressed directly. And so it comes about that the horrible and dreadful character of primitive images and pictures of gods, which seems to us to-day frequently so repellent, has even yet among naïve and primitive natures—nay, occasionally even among ourselves —the effect of arousing genuine feelings of authentic religious awe. And, vice versa, this awe operates as a supremely potent stimulus to express the element of terror in different forms of imaginative representation. The hard, stern, and somewhat grim pictures of the Madonna in ancient Byzantine art attract the worship of many Catholics more than the tender charm of the Madonnas of Raphael. This trait is most signally evident in the case of certain figures of gods in the

程立即开始,无须任何激励。“以灵性的方式”阅读书写下的文字的人,生活在神秘之中,尽管他可能既不了解它也不知道它的名字,而且,尽管他可能不能分析自己的任何感受,因此也不能使自己明白那贯穿在宗教经验中的神秘线索的性质。

2.间接的方式

对于其余的人来说,神秘感受得以表达和唤起的方式是间接的;也就是说,这些方式存在于我们表达属于“自然的”领域的同族的与类似的感受的方式之中。我们已经很熟悉这一类感受了,而且,只要我们对宗教在一切时代、一切国家所采用过的那些表达方式加以思考,我们立刻就可以识别出这些感受来。

这些感受中最原始的一种——后面会越来越感到它的不充分,直到最后它被当做“无价值的”而整个被抛弃掉——自然就是“害怕”和恐惧,而且甚至有时是厌恶与讨厌。由于这种相应的感受十分类似于那种畏惧的感受,因此表达它们的渠道和方式可以成为表达这种特殊的“神秘的敬畏”的间接方式——这种神秘的敬畏是不能被直接地表达出来的。于是就产生了这样的结果:神灵的原始形象的那种令人讨厌畏惧的性质——这在今天对我们来说似乎也常常是令人反感的——即便是处于淳朴原始的本质之中(而且有时甚至存在于我们中间),依然具有引发可信的宗教敬畏的真实感受的作用。而且,反之亦然,这种敬畏作为一种最强有力的刺激,以不同的想象性陈述方式表达了这种恐惧的因素。在古代拜占庭艺术中那僵硬的、严肃的、而且多少有些冷酷的圣母画像,比拉斐尔笔下那位温柔优雅的圣母更加吸引了众多天主

Indian pantheon. Durgā, the 'great Mother' of Bengal, whose worship can appear steeped in an atmosphere of profoundest devotional awe, is represented in the orthodox tradition with the visage of a fiend. And this same blending of appalling frightfulness and most exalted holiness can perhaps be even more clearly studied in the eleventh book of the Bhagavad-Gītā,① in which Vishnu—who is yet to his votaries the very principle of goodness—displays himself to Aryuna in the true height of his divinity. Here, too, the mind has recourse for mode of expression first to the fearful and dreadful, though this is at the same time permeated with that element of 'the grand' to which we next turn.

This mode of expression, by way of 'grandeur' or 'sublimity', is found on higher levels, where it replaces mere 'terror' and 'dread'. We meet it in an unsurpassable form in the sixth chapter of Isaiah, where there is sublimity alike in the lofty throne and the sovereign figure of God, the skirts of His raiment 'filling the temple' and the solemn majesty of the attendant angels about Him. While the element of 'dread' is gradually overborne, the connexion of 'the sublime' and 'the holy' becomes firmly established as a legitimate schematization and is carried on into the highest forms of religious consciousness—a proof that there exists a hidden kinship between the numinous and the sublime which is something more than a merely accidental analogy, and to which Kant's *Critique of Judgement* bears distant witness.

So far we have been concerned with that element or factor of the numinous which was the first our analysis noted and which we

---

① See Appendix II. Nowhere can the non-rational element of ὀργή be better studied than in this chapter, one of the perfectly classical passages for the theory of Religion.

教徒的崇拜。在印度万神殿里有许多神祇的情形中,这一特点更加显著。杜尔迦——这位孟加拉的“难近母”——对她的崇拜可以表现为沉浸在最为虔敬的畏惧气氛之中——在正统的传统中就是以恶魔的形象被表现出来的。同样,这种骇人听闻的恐惧与最尊贵的神圣的结合或许可以更加清楚地在《薄伽梵歌》(*Bhagavad-Gītā*)[①]第11章中找到,在这一章中,毗湿奴(*Vishnu*)——对于他的信仰者来说依然代表着善的原则——在他的神性的真正高度上将自身现实为阿周那(*Aryuna*)。在此,心灵同样首先求助于害怕和畏惧的表达方式,尽管这种畏惧同时渗透着下面我们就要讲到的“崇高”因素。

这种表达方式即采用“庄严”或者“崇高”的方式,在更高的层次上被发现,在此,它已取代了纯粹的“恐惧”与“畏惧”。在《以赛亚书》第6章中,我们遇到了这个无法超越的表达方式,在这里,在崇高的王座上和上帝的统御身份上,同样有崇高存在,他御衣的裙裾“充塞殿堂”,身边环绕着庄严肃穆的天使臣仆。当“畏惧”的因素逐渐被克服时,“崇高”与“神圣”的联系却作为一种合理的图示化而被牢固地建立起来,并继而成为宗教仪式的最高的形式——这是在神秘与崇高之间存在着隐蔽的亲缘关系的一个实证,这种关系远非仅仅偶然的类似,在康德的《判断力批判》中对此有隐约的证明。

至此,我们已经讨论过了神秘的一个因素,即那个我们的分

---

① 参见附录二,对愤怒(ὀργή)这个非理性因素的研究没有哪一章比在这一章中做得好,对于宗教理论来说,这是最完美的经典章节之一。

proposed to name symbolically 'the aweful' (*tremendum*). We pass now to consider the means by which the second—the element of 'the mysterious' (*mysterium*)—is expressed. Here we light upon the analogical mode of manifestation that in every religion occupies a foremost and extraordinary place, and the theory of which we are now in a position to give. I refer to *miracle*. 'Miracle is the dearest child of Faith'; if the history of religions had not already taught us the truth of Schiller's saying, we might have reached it by anticipation *a priori* from the element of 'the mysterious', as already shown. Nothing can be found in all the world of 'natural' feelings bearing so immediate an analogy—*mutatis mutandis*—to the religious consciousness of ineffable, unutterable mystery, the 'absolute other', as the incomprehensible, unwonted, enigmatic thing, in whatever place or guise it may confront us. This will be all the more true if the uncomprehended thing is something at once *mighty* and *fearful*, for then there is a twofold analogy with the numinous—that is to say, an analogy not only with the *mysterium* aspect of it, but with the *tremendum* aspect, and the latter again in the two directions already suggested of *fearfulness* proper and *sublimity*. This exemplifies the general truth already considered that any form of the numinous consciousness may be stirred by means of feelings analogous to it of a 'natural' kind, and then itself pass over into these, or, more properly, be replaced by them. And, in fact, this is everywhere manifest in the experience of man. Whatever has loomed upon the world of his ordinary concerns as something terrifying and baffling to the intellect; whatever among natural occurrences or events in the human, animal, or vegetable kingdoms has set him astare in wonder and astonishment—such things have ever aroused in man, and become endued with, the 'daemonic dread' and numinous feeling, so as to become 'portents', 'prodigies', and 'marvels'. Thus and only thus is it that 'the

析所针对的首要的对象,我们象征性地命名为“畏惧”。现在我们要进而考虑第二个因素,即“神秘的”因素得以表达的方式。这里我们要阐明那种在各种宗教中都占据首要和超常地位的类比的表达方式,以及那种我们正要给出的理论。我指的是奇迹。“奇迹是信仰最亲爱的孩子”;即便宗教史没有告诉我们席勒所说的这一真理,我们也可以通过从这一“神秘”因素中先验的预期来得出这结论,就像已经显示的那样。在“自然”感受的整个世界中,根本找不到任何可以对这种宗教意识作直接类比的东西,这种宗教意识是关于那个无法言表的神秘,即“绝对的他者”的,而这种绝对的他者,无论在何处、以何种形象与我们相遇,都是一种不可理解的、不同寻常的、高深莫测的东西。如果这种不可理解的东西同时又是强有力的和令人害怕的,情况就更是如此,因为这时有着与神秘的双重类似——也就是说,不仅与它的神秘的方面相类似,而且还和它的恐惧的方面相类似,而后者又存在于我们已经提到过的畏惧与崇高这两个路向中。这一点具体说明了我们已经思考过的那个一半真理,即任何形式的神秘意识都可以通过与之类似的“自然”感受的方式被激发,并进而进入到这些“自然”感受中,或者更准确地说,被这些“自然”感受所替代。而事实上,在人类的经验中,这一点是随处可见的。无论这种隐现在人日常关注的世界中的、使理智感到恐惧与困惑的东西是什么;也无论在人类、动物或者植物王国中的自然过程或者事件中使人震惊到目瞪口呆的是什么——这些东西都曾经在人们中间激发起并被赋予了“对魔鬼的畏惧”与神秘的感受,以至于变成了“征兆”、“奇观”和“奇迹”。这样并且只有这样,“奇迹”才生

miraculous' rose. And, in the reverse direction, the feeling of the *numen* as 'the mysterious' worked as a potent stimulus on the naive imagination, inciting it to expect miracles, to invent them, to 'experience' them, to recount them, just as before the felt awefulness of the numen became a stimulus to select or fashion inventively, as a means of religious expression, images of fear and dread. 'The mysterious' became an untiring impulse, prompting to inexhaustible invention in folk-tale and myth, saga and legend, permeating ritual and the forms of worship, and remaining till to-day to naïve minds, whether in the form of narrative or sacrament, the most powerful factor that keeps the religious consciousness alive. But here too, as in the case of the fearful and terrible, progress to a higher stage of development shows the gradual elimination of this merely external analogue to the numinous, viz. the miraculous; and so we see how, on the more enlightened levels, 'miracle' begins to fade away; how Christ is at one with Mohammed and Buddha in declining the role of mere wonderworker; how Luther dismisses the 'outward miracles' disparagingly as 'jugglery' or 'apples and nuts for children'; and finally how the 'supernaturalism' of miracle is purged from religion as something that is only an imperfect analogue and no genuine 'schema' of the numinous.

There are other manifestations of this tendency of the feeling of the 'mysterious' to be attracted to objects and aspects of experience analogous to it in being 'uncomprehended'. It finds its most unqualified expression in the spell exercised by the only half intelligible or wholly unintelligible language of devotion, and in the unquestionably real enhancement of the awe of the worshipper which this produces. Instances of this are—the ancient traditional expressions, still retained despite their obscurity, in our Bible and hymnals; the special emotional virtue attaching to words like 'Hallelujah', *Kyrie eleison*,

发出来。而在相反的方向上,作为“神秘”的神秘的感受以一种强有力的刺激在质朴的想象上发生作用,刺激它去期待奇迹、创造奇迹、“体验”奇迹、描述奇迹,就像先前被感受到的对神秘的敬畏,作为宗教表达的一种方式,变成了创造性地去选择和塑造惧怕意象的一种刺激。“神秘”变成了一种不倦的推动力,在民间故事、神话、传说以及传奇中激起了无穷无尽的发明创造,渗入了宗教仪式和崇拜的各种形式中,并且,无论是以叙述的形式还是以圣礼的形式,直到今天,它都为那些质朴的心灵保留了维持宗教意识存活的最强大的因素。但是在这里,正像在害怕和恐惧的情形中一样,向更高发展阶段的演进也显示出对这种纯粹外在的神秘亦即奇迹的相似性的逐渐消除;由此在更加显明的层面上,我们看到,“奇迹”是如何开始渐渐消退的;看到耶稣基督在削弱这一纯粹的“奇迹制造者”的角色上是如何与穆罕默德及佛陀一致的;看到路德是如何把“外在的奇迹”贬斥为“杂耍”或者“哄孩子的苹果和栗子”而打发掉的;最后,看到关于奇迹的“超自然主义”作为仅仅是神秘的不完善的类比和非本真的“图解”的某种东西,是如何从宗教中被清除掉的。

还有其他的关于“神秘的”感受的这种趋势的表现形式,被吸引到了类似于这种“不能被理解的”体验的诸对象和诸方面上来。在那些通过只能被部分理解或者整个都无法理解的祈祷语言所运用的符咒中,以及在由于这一符咒的使用而使信徒的敬畏无疑得到真正的增强的情况下,都可以找到它最不合格的表达。这方面的例子有:尽管含糊,但是依然保留在我们的《圣经》和赞美诗中的那种古代的传统的表达;仅仅因为它们是“完全的他者”以及没有传达任何清晰的含义,而被附丽

'Selah', just because they are 'wholly other' and convey no clear meaning; the Latin in the service of the Mass, felt by the Catholic to be, not a necessary evil, but something especially holy; the Sanskrit in the Buddhist Mass of China and Japan; the 'language of the gods' in the ritual of sacrifice in Homer; and many similar cases. Especially noticeable in this connexion are the halfrevealed, half-concealed elements in the service of the Mass, in the Greek Church liturgy, and so many others; we can see here one factor that justifies and warrants them. And the same is true of the remaining portions of the old Mass which recur in the Lutheran ritual. Just because their design shows but little of regularity or conceptual arrangement, they preserve in themselves far more of the spirit of worship than the proposed recastings of the service put forward by the most recent practical reformers. In these we find carefully arranged schemes worked out with the balance and coherence of an essay, but nothing unaccountable, and for that very reason suggestive; nothing accidental, and for that very reason pregnant in meaning; nothing that rises from the deeps below consciousness to break the rounded unity of the wonted disposition, and thereby point to a unity of a higher order-in a word, little that is really spiritual. All the cases cited, then, derive their power of suggestion from the same source; they are all instances of the analogy to 'the mysterious' afforded by that which is not wholly understood, unwonted and at the same time venerable through age; and in the resemblance they present to the 'mysterious' they arouse it in the mind by a sort of 'anamnēsis' or reminder, and at the same time constitute its outward analogical representation.

于比如“哈利路亚(*Hallelujah*)”、“基立—依莱依桑(*Kyrie eleison*)”、“细拉(*Selah*)”等语词上的特殊的情感效力;在做弥撒时所用的拉丁语,在天主教徒看来,那不是一种必然的恶,而是某种特别的神圣;中国与日本在佛教道场中使用的梵语;在荷马史诗中出现在献祭仪式中的“神的语言”,以及很多类似的例子。在这个联系中有其值得注意的,是出现在弥撒过程中、出现在希腊教堂礼拜中以及在其他很多仪式中的那种半隐半现的因素;在这里我们能够看到确保这些仪式的正当性的一个因素。重现在路德宗仪式中的老式弥撒的存留部分也同样存有这种因素。正是因为这些仪式的设计表现出了很少的规则性或者概念性安排,比起由最近的实践的改革家们提出的重新设计过的宗教仪式来,他们在自身中保留了更多的崇拜精神。在这些新设计的仪式中,我们看到被仔细安排好的方案,这是按照一篇文章所要有的平衡和内在关联而搞出来的,但是没有丝毫无法解释的、因而富于暗示的东西;没有丝毫偶然的、因而含义丰富的东西;没有丝毫出自意识深处、去打破习惯性部署的全面统一,并进而指向一种更高层面上的统一的东西——一句话,很少有真正精神性的东西。上面所援引的全部例子,都是从同一个源泉获得其暗示的力量的;它们都是些与“神秘”相类似的例子,这种类似是由那种不能完全被理解的、不同寻常的、同时又因为古老而值得尊重的东西所给予的;在它们表现给“神秘”的那种相似性中,它们以一种“回忆(*anamnésis*)”或者暗示的方式在心中唤醒了神圣,并同时构建起了它外在的类似表现。

3. *Means by which the Numinous is expressed in Art*

In the arts nearly everywhere the most effective means of representing the numinous is 'the sublime'. This is especially true of architecture, in which it would appear to have first been realized. One can hardly escape the idea that this feeling for expression must have begun to awaken far back in the remote Megalithic Age. The motive underlying the erection of those gigantic blocks of rock, hewn or unworked, single monoliths or titanic rings of stone, as at Stonehenge, may have well been originally to localize and preserve and, as it were, to store up the numen in solid presence by magic; but the change to the motive of *expression* must have been from the outset far too vividly stimulated not to occur at a very early date. In fact the bare feeling for solemn and imposing magnitude and for the pomp of sublime pose and gesture is a fairly elementary one, and we cannot doubt that this stage had been reached when the *mastabas*, obelisks and pyramids were built in Egypt. It is indeed beyond question that the builders of these temples, and of the Sphinx of Gizeh, which set the feeling of the sublime, and together with and through it that of the numinous, throbbing in the soul almost like a mechanical reflex, must themselves have been conscious of this effect and have intended it.

Further, we often say of a building, or indeed of a song, a formula, a succession of gestures or musical notes, and in particular of certain manifestations of ornamental and decorative art, symbols, and emblems, that they make a 'downright magical' impression, and we feel we can detect the special characteristic of this 'magical' note in art with fair assurance even under the most varying conditions and in the most diverse relationships. The art of China, Japan, and Tibet, whose specific character has been determined by Taoism and Buddhism, surpasses all others in the unusual richness and depth of such impressions of the 'magical', and

3.神秘得以表现在艺术中的方式

在几乎各个地方的艺术中，给人印象最深刻的表现神秘的就是“崇高”。对建筑来说尤其如此，在建筑中，崇高的因素显然是最早被人认识到的。人们很难回避这样的看法，早在遥远的巨石时代，这种为表现而生的感受就已经开始苏醒了。无论是砍削过的还是未经加工过的，无论是单个的整块巨石还是像英国史前巨石阵那样的巨大的石头圈，那些巨大石块的耸立所包含的动机，或许最初是想要通过魔法把神秘放置并储存于坚固的存在物中，但是向这种表达的动机的转变一定从一开始就受到了非常鲜明的刺激，以至它会在很早的时候出现。事实上，这种对庄严与宏大，以及对崇高的形象与姿态的赤裸裸的感受是一种非常基本的感受，而且当平顶斜纹墓、方尖碑以及金字塔在埃及已经被建造起来时，我们不能怀疑这种感受已经达到了这一阶段。毫无疑问，这些神庙与斯芬克斯像——它们能够使崇高感与神秘感（与崇高感一同产生并通过崇高感表现出来）几乎像机械反应一样在灵魂中颤动——的建造者们本人一定已经意识到了这种作用并力图表现它。

还有，我们经常谈及一座建筑，或者一首歌，一套规则，一组姿态或音符，尤其是在谈到装饰与装潢艺术、象征、符号的某种表现，说到它们给了我们一种“全然魔幻的”印象，而且我们感到，即使是在对多变的条件下、在最不同的关系中，我们也能够很有把握地在艺术中找到这种“魔幻”暗示的特殊性质。中国、日本和西藏的艺术——其特点是由道教和佛教所决定的——在这种“魔幻”印象的不同寻常的丰富和深刻上超越了其他所有的艺术，甚

even an inexpert observer responds to them readily. The designation 'magical' is here correct even from the historical point of view, since the origin of this language of form was properly magical representations, emblems, formularies, and contrivances. But the actual impression of 'magic' is quite independent of this historical bond of connexion with magical practices. It occurs even when nothing is known of the latter; nay, in that case it comes out most strongly and unbrokenly. Beyond dispute art has here a means of creating a unique impression—that of the magical—apart from and independent of reflection. Now the magical is nothing but a suppressed and dimmed form of the numinous, a crude form of it which great art purifies and ennobles. In great art the point is reached at which we may no longer speak of the 'magical', but rather are confronted with the numinous itself, with all its impelling motive power, transcending reason, expressed in sweeping lines and rhythm. ①In no art, perhaps, is this more fully realized than in the great landscape painting and religious painting of China in the classical period of the T'ang and Sung dynasties. It has been said of this great art:

These works are to be classed with the profoundest and sublimest of the creations of human art. The spectator who, as it were, immerses himself in them feels behind these waters and clouds and mountains the mysterious breath of the primeval Tao,

---

① This numinous-magical character is specially noticeable in the strangely impressive figures of the Buddha in early Chinese art; and here too it affects the observer independently of 'ideas', i. e. without his knowing anything about the speculative doctrines of Buddhism. Thus Sirén justly says of the great Buddha from the Lung-Men Caves (T'ang Dynasty):

'Anyone who approaches this figure will realize that it has a religious significance without knowing anything about its *motif*.... It matters little whether we call it a prophet or a god, because it is a complete work of art permeated by a spiritual will, which communicates itself to the beholder.... The religious element of such a figure is immanent; it is "a presence" or an atmosphere rather than a formulated idea. ... It cannot be described in words, because it lies beyond intellectual definition.'

(Oswald Sirén, *Chinese Sculpture*, London, 1925, vol. i, p. 20.)

至连不熟练的观察者都很容易对它们作出反应。在此,“魔幻”这一名称即使从历史的观点上来看也是正确的,因为这种形式语言的起源正是魔力的表现、符号、规定与发明。但是,对“魔法”的真正印象却完全独立于这种魔法实践的历史关联。即使对后者[1]一无所知,这种魔幻印象也会产生;不仅如此,在此情形中,它会最激烈最完整地浮现出来。无疑,在这里艺术是一种创造某种独特印象(即关于魔力的印象)的方式,而这种印象与反映是毫不相干的。这种魔法不是别的,正是神秘的被压抑形式与模糊形式,是伟大的艺术要对之加以净化和提升的一种天然形式。在伟大的艺术中,这一点已经达到,即我们可以不再讨论“魔幻”,而是直接面对神秘本身,这种神秘带着其强大的动力、超越的理性,被表现在规模宏大的线条和韵律中。① 或许,没有任何艺术比得上在中国唐宋时期的伟大山水画和宗教画中将这一点更加充分地表现出来。对于这种伟大的艺术,有人曾这样说道:

这些作品应当被列入最深刻、最崇高的人类艺术之林。观众宛如将自身沉浸在这些艺术品种中,可以从这些水、云、和山中感受

---

① 在中国早期的艺术中,这种神秘—魔幻的性质在那些给人以非常奇特印象的佛陀形象中特别引人注目;在此,它不以“观念”来影响观察者,也就是说,观看者无须了解佛教的思辨教条。这样,西伦很公正地谈到唐代龙门石窟的大佛:

“任何一个接近这尊大佛的人都会体认到它的宗教意蕴,而无需知道有关它主旨的任何东西。……无论我们把这尊佛称为先知还是神,都无关宏旨,因为它是一件完整的艺术品,浸透着某种精神性的意愿,这种意愿把自己传达给观看者。……这样一尊佛像的宗教因素是内在的,是‘某种呈现’或某种氛围,而不是一种清楚表述的观念。……这种因素不能用言语来加以描述,因为它存在于理智的界限之外。”

(奥斯瓦尔德·西伦:《中国石刻》,伦敦,1925,第1卷第20页)

〔1〕 即魔法实践。

the pulse of innermost being. Many a mystery lies half-concealed and half-revealed in these pictures. They contain the knowledge of the 'nothingness' and the 'void', of the 'Tao' of heaven and earth, which is also the Tao of the human heart. And so, despite their perpetual agitation, they seem as remotely distant and as profoundly calm as though they drew secret breath at the bottom of a sea. ①

To us of the West the Gothic appears as the most numinous of all types of art. This is due in the first place to its sublimity; but Worringer in his work, *Probleme der Gothik*, has done a real service in showing that the peculiar impressiveness of Gothic *does* not consist in its sublimity alone, but draws upon a strain inherited from primitive magic, of which he tries to show the historical derivation. To Worringer, then, the impression Gothic makes is one of magic; and, whatever may be said of his historical account of the matter, it is certain that in this at least he is on the right track. Gothic does instil a spell that is more than the effect of sublimity. But 'magic' is too low a word: the tower of the Cathedral of Ulm is emphatically not 'magical', it is *numinous*. And the difference between the numinous and the merely magical can nowhere be felt more clearly than in the splendid plate Worringer gives in his book of this marvellous work of architecture. But when this is said, we may still keep the word 'magic' in use to denote the style and means of artistic expression by which the impression of the numinous comes into being.

But in neither the sublime nor the magical, effective as they are, has art more than an indirect means of representing the numinous.

---

① From an article by Otto Fischer on Chinese landscape painting in *Das Kunstblatt*, Jan. 1920.

到那种隐匿其后的原初之道的神秘气息，即那种最内在存在的脉动。在这些画作中隐现着许多神秘，它们包含着“无”与“空”的知识，包含着天地之“道”也就是人心之“道”的知识。因此，尽管它们具有永久的激发性，但是它们却显得悠远恬静，就好像它们从海底深处汲取了隐秘的气息。①

对我们西方人来说，哥特式风格在所有艺术类型中表现出了最多的神秘因素。这首先要归之于它的崇高性，但是沃林格在他的著作《关于哥特式建筑的一些问题》(*Probleme der Gothik*)中，在表明哥特式建筑给人的特殊印象不仅仅在于它的崇高性，而且也吸取了继承自原始魔法的某种天性方面做了一件真正的工作，而他则试图展示这一天性的历史渊源。在沃林格看来，哥特式风格所造成的印象是魔力的一种，而且，无论关于他对这一问题的历史说明会有怎样的说道，但是有一点是确定的，即至少在这一点上，他是正确的。哥特式建筑的确渗透着一种远高于崇高印象的魅力，但是“魔幻”是一个太低层次的词：乌尔姆大教堂的塔绝不是“魔幻的”，而是神秘的。神秘与纯粹魔幻之间的区别，在那个辉煌的盘子(在沃林格关于这一绝妙的建筑作品的书中所提到的)中，比在其他任何地方都可以更清晰地感受到。不过，在这样说时，我们仍然可以使用“魔幻”一词来指称艺术表现的风格与手段，也正是通过这些风格与手段，神秘印象得以显示出来。

但是，艺术比表达神秘的一种间接方式所拥有的更多的东西，既不在崇高中，也不在魔幻中，尽管它们都很有效。在所有更

① 引自奥托·费歇发表在《艺术报》(*Das Kunstblatt*，1920 年 1 月)上的一篇论中国山水画的文章。

Of directer methods our Western art has only two, and they are in a noteworthy way *negative*, viz. *darkness* and *silence*. The darkness must be such as is enhanced and made all the more perceptible by contrast with some last vestige of brightness, which it is, as it were, on the point of extinguishing; hence the 'mystical' effect begins with semidarkness. Its impression is rendered complete if the factor of the 'sublime' comes to unite with and supplement it. The semi-darkness that glimmers in vaulted halls, or beneath the branches of a lofty forest glade, strangely quickened and stirred by the mysterious play of half-lights, has always spoken eloquently to the soul, and the builders of temples, mosques, and churches have made full use of it.

Silence is what corresponds to this in the language of musical sounds. 'Yahweh is in his holy temple, let all the earth keep silence before him.' (Hab. ii. 20.) Neither we nor (probably) the prophet any longer bear in mind that this 'keeping silence' (as *εὐφημεῖν* in Greek), if regarded from the historical, 'genetic' standpoint, springs from the fear of using words of evil omen, which therefore prefers to be altogether speechless. It is the same with Tersteegen in his 'God is present, let all in us be silent'. With prophet and psalmist and poet we feel the necessity of silence from another and quite independent motive. It is a spontaneous reaction to the feeling of the actual *numen praesens*. Once again, what is found coming upon the scene at a higher level of evolution cannot be explained by merely interpolating links in a 'historico-genetic' chain of development; and the Psalmist and Tersteegen and even we ourselves are at least as interesting subjects for the analysis of the psychologist of religion as are the 'primitives', with their habitual practice of *εὐφημία*, the silence that merely avoids words of ill augury.

加直接的方式中,我们西方艺术只拥有两种,而且它们处于一种明显的否定的方式中,即黑暗和静默。黑暗必须是这样一种东西,通过与某种光明的最后余晖的对比,它得到强化并使所有的一切更加显而易见,而这种光明的余晖好像正要熄灭;因此这种"魔幻"影响开始于这种半暗。如果"崇高"的因素能与之相结合、相补充,那么,它的影响会被表现得更加完满。那种闪烁在拱形大厅中或者处于高大的森林空地的树枝下面的半暗——它因半明的神秘作用而被神奇地加强和激发——总是能雄辩有力地感染灵魂,而庙宇、清真寺与教堂的建造者们充分地运用了它。

静默是在乐音语言中与之对应的东西。"惟耶和华在他的圣殿中,众生都应当在他面前保持静默。"(《哈巴谷书》第 2 章第 20 节)无论是我们还是先知(很有可能)都忘记了,如果从历史的、"发生学的"观点来看,这个"保持静默"(正如希腊语的 εὐφημεῖν)产生于害怕使用带有不祥征兆的词,因而宁愿保持完全的沉默。这一点与特尔斯特根(*Tersteegen*)所说的"上帝在此,让我们都静默"的含义是相同的。与先知、赞美诗作者以及诗人一样,我们从另一个完全独立的动机感受到静默的必要性。静默是对实际的神秘在场的感受的自发反应。此外,那种在进化的较高水平上出现的东西,是不能只靠着单纯在发展的"历史发生学"链条中插入一些环节来解释的,而且赞美诗作者、特尔斯特根以及甚至我们自己,至少都是宗教心理学家的分析所感兴趣的对象,就像那些仅仅为了避开不祥词句而习惯于静默(εὐφημεία)的"原始人"也是他们的兴趣对象一样。

Besides silence and darkness oriental art knows a third direct means for producing a strongly numinous impression, to wit, *emptiness* and *empty distances*. Empty distance, remote vacancy, is, as it were, the sublime in the horizontal. The wide-stretching desert, the boundless uniformity of the steppe, have real sublimity, and even in us Westerners they set vibrating chords of the numinous along with the note of the sublime, according to the principle of the association of feelings. Chinese architecture, which is essentially an art in the laying out and grouping of buildings, makes a wise and very striking use of this fact. It does not achieve the impression of solemnity by lofty vaulted halls or imposing altitudes, but nothing could well be more solemn than the silent amplitude of the enclosed spaces, courtyards, and vestibules which it employs. The imperial tombs of the Ming emperors at Nanking and Peking are, perhaps, the strongest example of this, including, as they do, in their plan the empty distances of an entire landscape. Still more interesting is the part played by the factor of void or emptiness in Chinese painting. There it has almost become a special art to paint empty space, to make it palpable, and to develop variations upon this singular theme. Not only are there pictures upon which 'almost nothing' is painted, not only is it an essential feature of their style to make the strongest impression with the fewest strokes and the scantiest means, but there are very many pictures—especially such as are connected with contemplation—which impress the observer with the feeling that the void itself is depicted as a subject, is indeed the main subject of the picture. We can only understand this by recalling what was said above on the 'nothingness' and the 'void' of the mystics and on the enchantment and spell exercised by the 'negative hymns'. For 'void' is, like darkness and silence, a negation, but a negation that does away with every 'this' and 'here', in order that the 'wholly other' may become actual.

Not even music, which else can give manifold expression to all the feelings of the mind, has any positive way to express 'the holy'. Even the most consummate Mass-music can only give utterance to the holiest, most numinous moment in the Mass—the moment of

除了静默和黑暗，东方艺术还知道能够产生强烈的神秘印象的第三种直接方式，这就是空与空阔。空阔，即辽远的空白，可以说就是地平线上的崇高。那向远处伸展的沙漠，具有无限的一致性的大草原，都具有真正的崇高性，甚至在我们西方人心中，根据感受联想的原则，它们也能和着崇高的调子而拨动神秘的和弦。中国建筑，这种在本质上就是建筑物的安排与组合的一种艺术，对这一事实作了明智而非常显著的应用。它并不以高大的拱形大厅或者恢宏的高度来达到崇高的印象，但是没有什么能够比封闭的空间、庭院和门廊所具有的无言的广阔更加庄严了。在南京和北京的明代帝王的陵墓或许就是这方面的最有力的例证，在它们的规划中包含了整个风景区的空阔设计。更加有趣的是在中国绘画中空白或者空无的因素所起的作用。在中国绘画中，画出空白的空间，使其清晰可见，并在这一单一主题上展开多种变化，这几乎成了一种特殊的艺术。在中国画中不仅有画面上"几乎无物"的作品，不仅用最少的笔画和最简约的手段来造成最强烈的印象是其本质特征，而且还有大量的作品，尤其是与凝思相关的作品，会给观看者这样的感受，即空无本身是被当做一个对象来描述的，它确实就是这幅画作的核心主题。只有通过回想起我们在上面所谈论过的神秘主义的"无"与"空"，以及由"否定性的赞美诗"所激发出的魔法与魅力，我们才能理解这一点。因为，就像黑暗和静默，"空无"也是一种否定，但它是一种将"这个"与"此处"废除掉的否定，目的是使那个"完全的他者"得以出现。

甚至连对心灵中所有的感受都能够给以多种表达的音乐，也没有任何肯定的方式来表现"神圣"，甚至最完美的弥撒音乐也只能通过沉浸入静默之中，来表现弥撒中最神圣、最神秘的瞬

transubstantiation—by sinking into stillness: no mere momentary pause, but an absolute cessation of sound long enough for us to 'hear the silence' itself; and no devotional moment in the whole Mass approximates in impressiveness to this 'keeping silence before the Lord'. It is instructive to submit Bach's Mass in B minor to the test in this matter. Its most mystical portion is the 'Incarnatus' in the 'Credo', and there the effect is due to the faint, whispering, lingering sequence in the fugue structure, dying away *pianissimo*. The held breath and hushed sound of the passage, its weird cadences, sinking away in lessened thirds, its pauses and syncopations, and its rise and fall in astonishing semitones, which render so well the sense of awe-struck wonder—all this serves to express the *mysterium* by way of intimation, rather than in forthright utterance. And by this means Bach attains his aim here far better than in the 'Sanctus'. This latter is, indeed, an incomparably successful expression of Him, whose is 'the power and the glory', an enraptured and triumphant choric hymn to perfect and absolute sovereignty. But it is very far distant from the mood of the text that accompanies the music, which is taken from Isa. vi, and which the composer should have interpreted in accordance with that passage as a whole. No one would gather from this magnificent chorus that the Seraphim covered their faces with two of their wings. ① In this point Mendelssohn shows very fine sensibility in his musical setting of Ps. ii at the words

① The Jewish tradition has been, however, very well aware of the import ofthe matter. In the splendid New Year's Day Hymn of Melek Elyōn the wordsrun: 'All the mighty ones on high *whisper low*: Yahweh is King.'

间——圣餐的变体的瞬间：这不仅仅是瞬间的停顿，而且是声音的绝对停止，这一停止的时间长到足以让我们“听到静默”本身，而且，在整个弥撒中，没有哪个虔敬的瞬间类似于“在主面前保持静默”给我们以深刻的印象。如果用这一点来验证一下巴赫的《B小调弥撒曲》，那将是富有启发意义的。这首曲子最神秘的部分是“信条”中的“道成肉身(Incarnatus)”，而这一效果要归功于在赋格曲调结构中那种微弱的、喃喃细语般的、逡巡缠绵的一组乐句，渐渐极弱地消逝下去。这一节乐句中那屏住的呼吸与压抑的声音，它沉浸在缩减了的三分音程中的奇异节奏，它的停顿与切分音，以及在令人惊异的半音中它的起起落落(这很好地表现了对那种充满了敬畏的奇迹的感觉)——所有这一切都有助于通过暗示，而不是以直接的言说来表现神秘。通过这种方式，巴赫在这里，比在“神圣尊严者”中更好地达到了他的目的。的确，后者是对上帝是“权力与荣耀”的无比成功的表达——“权力与荣耀”是一首献给完美的绝对的君主的充满狂欢与喜悦的合唱赞美诗。然而，这首合唱的乐曲与取自《以赛亚书》第6章的文本的情绪相差甚远，作曲家应当将这段音乐阐释得与作为一个整体的文本段落一致起来。没有人能够从这一宏伟壮丽的合唱中推测出撒拉弗用他们的两个翅膀遮住他们的脸。[①] 在这一点上，门德尔松在为《诗篇》第2篇第11节“当存畏惧事奉耶和华，又当存战兢而快乐”配曲时，显示了他非

① 然而，犹太传统却非常了解这件事情的重要性。在梅里克·伊尔约所写的极好的《元旦歌》中有这样的句子：“空中一切有力者，齐来低声语：耶和华是王。”

(v. II): 'Serve the Lord with fear, and rejoice with trembling.' And here too the matter is expressed less in the music itself than in the way the music is restrained and repressed-one might almost say, abashed—as the Cathedral choir at Berlin so well knows how to render it. And, if a final example may be cited, the 'Populе meus' of Thomas Luiz gets as near to the heart of the matter as any music can. In this the first chorus sings the first words of the *Trisagion*: 'Hagios, ho theos, hagios ischyros, hagios athanatos', and the second chorus sings in response the Latin rendering of the words: 'Sanctus deus, sanctus fortis, sanctus immortalis', each chorus thrilling with a sort of muffled tremor. But the *Trisagion* itself, sung *pianissimo* by singers kept out of sight far at the back, is like a whisper floating down through space, and is assuredly a consummate reproduction of the scene in the vision of Isaiah.

常杰出的敏感性。在这里,同样,有问题的东西与其说是被表现在音乐本身中,不如说是被表现在音乐被限制被压抑的方式中(有人或许会非常窘迫地说此事),就像柏林大教堂唱诗班就非常清楚怎样去阐释它。我们再举最后一个例子吧,托马斯·鲁一兹的《我的百姓》(Popule meus)以音乐之所能尽可能地接近了问题的核心。在这一作品中,第一合唱队唱出了《三圣颂》的最初几个词:"Hagios, hotheos, hagios ischyros, hagios athanatos",第二合唱队吟唱出这些歌词的对应拉丁语译文:"Sanctus deus, sanctus fortis, sanctus immortalis",[1]每一合唱队都怀着一种压抑的恐惧而战栗不已。而《三圣颂》本身——它由远在背景后的看不见的歌者极低地唱出——就像从空中飘下的呢喃细语,并确实完美地再现了以赛亚想象中的景象。

〔1〕 这句歌词的含义是:"神圣的天主,神圣的威严者,神圣的永在者。"

CHAPTER X

The Numinous In The Old Testament

While the feelings of the non-rational and numinous constitute a vital factor in every form religion may take, they are pre-eminently in evidence in Semitic religion and most of all in the religion of the Bible. Here mystery lives and moves in all its potency. It is present in the ideas of the daemonic and angelic world, which, as a 'wholly other', surrounds, transcends, and permeates this world of ours; it is potent in the Biblical eschatology and the ideal of a 'kingdom of God' contrasted with the natural order, now as being future in time, now as being eternal, but always as the downright marvellous and 'other'; and finally it impresses itself on the character of Yahweh and Elohim—that God who is nevertheless the 'Heavenly Father' of Jesus and as such fulfils, not loses, His character as Yahweh.

The lower stage of numinous consciousness, viz. daemonic dread, has already been long superseded by the time we reach the Prophets and Psalmists. But there are not wanting occasional echoes of it, found especially in the earlier narrative literature. The story in Exod. iv. 24, of how Yahweh in his *όργὸ* met Moses by the way 'and sought to kill him', still bears this 'daemonic' character strongly, and the tale leaves us almost with the suggestion of a ghostly apparition. And from the standpoint of the more highly developed 'fear of God' one might easily get from this and similar stories the impression that this is not yet religion at all, but a sort of prereligious, vulgar fear of demons or the like. That would, however, be a misconception; a 'vulgar fear of demons' would

第十章　《旧约》中的神秘

尽管非理性感受和神秘感受构成了宗教所能采取的所有形式的至关重要因素，但是它们卓越地表现在闪米特人的宗教中，而且，尤其是表现在有关《圣经》的宗教中。在此，它表现得最为有力。它表现在有关魔鬼和天使的世界的观念中，这一世界作为一个"完全的他者"，环绕着、超越着并渗透着我们这个世界；它还有力地表现在《圣经》的末世论中，表现在那个与自然秩序相对立的"上帝之国"的理想中，无论是在将来，还是在永恒中，它总是作为一种全然的奇迹和"他者"；而最后，它将自身表现在耶和华和艾洛辛的特性中——上帝仍然是耶稣的"天父"，并且因此上帝充实了，而不是丧失了他作为耶和华的性质。

神秘意识的低级阶段，也就是对魔鬼的畏惧的阶段，早已经被我们所达到的先知与赞美诗作者的时代所取代，但是，依然存在着对魔鬼畏惧的偶尔重现，尤其是在早期叙事性文献中可以发现。《出埃及记》第 4 章第 24 节在讲到耶和华在愤怒（ὀργή）中怎样以"试图杀掉他"的方式遇到摩西的故事中，依然强烈地带有这种"魔鬼之畏"的特征，而这段故事给我们的几乎是一种鬼怪幻影的暗示。如果从更高发展阶段的"对上帝之畏"的立场出发，那么，从这个或者类似的故事中，人们可以很容易地得出一个印象：即这根本算不上宗教，只不过是对于鬼怪之类东西的前宗教的、粗鄙的害怕而已。然而，那有可能是一种误解；"对鬼怪的粗鄙的

refer to a 'demon' in the narrower sense of the word, in which it is a synonym for devil, fiend, or goblin, and is *contrasted* with the divine. But 'demon' in this sense has not been, any more than 'ghost' or 'spectre', a point in the transition, or, if it be preferred, a link in the chain of development which religious consciousness has undergone. Both 'demon' (= fiend) and 'spectre' are, so to speak, offshoots from the true line of progress, spurious fabrications of the fancy accompanying the numinous feeling. We must carefully distinguish from such a 'demon' the *δαίμων* or 'daemon' in the more general sense of the word, which, if it is not yet itself a 'god', is still less an anti-god, but must be termed a 'pre-god', the numen at a lower stage, in which it is still trammelled and suppressed, but out of which the 'god' gradually grows to more and more lofty manifestations. *This is* the phase whose after-effects can be detected in these ancient stories.

It will be worth while to consider this matter further. Two things may help to an understanding of the real relation with which we are here concerned. First, we may refer back to what was said on an earlier page upon the capacity of 'the dreadful' and 'terrible' in general to attract and arouse, and also to express, the true numinous consciousness or emotion. In the second place, we may refer to the parallel case of music. A man with a pronounced musical faculty, so long as he is a mere raw tyro, may be enraptured by the sound of the bagpipes or the hurdy-gurdy, though perhaps both become intolerable to him when his musical education has been completed. But, if he then recalls the qualitative character of his earlier musical experience and compares it with his present one, he will have to admit that, in both, one and the same side of his mind is functioning, and that what has taken place in the rise of his feeling for music to a more elevated form is no transition to something different in kind, but a process

害怕”可以指该词狭义上的“魔鬼”,在此含义上,它和恶魔、鬼魅或者妖精是同义的,并且是与神性相对立的,但是在这种含义上的“魔鬼”如同“鬼怪”或者“幽灵”一样,并没有如它被期望的那样,成为宗教意识发展过程中的一个转折点,或者发展链条上的一个环节。可以说,“魔鬼”(=鬼怪)和“幽灵”都是从真实的前进主线上生发出来的分支,即伴随着神秘感受的不真实想象的生成物。我们必须仔细地把这种狭义的“魔鬼”与这个词汇更加一般意义上的“魔鬼”(δαίμων)区分开来,如果说一般意义上的“魔鬼”本身还不是“神”,因此更不是与神相反的东西,而必须被命名为“前神”,即处于较低阶段上的神秘者,在这一阶段上,神秘依然受到束缚与压抑,但是正是在此之中,“神”逐渐发展出越来越崇高的表现形式。这就是其影响可以在这些古代故事中被察觉出来的那个阶段。

有必要对此作进一步的思考。有两件事情或许有助于理解我们在此处所关注的那种真实关系:第一,我们可以往回翻阅一下,看看前面页面上就一般的“畏惧”和“恐怖”所具有的引起、唤醒还有表达真正的神秘意识或者感受的能力所说过的那些话。第二,我们可以参考音乐的类似情形。一个拥有明显音乐才能的人,即便他只是一个新手,也会被风笛或者手风琴的乐声迷住,尽管他在完成音乐教育之后又可能对这两种乐器都难以忍受。但是,如果他那时回想一下他早期音乐体验的质的特点,并将这种体验与他现在的相比较,那么,他将不得不承认,在两种情形中,起作用的是他心灵中的一个方面,而且是同一个方面,在他对音乐的感受被提升到一种更高的形式中所发生的东西,绝不是向不同种类的某种东西的转化,而是一种我们可以称

which we may call 'development' or 'growth to maturity', but can hardly further specify. Were we to hear to-day the music of Confucius, it would probably be to us merely a succession of queer noises. Yet already Confucius speaks of the power of music on the mind in a way we moderns cannot better, and touches upon just those elements which we also must recognize in the experience of music. But the most striking consideration in this regard is the way in which some savage tribes are endowed with a capacity for a ready appreciation of our music, which they grasp quickly, practise assiduously, and enjoy intensely, when it is brought before them. This endowment did not first enter their minds at the moment they heard the music by a 'heterogony', 'epigenesis', or other miracle; it simply existed all the time as a natural predisposition or latent capacity. It was aroused and began to develop as soon as the proper incitement came to stimulate it, but to the end it was yet *the selfsame* disposition that had been formerly excited to such primitive and crude manifestations. This 'crude', 'primitive' form of music is often almost or wholly unrecognizable as real music by our developed musical taste, although it was the manifestation of the same impulse and the same element of our psychical nature. Now it is exactly a parallel case when the 'Godfearing' man of to-day finds it hard to detect in the narrative of Exod. iv that which is akin to his own religious experience, or misjudges it altogether. All this involves a point of view which should be taken into consideration more generally with respect to the religion of 'primitive man', though naturally great caution should be used in applying it, seeing that very mistaken conclusions can be drawn from it and there is a real danger of confounding the lower with the higher levels of development and of making too little of the interval between them. However, it is still more dangerous to exclude this point of view altogether, as is unfortunately very commonly done. ①

① In this regard Mr. Marett in particular has important and novel considerations to offer.

之为“发展”或者“成熟”的过程，对这一过程我们很难作进一步的详细说明。如果我们今天去听孔子时代的音乐，对我们来说，它很有可能只是一连串奇怪的噪音。然而，孔子早就以一种远胜于我们现代人的方式谈到了音乐影响心灵的力量了，而且正好触及到了我们在音乐体验中也必须认识的那些因素。但是在这一点上最值得思考的，某些原始部落是以何种方式被赋予了一种迅速接受我们的音乐的能力，一旦音乐被呈现于他们面前，他们能迅速地领会它、勤勉地练习它、并充满激情地享受它。这种天赋并不是在他们听到音乐的那一刻以“形变”、“渐成”或者别的什么奇迹的方式第一次进入他们的心灵；它作为一种自然的倾向或者潜在的能力一直都完全存在着。一旦有适当的刺激来激活这种天赋，它就会被唤醒并开始发展，但是归根结底它还是完全相同的倾向，即先前被激起的那种原始粗糙的表现形式。音乐的这种“粗糙”、“原始”的形式常常是几乎不被或者完全不被我们的高级的音乐品味认作为真正的音乐，尽管它是我们精神本性的同样冲动与同样因素的表现形式。当今天“害怕上帝”的人发现很难从《出埃及记》第4章的叙述中找到那种与他自己的宗教经验相近的东西，或者完全误解他，情况与此完全类似。所有这一切都牵涉到一个观点，在谈到“原始人”的宗教时，这一观点必须被更加一般地予以考察，尽管在应用这一观点时我们必须万分小心，因为很可能从中引出错误的结论，而且还存在着混淆发展的较高水平与较低水平的真正危险，存在着在二者之间几乎无法划清界限的真正危险。然而不幸的是，正如人们通常所做的那样，更加危险的在于完全摒弃这一观点。①

① 在这个问题上，马雷特先生尤其可以提供重要而且新颖的观点。

Recent research has sought to discover a difference in character between Yahweh, the austere and stern, and Elohim, the familiar, patriarchal God, and there is something very illuminating in the suggestion. Söderblom's supposition[①] is that the notion of Yahweh had its point of origin in earlier 'animistic' ideas. I do not dispute the importance of such 'animistic' ideas in the religious evolutionary process; in fact, I should go even farther than Söderblom in that respect, for he would explain them as a sort of primitive 'philosophy', and therefore has to exclude them altogether from the domain of genuinely *religious* imagination. It would be perfectly compatible with my own view to hold that where ideas of an animistic character had been framed they could serve as an important link in the 'chain of stimulation' by which true numinous consciousness is aroused (namely, in so far as they served to disengage and free the obscure feeling-element of 'existent being', latent in it). But what distinguishes Yahweh from El-Shaddai-Elohim is not that the former is an 'anima', but (and the distinction may be applied to differentiate all god-types) that, whereas in Yahweh the numinous preponderates over the familiar 'rational' character, in Elohim the rational aspect outweighs the numinous. 'Outweighs' is as much as we can say, for in Elohim too the numinous element is certainly present; Elohim is, for instance, the subject of the genuinely numinous narrative of the theophany in the burning bush, with the characteristic verse (Exod. iii. 6): 'And Moses hid his face; for he was afraid to look upon God.'

For the copious and diverse characteristics of the idea of God of the ancient Israelites which might be instanced here the reader is

---

① Söderblom, *Das Werden des Gottesglaubens*, 1916, pp. 297 ff.

近来的研究发现了严峻苛刻的耶和华与熟悉慈爱的艾洛辛，即神，是古代犹太教对上帝的另一种称呼）在性格上的差异，而且在这种差异中存在着很有启发性的东西。索德布洛姆提出的推测[①]是关于耶和华的观念在早期的“泛灵论”观念中就已经有其端倪。我不想就这种“泛灵论”观念在宗教进化进程中的重要性展开争论；事实上，我在那一方面要比索德布洛姆走得更远一些，因为他会把它们解释为一种原始“哲学”，并因此不得不将它们完全从真正宗教想象的领域中排斥出来。有一种看法与我的观点完全一致，它认为，泛灵论性质的观念一旦形成，它们就会成为“刺激之链”的一个重要环节，通过它们，真正的神秘意识才能够被激发（也就是，就它们将隐含于泛灵论观念中的那种关于“现存的存在”的模糊的感受因素释放出来而言）。但是，将耶和华和艾洛辛区别开来的，并不是前者（即耶和华）是一种“灵魂”，而是在耶和华身上，神秘压倒了那种熟悉的“理性”的性质，在艾洛辛那里则是理性方面超过了神秘方面（而这种差别可以应用于区分所有类型的神）。我们所能说的只是“超过”，因为在艾洛辛那里也确实存在神秘因素；例如，艾洛辛就是神在燃烧的荆棘中现身那个真正神秘的故事中的主体，以典型的诗句表现为：“摩西蒙上脸，因为怕见上帝。”（《出埃及记》，第3章第6节）

有关在此可以作为例证说明的古代以色列人的上帝观念的

---

① 索德布洛姆：《上帝信仰的形成》（*Das Werden des Gottesglaubens*），1916年版，第297页以后的段落。

referred to works upon the history of religion. [1] The venerable religion of Moses marks the beginning of a process which from that point onward proceeds with ever increasing momentum, by which the numinous is throughout rationalized and moralized, i. e. charged with ethical import, until it becomes the 'holy' in the fullest sense of the word. The culmination of the process is found in the Prophets and in the Gospels. And it is in this that the special nobility of the religion revealed to us by the Bible is to be found, which, when the stage represented by the 'deutero-Isaiah' is reached, justifies its claim to be a universal world-religion. Here is to be found its manifest superiority over, e. g., Islam, in which Allah is mere 'numen', and is in fact precisely Yahweh in His pre-Mosaic form and upon a larger scale. But this moralizing and rationalizing process does not mean that the numinous itself has been overcome, but merely that its preponderance has been overcome. The numinous is at once the basis upon which and the setting within which the ethical and rational meaning is consummated.

The capital instance of the intimate mutual interpenetration of the numinous with the rational and moral is Isaiah. The note struck in the vision of his call is the keynote of his entire prophecy. And nothing is in this regard more significant than the fact that it is in Isaiah that the expression 'the Holy One of Israel' first becomes established as the expression, *par excellence*, for the deity, prevailing over all others by its mysterious potency. This remains so in the writings of the 'deutero-Isaiah', who follows the tradition of the earlier

① They are given exhaustively in the Encyclopaedia *Die Religion in Geschichte und Gegenwart*, vol. ii, pp. 1530, 2036.

丰富而多变的特征，读者可以参考有关宗教史的著作。[①] 摩西的古老的宗教标志着一个过程的开始，从那一点开始，这一过程就伴随着不断增长的动力向前发展，通过这个过程，神秘被彻底地理性化或者道德化了，也就是说，神秘被装载着伦理的重要性，直到它变成最完全意义上的“神圣”。在各类先知书与福音书中，可以找到这一发展进程的顶点。而正是在这一点上，由《圣经》揭示给我们的宗教的特殊的高贵才得以发现，当这种高贵达到了通过“后一以赛亚”表现出来的阶段时，它便可以确证自己要成为普遍的世界宗教的主张。在这里可以看到它明显优越于其他宗教的地方，比如在伊斯兰教中，安拉仅仅是“神秘”，而且事实上正好是在前摩西形式中的和在更大规模上的耶和华。但是，这一道德化和理性化的过程并不意味着神秘本身已经被克服，而仅仅意味着它的优势被克服了。神秘立刻就成为那种伦理的与理性的意义得以在其上和在其中完成的基础与背景。

神秘与理性和道德之间相互渗透的重要的例子就是《以赛亚书》。那种回响在以赛亚的呼唤的幻象中的调子就是他整个预言的基调。在这个方面，没有什么比这个事实更有意义了，即正是在《以赛亚书》中，“以色列的圣者”这一表达才第一次被确立为对神性的卓越表达，这一表达因其神秘力量而优越于其他所有的表达方式。这一点在关于“后一以赛亚”追随着较早的《以赛亚书》的传统的那些著作中依然保持着这个样子。无疑，在后一以

① 这些特征在《古今宗教》(*Die Religion in Geschichte und Gegenwart*)这部百科全书的第 2 卷第 1530 页和第 2036 页有详尽的描述。

Isaiah. Assuredly in deutero-Isaiah, if in any writer, we have to do with a God whose attributes are clear to conceptual thought: omnipotence, goodness, wisdom, truth; and yet all the time these are attributes of 'the Holy One', whose strange name deutero-Isaiah too repeats no less than fifteen times and always in passages where it has a special impressiveness.

Related expressions akin to the 'holiness' of Yahweh are His 'fury', His 'jealousy', His 'wrath', the 'consuming fire', and the like. The import of them all is not only the allrequiting righteousness of God, not even merely His susceptibility to strong and living emotions, but all this ever enclosed in and permeated with the 'awefulness' and the 'majesty', the 'mystery' and the 'augustness', of His non-rational divine nature.

And this holds good, also, of the expression 'the living God'. God's 'livingness' is perceptibly akin to His 'jealousy' and is manifested in and through this, as in His other 'passions' generally. ①'It is by His 'life' that this God is differentiated

① Cf. Deut. v. 26: 'For who is there of all flesh, that hath heard the voice of the *living* God speaking out of the midst of the fire, as we have, *and lived*?' Cf. also Josh. iii. 10; I Sam. xvii. 26, 36; 2 Kings xix. 4; Isa. xxxvii. 4, 17; Jer. x. 10: 'He is the *living* God: ... at His *wrath* the earth shall tremble and the nations shall not be able to abide His *indignation*'; Jer. xxiii. 36; 2 Macc. vii. 33; Matt. xxvi. 63 (the adjuration 'by the *living* God', the God of terror and dread); and Heb. x. 31: 'It is a fearful thing to fall into the hands of the *living* God.' The Old Testament idea of the terrible 'living' God reaches its completion in the ideas of the 'avenging God', of which the most ruthless expression is in the almost appalling image of the treader of the wine-press, Isa. lxiii. 3: 'I will tread them in mine anger, and trample them in my fury; and their blood shall be sprinkled upon my garments and I will stain all my raiment.' The dreadful image recurs in the New Testament in Rev. xix. 15: 'He treadeth the wine-press of the fierceness and wrath of Almighty God.'

赛亚中,如果在任何作者中,我们都不得不忍受这样一个上帝,它的性质对于概念性思维来说是清清楚楚的:全能、善良、智慧、真理;而这些又总是"圣者"的性质,它的这一奇怪的名称被后以赛亚重复了不止十五次,而且总是在它具有某种特殊影响力的那些段落中被重复提及的。

与耶和华的"神圣"相近的相关表述还有耶和华的"狂怒"、耶和华的"嫉妒"、耶和华的"愤怒"以及耶和华的"烈焰"等。所有这些表述的含义不仅是指上帝善恶必报、毫厘不爽的公正,甚至不单单是上帝对强烈和生动情感的易感性,而且指所有这些表达都为上帝的非理性的神圣性质的"畏惧"、"威严"、"神秘"以及"庄严"所围绕与渗透。

这对于"活的上帝"这一表述同样有效。上帝的"活力"明显类似于上帝的"嫉妒",并且是在这种"嫉妒"中并通过这种"嫉妒"表现出来的,正如通常在它的其他"激情"中表现出来一样。[①] 正是通过上帝的"生命",这个上帝才与所

---

① 参见《申命记》第5章第26节:"凡有血气的,曾有何人听见永生上帝的声音从火中出来还能存活呢?"亦见《约书亚记》第3章第10节;《撒姆耳记上》第17章第26、36节;《列王纪下》第19章第4节;《以赛亚书》第37章第4、17节;《耶利米书》第10章第10节:"耶和华是活上帝:……他一发怒,大地震动,他一恼怒,列国都担当不起";《耶利米书》第23章36节;《马太福音》第6章第63节("以永生上帝",即令人恐怖与畏惧的上帝起誓);《希伯来书》第10章第31节:"落在永生上帝的手里,真是可怕之事。"在《旧约》中,关于可怕的永生上帝的观念在"复仇的上帝"这一概念中达到极致,这一概念的最冷酷无情的表达见于《以赛亚书》第63章第3节中那个踩酒榨机的人那令人恐惧的形象上:"我发怒将他们踹下,发怒将他们践踏。他们的血溅在我的衣服上,并且污染了我所有的衣袍。"这一可怕的形象后来又出现在《新约·启示录》第19章第15节中:"他要踹全能上帝烈怒的酒榨机。"

from all mere ‘world reason’, and becomes this ultimately non-rational essence, that eludes all philosophic treatment. This is the God that lives in the consciousness of all prophets and apostles of the Old and the New Dispensation alike. And all those who later championed against the ‘God of philosophy’ the ‘living God’ and the God of anger and love and the emotions have unwittingly been defending the nonrational core of the Biblical conception of God from all excessive rationalization. And so far they were right. Where they were wrong and sank into anthropomorphism was in defending, not figurative ‘anger’ and ‘emotion’, but literal anger and emotion, misconceiving the numinous character of the attributes in question and holding them simply to be ‘natural’ attributes, taken absolutely, instead of realizing that they can only be admitted as figurative indications of something essentially non-rational by means of symbols drawn from feelings that have analogy to it.

We find the power of the numinous—in its phase of the mysterious—to excite and intensify the imagination displayed with particular vividness in Ezekiel. Here are to be classed Ezekiel's dreams and parables and fanciful delineation of God's being and sovereign state, which are, as it were, an example by anticipation of the later more spurious sort of excitement of the religious impulse to the mysterious, leading (in accordance with analogies already expounded) to the merely strange, the extraordinary, the marvellous, and the fantastic. When such an operation of the religious consciousness works itself out in accordance with a wrong analogy, the way is prepared for miracle and legend and the whole dreamworld of pseudo-mysticism; and, though these are all truly enough emanations from the genuine religious experience, they are emanations broken by the opaque, dull medium through which they pass, a mere substitute for the genuine thing, and they end in a vulgar rankness of growth that over-

有的“世界理性”区分开来，并成为这个躲避一切哲学处理的根本的非理性本质。这就是存活于所有的新、旧天启之类的先知与使徒们中间的那个上帝。所有那些后来反对“哲学的上帝”而拥护“活的上帝”以及愤怒的上帝、爱的上帝和情感的上帝的人，一直在无意地维护着上帝的圣经概念的非理性之核，以免被过分地理性化。而且就此范围而言，他们是正确的。他们出错并且陷入到神人同形同性论之中，是在于他们所捍卫的是比喻性的“愤怒”与“感受”，而不是字面上的愤怒与感受，他们误解了这些正被讨论的性质的神秘特征，仅仅把它们当做是“自然的”性质，并对这些性质作了绝对的理解，而不是将其理解为，只有通过取自与它们类似的感受的某些象征符号，这些性质才能被确认为对某种在本质上是非理性的东西的比喻性指称。

我们发现了神秘者在处于神秘阶段中的力量，这种力量能够激发和强化那种特别生动地表现在《以西结书》中的想象。在这里要把以西结的梦、比喻以及关于上帝的存在的和统治状态的想象的描述归为一类，这些东西宛如一个实例，它们通过对后来更具欺骗性的某种对神秘的宗教冲动的刺激的预期，导致(与我们前面已经详细阐明了的类似相一致)纯粹怪异的、反常的、奇迹的以及想象的东西。当宗教意识的这种运作依照着一种错误的类比将自身显示出来时，一条通往奇迹、传说以及关于虚假的神秘主义的整个梦幻王国的道路就开辟出来了；而且，尽管这些全部都是从真正的宗教经验中散发出来的，但是它们却被那些通过其来表现自身的不透明的、沉闷的媒介搞得支离破碎，成了真实事物的纯粹的替代品，而且它们最终成为一种粗俗的生长繁茂

spreads the pure feeling of the *mysterium* as it really is and chokes its direct and forthright emotional expression.

But, if Ezekiel hardly shows the numinous moment apart from an admixture of excessive fantasy and imagination, the same is not true of the Book of Job. In the 38th chapter of Job we have the element of the mysterious displayed in rare purity and completeness, and this chapter may well rank among the most remarkable in the history of religion. Job has been reasoning with his friends against Elohim, and—as far as concerns them—he has been obviously in the right. They are compelled to be dumb before him. And then Elohim Himself appears to conduct His own defence in person. And He conducts it to such effect that Job avows himself to be overpowered, truly and rightly overpowered, not merely silenced by superior strength. Then he confesses: 'Therefore I abhor myself and *repent* in dust and ashes.' That is an admission of inward *convincement* and conviction, not of impotent collapse and submission to merely superior power. Nor is there here at all the frame of mind to which St. Paul now and then gives utterance; e. g. Rom. ix. 20: 'Shall the thing formed say to him that formed it, Why hast thou made me thus? Hath not the potter power over the clay, of the same lump to make one vessel unto honour, and another unto dishonour?' To interpret the passage in Job thus would be a misunderstanding of it. This chapter does not proclaim, as Paul does, the renunciation of, the realization of the impossibility of, a 'theodicy'; rather, it aims at putting forward a real theodicy of its own, and a better one than that of Job's friends; a theodicy able to convict even a Job, and not only to convict him, but utterly to still every inward doubt that assailed his soul. For latent in the weird experience that Job underwent in the revelation of Elohim is at once an inward relaxing of his soul's anguish and an appeasement, an appeasement which would alone and in itself perfectly suffice as the solution of the problem of the Book of Job, even whitout job's

的东西,实际地遍布在纯粹的神秘感受中,并堵塞了它的直接的坦白的情感的表达。

但是,如果《以西结书》除了显示出过分的幻想与想象的混合物之外,几乎没有显示出神秘因素,那么,《约伯记》就不是这样。在《约伯记》第38章中,我们看到了以稀有的纯粹性和完整性显示出来的神秘因素,这一章完全应当列入宗教史上最显著的章节之中。约伯一直与他的朋友们论争反对艾洛辛的问题,而就他的朋友们而言,约伯显然是正确的,他们被迫在他面前保持缄默。这时,艾洛辛本身显现出来,亲自捍卫自己。艾洛辛这样做的结果是约伯承认自己被制服了,真正地和公正地被制服了,而不仅仅是被超常力量所压制。于是约伯承认:"因此我厌恶自己,在尘土和炉灰中懊悔。"这是一种对于内在有罪和服罪的承认,而不是虚弱地坍塌或者臣服于纯粹超常的力量。这里根本不存在圣保罗时不时地以言语表达出来的心境,例如在《罗马书》第9章第20节:"被造之物岂能对那造物者说,你为什么这样造我呢? 陶工难道没有权柄,从一团泥里拿一块做成贵重的器皿又拿一块做成卑贱的器皿么?"如果这样来理解《约伯记》中的那段话,将是对它的误解。这一章并没有像保罗那样宣称要放弃"神正论",即声称认识"神正论"是不可能的;相反,该章的目的在于提出一种真正的"神正论",一种要远远好于约伯的朋友们的那种"神正论",一种能够使即便是像约伯这样的人知罪的"神正论",而且不仅宣称他有罪,还能完全地平息攻击他的灵魂的每一种内在的疑问。因为潜藏在约伯的怪异的体验(他在艾洛辛的启示中所经历的)中的东西,立刻就成为一种缓解他的灵魂痛苦的内在的放松和抚慰,单单是这种抚慰就足以充当《约伯记》一书

rehabilitation in Chapter xlii, where recovered prosperity comes as an extra payment thrown in after quittance has been already rendered. But what is this strange 'moment' of experience that here operates at once as a vindication of God to Job and a reconciliation of Job to God?

In the words put into the mouth of Elohim nearly every note is sounded which the situation may prepare one to expect a *priori*: the summons to Job, and the demonstration of God's overwhelming power, His sublimity and greatness, and His surpassing wisdom. This last would yield forthwith a plausible and rational solution of the whole problem, if only the argument were here completed with some such sentences as: 'My ways are higher than your ways; in my deeds and my actions I have ends that you understand not'; viz. the testing or purification of the godly man, or ends that concern the whole universe as such, into which the single man must fit himself with all his sufferings. It you start from rational ideas and concepts, you absolutely *thirst* for such a conclusion to the discourse. But nothing of the kind follows: nor does the chapter intend at all to suggest such teleological reflections or solutions. In the last resort it relies on something quite different from anything that can be exhaustively rendered in rational concepts, namely, on the sheer absolute wondrousness that transcends thought, on the *mysterium*, presented in its pure, non-rational form. All the glorious examples from nature speak very plainly in this sense. The eagle, that 'dwelleth and abideth on the rock, upon the crag of the rock, and the strong place', whose 'eyes behold afar off' her prey, and whose 'young ones also suck up blood, and where the slain are, there is she'—this eagle is in truth no evidence for the *teleological* wisdom that 'prepares all cunningly and well', but is rather the creature of *strangeness* and *marvel*, in whom the wondrousness of its creator becomes apparent. And the same is true of the ostrich (xxxix. 13-18) with its *inexplicable* instincts. The ostrich is indeed, as here depicted, and 'ration-

中问题的解答了,甚至无需在第42章中约伯的财产的复原——在这一章中,被恢复的财产是作为一种额外的报偿,在约伯已经放弃报答之后而给与他的。然而,这种奇怪经验的"要素",即在这里同时作为上帝对约伯的辩护和约伯对上帝的顺从的因素是什么呢?

在艾洛辛所说的那些话中,几乎每一个字都非常合理,这一情形使人期待着某种先验的东西:对约伯的召唤,对上帝无法抵抗的能力的示范,上帝的崇高与伟大,以及上帝的卓越的智慧。只要这里的争论是以这样的句子来完成:"我的方式高于你的方式;我的行为与行动中包含有你所不能理解的目的",那么,最后这一点,即上帝的卓越的智慧就会立刻产生出对整个问题的振振有词的、理性的解答,即,对敬神之人的考验与净化,或者同样地关涉到整个宇宙的目的,个人必须以其忍受所有的痛苦来适应这一宇宙。如果你是从理性的观念和概念出发,那么,你对此谈话绝对会渴望着这样一个结论。但是根本就没有这种结论:这一章也完全无意于去提出这种神学的思考与解答。最后它所求助于的是某种完全不同于那种能够以理性的概念彻底地解释的东西,也就是说,它所依赖的是超越思想的完全绝对的奇迹,是表现在它的纯粹的非理性形式中的那个神秘。所有那些取自大自然的精彩的例子都非常明白地道出了这一意思。那只鹰"住在山岩,以山峰和坚固之所为家",它的"眼睛远远观望"着它的猎物,而且"它的雏儿也咂血,被杀的人在哪里,它也在哪里"——这只鹰确实没有证明那种"巧妙安排一切"的目的论的智慧,但是确实创造了奇异与奇迹,通过这只雄鹰,造物主的神奇变得明朗起来。这一点也适用于那只有着莫名其妙的本能的鸵鸟(第39章第13~18节)。正如这里所描写的,以及"理性地"思考的,这只鸵鸟

ally' considered, a crucial difficulty rather than an evidence of wisdom, and it affords singularly little help if we are seeking *purpose* in nature: 'which leaveth her eggs in the earth, and warmeth them in the dust, and forgetteth that the foot may crush them or that the wild beast may break them. She is hardened against her young ones as though they were not hers: her labour is in vain without fear; because God hath *deprived her of wisdom*, neither hath he imparted to her *understanding*'.

It is the same with the 'wild ass' (verse 5) and the unicorn (verse 9). These are beasts whose complete 'dysteleology' or negation of purposiveness is truly magnificently depicted; but, nevertheless, with their mysterious instincts and their inexplicable behaviour, this very negation of purpose becomes a thing of baffling significance, as in the case of the 'wild goat' (verse I) and the hind. The 'wisdom' of the inward parts (xxxviii. 36), and the 'knowledge' of dayspring, winds, and clouds, with the mysterious ways in which they come and go, arise and vanish, shift and veer and re-form; and the wonderful Pleiades aloft in heaven, with Orion and 'Arcturus and his sons'—these serve but to emphasize the same lesson. It is conjectured that the descriptions of the hippopotamus (behemoth) and crocodile (leviathan) in xl. 15 ff. are a later interpolation. This may well be the fact; but, if so, it must be admitted that the interpolator has felt the point of the entire section extraordinarily well. He only brings to its grossest expression the thought intended by all the other examples of animals; they gave portents only, he gives us 'monsters'—but 'the monstrous' is just the 'mysterious' in a gross form. Assuredly these beasts would be the most unfortunate examples that one could hit upon if searching for evidences of the purposefulness of the divine 'wisdom'. But they, no less than all the previous examples and the whole context, tenor, and sense of the entire passage, do express in

事实上是一个决定性的困难，而非智慧的证据，如果我们在自然中寻求目的，那么，它所能提供的帮助将是微乎其微的："它把蛋留在地上，在尘土中温暖它们，却想不到被脚踹碎，或者可能被野兽践踏。它忍心待雏，似乎不是自己生的；虽然徒受劳苦，也不为雏惧怕；因为上帝使它没有智慧，也未将悟性赐予它。"[1]

野驴（第5节）与野牛（第9节）的情形也是如此。这些都是野兽，它们完全的"无目的论"或者对目的的否定得到了真正华丽的描述；然而，由于这些野兽的神秘的本能和无法言说的行为，这种对目的的十足的否定变成了一种带有使人困惑的意义的东西，就像在"野山羊"（第1节）以及其后段落中的情形一样。内在的"智慧"（第38章第36节）以及关于黎明、风和云的"知识"，还有它们在其中来来去去、涨涨消消、转换变向以及重新形成的神秘方式；与参星、"北斗及其随星"一道高悬天宇的神奇的昴宿星——所有这一切都是要强调同样的教诲。可以推测出第40章第15节以下关于河马（behemoth）与鳄鱼（leviathan）的描述是后来添加进去的。这很可能是事实；但是，即便如此，也必须承认，那个添加者非常好地理解了整段的要点。他只是对于通过所有其他的动物例子所要表达的思想作了最粗糙的表达；那些例子仅仅给出了征兆，而添加者却给出了"怪物"——但是，这个"怪异"正是以粗糙形式表现出来的"神秘"。如果从中去寻找神性"智慧"的目的的证据，那么，毫无疑问，这些野兽是一个人所遇到的最不适宜的例子。但是，它们同前面所有的例子以及整个段落的全部内容、要

[1] 《约伯记》第39章第14~16节。

masterly fashion the downright stupendousness, the wellnigh daemonic and wholly incomprehensible character of the eternal creative power; how, incalculable and 'wholly other', it mocks at all conceiving but can yet stir the mind to its depths, fascinate and overbrim the heart. What is meant is the *mysterium* not as mysterious simply, but at the same time also as 'fascinating' and 'august'; and here, too, these latter meanings live, not in any explicit concepts, but in the tone, the enthusiasm, in the very rhythm of the entire exposition. And here is indeed the point of the whole passage, comprising alike the theodicy and the appeasement and calming of Job's soul. The *mysterium*, simply as such, would merely (as discussed above) be a part of the 'absolute inconceivability' of the numen, and that, though it might strike Job utterly dumb, could not convict him inwardly. That of which, we are conscious is rather an *intrinsic value* in the incomprehensible—a value inexpressible, positive, and 'fascinating'. This is incommensurable with thoughts of rational human teleology and is not assimilated to them: it remains in all its mystery. But it is as it becomes felt in consciousness that Elohim is justified and at the same time Job's soul brought to peace.

* * * * * *

A very real parallel to this experience of Job is to be found in the work of a writer of our own day, which is not the less deeply impressive because it is found in the fictitious context of a novel. Max Eyth recounts in his story *Berufs-Tragik* (in the collection *Hinter Pflug und Schraubstock*) the building of the mighty bridge over the estuary of the Ennobucht. The most profound and thorough labour of the intellect, the most assiduous and devoted professional toil, had gone to the

旨和意义都是一样的，的确以精巧的方式表达了那种清楚明白的巨大——那永恒的创造力所具有的几乎像魔鬼一样的、完全无法理解的性质；作为不可计量的东西和“完全的他者”，无论它怎样嘲笑对它所有的构想，但是它依然能够深刻地激动心灵，使内心着迷、衷心荡漾。在这里所说的神秘并不仅仅作为神秘的东西，而是同时也作为“沉迷”于“威严”的东西；同样，在这里，后两层含义并不时存活于任何清晰的概念之中，而是存活于语调、热情和整个展示出来的节奏之中。这正是整段文章的要点所在，同样包含了神正论、抚慰以及对约伯的灵魂的镇静。单纯的神秘，正如上面所讨论过的，会仅仅成为那种神秘者的“绝对不可理解性”的一部分，而这一部分，尽管它能够使约伯完全哑口无言，但是无法使他从内心里服罪。那种我们所能意识到的部分毋宁说是不可理解的内在价值——一种无法言表的、肯定的并且是“令人着迷的”价值。这种东西与有理性的人们的目的论思想无法比较，并且不能被比作它们：它将自己保持在完全的神秘之中。但是，当它在意识中被感受到上帝是被证明为正当的，而且同时约伯的灵魂也得到了安抚，它才保持其完全的神秘。

* * * * * * * *

与约伯的这种经验真正非常相似的经验可以在我们自己时代的一位作家的一部作品中找到，由于它出现在小说的虚构的文本中，这种经验具有同样深刻的感染力。马克斯·艾特在他的小说《不幸的职业》（载于小说集《在犁和虎钳的后面》）中描写了在埃诺布赫特港湾建造一座特大桥的事。最深邃最全面的智力劳动，最勤勉最虔敬的

construction of the great edifice, making it in all its significance and purposefulness a marvel of human achievement. In spite of endless difficulties and gigantic obstacles, the bridge is at length finished, and stands defying wind and waves. Then there comes a raging cyclone, and building and builder are swept into the deep. Utter meaninglessness seems to triumph over richest significance, blind 'destiny' seems to stride on its way over prostrate virtue and merit. The narrator tells how he visits the scene of the tragedy and returns again.

When we got to the end of the bridge, there was hardly a breath of wind; high above, the sky showed blue-green, and with an eerie brightness. Behind us, like a great open grave, lay the Ennobucht. The Lord of life and death hovered over the waters in silent majesty. We felt His presence, as one feels one's own hand. And the old man and I knelt down before the open grave and before Him.

Why did they kneel? Why did they feel constrained to do so? One does not kneel before a cyclone or the blind forces of nature, nor even before Omnipotence merely as such. But one does kneel before the wholly uncomprehended Mystery, revealed yet unrevealed, and one's soul is stilled by feeling the way of its working, and therein its justification.

It would be possible to cite many other traces of numinous feeling in the Old Testament. But they have already been admirably put together by one who wrote sixteen hundred years ago in the same sense as we 'upon the non-rational'. This was Chrysostom. We shall be considering him later on and will not anticipate further in this place. ①

---

① See Appendix I.

专业化工具都投入到这一伟大工程的建设当中,其所有的意义与目的就在于将它建造成人类建筑成就的奇迹。尽管有无数的困难和巨大的障碍,大桥最终还是建成了,并且迎着风浪屹立起来。这时,一股狂烈的飓风袭来,桥和建桥的人都被卷进了深渊之中。极度的无意义似乎战胜了最丰富的意义,盲目的"命运"似乎征服了英勇和业绩。叙说者讲述了他是如何访问了悲剧的现场以及返回的情况。

当我们到达桥边的时候,风已经差不多完全停止了;天很高,呈蓝绿色,还闪着奇异的亮光。在我们后面是埃诺布赫特湾,就像一个巨大的露天坟场。主宰生与死的上帝在静默的庄严中盘旋在水面上。我们感到了他的在场,就像一个人感到他自己的手一样。我和那个老人跪下来,面对着那个露天的坟场,面对着上帝。

为什么他们要下跪?为什么他们感到必须这样做呢?人是不会向飓风或者大自然的一种盲目的力量下跪的,甚至不会拜倒在纯粹如此的全能者面前。但是人的确会拜倒在那种完全无法理解的若隐若现的神秘面前,而人的灵魂则会通过感到它起作用的方式,以及它在那里得到辩护的方式而受到安抚。

在《旧约》中,本来还可以摘引很多其他的神秘感受的踪迹,但是这些踪迹已经被一个人极好地收集起来了,他在一千六百年前就在我们所讨论的"基于非理性"的同样的意义上对其作了论述。这个人就是克里索斯托姆,我们将在后面谈到他,[1]此处就不再作进一步的论述了。

---

① 见附录1。

CHAPTER XI

The Numinous In The New Testament

In the Gospel of Jesus we see the consummation of that process tending to rationalize, moralize, and humanize the idea of God, which began with the earliest period of the old Hebrew tradition and became specially prominent as a living factor in the Prophets and the Psalms, continually bringing the apprehension of the numinous to a richer fulfilment by recognizing in it attributes of clear and profound value for the reason. The result was the faith in 'the fatherhood of God' in that unsurpassable form in which it is peculiar to Christianity.

But in this case, too, it would be a mistake to think that such a rationalization means that 'the numinous' is excluded or superseded. That is a misunderstanding into which we are led by the all-too-plausible delineations of 'Jesus's faith in the fatherhood of God' now prevalent, but it certainly misrepresents the attitude of the first Christian congregations. The error is only possible if we disregard in the message of Christ that which it really purports to be, first, last, and all the time, viz. 'the gospel *of the kingdom*'. As against all rationalizing attempts to tone it down into something less startling, the most recent research shows quite decisively that the 'kingdom' is just greatness and marvel absolute, the 'wholly other' 'heavenly' thing, set in contrast to the world of here and now, 'the mysterious' itself in its dual character as awe-compelling yet all-attracting, glimmering in an atmosphere of genuine 'religious awe'. As such, it sheds a colour,

第十一章 《新约》中的神秘

在关于耶稣的福音中,我们看到了那种倾向于将上帝观念理性化、道德化和人性化的全过程,这一过程始于古希伯来传统的最初时期,并且在各种先知书和赞美诗篇中,作为一种活跃的因素变得特别突出,而这一过程通过在神秘中识别出那些对于理性有着清晰而深刻的价值的性质,不断地将对于神秘的理解带入到一个更加丰富的实现阶段。其结果就是基督教所独有的、以一种无法超越的形式表现出来的信仰:对“上帝的父性”的信仰。

但是在这种情形中,如果认为这种理性化意味着对“神秘”的消解与替代,那也将是错误的。通过对当今非常流行的有关“耶稣对上帝的父性的信仰”的过于似是而非的描述,我们被引入了一种误解,不过这个描述肯定错误地表达了最早的基督教会众的态度。只有在我们始终无视在耶稣基督的预言中所真正声称的东西,即“关于天国的福音”时,这一错误才是可能的。与一切要把天国变得平易近人的理性化意图相反,最近的研究非常果断地表明,“天国”正是伟大与神奇的绝对者,是“完全的他者”,是“天上的”东西,作为与当下的此世的世界的对立,“神秘”本身在其既令人敬畏又具有完全的吸引力的二元性质中,隐身于一种真正的“宗教敬畏”的氛围当中。同样地,神秘将把某种色

a mood, a tone, upon whatever stands in relation to it, upon the men who proclaim it or prepare for it, upon the life and practice that are its precondition, upon the tidings of it, upon the congregation of those who await it and attain it. All is made into a mystery—all, that is, becomes numinous. This is shown most strikingly in the name by which the company of the disciples call themselves collectively and each other individually, the numinous 'technical term' *οἱ ἅγιοι*, the holy ones or 'the saints'. It is manifest at once that this does not mean 'the morally perfect' people: it means the people who participate in the mystery of the final Day. Their title is the clear and unambiguous antithesis to the term 'the profane', which we have already met with. For this reason the early Christians are able later to call themselves also actually a 'priestly'—or sacerdotal—'people', that is, a group of 'consecrated' persons. But the precondition of all this was given with the gospel itself and its claim to be the preaching of the coming kingdom.

What of the Lord of this kingdom, the 'heavenly Father'? As its Lord He is not less, but far more 'holy', 'numinous', mysterious, *qādôsh*, *ἅγιος*, *sacer*, and *sanctus* than His kingdom. He is all these in an absolute degree, and in this aspect of His nature He represents the sublimation and the consummation of all that the old covenant had grasped by way of 'creature-consciousness', 'holy awe', and the like. Not to realize this is to turn the gospel of Jesus into a mere idyll. That these moments do not occur severally in Jesus's message in the form of special 'doctrines' is due to the circumstances already mentioned more than once. But apart from the

彩、某种心境、某种情调投射到任何与之发生联系的东西上去，投射到那些宣扬它并准备接受它的人们身上去，投射到作为它的前提的生活和实践中去，投射到关于它的消息中去，投射到那些等待着它并且获得它的会众身上。所有的一切都被变成了一种神秘，也就是说，所有的一切都变成了神秘的。这一点在信徒们用来称呼他们全体或者彼此个人的称谓中表现得最为突出，这就是那种神秘的“技术术语”*οί ἅγιοι*，即神圣者或者圣徒。它同时也表明，“圣徒”这一称谓并不意味着“道德完美”的人：它指的是那些参加到末日的神秘中去的人。这些称谓是“俗人”这个我们已经提到过的术语的清晰明确的对立面。基于这个原因，早期的基督徒能够在后来也实际将自己称呼为一种“教士式的”——或者“僧侣式的”——“人”，即一群“神圣的”人。但是，这一切的前提都是由福音本身以及它所宣传的即将到来的天国的讲道所提供的。

那么，这个天国的主，即“天父”的情形如何呢？作为天国之主，上帝不比他的王国更少，而是更多神圣，神秘，玄奥，*qādôsh*（神圣），*ἅγιος*（神圣），可敬，威严。天父在绝对的程度上是所有这一切，而且在他的本性这一方面，他表现出了《旧约》以“被造物意识”、“神圣的敬畏”以及与之类似的方式所把握到的所有的崇高与完满。如果认识不到这一点，就会把耶稣的福音变成一首纯粹的田园诗。这些因素之所以没有多次以特殊的“信条”的形式出现在耶稣的启示中，是因为那些不止一次提到过的事实。但是，除了根本不可能教给他们之外，

inherent impossibility of *teaching* them, how could He have had need of 'teaching' what was simply the primary, selfevident fact to every Jew, and especially to every believer in 'the kingdom', namely, that God was 'the Holy One of Israel'? Christ had rather to teach and to proclaim what was *not* self-evident to the Jews, but His own original discovery and revelation, that this very 'Holy One' is a 'heavenly Father'. This point of view necessarily occupied the whole of His 'teaching', and all the more so because it was the point of view thrust sharply into the foreground by the two opposed influences of His time, against both of which the Gospel came historically as a reaction. On the one hand was Pharisaism, with its servitude to Law; on the other, John the Baptist, with his harsh, ascetic interpretation of God; and, in contrast to both, the gospel of the sonhood of man and the fatherhood of God came as the easy yoke, the light burden. But though it is necessarily this new message that the parables and discourses and pronouncements of Jesus complete and fill out, it is in such a way that it always remains an overwhelming and daring paradox, claiming our utmost homage, that He who is 'in heaven' is yet 'our Father'. That that 'heavenly' Being of marvel and mystery and awe is Himself the eternal, benignant, gracious will: this is the resolved contrast that first brings out the deep-felt harmony in true Christian experience; and the harmony cannot be heard aright by the man whose ear does not detect always sounding in it this sublimated 'seventh'.

It is significant, and yet again so natural, that the first petition in the prayer of the Christian fellowship is: 'Hallowed be Thy name.' What I have already said should make the meaning of this clear in its connexion with the Biblical meaning of the word. And we can sometimes detect, even in the teaching of Jesus, notes still vibrating which seem to suggest

耶稣又有什么必要把这些对于每一个犹太人,尤其是对于每一个“天国”的信仰者,也就是信仰上帝是“以色列的圣者”的人来说,都纯粹是基本的、自明的事实去“教诲”他们呢?相反,基督必须教给并且宣称那些对于犹太人来说不是自明的东西,而是他自己独创的发现与启示,即这位“圣者”正是“天父”。这一观点必然占据了他的整个“教诲”并且因下述事实而尤其如此:这一观点被他同时代的两种反面的影响急剧地推进到了显著的位置,作为对抗者,福音书作为一种反应历史地出现了。这两种反面影响,一个是法利赛主义及其受法律的奴役状况;另一个是施洗约翰及其对上帝的苛刻的苦行的理解;而与这两者相反,关于人的子性与上帝的父性的福音是作为一种轻松的束缚,即较轻的负担而到来的。但是,尽管耶稣的寓言、谈话、声明所要完成和实现的必然是这种新的福音,然而,它却是以这种方式来完成与实现的:这种福音总是处于一种无法抵抗的、大胆的矛盾之中而要求着我们最大的敬意,即上帝虽然“在天上”,但是他仍然是“我们的父亲”。那种奇迹的、神秘的和敬畏的“天国的”存在本身就是永恒的、仁慈的和高尚的意志:正是这种断然的对立首先在真正基督徒的经验中显示出那种被深刻感受到的和谐;而这种和谐是不能被那种人所正确地听到的——他们的耳朵无法察觉到那总是在其中奏鸣着的这种被升华了的“第七重天”。

在基督教团体的祈祷中,第一句祷词是:“愿你的名为生。”这是很有意义,而又非常自然的。我已经说过的那些话应当使这句祷词的含义在它与该词的圣经的含义的联系中变得清晰起来。甚至在耶稣的教诲中,我们有时也能察觉到那依然在振动着的音

a trace of that weird awe and shuddering dread before the mysteries of the transcendent of which we have already spoken. Such a passage is Matt. x. 28: 'But fear him which is able to *destroy both soul and body in hell.*'

The dark and awful ring of this saying cannot be missed, and it is a rationalization of it merely to refer it to the Judge and His judgement on the Last Day. The same note rings out again clearly in the saying in Heb. x. 31: 'It is a fearful thing to fall into the hands of the living God'; and in Heb. xii. 29: 'Our God is a consuming fire.' (Here the adaptation of Deut. iv. 24: 'The Lord is a consuming fire' into 'Our God is a consuming fire' gives a contrast whose effect enhances the horror of the saying.) And when occasion demands it the Old Testament God of 'vengeance' recurs even in the teaching of Jesus Himself, unveiled and in His own authentic character; as, for instance, in Matt. xxi. 41: 'He will miserably destroy those wicked men.'

Finally, it is in the light of, and with the background of, this numinous experience, with its mystery and its awe—its *mysterium tremendum*—that Christ's Agony in the night of Gethsemane must be viewed, if we are to comprehend or realize at all in our own experience what the import of that agony was. What is the cause of this 'sore amazement' and 'heaviness', this soul shaken to its depths, 'exceeding sorrowful even unto death', and this sweat that falls to the ground like great drops of blood? Can it be ordinary fear of death in the case of one who had had death before his eyes for weeks past and who had just celebrated with clear intent his death-feast with his disciples? No, there is more here than the fear of death; there is the awe of the creature before the *mysterium tremendum*, before the shuddering secret of the

调,它仿佛暗示着在面对我们已经讲到过的超越的神秘时的某种奇异的敬畏和令人战栗的恐惧。这一段话是《马太福音》第 10 章第 28 节:“所要怕的,乃是能把身体和灵魂都毁灭在地狱里的那个人。”

这句话中阴森恐怖的语调是不能被忽略的,而且只有在它指的是审判或者上帝的末日审判时它才是一种理性化。同样的语调还清晰地回荡在《希伯来书》第 10 章第 31 节中:“落在永生上帝手中,真是可怕”;在《希伯来书》第 12 章第 29 节中:“我们的上帝乃是一团烈火。”(这里,将《申命记》第 4 章第 24 节的“上帝是一团烈火”改写为“我们的上帝是一团烈火”,它带来了一个对比,其结果是增强了这句话的恐怖性。)在必要时,《旧约》中的那个“复仇”的上帝甚至会在耶稣本人的教诲中重现出来,毫不遮掩地重现在他自己的真实的性格之中;例如,在《马太福音》第 21 章第 41 节:“他要下毒手除灭那些恶人。”

最后,如果我们想要从根本上去理解或者认识在我们的经验中那种痛苦的重要性,那么,就必须按照那种包含有其神秘性和敬畏性的神秘经验——即令人敬畏的神秘性,或者以之为基础来加以考察,这种神秘体验就是耶稣基督在客西马尼(Gethsemane,即蒙难地)的那个晚上的痛苦。引起这种“极度的震惊”和“沉重的心情”,这种灵魂的深度振颤与“悲痛欲绝”,以及汗水就像巨大的血滴一样滚落在大地上的原因是什么呢?它能是一个人对死亡的普通的害怕吗?这个人在过去的几周里已经见识了死亡并且与其门徒一道怀着清晰的意图庆祝了自己的死宴?不,这里有着比对死亡的害怕更多的东西;这里有在令人敬畏的神秘面前、在令人战栗的神秘者的秘密面前的

numen. And the old tales come back into our mind as strangely parallel and, as it were, prophetically significant, the tales of Yahweh who waylaid Moses by night, and of Jacob who wrestled with God 'until the breaking of the day'. 'He had power with God ... and prevailed', with the God of 'wrath' and 'fury', with the *numen*, which yet is itself '*my Father*'. In truth even those who cannot recognize 'the Holy One of Israel' elsewhere in the God of the Gospel must at least discover Him here, if they have eyes to see at all.

I have no need to dwell upon the numinous atmosphere pervading the writings of St. Paul. 'God dwelleth in a light that none may come nigh.' The 'over-aboundingness' ('exuberance') of the idea of God and the feeling of God leads with Paul to the special terminology and experiences of mysticism. ①But it is not confined to these: it can be seen alive through all his utterances in the feelings of exalted enthusiasm and his spiritual terminology of the *pneuma*, which are alike far removed from the merely rational side of Christian piety. His dualistic depreciation of 'the flesh', as of all that pertains to creaturehood, is that numinous selfdisvaluation spoken of on pp. 49 ff. carried to its extreme. These catastrophes and sudden reversals that befall the religious consciousness, the tragedy of sin and guilt, or again the glow of beatific joy, are only possible and intelligible on the basis of numinous experience.

---

① As a provisional definition of mysticism I would suggest that, while sharing the nature of religion, it shows a preponderance of its non-rational elements and an over-stressing of them in respect to the 'over-abounding' aspect of the 'numen'. A type of religious experience acquires 'mystical colouring' if it shows an inclination to mysticism. In this sense Christianity since St. Paul and St. John is not mysticism, but religion with a mystical colouring. And this is justified.

那种被造物的敬畏。这让我们回想起那些与此非常类似并且可以说具有这预言的意义的老故事,即耶和华趁着夜色拦劫摩西的故事,以及雅各与上帝搏斗“直到黎明”的故事。“他与神较力……并得了胜”,与“愤怒”的“狂怒”的上帝较力,与神秘较力,而它本身却是“我的父亲”。事实上,那些在福音书中的上帝身上看不出“以色列的圣者”的人,至少能在这里发现他,如果他们的眼睛还能看东西的话。

我没有必要详细论述那种弥漫在圣保罗的著作中的神秘气氛。“上帝栖居在无人能够接近的光明之中。”那种“极为丰富”(茂盛)的关于上帝的观念和关于上帝的感受带给圣保罗的是特殊的术语以及关于神秘主义的特殊的体验。① 但它还不止于此:通过他在激情中所说的所有话语以及他给予灵魂的精神性的术语——这二者与基督教的虔敬的纯粹理性的方面都相差甚远——都能看到非常活跃的神秘气氛。他对“肉体”的双重的贬抑,正如对于所有被造物的贬抑一样,是在前面已经讲到过、在第 49 页及以下段落中达到其顶点的那种神秘的自我贬抑。

这些加之于宗教意识的大灾难和突然剧变,那种关于原罪与罪恶的悲剧,或者再次闪现的祝福之光,都只有在神秘经验的基础上才是可能的和可以理解的。正如在圣保罗看来,主的盛怒

① 作为对神秘主义的一种临时定义,我认为:神秘主义虽然分有宗教性质,但是它显示出了非理性因素的优越性,并且非常突出地强调了这些非理性因素的“神秘的”“非常丰富的”方面。如果一种宗教经验表现出某种神秘主义的倾向,那么这种宗教经验就获得了“神秘色彩”。在这个意义上,自圣保罗和圣约翰以来的基督教不是神秘主义,而是带有神秘色彩的宗教。这是有道理的。

And just as the o’ργή Θεοû with St. Paul is more than the mere reaction of righteous retribution, just as it is permeated by the ‘awefulness’ of the numinous, so on the other side is the ‘fascination’ of the experienced love of God, that bears the spirit beyond its boundaries into the third heaven, more than the mere consummation of the natural human feeling of a child for its parent. The *ὀργή Θεοû* is potently and vividly present in the grand passage in Rom. i. 18 ff., where we recognize directly the jealous, passionate Yahweh of the Old Testament, here grown to a God of the universe of fearful power, who pours out the blazing vials of His wrath over the whole world. In this passage there is an intuition, genuinely non-rational in character, the sublimity of which has an almost horrible quality: that the commission of sin is the angry God’s punishment for sin. St. Paul reiterates this thought—so intolerable, if considered ‘rationally’—in three separate verses. ‘Wherefore God also gave them up to uncleanness through the lusts of their own hearts, to dishonour their own bodies between themselves’ (Rom. i. 24); ‘For this cause God gave them up unto vile affections’ (i. 26); ‘God gave them over to a reprobate mind, . . . being filled with all unrighteousness’, &c. (i. 28, 29).

To feel the full weight and force of this intuition it is necessary to escape as far as possible from the mental atmosphere of our dogmatic interpretations and judiciously toneddown catechisms, and to try to recapture the awe that could be felt by the Jew toward the fury of Yahweh, by the Hellenistic Greek toward the horror of *heimarmenē* or Destiny, and by primitive man in general toward the *ira deorum* or anger of the gods.

There is one other point in the teaching of Paul that demands notice in this connexion—his doctrine of predestination. It is perhaps precisely the ‘rationalist’ who feels most directly that with the idea of predestination we are standing on downright non-rational ground. Nothing remains so

(o'ργή Θεοῦ)远不止于正义的报偿反应,正如这种盛怒被神秘的"敬畏"所浸渍一样,因此,在另一方面,这种被体验为"沉迷"的对上帝的爱,远远超出了一个孩子对于其父母的这种自然人类感情的最完美的表现,这种对上帝的爱承载着超出自身边界而进入到第三重天的精神。这种主的盛怒有力而且生动地表现在《罗马人书》第1章第18节以下的重要段落中,在这些句子中我们直接认出了那个《旧约》中的妒忌的、易怒的耶和华,在此,他变成了拥有可怕力量的宇宙的上帝,他要将其愤怒倾向全世界。在这一段中有一种在性质上是真正非理性的直觉,这种直觉所具有的崇高有一种几乎可怕的性质:即犯罪是愤怒的上帝对罪的惩罚。圣保罗分别在三段话中重申了这一思想——如果"理性地"思考这一思想,那将是令人难以忍受的。"所以上帝任凭他们逞着心里的情欲行污秽的事,以致彼此玷辱自己的身体"(《罗马人书》,第1章第24节);"上帝就任凭他们存邪恶的心……充满各种不义"(《罗马人书》第1章第28、29节)。

要感受这种直觉的全部的分量和力量,就必须尽量远离我们的教条式解释与明智低调的问答所具有的精神氛围,并且尽力去重新体验犹太人对耶和华的狂怒所感受到的敬畏、希腊人对命运(*heimarmené*)的可怕所感受到的敬畏以及原始人通常对于神祇的愤怒(*ira deorum*)所感受到的敬畏。

在圣保罗的教诲中还有另外一点需要注意到,即他的命定论的学说。或许正是这种"理性主义者"最直接地感受到,只要接受了命定论的观念,我们就站到了彻底非理性的立场上了。对于理性主义者来说,没有什么比这种命定论更加陌生的

alien to the rationalist as this doctrine. And from his point of view he is quite right; from the standpoint of the rational this notion of predestination is a sheer absurdity, an absolute offence. Let him acquiesce in all the paradoxes of the Trinity and Christology, predestination will yet remain perpetually to confront him as a stumbling-block.

Not, as need hardly be said, in the form in which it has been put forward since the time of Schleiermacher, following the tradition of Leibniz and Spinoza. That is simply a capitulation to natural law and *causae secundae*, a surrender to the claim of modern psychology that all human resolves and actions are subject to the compelling force of motives, so that a man is unfree and predetermined thereby. And so, this predetermination by *nature*, having been identified with the all-embracing efficacy of God, in the end the outcome of the profound and purely religious intuition of divine predetermination—which has no concern at all with 'laws of nature'—is the comparatively trivial 'scientific' notion of universal causal connexion. There can be no more spurious product of theological speculation, no more fundamental falsification of religious conceptions than this; and it is certainly not against this that the rationalist feels an antagonism, for it is itself a piece of solid rationalism, but at the same time a complete abandonment of the real religious idea of 'predestination'.

This false 'scientific' interpretation of 'predestination' having been put aside, it may be shown that as a religious idea it springs from two sources and has two quite distinct aspects, which should be distinguished by separate names. The one is 'election', the other—striking an essentially different note—'predestination' proper.

The idea of 'election'—i. e. of having been chosen out and pre-ordained by God *unto salvation*—is an immediate and pure expression of the actual religious experience of grace. The

了。从他自己的这个观点来看,他是完全正确的;从理性的立场来看,这种命定论的观点是一种纯粹的谬论,一种绝对的冒犯。即便理性主义者勉强同意了三位一体与基督学的所有悖论,命定论也将永远作为一种障碍物横亘在他的面前。

几乎无须多说,这种命定论并不是存在于从施莱尔马赫时代遵循着莱布尼茨和斯宾诺莎的传统所提出的那种形式中。那种命定论的观点纯粹是对自然法则和因果律(*causae secundae*)的一种屈服,一种对现代心理学的看法的屈服,现代心理学声称,人的所有决断与行为都受动机的强制力的支配,因此,人是不自由的,是被预先确定的。因此,这种基于自然的命定论——由于被等同于上帝的包容一切的功效,最后形成了这种深刻的并且是纯粹宗教的神学命定论的、根本不涉及"自然法则"的直觉——是一种关于普遍的因果联系的比较琐碎的"科学的"观念。与这种"科学的"观点相比较,没有什么东西是神学反思的更加虚假的产物,没有什么东西比它对宗教概念的歪曲更加根本;而且它确实不会反对这一点,即理性主义者所感受到的对它的反抗就是它自身,即坚实的理性主义的一部分,但是与此同时,却完全放弃了"命定论"的真正宗教的观念。

这种对"命定论"的虚假的"科学"解释被撇开了,这或许显示出,作为一种宗教观念,它来自于两个来源,并且具有两个截然不同的方面,这两个方面应当以不同的名称加以区分。一个是"选择",另一个就是"命定论"本身——它奏出了根本不同的一个调子。

"选择"的观念,也就是被上帝挑选出来并且预先定为拯救的对象,是对恩赐这种实际的宗教经验的直接和纯粹的表达。神的

recipient of divine grace feels and knows ever more and more surely, as he looks back on his past, that he has not grown into his present self through any achievement or effort of his own, and that, apart from his own will or power, grace was imparted to him, grasped him, impelled, and led him. And even the resolves and decisions that were most his own and most free become to him, without losing the element of freedom, something that he *experienced* rather than *did*. Before every deed of his own he sees love the deliverer in action, seeking and selecting, and acknowledges that an eternal gracious purpose is watching over his life. But this 'preordainment' is purely a preordainment unto salvation and has in itself nothing to do with the *praedestinatio ambigua*, the predetermination of all men *either* to be saved or to be damned. The rational and logical conclusion of course would be that, if he is elected of God but others are not, God, in appointing the elect to bliss; determines also the rejected for damnation. But this conclusion is not, and must not be, drawn, for what we are concerned with is a religious intuition which, as such, stands alone and is only warrant for itself, and which indeed is outraged by any attempt to weave it into a system or make it yield a series of inferences. In this respect Schleiermacher is quite right when he says in his *Discourses upon Religion*:① 'Every (sc. religious) intuition is a self-subsistent work ... knowing nothing of derivation and point of connexion.'

So much for 'election'. From it must be distinguished 'predestination' proper, as it appears in St. Paul, e. g. Rom. ix. 18: 'Therefore hath he mercy on whom he will, and whom he will he hardeneth.'

---

① Schleiermacher, *Reden über die Religion*, ed. R. Otto, 4th ed., pp. 37-8.

恩赐的接受者在回顾他自己的过去时，越来越确切地感受和认识到，他尚未通过自己的任何成就与努力而成长为他的当下自我，而且，除了他自己的意愿与力量外，神的恩赐被施与他，并且抓住他、强迫他、引导他。甚至那些主要是他自己的而且也是最自由的决断与决心，对于他来说也变成了那种与其说是他做过的，不如说是体验到的——没有失去自由的因素。在他自己的每一个行为之前，他都看到了正在寻觅和挑选着的神恩的施予者在行动中的爱，并且承认一种永恒的恩赐的目的在关注着他的生活。但是，这种“预先注定的命运”纯粹是一种通向拯救的预定，它本身与那种含糊的命定论，即所有的人要么被拯救要么被惩罚的命定论毫不相干。理性的与逻辑的结论当然应当是这样的，如果是他而不是别的人被上帝选中了，那么，上帝在赐福给他这个被选中者的同时，注定了也要给落选者以惩罚。然而这一结论没有被得出，也不应当被得出，因为我们所关注的是某种宗教直觉，这种宗教直觉同样特立独行并仅仅以自身为据，而且任何要把这种直觉纳入到某种系统或者使之产生一系列的推论的企图都确实是对它的侮辱。在这一点上，施莱尔马赫在他的《关于宗教的谈话》①中讲得非常对：“每一种（即宗教的）直觉都是一种独立自存的东西……与派生的以及相联系的观点毫不相关。”

关于“选择”就讲这么多。必须将它与“命定论”适当地区分开来，如同它出现在圣保罗那里，例如在《罗马人书》第 9 章第 18 节：“如此看来，上帝要怜悯谁就怜悯谁，要叫谁刚硬就叫谁刚硬。”

① 施莱尔马赫《关于宗教的谈话》(*Reden über die Religion*)，由 R. 奥托编辑出版，第 4 版第 37 ~ 38 页。

It is true that the thought of 'election', prominent in St. Paul, can be detected here as well. But the reflection in v. 20 is obviously the utterance of quite a different frame or mind: 'Nay, but, O man, who art thou that repliest against God? Shall the thing formed say to him that formed it, Why hast thou made me thus?' That is a line of thought wholly out of keeping with the set of ideas centring about 'election'. And yet even less can it be derived from any abstractly theoretic 'doctrine' of the all-causing nature of God. Such a doctrine we find in Zwingli, and with him it does indeed give rise to a 'doctrine of predestination', but one that is rather the artificial product of philosophical speculation than the result of immediate religious experience. The true 'predestination', springing directly from religious intuition, has its origin beyond question in St. Paul. But in him it is easily recognized as the numinous feeling in face of the *mysterium tremendum*; and that unique phase of it that we met with above (pp. 9 ff.) in the narrative of Abraham recurs here in a signally intensified form. For the religious conception in the notion of predestination is nothing but that 'creature-consciousness', that self-abasement and the annulment of personal strength and claims and achievements in the presence of the transcendent, as such. The numen, overpoweringly experienced, becomes the all-in-all. The creature, with his being and doing, his 'willing' and 'running' (Rom. ix. 16), his schemes and resolves, becomes nothing. The conceptual expression to indicate such a felt submergence and annihilation over against the numen is then—here impotence and there omnipotence; here the futility of one's own choice, there the will that ordains all and determines all.

It is next to be noted that 'predestination' in this sense, as identical with the absolute supremacy of the numen, has nothing whatever to do with the 'unfree will' of 'Determinism'. Rather, it finds very frequently precisely in the 'free will' of the creature the contrast which makes it stand out so prominently.

的确,在圣保罗那里非常著名的关于“选择”的思想在这里也同样可以找到。但是,反映在第20节中的却明显是另一种不同的心态的表述:“人哪,你是谁,竟敢与上帝顶嘴?被造之物岂能对造它者说,你为什么要这样造我呢?”那是一种完全不同于集中于“选择”那一套观念的思想。然而,它更不可能来自上帝是万物的始因这一抽象神学的“教条”。我们在慈温利那里看到了这一教条,而且,在他那里,这一教条的确引申出了“命定论的教条”,但是这种命定论的教条却是一种哲学反思的人造物,而不是直接宗教经验的结果。那种真正的直接产生于宗教直觉的“命定论”,在圣保罗那里无疑有其根源。但是,在他那里,这种命定论很容易被当做是面对令人畏惧的神秘时的那种神秘感受;我们在前面(第9页及以下段落)在亚伯拉罕的叙述中所遇到的那种独特的状态在这里以显著增强了的方式重新出现了。因为包含在命定论的观念中的宗教概念不是别的,正是那种“被造物意识”,即在超验者面前的自卑以及同样地,对个人力量、要求和成就的取消。那个被无法抵抗地体验到的神秘者变成了凌驾一切的东西。被造物及其存在与行为、他的“定意”与“奔跑”(《罗马人书》第9章第16节)、他的谋划与决断,全都变成了虚无。如果用概念性的表达方式来指称那种对应着神圣者的被感受到的浸没与泯灭,那就是,此处是无能为力而彼处则全知全能;此处是个人在选择上的一无所是,彼处则是规定一切和决定一切的意志。

接着要指出的是,在这种意义上的“命定论”,作为同一于神秘者的绝对的至高无上,与“宿命论”的“不自由意志”没有任何关系。相反,正是在被造物的“自由意志”中,才非常频繁地发现那种使“命定论”变得十分突出的那种

'Will what thou wilt and how thou canst; plan and choose; yet must all come about as it shall and as is determined' : that is the earliest and most genuine expression of the matter. In face of the eternal power man is reduced to naught, *together with* his free choice and action. And the eternal power waxes immeasurable just because it fulfils its decrees *despite* the freedom of human will. This is the aspect of the matter designedly thrust into the foreground in many typical Mohammedan narratives which profess to display the inflexibility of the decrees of Allah. In these, men are *able* to devise and decide and reject; but, however they choose or act, Allah's eternal will is accomplished to the very day and hour that was ordained. The purport of this is precisely, *not* that God and God alone is an active cause, but rather that the activity of the creature, be it never so vigorous and free, is overborne and determined absolutely by the eternal operative purpose. ①The thought of the deity as the absolutely sole and all-embracing active cause first occurs where the creaturefeeling is intensified still further, and is at the same time combined with theoretic considerations. It then leads to mysticism; and it is only again a further consequence if the speculations about being, peculiar to and characteristic of mysticism, become then attached to the thought of God as sole cause. To the creature then is denied, not merely *efficacy* as

---

① The story told by Beidhavi, an expositor of the Koran, illustrates this: Once when Azrael, the angel of Death, came before Solomon he directed his gaze upon one of the king's companions. 'Who is that?' asked the man. 'The angel of Death,' replied Solomon. 'He seems to be looking at me,' continued the other, 'so command the wind that it bear me hence and set me down in India.' Solomon did so. Then said the angel, 'I gazed upon him for so long out of astonishment, seeing it had been commanded me to fetch his soul out of India, while he was yet with thee in Canaan.' This is a predestination which presupposes free will just as its foil. However freely man makes his plans, Allah has always set his countermine.

[This story is told in verse by Leigh Hunt in his poem 'The Inevitable'; cf. Oxford ed. (1922), pp. 95-6. (*Trans.*)]

对比。“如你所愿如你所能地去谋划与选择;但一切都要像被决定了的那样发生”:这是对命定问题的最早、最准确的表述。面对着这种永恒的力量,人连同其自由选择与自由行为,都被削减为零。而那种永恒的力量增大到不可量度,就是因为他在实现自己的天命时置人的意志自由于不顾。在许多关于默罕默德的典型叙事中被故意地推向前台的正是命定论的这个方面,它做要变现的是安拉意旨的不可更改性。在这些叙事中,人能够谋划、决定和拒斥,但是,无论人们怎样选择与行动,安拉的永恒意志都会在被规定好的那个时刻得到实现。这种命定论的主旨并不正好就是说,上帝而且只有上帝是能动的原因,而事实上,被造物的活动,无论它是多么的有力与自由,都绝对地被永恒运作的目的所压服着和决定着。① 把神性视作那种绝对唯一的和包容一切的能动原因的思想,最初出现于被造感被进一步增强,并且同时又与理论思维结合在一起的地方。因而,它导致了神秘主义;只有在关于存在的思索——这种思索是神秘主义所独有并且是其特征——被纳入到那种将上帝视为唯一的原因的思想中去时,这种命定论才再次具有了进一步的重要性。那么,对于被

① 这个故事是由《古兰经》的研究者拜德哈维讲述的,它讲到:从前,当死神阿斯内尔来到所罗门王面前,他盯着国王的一个随从。“那是谁?”这个随从问。所罗门答道:“死神。”随从接着说:“它好像在盯着我,请让风把我吹到印度去吧。”所罗门王照办了。然后死神说:“我之所以盯着他看那么久,是出于惊讶,因为我发现我曾经受命要从印度取他的灵魂,而他却在迦南(Canaan)与你在一起。”这正是一种将自由意志预设为陪衬的命定论。无论人多么自由地制定他的计划,安拉总是能够将计就计。

[这个故事是由莱·亨特在他的诗《命定》中所讲述的;参见 1922 年牛津版第 95 ~96 页。英译注]

a cause, but true *reality* and complete being, and all existence and fullness of being is ascribed to the absolute entity, who alone really *is*, while all 'being' of creatures is either a function of this absolute Being—which brings them into existence —or mere illusion. This sequence of ideas is found in particularly explicit form in the mysticism of Geulincx and the Occasionalists. 'Ubi nihil vales, ibi nihil velis.' Sometimes we hear the same mystical chord in St. Paul also, as in his mysterious saying about the final issue of all things, where 'God shall be all in all'. But the passage in Romans is different. It goes no farther than the thought of predestination itself; and predestination we have found to be nothing but the intensified 'creature-feeling' in conceptual expression, and to be altogether rooted in the numinous consciousness.

A further consideration may make it plainer that this must be so. If it be really true that the consciousness of the numinous, as 'creature-feeling', is the root of the predestination idea, then we should expect that the form of religious faith marked by an undue and exaggerated insistence on the non-rational elements in the idea of God would also lean most markedly to predestination. And such is obviously the case. No religion has such a leaning to predestination as Islam; and the special quality of Islam is just that in it, from its commencement onwards, the rational and specifically moral aspect of the idea of God was unable to acquire the firm and clear impress that it won, e.g., in Christianity or Judaism. In Allah the numinous is absolutely preponderant over everything else. So that, when Islam is criticized for giving a merely 'fortuitous' character to the claim of morality, as though the moral law were only valid through the chance caprice of the deity, the criticism is well justified, only 'chance' and fortuitousness have nothing to do with the matter. The explanation is rather that the numinous inAllah, nay, even his uncanny

造物来说,被否定的就不仅仅是作为一种原因的功效,而是真正的实体和全部的存在,而且,存在的全部实存与完满都被归之于绝对的实体,只有这种存在才真正地存在着,而被造物的所有“存在”要么是这个绝对存在者的功能——它使被造物进入到存在中,要么仅仅是它的幻象。这一系列观念以一种特别清晰的形式表现在格林克斯和偶因论者那里。“哪里你一无所得,哪里你也一无所求。”有时我们也在圣保罗关于万事万物的最后结局的神秘言论中听到这种同样神秘的旋律,如“上帝将成为一切的一切”,但是在《罗马人书》中的这段话则不同。这段话并没有超过命定思想本身;而我们已经发现的命定论不是别的,而只是以概念化的表达方式增强了的“被造感”,并且完全被植根于神秘意识之中。

进一步的思考或许可以使这一点变得更加清晰起来。如果作为“被造感”的关于神秘的意识确实真的是命定观念的根基,那么,我们就可以预期,那种被在上帝观念的非理性因素上的某种不适当的、言过其实的执著打下烙印的宗教信仰的形式,也将会最显著地倾向于命定论,而上述情形显然正是如此。没有哪种宗教像伊斯兰教这样如此倾向于命定论,而且伊斯兰教的独特性质正在于此,从这种宗教创立以来,上帝观念中的理性方面,尤其是道德方面就无法获得如其在基督教或者犹太教中所获得的那种坚定的、清晰的印象。在安拉那里,神秘绝对地优越于其他的所有东西。因此,当伊斯兰教因为仅仅把“偶然的”性质给予了道德要求(似乎道德律令只有在通过神的任意裁决才是有效的)而被批判时,这种批判是完全正确的,单纯的“或然性”以及偶然性与命定论没有丝毫关系。这一解释更确切地说,在于安拉身上的

and daemonic character, outweighs what is rational in him. And this will account for what is commonly called the 'fanatical' character of this religion. Strongly excited feeling of the numen, that runs to frenzy, untempered by the more rational elements of religious experience—that is everywhere the very essence of fanaticism.

The above interpretation of the notion of predestination gives at the same time our estimate of it. It is an attempted statement, in conceptual terms and by *analogy*, of something that at bottom is incapable of explication by concepts. Fully justified in this sense as an analogical expression, it is wholly unjustified (*summum jus* becoming *summa injuria*) if its character as analogy is missed, so that it is taken as an adequate formulation of theological theory. In that case it is disastrous and intolerable to a rational religion like Christianity, in spite of the attempts that are made to render it innocuous by all the arts of evasion and mitigation.

There is another element in the thought of Paul besides his notion of predestination that is rooted in the numinous: I refer to his utter depreciation of 'the flesh'. 'The flesh' with Paul is simply the condition of the creature in general. And this is utterly disparaged and depreciated by the numinous consciousness (as we saw on pp. 9 ff., 49 ff.) in contrast to the transcendent, both in regard to its existence and its value; in respect to the first as 'dust and ashes', 'nothingness', insufficient, weak, transient, and perishing, and in respect to the second as the 'profane', the impure, which is unable to assume the worth of holiness or to come into its presence. We

神秘,不仅如此,甚至他的离奇的恶魔般的性质,都远远超出了他身上的理性因素,而这一点将可说明那种通常被称做这一宗教的“狂热”性质的东西。被强烈激发出来的神秘感受迅速达到了狂暴,而不受宗教经验中更加理性的因素的节制——这就是一切狂热的确切本质。

上述对命定论观念的解释同时也给出了我们对它的评价。它是一种以概念性的术语以及通过类比的方式所做的尝试性陈述,它所要叙说的是某种实际上无法通过概念来界说的东西。在这种作为类比的表达方式的意义上,命定论是完全合理的,但是如果它的作为类比的性质被忽略掉,由此导致它被当做一种神学理论的充分表述,那么它就是完全不合理的了(完全的合理变成了完全的不合理 *summum jus* becoming *summa injuria*)。在那种情形中,它对于像基督教这样理性的宗教来说是有害的和无法忍受的,尽管人们采取了很多的努力,通过所有的回避与缓解的方法,来使其变得没有危害。

除了他的命定论的观念之外,在圣保罗的思想中,还有另外一种因素,也根植于这种神秘之中:我指的是他对“肉体”的绝对贬抑。在圣保罗看来,“肉体”只不过是一般被造物的条件而已。在同超验者——不仅关于其存在,而且关于其价值——的对比中,这是被神秘意识全然地轻蔑与贬抑(正如我们在第9页及以下各段以及第49页及以下各段中所看到的那样);与前者即超验者的存在相对应,“肉体”相当于“尘土与灰烬”、“虚无”、不足、虚弱、暂时的而且是令人生厌的,与后者即超验者的价值相对应,“肉体”相当于“粗俗的”、不纯净的,是不能呈现出神圣的价值或者不能进入到神圣之中的。我们在圣保罗的思想中找到了这两

find these two same sorts of depreciation among the ideas of Paul, and the specifically Pauline feature in them is only the vigour and completeness with which he expresses them. It is a quite separate question whence Paul derives this intensity in his denunciation and depreciation of 'the flesh', whether it is original to him or stimulated by the 'dualistic' environment of thought in which he moved. As has been already said, one can determine nothing about the essential nature or the value of a thing by tracing its genesis and continuous historic derivation from other sources. And at least we may maintain that Paul might well be stimulated to this emphatic expression by many genuine cases of the numinous experience recorded in the Old Testament. There too *bāsār*, the flesh, is both the principle of being 'dust and ashes' and the principle of the 'pollution' of the creature in the presence of holiness.

In St. John, no less than in St. Paul, there is a strong strain of the numinous. The element of 'awefulness', it is true, dies away in him, as so commonly in mysticism, without ever quite vanishing, for, *pace* Ritschl, even in John 'the wrath of God abideth' (John iii. 36); but this only makes the elements of 'mystery' and 'fascination' the stronger, even in their mystical form. In John, Christianity absorbs Φώς and ξωή, 'light' and 'life', into itself from the religions at rivalry with it;① and justly so, for only in Christianity do they win home.

---

① And thereby drains these religions of their life-blood, according to 'the right of the stronger'. And henceforth these elements belong to Christianity indissolubly as its very own. For

Wenn starke Geisteskraft
Die Elemente
An sich herangerafft:
Kein Engel trennte
Geeinte Zwienatur
Der innigen Beiden-

and still less can the criticism of scholars! ['When the vigour of the spirit has gathered the elements into itself, then may no angel sunder the double nature now made single of the united twain.']

种同样的贬抑,而在这两种相同的贬抑中,那种独特的圣保罗风格仅仅在于他将它们表述得更加有力和更加完整了。至于圣保罗在谴责与贬抑"肉体"时的这种强度来自何处,无论是他原来就有的,还是由于他活动于其中的那种"二元论的"思想环境的激发的结果,那完全是另外一个问题。就像前面已经说过的,一个人通过从另外的根源来追踪一事物的起源及其后来的历史发展,是不可能确定这一事物的根本本质或者价值的。至少我们可以坚持一点,这就是圣保罗很有可能是受到了在《旧约》中记载的许多关于神秘体验的真实例子的刺激,而作出了这种强烈的表达。在《旧约》中,同样的,bāsār 即肉体,既是变成"尘土与灰烬"的成分,又是被造物在面对着神圣者时的"污染"的成分。

在圣约翰那里,正如在圣保罗那里一样,也存在着某种强烈的神秘的张力。的确,"敬畏"的因素在约翰这里就像通常在神秘主义那里一样减弱了,但却从来没有完全消失,因为,说一句冒犯利奇尔的话,即便是在圣约翰那里,"上帝的震怒"(《约翰福音》第 3 章第 36 节)也从来没有完全消失;但是这样只会使"神秘"与"沉迷"的因素变得更加强大,即便在它们的神秘主义的形式中也是如此。在圣约翰那里,基督教从与其敌对的宗教中吸收了"光"(φώs)与"生命"(ξωή)到其自身中来;[①]而且正是如

---

① 因而,根据"强者的权利",从这些宗教中吸取了它们的生命力。而自此以后,这些因素就成了基督教不能分割的一部分。因为"一旦精神所具有的活力把诸因素纳入自身之中,就没有任何神祇能再把这种合而为一的东西分成两截。"

Wenn starke Geisteskraft
Die Elemente
An sich herangerafft:
Kein Engel trennte
Geeinte Zwienatur
Der innigen Beiden-而学者的批判就更不能做到这一些了!

But what is this 'light' and this 'life'? Not to *feel* what they are is to be made of wood, but none can express it. They are a sheer abounding overplus of the non-rational element in religion.

And the same is true even of that saying of St. John to which the 'rationalists' are so specially fond of referring: 'God is a Spirit' (John iv. 24). This was the text on account of which Hegel held Christianity to be the highest because the most truly spiritual (*geistig*) religion. But Hegel meant by 'spirit' the 'absolute reason'. St. John when he speaks of πνεῦμα is not thinking of 'absolute reason' but of that which is in absolute contrast to everything of 'the world' and 'the flesh', the utterly mysterious and miraculous heavenly Being who surpasses all the understanding and reason of the 'natural' man. He is thinking of that 'Spirit' which 'bloweth where it listeth, and thou hearest the sound thereof, but canst not tell whence it cometh and whither it goeth'—the Spirit which just on that account is not confined to Zion or Gerizim, and whose worship is only for those who are themselves 'in spirit and in truth'. So that this saying, apparently wholly 'rational' in import, is itself the strongest and clearest indication of the non-rational element in the Biblical idea of God. ①

---

① Compare with this chapter my book Reich *Gottes und Menschensohn* (*The Kingdom of God and the Son of Man*).

此，因为在基督教中，它们才找到了自己的家。但是，什么是这种“光”与这种“生命”呢？只有用木头做的人才感受不到它们是什么，但却无人能够将其表达出来。它们就是宗教中绝对丰富而过剩的非理性因素。

甚至那些“理性主义者们”特别热衷于引用的圣约翰的“上帝是个灵”(《约翰福音》第4章第24节)这句话，也同样充满着非理性因素。正是基于这句话，黑格尔把基督教看做是最高的宗教，因为它是最真实的精神性(*geistig*)的宗教，但是，黑格尔所说的“精神”指的是“绝对理性”。当圣约翰说到 *πνεῦμα* 时，绝没有想到“绝对理性”，而是那种同“此岸”的以及“肉体”的每一种东西绝对相对立的东西，即那种绝对神秘的、不可思议的神圣的存在，这种存在超越了“自然的”人的全部的理解力和理性。他所想到的，是那种“随着意思吹，你听见风的声音，却不知道从哪儿来，往哪儿去”的“精神”——这种精神正是由于这个缘故，才并不只为锡安山或者盖里济姆山所拥有，而对于这种精神的崇拜也仅仅属于那些本身就“处于精神与真理之中”的人。因此，圣约翰的这句话尽管显然完全是“理性的”含义，但是它本身却是对圣经的上帝观念的非理性因素的最强烈和最清晰的指称。[①]

① 请将本章与我的《神国与人子》(*Reich Gottes und Menschensohn*)一书相对照。

CHAPTER XII

The Numinous In Luther

In Catholicism the feeling of the numinous is to be found as a living factor of singular power. It is seen in Catholic forms of worship and sacramental symbolism, in the less authentic forms assumed by legend and miracle, in the paradoxes and mysteries of Catholic dogma, in the Platonic and neo-Platonic strands woven into the fabric of its religious conceptions, in the solemnity of churches and ceremonies, and especially in the intimate *rapport* of Catholic piety with mysticism. For reasons already suggested, the mysterious is much less in evidence in the official systems of doctrine, whether Catholic or Protestant. Particularly since the time when the great medieval scholastics (the *theologi moderni*, so called) replaced Plato by Aristotle and welded the latter and his method on to the doctrines of the Church, Catholic orthodoxy has been subjected to a strong rationalizing influence, to which, however, actual living religious practice and feeling never conformed or corresponded. The battle here joined between so-called 'Platonism' and 'Aristotelianism', and in general the long persistent protest against the scholastics, is itself in large part nothing but the struggle between the rational and the non-rational elements in the Christian religion. And the same antithesis is clearly operative as a factor in Luther's protest against Aristotle and the *theologi modemi*.

At that time Plato himself was known (very imperfectly) chiefly through the interpretations—and misinterpretations —of him by Augustine, Plotinus, and Dionysius the Areopagite. Yet it was a true feeling that led the contrasted attitudes of mind to choose the names of Plato and Aristotle

第十二章　路德思想中的神秘

在天主教教义中，对神秘的感受是一种活跃的具有非凡力量的因素。它存在于天主教的各种崇拜形式中以及圣礼的象征主义中，存在于经由传奇与奇迹所表达出的宗教色彩稍弱的形式中，存在于天主教教条的种种矛盾冲突与神话中，存在于被织入宗教概念的体系的柏拉图主义与新柏拉图主义之中，存在于教堂与宗教仪式的庄严肃穆之中，尤其是存在于天主教的虔敬与神秘主义之间的亲密关系之中。由于已经提及的原因，这种神秘性在官方的教义系统中，无论是天主教还是新教，都很不明显。特别是自从伟大的中世纪经院哲学家(即所谓的神学思想家)以亚里士多德取代了柏拉图，并且将亚里士多德及其方法与教会的教条紧密结合起来以来，天主教的正统就遭受到某种强烈的理性化的影响，然而，实际起作用的宗教实践与宗教感受从来没有遵从或者符合这一影响。此处纠缠在所谓的“柏拉图主义”与“亚里士多德主义”之间的战争，以及总的说来，对于哲学家长期坚持不懈的反抗，它本身在很大程度上不是别的，正是基督教宗教中的理性因素与非理性因素之间的斗争。在路德反对亚里士多德以及那些所谓的神学思想家们时，那种同样的对立面作为一种因素清晰地起着作用。

在那个时候，柏拉图本人主要是通过奥古斯丁、普罗提诺以及雅典大法官狄俄尼西斯等人对他的解释和误解而为人所知的(非常不全面)。然而，那导致两种对立心态去选择柏拉图与亚里士多德的名字作为其论战旗帜的，是一种真实的感受。柏拉图在

as their battle-cries. Plato did indeed make a powerful contribution towards the rationalization of his religion, for according to his *philosophy* the deity had to become identical with the 'Idea of the Good', and consequently something wholly rational and conceivable. But the most remarkable characteristic of Plato's thought is just that he himself finds science and philosophy too narrow to comprise the whole of man's mental life. He has indeed properly no philosophy of religion; he grasps the object of religion by quite different means than those of conceptual thinking, viz. by the 'ideograms' of myth, by 'enthusiasm' or inspiration, 'erôs' or love, 'mania' or the divine frenzy. He abandons the attempt to bring the object of religion into one system of knowledge with the objects of 'science' (έπιστήμη), i. e. reason, and it becomes something not less but greater thereby; while at the same time it is just this that allows the sheer non-rational aspect of it to be so vividly felt in Plato, and indeed vividly expressed as well as felt. No one has enunciated more definitively than this master-thinker that God transcends all reason, in the sense that He is beyond the powers of our conceiving, not merely beyond our powers of comprehension.

'Therefore is it an *impossible* task both to discover the creator and father of this whole universe and to publish the discovery of him in words for all to understand.'①

---

① *Timacus*, 28 *Cτὸν μὸν οὔν ποιητήν καί πατέρα τοῦδε τοῦ παντὸs εὕρεῖν τεέργον καί εὑρόντα είs πάντας άδύνατον λέγειν*. For the non-rational and supra-rational strain in Plato the reader is referred to von Wilamowitz Möllendorff, *Plato*, i. 418: and especially to the splendid passage from Plato's seventh letter: 341 c: 'Concerning these things [sc. ultimate truth] there is not, nor will there be, any treatise written by me. For they do not at all admit of being expounded in writing, as do objects of other [scientific] studies... Only after long, arduous conversance with the matter itself... a light suddenly breaks upon the soul as from a kindled flame, and once born keeps alive of itself... Only to a few men is the exposition of these things of any profit, and they only need a slight indication of them for their discovery.'

将其宗教理性化方面的确做出了影响巨大的贡献，因为按照他的哲学，神必须等同于“关于善的理念”，并且因此，神就变成了某种完全理性的和可以想象的东西。但是，柏拉图思想最显著的特征正在于他本人发现科学与哲学都太过于狭窄，以至于不能包容人类全部的精神生活。柏拉图的确完全没有关于宗教的哲学，他通过大大不同于概念性思维的方式来掌握宗教的对象，即，通过神话的“表意符号”，通过“激情”或者灵感，“厄洛斯”（erôs）或者爱，“癫狂”（mania）或者神性的迷狂来掌握。他摒弃了试图把宗教的对象与科学（ἐπιστήμη）的对象，也就是理性的对象一道纳入一个知识体系的做法，因此这种宗教对象变成了某种比科学对象更加伟大的东西；而与此同时，正是这一点，才使得它的那种纯粹非理性的方面在柏拉图那里被如此生动地感受到，并且如其被感受到的状况一样，被真正生动地表达了出来。没有任何人比这位思想大师更明确地阐明了上帝是超越一切理性的，其意义在于，上帝超越了我们的想象能力，而不仅仅是超越了我们的理解能力。

“因此，不仅要发现这整个宇宙的创造者与父亲，而且要把这种发现以文字表达出来，以便所有的人都能理解，这是一项不可能的任务。”①

① 《蒂迈欧篇》，28（Cτὸν μέν οὖν ποιητήν καί πατέρα τοῦδε τοῦ παντὸς εὑρεῖν τεέργον καί εὑρόντα εἰς πάντας ἀδύνατον λέγειν）。关于柏拉图思想中的非理性与超理性因素，读者可以参考冯·莫伦多夫的《柏拉图》一书（i. 418），特别是摘引自柏拉图第七封信的那一段精彩的话（341c）：“关于这类事（即终极真理），我现在不会，将来也不会写任何东西。因为它们不像其他（科学的）研究的对象那样，根本就不允许在著作中进行详细说明……只有经过长期的、艰辛的熟悉这种事物本身之后……灵魂突然被某种像是来自燃烧着的火焰的光芒所照亮，而这种光芒一旦产生，就能够永久地保持其自身的活力……只是对于很少的人来说，对这些事物的阐释才具有某些益处，而他们只需要一点点的暗示，就足以得出这些发现。”

Aristotle's thought is much more theological than Plato's, but his temper is far less religious; and at the same time his theology is absolutely rationalistic. And this contrast between the two is repeated among those who profess themselves 'Platonists' or 'Aristotelians'.

Another influence which orthodox doctrine underwent, from the earliest patristic period onwards, and which tended to weaken the nonrational element in religion, came from the acceptance of the ancient theory of the divine *ἀπάθεια* or immunity from passion. The God of Greek, and especially of Stoic, theology was constructed after the ideal of the 'wise man', who achieves this 'apathy' by the overcoming of his 'passions' and 'affections'; and the attempt was now made to assimilate this God to the 'living God' of Scripture. And, as intimated above, an effective if unconscious factor in this contest was the antithesis between the non-rational and the rational aspects of the deity. Lactantius, in his treatise De *Ira Dei*, illustrates particularly strikingly this fight against the God of the philosophers. He uses the same wholly rational terms, taken from man's emotional life, as do his opponents, but raises them to a higher power, so that he makes God, as it were, a gigantic mind, quick with an immense vitality. But whoever in this way contends for the 'living God' is at the same time contending unwittingly for the divine in God, that which cannot be reduced to idea, world-order, moral order, principle of being, or purposive will. And many or Lactantius' own expressions point of themselves to something beyond. Thus, quoting Plato, he says: 'Quid omnino sit Deus, non esse quaerendum: quia nec inveniri possit nec enarrari.'① He is in general fond of emphasizing the *incombrehensibilitas*

① Ed. Fritzsche, p. 227: 'We ought not to ask what God is altogether; for it can neither be discovered by any nor stated in words.'

亚里士多德的思想要比柏拉图的思想更富于神学性，但是其特征却不如柏拉图思想更具宗教性；并且同时，他的神学完全是理性主义的。二人之间的这种差异也反复出现于那些自称为“柏拉图主义者”或者“亚里士多德主义者”的人们中间。

从最早的教父时期以来，正统教义所受到的另一个影响来自人们接受了古代神性的麻木（*ἀπάθεια*）或者不动情的理论——这一影响倾向于削弱宗教中的非理性因素。希腊神学的，尤其是斯多葛派神学的上帝，是按照那种关于“智者”，即那些通过克服他的“激情”与“倾向”而达到这种“冷漠”的人的理想而构建起来的；而这一意图现在却将这一上帝同化为《圣经》中的那个“活的上帝”。而正如上面所明确阐释的，在这场论战中，无意识因素的有效条件正在于它是神性的非理性与理性方面之间的对立。拉克坦修斯在其《论上帝的愤怒》（*De Ira Dei*）一文中，特别突出地描绘了这场反对哲学家的上帝的论战。他和他的论敌一样，采用了那些取自人的情感生活的同样完全理性的术语，但是，他将这些术语提高到了一种更大的力量，因此他使得上帝宛如一种巨大的力量，躁动着一种无限的生命力。但是，无论谁以这种方式为“活的上帝”而论争，他就会同时无意地为上帝中的神性而论争，这种上帝中的神性是不能被归纳为理念、世界秩序、道德秩序、存在原则或者有目的的意志的。而拉克坦修斯自己的许多表述本身，也指向了某种超越的东西。因此，若柏拉图所言：“我们不应追问上帝整个是什么，因为这一点既不能为任何人观察到，也无法用语言加以表述，（Quid omninosit Deus，non esse quaerendum：quia nec inveniri possit nec enarrari.）。”[①]总体上来

① 见弗莱彻版，第 227 页：“我们不应追问上帝整个是什么，因为这一点既不能为任何人观察到，也无法用语言加以表述，。”

of God: 'quem nec aestimare sensu valeat humana mens nec eloqui lingua mortalis. Sublimior enim ac maior est, quam ut possit aut cogitatione hominis aut sermone comprehendi.'① He is fond of the expression *maiestas Dei*, and blames the philosophers for misjudging the 'unique majesty' of God. And he feels the *tremendum* in the *maiestas* when he asserts that God 'is wroth', and demands 'awe' as a fundamental characteristic of religion when he says: 'Ita fit, ut religio et maiestas et honor *metu* constet. Metus autem non est, ubi nullus irascitur.'② He says that a God who cannot be angry cannot love either: and a God that knows neither love nor anger would be *immobilis* and not the 'Deus *vivus*', the *living* God of Scripture.

This ancient battle of Lactantius against the *deus philosophorum* comes to life again in the Middle Ages in Duns Scotus's battle for the God of 'willing', as opposed to the God of 'being', and for the validity of volition as an essential in religion, as opposed to cognition. And the non-rational elements which are still latent in Duns Scotus break out openly in Luther in a whole series of some of his most characteristic thoughts.

---

① Ibid., p. 116: '[God] whom the human mind has no power to appraise, nor tongue of mortals to utter. For he is too sublime and too great to be grasped in the thought or the speech of man.'

② 'Thus it comes that religion and majesty and honour depend upon fear. But there is no fear where none is angry.'

说,拉克坦修斯喜欢强调上帝的不可理解性:“人的心灵既没有评价上帝的能力,也没有表达的言辞。因为上帝太崇高、太伟大,以至人的思想和语言都把握不住他。(quem nec aestimare sensu valeat humana mens nec eloqui lingua mortalis. Sublimior enim ac maior est, quam ut possit aut cogitatione hominis aut sermone comprehendi.)”①他喜欢威严的上帝这个表达方式,而责备那些哲学家们错误地判断了上帝的“独一无二的权威”。当他断言上帝是“值得”,并且要求作为一种宗教的根本特征而“敬畏”时,他在威严中感受到了畏惧,他说:“因此这就很清楚,宗教、权威与荣耀都建立在恐惧之上,但是,哪儿没有愤怒,哪儿就不会有恐惧。(Ita fit, ut religio et maiestas et honor metu constet. Metus autem non est, ubi nullus irascitur.)”②他认为,一个不能发怒的上帝同样也不能去爱:一个既不知道爱又不知道愤怒的上帝将会是静态的,而不是“动态的”,即《圣经》中的那个活的上帝。

这场拉克坦修斯反对那种哲学家的上帝的古老的战争在中世纪,在邓斯·司各脱为了作为“意愿”的上帝(对立与所谓一种“存在”的上帝),为了作为宗教本质的意志的有效性(对立于对意志的认知)的战斗中再次重现出来。而那种在邓斯·司各脱那里还仍然处于潜在状态的非理性因素,在路德那里公然地迸发出来,成为路德思想的整个系列的某些最有特色的思想。

---

① 同前,第116页:“人的心灵既没有评价上帝的能力,也没有表达的言辞。因为上帝太崇高、太伟大,以至人的思想和语言都把握不住他。”

② “因此这就很清楚,宗教、权威与荣耀都建立在恐惧之上,但是,哪儿没有愤怒,哪儿就不会有恐惧。”

This aspect of Luther's religion was later tacitly expunged, and is to-day readily dismissed as 'not the authentic Luther', or as 'a residuum of the scholastic speculations of the nominalists'. But, if that is so, it is strange that this 'residuum of Scholasticism' exercised such a power in Luther's own mental life as it palpably did. In point of fact this is not a 'residuum' .at all, but beyond all question the mysterious background of his religious life, obscure and 'uncanny', and to estimate it in all its power and profundity we need to abstract the lucid bliss and joyfulness of Luther's faith in the divine grace, and to see this faith in relation to the background of that mysterious experience on which it rests. It matters not from what source, whether 'nominalism' or the traditional teaching of his Order, his consciousness was first stirred; we have in any case in Luther the numinous consciousness at first hand, stirred and agitated through its typical 'moments', as we have come to know them. It is a corroboration that these 'moments' appear in Luther in their completed series, and so point back to the common basis that unites them all.

1. We are not here concerned with the many strands, strong at the outset, weaker later, but never altogether dis-appearing, that connect him with mysticism. Nor are we concerned with the surviving effects of the 'numinous' element of the Catholic worship in his doctrine of the Eucharist, which cannot be wholly derived either from his doctrine of the forgiveness of sins or from his deference to the written word of scripture. Let us rather consider Luther's *mirae speculationes* upon the 'unrevealed' in God in contrast to the *facies Dei revelata* (revealed face of God), upon the *divina maiestas* and the *omnipotentia Dei* in contrast to His *gratia*, as he treats of them in his work *De Servo Arbitrio*. The investigation as to how far Luther took over 'doctrines' from Scotus does not amount to much; they stand in most intimate connexion with his own innermost religious life, of which they are a

在路德的宗教中的这种非理性的方面后来被悄然抹去,而且在今天,这一方面也很容易被当做“并非真正的路德”或者作为“唯名论者的经院哲学反思的残余”而抛弃掉。但是,如果那样的话,这种“经院哲学的残余”在路德本人的精神生活中起着如此明显的、有利的作用,那可真是怪事了。事实上,这一方面根本就不是什么“残余”,而正是路德的宗教生活的晦涩而又“离奇”的神秘背景,要全面评价这一背景的力度与深度,我们需要把路德因信仰神的恩赐而得到的明晰的至福与快乐概括出来,而且要联系到信仰所栖居其上的那种神秘经验的背景来考察这种信仰。至于究竟路德的宗教意识最初是从哪里被激发出来的,是从“唯名论”还是他所在的阶层接受的传统教育,这并不重要;我们随时随地都能够在路德那里看到第一手的神秘意识,如我们知道的那样,这种意识通过它的那些典型的“要素”而被激发起来。这些“要素”以其完整的系列在路德那里表现出来,并由此向回指向那将它们全部统一起来的共同的基础,这是一个确证的事实。

1. 我们在这里并不关注那些将路德和神秘主义联系起来的线索,它们初始强劲,继而疲弱,但是从来都不会完全消失。我们也不关注在路德关于圣餐的教义中所残存下来的对天主教信仰的“神秘”因素的影响,这种影响既不能完全从他关于宽恕原罪的教条、也不能从他对《圣经》文本的顺从得来。让我们更进一步地思考一下路德关于上帝中被遮掩的部分对于 *facies Dei revelata*(上帝的开显面),关于神圣的威严与全能的神对上帝的恩赐的神奇的思考,就像他在其著作《论对意志的束缚》(*De Servo Arbitrio*)中对他们所做的思考。对于路德在多大程度上接受了司各脱的“教义”的调查并没有多大意义;这些教义与他自己最内在的

genuine first-hand utterance, and should be examined as such. Luther himself guarantees expressly that he does not teach such things merely as subjects of dispute in the schools or as philosophical deductions and corollaries, but because they are a central part of the religious experience of the Christian, who must know them in order to have faith and to have life. He rejects the cautious foresight of Erasmus's view, that such things should at least be withheld from the common people, preaching them himself in public sermons (for example, upon Exodus, in reference to the hardening of Pharaoh's heart) and writing them in his letter to the men of Antwerp. And again, just before his death, speaking of his book *De Servo Arbitrio*, in which these ideas stand clearly expressed, Luther acknowledges that nothing he wrote was so truly his own.

Is this borne out in his general teaching? His words in the *Great Catechism*, 'To have a God is nothing else than to trust Him from the heart', might seem to imply the negative. And certainly to Luther God is He who 'overbrims with pure goodness'. Yet this same Luther knows depths and abysses in the Godhead that make his heart despond, from which he flees for refuge to the 'Word', like a 'hare to his cleft in the rocks', flees, it may be, to the Sacrament or to absolution, or to the comforting official pronouncements of Dr. Pommeranus, but in general no less to every word of comfort or promise in the Psalms and the Prophets. But that before which his soul quails again and again in awe is not merely the stern Judge, demanding righteousness—for He is wholly a 'God of revelation'—but rather at the same time God in His 'unrevealedness', in the awful majesty of His very God-

宗教生活有着极为密切的关系,同时它们又是他这种最内在的宗教生活的真实而直接的表达,因此这些教义应当被如此考察。路德本人曾清楚明白地保证,他不会把这些教义在学校中仅仅当做讨论的主题或者当做哲学的演绎与推论来教授,但是,因为它们是基督徒的宗教经验的核心部分,基督徒必须知道它们以便拥有信仰、拥有生活。他反对伊拉斯谟的那种审慎的深谋远虑,即认为这些教义至少不应被普通民众知晓的看法,并且在公开的布道中亲自讲述它们(例如,在讲到《出埃及记》时,就讲到法老的心肠是如何变硬的),还在写给安特卫普的人们的信中谈论这些教义。除此之外,就在他去世之前,在谈到他的《论对意志的束缚》一书时——这些观念在这本书中得到了清晰表述——路德承认,在他所写的所有著作中,没有什么比得上这本书更真实地表达了他自己的观点。

这一点在他的一般教义中得到了验证了么?他在《大教义问答》一书中所说的“拥有上帝无非是要从心底里相信他”,看起来意味着否定的回答。对于路德来说,的确,上帝就是“充溢着纯粹的善”。然而,同样是这个路德,他也知道存在于神性中的深渊,这种深渊使他内心沮丧,由此他逃向“圣言”寻求避难,就像一只“兔子或许会逃向它筑于岩石罅隙中的窝”,他逃向了圣礼或者是赦免,或者是逃向波麦兰努斯博士的那些安慰性的官方声明,但是,总体上说来,他并不在圣歌和先知的每一个安慰性的或者承诺性的话语中寻求逃避。但是,那种使得他的灵魂在其面前陷入敬畏之中一再感到恐惧的,并不单单是那要求正义的严厉的最高审判——因为上帝完全是一个“启示的上帝”——但是同时,上帝又处于他的“未开显”之中,处于他真正神性的令人敬畏的威严

head; He before whom trembles not simply the transgressor of the law, but the creature, as such, in his 'uncovered' creaturehood. Luther even ventures to designate this aweinspiring, non-rational character of deity as 'Deus ipse, ut est in sua natura et maiestate'[①] (an assumption which would be in fact a dangerous and erroneous one; for no distinction of the non-rational and the rational aspects of God should imply that the latter is less essential than the former).

The passages relevant in this connexion from Luther's *De Servo Arbitrio* are cited often enough: but to understand the wellnigh daemonic character of this numinous feeling the reader should particularly note the effect of the following passage from Luther's sermon on Exod. xx. The preacher leaves no means untried to bring out effectively the element of numinous horror in his text:

Yea, for the world it seemeth as though God were a mere silly yawner, with mouth ever agape, or a cuckold, who lets another lie with his wife and feigneth that he sees it not.

But He assaileth a man, and *hath such a delight* therein that He is of His jealousy and wrath impelled to *consume* the wicked.

Then shall we learn how that God is a consuming fire...

That is then the consuming, devouring fire... Wilt thou sin? Then will He *devour thee up*... For God is a fire, that consumeth, devoureth, rageth; verily He is your undoing, as fire consumeth a house and maketh it dust and ashes.

And in another place:

Yea, He is more terrible and frightful than the Devil. For He

① 'God Himself, as He is in his own very nature and majesty.'

之中;他就在这样的上帝面前颤抖着,不单纯是作为一个律法的违反者,而是作为一个被造物,同样地,处于其"未加遮掩的"被造性之中。路德甚至大胆地将神的这种引起敬畏的非理性因素解释为"Deus ipse, ut est in sua natura et maiestate"①(这种假定事实上是一种危险而错误的提法;因为在上帝的非理性方面和理性方面之间的区别并不意味着后者没有前者重要)。

在路德的《论对意志的束缚》一书中与之有关系的段落已经被引用得够多了:但是要理解这种神秘感受的几乎是魔鬼般的特征,读者需要特别注意一下段落的作用,这些段落出自路德关于《出埃及记》第20章的布道。在这段话中,路德采用了所有的手段有效地阐发了这种神秘恐惧的因素:

的确,在这个世界看来,似乎上帝只是一个咧着嘴、傻乎乎地睡大觉的人,或者说是一个任凭别人与自己老婆睡觉却佯装不见的戴绿帽子的人。

但是上帝攻击人并以此为乐,因为上帝怀有不得不毁灭恶人的那种妒嫉和愤怒。

这样我们就将认识到何以这个上帝是一团毁灭之火……这是毁灭性的、吞噬一切的火焰……他将使你的罪过退缩? 不,他会整个地将你吞噬。因为上帝是一团毁灭的、吞噬的和狂暴的火焰;他确实是你的毁灭,就像火焰毁灭一所房屋,并将其变成灰烬一样。

在另一个地方,路德写道:

的确,他(上帝)比魔鬼还要恐怖和可怕。因为他与我们打交

---

① "上帝作为其本身,是处于他自己的真实本质和威严之中的。"

dealeth with us and bringeth us to ruin with power, smiteth and hammereth us and payeth no heed to us... In His majesty He is a consuming fire ... For therefrom can no man refrain: if he thinketh on God aright, his heart in his body is struck with terror... Yea, as soon as he heareth God named, he is filled with trepidation and fear. ①

It is the absolute numen, felt here partially in its aspect of *maiestas* and *tremendum*. And the reason I introduced these terms above to denote the one side of the numinous experience was in fact just because I recalled Luther's own expressions, and borrowed them from his *divina maiestas* and *metuenda voluntas*, which have rung in my ears from the time of my earliest study of Luther. Indeed, I grew to understand the numinous and its difference from the rational in Luther's *De Servo Arbitrio* long before I identified it in the *qādôsh* of the Old Testament and in the elements of 'religious awe' in the history of religion in general.

One must have beheld these gulfs and abysses in Luther to understand aright how significant it is that it is the same man who, on the other hand, endeavours to put the whole of Christianity into a confiding faith. The same contrast noted above in the religion of the Gospel and in the paradoxes of the 'faith in God the Father', recurs in the religious experience of Luther, but in unexampled intensity. That it is the *unapproachable* which becomes approachable, the *Holy One* who is pure goodness, that it is '*Majesty*' which makes itself familiar and intimate—there is the inwardness of the matter,

---

① *Vide* the Erlangen edition of Luther's works, xxxvi, pp. 210 ff., 222, 231, 237; xxxv, p. 167; xlvii, p. 145; l, p. 200.

道并以强力把我们带向毁灭，他打击我们并对我们毫不在乎……在其威严中，上帝是一团毁灭的火焰……因为没有任何人能够从那里避免：如果他正确地思考上帝，他的内心深处就会受到恐惧的袭击……的确，一旦他听到提起上帝的名字，心中立刻就充满了战栗与恐惧。①

这就是在此处部分地从其威严和恐惧的方面所感受到的那种绝对的神秘。而我要援引上述文字以便标示出那种神秘经验的一个方面的原因，事实上就在于我想起了路德自己的表达，并从他的神圣的威严和可怕的意志中借用了它们，这些东西从我最初研究路德时就一直在我的耳边回响。的确，在我将神秘等同于《旧约》中的 *qādôsh* 和一般的宗教历史上的"宗教敬畏"的诸多因素之前很久，我就在路德的《论对意志的束缚》一书中，逐渐理解了神秘及其与理性的区别。

人们必须看到在路德心中的这些深渊，以便正确地理解这件事情有多么重大的意义，即正是这同一个路德，在另一方面，他致力于将整个的基督教放置于易于相信的信仰之中。上面所提到的那种存在于福音的宗教中和存在于"天父信仰"这一悖论中的同样的冲突，在路德的宗教经验中重现出来，但却是处于一种前所未有的强烈程度中。那不可接近者变成了可接近者，即变成了作为至善的神圣者，原本的"威严"将自身变得和蔼可亲了——此处有事情的内在性，而这种内在性在路德之后的诸学派的片面的教义中只得到

① 参见艾尔南根版的《路德著作集》第 36 卷第 210 页，222 页，231 页，237 页；第 35 卷第 167 页；第 57 卷第 145 页；第 50 卷第 200 页。

and this finds only very dubious expression in the subsequent one-sided doctrine of the schools, where the mystical character of the 'wrath'—which is of the essence of 'holiness' infused with that of 'goodness'—is referred simply to the righteousness of God, and taken thus as righteous anger or indignation.

2. Once the numinous consciousness has been aroused, it is to be expected, seeing that it is a unity, that one of its 'moments' will be found to be bound up with the rest. In the case of Luther we find next after this element of 'wrath' the numinous manifesting itself in the set of ideas which we may fairly call those of Job. The Book of Job, as was seen above, is not so much concerned with the *awefulness* of the majesty of the numen as with its *mysteriousness*; it is concerned with the non-rational in the sense of the irrational, with sheer paradox baffling comprehension, with that which challenges the 'reasonable' and what might be reasonably expected, which goes directly against the grain of reason. To this place belong Luther's violent onslaughts upon the 'whore Reason', which must seem grotesque to anyone who has not rightly grasped the problem of the non-rational element in the idea of God. But certain set phrases, constantly recurring in Luther and very typical of him, are specially significant in this connexion, as showing the strong feeling he had for the non-rational aspect of the divine nature in general. The most interesting passages are not those in which he gives this feeling currency in the small change of popular edification, that soothes itself with the thought that God's ways are too high for us men; but those in which he lays hold of some startling paradox. He can indeed tell in quite a homely and popular way 'how strange a lord our God is', and refer this to the fact that God does not esteem or count as the world counts, and that He disciplines us by the strange ways of His guidance. Such expressions are of general currency; but others—and these the more characteristic—strike a loftier

了非常不确定的表达，在这些学派的片面教义中，“愤怒”的神秘的特征——那种浸渍着“善”的“神圣”的本质——仅仅被看作是上帝的公正性，并且被当作是正当的愤怒或者义愤。

2. 一旦神秘的意识被激发出来，因为它是一个统一体，那么，它的任何一个“因素”都会被发现是与其余的因素紧紧联系在一起的，这就是可以预料到的了。在路德的例子中，紧邻着“愤怒”这一因素，我们发现神秘将其自身展现于一系列我们应当公正地归之于约伯的观念中。如我们前面所看到的，《约伯记》与其说关涉神秘的威严的那种敬畏，不如说关涉它的神秘性；它在无理性的意义上关涉非理性，关涉阻碍理解的纯粹悖论，关涉那些向“合理的”或者能够被合理地预期的东西挑战的东西，这些东西直接地反对任何丝毫的理性。路德就是在这里向着“理性娼妓”发起猛烈的攻击的，这一点对于那些没有正确地把握上帝观念中的非理性因素这一问题的人来说，必定会显得荒诞不经。但是，某些在路德那里反复出现的并且非常具有路德特色的确定用语在这个关系中显得尤其重要，因为它们显示出了路德对于一般神性的本质的非理性方面所具有的强烈情绪。最有趣的并不是那些他在其中以稍作变动的大众教诲方式表达了这种情感流的段落，这种情感以上帝的行为方式对人类来说是高不可攀的这一思想来安抚自己，而是那些在其中他抓住了令人吃惊的悖论的段落。的确，路德能够以非常家常的通俗的方式讲述“我们的上帝是多么奇怪的主”，并指出这一事实，即上帝并不以世俗社会所看重的东西为重，他以奇特的引导方式来训练我们。这样一些表达方式是通用的；而另外一些，即那些更具特色的，则奏响了更加

note. God is altogether 'mysteriis suis et iudiciis impervestigabilis' ('beyond tracking out in His mysteries and His judgements'), displays—as in Job—His 'vera maiestas' 'in metuendis mirabilibus et iudiciis suis incomprehensibilibus' ('in His fearful marvels and incomprehensible judgements'), is in His essence hidden away from all reason, knows no measure, law, or aim, and is verified in the paradox: 'ut ergo fidei locus sit, opus est, ut omnia, quae creduntur, abscondantur' ('in order, therefore, that there may be a place for faith, all the things that are believed must be hidden away'). And his concern is not simply to note this as an inconceivable paradox, to acknowledge it and bow before it, but to recognize that such a paradox is essential to the nature of God and even its distinguishing characteristic.

Si enim talis esset eius iustitia, quae humano captu posset iudicari esse iusta, *plane non esset divina et* nihilo differret ab humana iustitia. At cum sit Deus verus et unus, deinde totus incomprehensibilis et inaccessibilis humana ratione, par est, immo necessarium est, ut et iustitia sua sit incomprehensibilis. ①

Theology gives expression to its perplexed endeavour to find a name for the elements of the non-rational and the mysterious

① 'For were His justice such as could be adjudged as just by the human understanding it were manifestly not divine, and would differ in nothing from human justice. But since God is true and single, yea in His entirety incomprehensible and inaccessible to human reason, it is right, nay it follows necessarily, that His justice also is incomprehensible.'

崇高的旋律。上帝是完全“隐藏于他的神秘与判决中而无法被追索的”(mysteriis suis et iudiciis impervestigabilis),就像在约伯那里一样,上帝“在其可怕的奇迹和无法理解的判断中”(in metuendis mirabilibus et iudiciis suis incomprehensibilibus)展示了他的“真正的威严”(vera maiestas),上帝在其本质上不为任何理性所知晓,不了解任何尺度、法则和目标,而只是在悖论中被确证:“以便为信仰留下地盘,所有信仰的东西都是必须被隐匿起来的东西。”(ut ergo fidei locus sit, opus est, ut omnia, quae creduntur, abscondantur)路德所关注的,并不仅仅是指出它是一个无法想象的悖论,从而去接受它并且拜倒在它的面前,而是要认识到,这样的悖论对于上帝的本性是本质性的,甚至是上帝本性的区别性的特征。

Si enim talis esset eius iustitia, quae humano captu posset iudicari esse iusta, *plane non esset divina et* nihilo differret ab humana iustitia. At cum sit Deus verus et unus, deinde totus incomprehensibilis et inaccessibilis humana ratione, par est, immo necessarium est, ut et iustitia sua sit incomprehensibilis. ①

神学要表达出它的那种不知所措的努力,去为那些表现在令人反感的教义中的非理性的和神秘的因素寻找一个名字,即上帝

① 因为,如果上帝的公正仅仅通过人的理智就可以判明为正义,那它就显然并不是神圣的,它与人的正义没什么差别。但是,因为上帝是真实独特的,它的完整性是人的理智所无法理解的和难于接近的,所以下面一点也必然是对的,即:上帝的正义也是无法理解的。

in the repulsive doctrine that God is *exlex* (outside the law), that good is good because God wills it, instead of that God wills it because it is good, a doctrine that results in attributing to God an absolutely fortuitous will, which would in fact turn Him into a 'capricious despot'. These doctrines are specially prominent in the theology of Islam, and this can be immediately understood if the two positions we maintain are sound, viz. that such doctrines are really perplexed expressions of the non-rational, numinous side of the divine nature, and that this is altogether the preponderant aspect in Islam. And we find them also in Luther in the same connexion. In this very fact, however, lies the excuse for doctrines in themselves so blasphemous and horrible: they are caricatures prompted by a deficient psychology and a mistaken choice of expressions, and not by any disregard of the absoluteness of moral values.

3. From the point of view already considered in detail it will be seen that, with such feelings as a basis, it was inevitable that the doctrine of predestination would in due course make its appearance in Luther's religion. And in his case we do not need, as we did in the case of Paul, to *postulate* the close inner connexion between this doctrine and the numinous temper, for in the *De Servo Arbitrio* it is palpably evident. The one explicitly depends upon the other, and the inward bond of union between the two is so unmistakable that this treatise of Luther's becomes a sort of psychological key to related phases of religious experience.

It is only occasionally that these purely numinous elements in Luther's religious consciousness are displayed so strongly and forcibly as in the treatise *De Servo Arbitrio*. But in his battles with '*desperatio*' and with Satan, in his constantly recurring religious catastrophes and fits of melancholy, in his wrestlings for grace, perpetually renewed, which bring him to the verge of mental disorder, in all these there are

是 *exlex*（在法则之外），也就是说，善之为善，是因为上帝愿意为善，而不是因为它是善，上帝才愿意去做，这样一种教义的结果就在于赋予了上帝一种绝对偶然的意志，而这种意志事实上会把上帝转变成一个“反复无常的暴君”。这些教义在伊斯兰神学中尤其突出，而只要我们所主张的这两点成立，这个问题立刻就能被理解，即，这些教义真正是对非理性——这一神性本质的神秘方面的令人困惑的表达，并且，这种表达在伊斯兰宗教中完全是占据优势的方面。我们在路德的宗教中也发现了这同样的关系。然而，正是在这一事实中，为那些就其本身来说是渎神的和可恶的教义提供了借口：它们是拙劣的模仿，是由不完善的心理学和对表达的错误选择所引发的，而不是由任何漠视道德价值的绝对性所导致的。

3. 从已经很详尽地讨论过的观点来看，我们会发现，以这些感觉作基础，预定论的教义必定会在适当的时间出现在路德的宗教中。在路德的例子中，我们不需要像在保罗的例子中那样，在这种教义与神秘性质之间去假定某种密切的内在的联系，因为在《论对意志的束缚》一书中，这种联系表现得非常明显。一个方面明确地依赖于另一个方面，而二者之间的内在联系是如此得明白无误，以至路德的这一篇论著变成了开启宗教经验的相关阶段的心理学的钥匙。

路德宗教意识中的这些纯粹神秘的因素就像在他的《论对意志的束缚》一书中表现得如此有力如此强烈，这只是偶然发生的。在他与“绝望”以及撒旦的战斗中，在他持续地反复出现的宗教悲怆与突发的忧郁中，在他为了获得不断更新的神恩的奋斗中——这种奋斗将他带到了精神错乱的边缘，在所有这一切中，路德的

more than merely rational elements at work in his soul.

Moreover, even when he is speaking solely in rational terms of judgement, punishment, and the wrath of God, we must, if we are to recapture the real Luther in these expressions, hear sounding in them the profoundly non-rational strain of 'religious awe'. For this wrath of God also has often, perhaps has always, something in it of that fury of Yahweh, that *ὀργή* of the numen.

4. This circumstance suggests a further point. The expressions 'unrevealed God' and '*tremenda maiestas*' manifestly repeated only those 'moments' of the numinous which we found first in our analysis of it (p. 13), especially the *tremendum*, the *daunting* aspect of the numinous. What of that of 'fascination' in Luther? Is it missing altogether, to be replaced merely by the rational attributes of trustworthiness and love and the corresponding element in the mind of the worshipper, viz. faith and trustfulness? No, beyond all question it is not. Only, the element of fascination is in Luther wholly interwoven with these rational elements and comes to utterance with them and in them. This can be felt forcibly in the boisterous, almost Dionysiac, blissfulness of his experience of God.

Christians are a blissful people, who can rejoice at heart and sing praises, stamp and dance and leap for joy. That is well pleasing to God and doth our heart good, when we trust in God and find in Him our pride and our joyfulness. Such a gift should only kindle a fire and a light in our heart, so that we should never cease dancing and leaping for joy.

Who will extol this enough or utter it forth? It is neither to be expressed or conceived.

If thou feelest it truly in the heart, it will be such a great thing

灵魂深处起作用的绝不仅仅是理性的因素。此外,甚至在他单单是谈论到审判、惩罚以及上帝的愤怒这些理性的术语时,如果我们要再次体验到在这些表述中的真正的路德,我们就必须听到那个回响在这些表述中的那种完全非理性的"宗教敬畏"的旋律。因为这种上帝的愤怒也经常——或许总是——包含有某种耶和华的盛怒,即神秘的愤怒(ὀργή)。

4. 这种情况还暗示了更深的一点。"未开显的上帝"与"可怕的威严"这些表达方式明显重复的,仅仅是神秘所包含的那些"要素",我们最初是在对神秘的分析(第 13 页),尤其是在分析畏惧——神秘的令人畏缩的方面时遇到了这些"要素"。在路德那里,"沉迷"的要素又是些什么呢?它是否完全缺乏这些要素,而只是用崇拜者心中的信赖、爱以及相关因素的理性性质,也就是信仰和信任来取代了呢?不,毫无疑问,绝非如此。只是在路德的宗教那里,沉迷的因素完全与这些理性因素交织在一起,与这些理性因素一道并且通过这些理性因素表达出来。这一点可以在路德对上帝的体验中所产生出来的那种狂烈的,几乎是酒神式的极乐中被有力地感受到。

基督徒是有福的人,他们能够由衷地欢欣和唱颂赞歌,并因为欢乐而手舞足蹈。如果我们信任上帝并在上帝那里找到我们的自豪与快乐,那就不仅能取悦上帝,而且对我们的心灵有也大有好处。只有这样一种天分才能在我们心中燃起火光,所以我们应永远为欢乐而雀跃。

谁能充分赞美这种天分或进一步把它表达出来呢?这种天赋是既不可表达又不可想象的。

如果你在心里确实感受到这种天赋,那么,对你来说至关重

to thee that thou wilt rather be silent than speak aught of it. ①

Here should be borne in mind what was remarked earlier (pp. 46 ff.) respecting the interweaving of the non-rational with the rational and the consequently deepened import of rational expressions. As the awe-inspiring character of the transcendent is comprised in the God of sternness and punishment and justice, so is its bliss-giving character included in the God who 'overbrims with pure goodness'. Indeed it is involved in the 'over-abounding' ('exuberant') and mystical tone of Luther's actual creed. Here, as elsewhere, there is no mistaking his connexion with mysticism. ② Though for Luther faith begins more and more to take the place of 'knowledge' and 'love of God' (*Gottes-Minne*)—which means a marked qualitative alteration of the whole religious temper, as compared with that of mysticism—yet, despite the change, it remains obvious that there are definite features in 'faith', as the term is used by Luther, which justify us in classing it with the mystical ways of response to which it is in apparent contrast, and clearly distinguish it from the *fides* taught by the Lutheran school with its determinate, well-ordered, unmystical temper. 'Faith' for Luther plays the same essential part, *mutatis mutandis*, as 'knowledge' and 'love' for the earlier mystics: it is the unique power of the soul, the *adhaesio Dei*, which *unites* man with God: and 'unity' is the very signature of the mystical. So that when Luther says that faith makes man 'one cake' (*ein Kuche*) with God or Christ, or holds him 'as a ring holds a jewel' (*sicut annulus gemmam*), he is not speak-

① Erlangen ed., xi. 194.

② See Appendix VI.

要的就是:宁愿保持缄默,也不可稍加泄漏。①

在这里,还要记住我们在前面(第46页及以下)所说过的关于非理性与理性的相互交织以及由此带来的理性的表达方式的被深化了的重要性的话语。正如那个超验者所具有的能够激起敬畏的特征被包含在上帝的威严、惩戒以及公正之中一样,这个超验者的赐福的性质也被包含在“充盈着纯粹的善”的上帝之中。的确,它涉及路德的实际信条所具有的那种“过于繁茂的”(“丰富的”)和神秘的色调。在此处与在别的地方一样,路德与神秘主义的关系是明白无误的。② 尽管对于路德来说,信仰开始越来越多地替代“对上帝的知”与“对上帝的爱”(*Gottes-Minne*)——与神秘主义者的观点比较,这意味着整个宗教性质的明显的质的改变——然而,尽管有这些转变,很明显,被路德所使用的“信仰”这一术语有着明确的特征,它使我们有理由将这种信仰与其反应的神秘方式归于一类,这种信仰与反应方式处于明显的对立,并且很显然,经由路德教派以其确定的、秩序井然的、不神秘的性质所教示出来的信念与这种反应方式区分开来了。对路德来说,“信仰”是同等重要的部分,就像“知”与“爱”(*mutatis mutandis*)对于早期的神秘主义者一样:信仰是灵魂的一种独特力量,即接近神的力量,这种力量将人与神联系起来:而“联系”正是神秘的信号。因此,当路德讲到,信仰使人与上帝或者基督成为“一块蛋糕”[1],或者说信仰就像“戒指镶嵌上了一颗宝石”那样掌握了人时,他所说的话并

① 艾尔兰根版,第11卷第194节。

② 参见附录六。

〔1〕 意即一个整体。

ing any more figuratively than when Tauler says the same of love. 'Faith' for Luther, as 'love' for Tauler and the mystics generally, is a something that cannot be exhaustively comprised in rational concepts, and to designate which 'figures' and 'images' are a necessity. To him 'faith' is the centre of the soul—the *fundus animae* or 'basis of the soul' of the mystics —in which the union of man with God fulfils itself. It is at the same time an independent faculty of knowledge, a mystical a *priori* element in the spirit of man, by which he receives and recognizes supra-sensible truth, and in this respect identical with the 'Holy Spirit in the heart' (*Spiritus Sanctus in corde*). 'Faith' is further the 'mighty creative thing' in us and the strongest of *affects*, most closely akin to the Greek 'enthusiasm' (*ἐνθουσιάζεσθαι*). It even takes over all the functions which all 'enthusiasts' from Paul onwards have ascribed to 'the Spirit'; for it is 'faith' that 'transforms us inwardly and brings us forth anew'. In this regard, different as it is in its inner attitude, 'faith' is very similar to the *amor mysticus*. And in the bliss of the 'assurance of salvation' (*certitudo salutis*) that it arouses, and the intensity of Luther's 'childlike faith', we have in a subdued form a recurrence of the 'childhood' feelings of Paul, which go beyond mere comfort of the soul, appeasement of conscience, or feeling of protectedness. All subsequent mystics from Johann Arndt to Spener and Arnold① have always felt these aspects of Luther's inner life to be congenial and akin to their own, and have carefully collected the relevant passages from his writings as a defence against the attacks of the rationalized doctrine of the Lutheran school.

---

① Johann Arndt, 1555-1621; Gottfried Arnold, 1666-1697; Philipp Jacob Spener, 1635-1705: the last-named was one of the founders of 'Pietism' in Germany. (*Trans.*) ‖

不比陶勒尔关于爱所说的同样的话有更多的象征意义。就像“爱”对于陶勒尔以及一般的神秘主义者一样,“信仰”对于路德,是某种不能完全被纳入到理性概念中的东西,而必须用“形象”与“图形”来加以指称。对他来说,“信仰”是灵魂的核心——此所谓神秘主义者的“灵魂的基础”——人与上帝的联合就在这一核心中实现自身。与此同时,信仰又是一种获得知识的独立的能力,是人的精神中的一种神秘的先验的因素,通过它,人得以接收和认识超越感觉的真理,并且在这一点上,它等同于“心中的圣灵”(*Spiritus sanctus in corde*)。“信仰”还是我们心中的“强有力的创造力量”和最强烈的感情,与希腊的“激情”(*ε ̓́νθουσιάξεσθαι*)最为接近。它甚至还涵盖了自从保罗以来所有的“激情主义者”归之于“圣灵”的全部功能;因为那“内在地改变我们并且使我们焕然一新的”,正是“信仰”。在这一点上,不管信仰在其内在的态度上有何不同,它都非常类似于“神秘的爱”(*amor mysticus*)。而且,在有信仰所激发的“确信得救”(*certitudo salutis*)的极乐中,在路德的那种“孩子般的信仰”的强度中,我们再次看到了以一种被抑制的形式出现的保罗的“孩子式的”感受,这种感受超越了灵魂的单纯抚慰、良知的缓和或者得到庇护的感受。所有后来的神秘主义者们,从约翰·阿恩特到斯皮纳和阿诺德[①],都总是感觉到路德的内心生活的这些方面与他们自己的非常类似,并且从路德的著作中仔细地收集了那些相关的段落,来对抗路德学派的理性化了的教义的攻击。

---

① 约翰·阿恩特,1555~1621年;哥特弗雷德·阿诺德,1666~1697年;菲利普·雅可布·斯皮纳,1635~1705年:最后提到的这个人是德国“虔信派”的创始人之一。(英译注)

For in opposition to the 'rationalizations' of the schools the non-rational elements are maintained and fostered in the western mysticism that came to its later flower both on Catholic and Protestant soil. In this, as in Christian mysticism as a whole from its first stirrings, the elements of the non-rational already detailed are easily recognizable, most prominently of all those of 'mystery', 'fascination', and 'majesty'. The element of 'awe', on the other hand, recedes and is subdued; there has never been in the West a mysticism of horror, such as we find in certain kinds of Indian mysticism, both Buddhist and Hindu—in Bhagavad-Gītā, ch. II①—in some forms of the Shiva and Durgā worship, and in the horrible form of Tantrism. Yet, though the *tremendum* element in Christian mysticism is subdued, it is not entirely lacking. It remains a living factor in the *caligo* and the *altum silentium*, in the 'abyss', the 'night', the 'deserts' of the divine nature, into which the soul must descend, in the 'agony', 'abandonment', 'barrenness', *taedium*, in which it must tarry, in the shuddering and shrinking from the loss and deprivation of selfhood and the 'annihilation' of personal identity. Thus Suso writes:

In this inconceivable mountain of the supra-divine Where (the 'height of the divine Majesty transcending substance') there is a precipitousness of which all pure spirits are sensible. Here the Soul enters a secret namelessness, a marvellous alienation. It is the bottomless abyss no creature can sound— . . . the spirit perishes there, to become all-living in the wonders of the Godhead. ②

And he can pray:

---

① See Appendix II.

② Suso, German writings, ed. Denifle, pp. 289 ff.

因为,与各个学派的“理性化处理”相反,非理性因素是在西方神秘主义那里得到了保持与培育,后来同时在天主教和新教的土壤中开出花来。在这一点上,就像在从一开始就是作为一个整体存在的基督教神秘主义中一样,已经详细论述过的这种非理性因素可以很容易很明显地从那些“神秘”、“沉迷”以及“威严”等多有的东西中被认出来。另一方面,“敬畏”的因素则退隐了或者被抑制了;在西方,还从来没有出现过一种关于恐惧的神秘主义,就像我们在某些印度神秘主义(包括佛教和印度教)中,在《薄伽梵歌》(Bhagavad-Gïtā)的第11章[①]中,在对湿婆(Shiva)和杜尔迦(Durgā)的某些崇拜形式中,以及在密宗的恐怖形式中所看到的那样。然而,尽管在基督教神秘主义中,恐惧因素被抑制了,但它并没有完全消失。在黑暗和寂静的苍穹中,在“深渊”中,在“黑夜”中,在灵魂必然陷入的神性的“荒漠”中,在灵魂必将在其中逗留的“痛苦”、“抛弃”、“荒凉”和烦恼中,在因为自我的丢失和被剥夺以及个人同一性的“毁灭”而产生的战栗与萎缩中,恐惧一直都保持为一种活生生的因素。因此,苏索写道:

在这个不可思议的超神性的山上,那里(即那个超越实在的神圣威严的“高处”)存在着一个所有的纯粹精神都能感觉到的峭壁。在此,灵魂进入一个隐秘的无名之所,一个神奇的陌生之地。这是任何被造物都无法谈论的无底深渊——……精神在那里死去,以便在上帝的奇迹之中永生。[②]

而且他祈求道:

---

① 参见附录二。

② 苏索:《德语著作集》,德尼弗尔版,第289页以下。

Ah, woe is me, Thy wrathful countenance is so full of fury.

Thy turning away in anger is so unendurable. Woe is me! And the words of Thy enmity are so fiery, they cleave through heart and soul. ①

This note is familiar also to the later mystics. Thus St. John of the Cross says:

As this clear sight of the divine comes like a violent assault upon the soul to subdue it, the soul feels such anguish in its weakness that all power and breath leave it together, while sense and spirit as though they stood burdened beneath a dark unmeasured load suffer such agony and are oppressed by such deadly fear that the soul would choose death as a mitigation and refreshment. ②

And again:

The fourth kind of anguish is brought into being in the soul... from the Majesty and Glory of God. ' ③

Once more:

Therefore He destroys, crushes and overwhelms (the soul) in such a deep darkness, that it feels as though melted and in its misery destroyed by a cruel death of the spirit. Even as though it were to feel it had been swallowed by some savage beast and buried in the darkness of his belly. ④

But in our Western mysticism the writer in whom the non-rationally 'dreadful' and even the 'daemonic' phase of the numinous remains a most living element is Jakob Böhme. For all his adoption of its motives, Böhme is in his speculation and

---

① Ibid., p. 353.

② St. John of the Cross, *The Ascent of Mount Carmel*.

③ Ibid.

④ Ibid.

啊,我真不幸啊!您那愤怒的面庞充满了狂怒。您在盛怒中转过脸去是多么不可忍受。我真不幸啊!您那带有敌意的话语是那么暴躁,它们简直穿透了我的心和灵魂。①

这种语调对于后来的神秘主义者来说也是熟悉的。十字架圣约翰也这样说:

当神的这一道清澈的目光就像对灵魂的猛烈一击将其制服时,灵魂在虚弱中感受到极度的痛苦,所有的力量和呼吸都离它而去,在这个时候,感觉和精神就像是承载着某种无法衡量的黑暗的重压,经受着这种痛苦,并且被这种致命的恐惧所压迫,以至灵魂宁可选择死亡来作为一种缓解和恢复。②

他又说道:

第四种痛苦被带到了灵魂那里……从上帝的威严与荣耀那里……③

他还说:

因此,上帝是在这样深沉的黑暗中毁灭、粉碎和制服了灵魂,以至灵魂感受到它似乎被熔化了,感受到它处于一种残酷的精神的死亡所摧毁的痛苦中,甚至还感受到它似乎要被某种野兽所吞噬,并且葬身于这只野兽的黑暗的腹脏之中。④

但是,在我们西方的神秘主义中,在其作品中那种非理性地"可怕的"甚至是"魔鬼般的"神秘的阶段还保持为一种最活跃因素的作家,就是雅可布·伯麦(Jakob Böhme)。尽管他采纳了

① 同上,第353页。
② 十字架圣约翰:《登卡麦山》。
③ 同上。
④ 同上。

'theosophy' sharply distinguished from the earlier mysticism. He is at one with this (as represented, for instance, by Eckhart) in aiming at a 'construction' and an understanding of God, and from Him of the world: and, like Eckhart, he finds as a starting-point for his speculation the 'primal bottom', the supra-comprehensible and inexpressible. But this stands to him, not for Being and Above-being, but for Stress and Will; it is not good and above-good, but a suprarational identification of good and evil in an Indifferent, in which is to be found the potentiality for evil as well as for good, and therewith the possibility of the dual nature of deity itself as at once goodness and love on the one hand and fury and wrath on the other. ①If the inventions and comparisons, with whose aid Böhme composes a sort of chemico-physical romance of God, strike us as extremely queer and bizarre, the strange intuitions of the religious feeling underlying them are yet highly significant. They are intuitions of the numinous, and are akin to those of Luther. With Böhme, as with Luther, the

① The 'ferocity' is the origin of Lucifer, in whom the mere potentiality of evil is actualized. It might be said that Lucifer is 'fury', the ὀργή, hypostatized, the *mysterium tremendum* cut loose from the other elements and intensified to *mysterium horrendum*. The roots at least of this may be found in the Bible and the early Church. The ideas of propitiation and ransom are not without reference to Satan as well as to the divine wrath. The rationalism of the myth of the 'fallen angel' does not render satisfactorily the horror of Satan and of the 'depths of Satan' (Rev. ii. 24) and the 'mystery of iniquity' (2 Thess. ii. 7). It is a horror that is in some sort numinous, and we might designate the object of it as the negatively numinous. This also holds good of other religions than that of the Bible. In all religions 'the devilish' plays its part and has its place as that which, opposed to the divine, has yet something in common with it. As such it should be the subject of a special inquiry, which must be an analysis of fundamental feelings, and something very different from a mere record of the 'evolution of the idea of the devil'.

早期神秘主义的动机，但是伯麦在他的思索以及他的"见神论"方面明显地区别于早期的神秘主义。他是与这样一种努力（例如，以艾克哈特为代表）相一致的，这种努力致力于对上帝的"建构"和理解，并通过理解上帝来理解世界：并且，就像艾克哈特一样，伯麦找到了作为他的思索的出发点的"原始基底"，即那种超越理解的、无法表达的东西。但是，这些东西对于伯麦来说，并不是代表着存在或者超越存在，而是压力与意志；并不是善和超越善的，而是善与恶在某种中立中的超越理性的同一，在这种中立中，既能找到善的可能性，也能找到恶的可能性，并且随其，又可以在找到神性自身的同时既是善与爱，又是狂暴与愤怒的二元本性的可能性。[①] 如果这些虚构与比较——伯麦在它们的帮助下构建了一种化学—物理学的上帝的故事——使我们感到极度离奇与怪异，那么，那种隐藏在这些虚构之中的宗教感情的奇怪直觉依然非常具有意义。它们是对于神秘的直觉，并且与路德的感觉相类似。正如对于路德一

① 这种"暴行"是撒旦的根源，撒旦就是把这种纯粹的恶的可能性加以现实化而已。可以说，撒旦就是实体化了的"盛怒"，狂怒，是从其他的因素中分离出来的令人畏惧的神秘，并且被强化到令人恐惧万分的神秘。至少这一现象的根源可以在《圣经》和早期教会中找到。就像与神的忿怒关系一样，抚慰和赎罪的观念并非与撒旦无关。有关"堕落的天使"的神话的理性主义的解释并不能令人满意地说明人们对撒旦与"撒旦的奥义"（《启示录》第2章第24节）的畏惧，和"邪恶所具有的神秘"（《帖撒落尼迦人后书》第2章第7节）。这是一种具有神秘性质的恐惧，我们可以把这种恐惧的对象叫做否定性的神秘。这对于那些完全不同于圣经宗教的其他宗教也是如此。在一切宗教中，"魔鬼"都有它既与神祇相对立，又与神祇相通的作用和地位。魔鬼的这种性质，应成为特殊的研究对象。这种研究应成为对基本感受的分析，应完全不同于那种对"魔鬼观念的进化"的纯粹记录。

non-rational energy and majesty of God and his 'awefulness' appear conceptualized and symbolized as 'Will'. And with Böhme, as with Luther, this is conceived as fundamentally independent of *moral* elevation or righteousness, and as indifferent toward good or evil action. It is rather a 'ferocity', a 'fiery wrath' about something unknown; or, better still, not about anything at all, but Wrath on its own account and without reference to any object; an aspect of character which would be quite meaningless if taken literally in the sense of a real conceivable and apprehensible anger. Who is not directly conscious that it is simply the non-rational element of 'awefulness', the *tremendum*, for which 'wrath', 'fire', 'fury', are excellent ideograms?[①] If such an ideogram is taken as an adequate concept, the result is anthropomorphism, such as mythology illustrates, and the writings of Lactantius (see p. 96). And if speculation follows, based upon such concepts, the result is the pseudo-science of theosophy. For the characteristic mark of all theosophy is just this: having confounded analogical and figurative ways of expressing feeling with rational concepts, it then systematizes them, and out of them spins, like a monstrous web, a 'science of God', which is and remains something monstrous, whether it employs, as Eckhart, the doctrinal terms of scholasticism; or as Böhme, the alchemical substances and mixtures of

① Böhme's disciple, Johann Pordage, has some feeling of this when he writes: 'So hope I then, that you will not be angered with me, if you find that I impute to God acerbity and bitterness, dread, wrath, fire, ... and the like. For even Jakob Böhme found no other words in which to express his exalted *sensation* (*Empfindung*) of God. You must then take all those forms of speech in a high divine sense, far removed from all imperfection' (*Divine and True Metaphysic*, i 166).

样,对于伯麦来说,上帝的非理性的能量与威严,以及他的“威慑力”都是作为“意志”的概念化和象征化而出现的。并且同样正如对于路德那样,对于伯麦来说,这种意志被理解为根本上独立于道德的崇高或者道德的公正,并被视为对善与恶的行为的漠视。它毋宁说是一种“暴行”,一种某种未知事物的“暴怒”;或者更好地形容它,它根本就不是针对任何别的事物,而是针对其自身的缘故,并且与任何别的事物都无关的一种“愤怒”;如果从字面上将其看作是某种真正的可想象的、可理解的愤怒,那么它这个方面的特征就会是毫无意义的。谁不是直接意识到它仅仅是“畏惧”(*tremendum*)的非理性因素,因为“愤怒”、“烈焰”、“狂怒”等不过是极好的表意符号而已呢?① 如果这样一种表意符号被当作一种充分的概念,就会导致如同神话学所阐明的那种拟人化,而拉克坦修斯的著作正是如此(参见第96页)。倘若反思也是建立在这个基础之上,就会导致伪科学的见神论。因为所有的见神论的特点正在于此:他们把表达感觉的类比的和比喻的方式与理性的概念混为一谈,然后将其系统化,并由这些概念旋转编织出一张令人恐惧的网,一种“关于上帝的科学”,它不仅是而且还保留着某种令人恐惧的东西,不管它采用的是经院哲学的教条的术语(如同艾克哈特所作的那样),还是帕拉舍尔萨斯的炼金

① 伯麦的学生约翰·波达格对此也有同样的感受,他写道:“如果你发现我把刻薄、尖酸、恐怖、愤怒以及烈焰等词语加之于上帝身上,那么,希望你不要生我的气。因为甚至连雅可布·伯麦也找不到别的词汇来表达他对上帝的崇高感受(*Empfindung*)。你必须在一种非常高的神圣的意义上来理解这些词汇,以扬弃它们所有的不完善性。”(《神性与真正的形而上学》,第1章第166页)

Paracelsus; or as Hegel, the categories of an animistic logic; or as Mrs. Besant, the elaborate diction of Indian religion. For the history of religion it is not on account of his theosophy that Böhme is interesting, but because in him behind the theosophy the consciousness of the numinous was astir and alive as an element of genuine value: so that herein Böhme was an heir of Luther, preserving what in Luther's own school came to be overlooked and disregarded.

For the Lutheran school has itself not done justice to the numinous side of the Christian idea of God. By the exclusively moral interpretation it gave to the terms, it distorted the meaning of 'holiness' and the 'wrath' of God, and already from the time of Johann Gerhardt and onwards Lutheranism was returning to the doctrine of divine *ἀπάθεια* or passionlessness. More and more it deprived the forms of worship of the genuinely contemplative and specifically 'devotional' elements in them. The conceptual and doctrinal—the ideal of orthodoxy—began to preponderate over the inexpressible, whose only life is in the conscious mental attitude of the devout soul. The Church became a school, and her com6munications, in truth, found a more and more contracted access to the mind, as Tyrrell has put it somewhere, 'through the narrow clefts of the understanding'.

Schleiermacher was the first to attempt to overcome this rationalism, most boldly and uncompromisingly in the rhapsody of his *Discourses*, with less heat and more subdued tone in his *Glaubenslehre* and his theory of the 'feeling of absolute dependence', which in point of fact give a representation—as has been pointed out already—of the first stirring of the feeling of the numinous. It will be a task for contemporary Christian teaching to follow in his traces and again to deepen the rational meaning of the Christian conception of God by permeating it with its non-rational elements.

术及其混合物(如同伯麦所作的那样),是泛灵论逻辑的范畴(如同黑格尔那样),还是印度宗教的精致的措辞(如同贝桑特夫人那样)。对于宗教历史来说,伯麦之所以让人们感兴趣,并不是因为他的见神论,而是在见神论的背后,在伯麦的内心深处,有一种神秘的意识作为一种真正价值的因素在骚动着、活跃着:因此,正是在这一点上,伯麦是路德的继承人,他保留了路德自己的学派所忽视和漠视的东西。

因为路德学派本身对于基督教上帝观念的神秘方面是有失公允的。由于它给予“神圣”、上帝的“愤怒”等概念以纯粹的道德的解释,路德学派曲解了这些术语的含义,并且从约翰·格哈德的时代以来,路德学派就已经开始回到了神的麻木(*ἀπάθεια*)或者不动情的教义上来了。路德学派越来越多地从崇拜的诸多形式中剥去了那些真正沉思冥想的和特别“虔敬”的因素。概念的与教条的成分——正统的理想——便开始超越不可表达的成分,这种不可表达的成分仅仅存在于虔敬的灵魂的有意识的精神态度之中。教会变成了一种学派,而它与心灵之间的交流却实实在在地表现为越来越收缩了,如同特列在某处所说的,“通过狭窄的理解的缝隙”。

在《布道集》(*Discourses*)这部狂想曲中,在其热情远远少于屈服的语调的《教义》(*Glaubenslehre*)一书中,以及在他关于“绝对的依赖感”的理论中——正如我们已经指出的那样,这一理论实际上表现出神秘感最初的骚动——施莱尔马赫是第一个最大胆、也是最坚决地试图克服这种理性主义的人。追寻着施莱尔马赫的道路,并且通过基督教的上帝感念的非理性因素的渗透,再次深化这一概念的理性含义,这将是当代基督教教义的一项任务。

CHAPTER XIII

The Two Processes Of Development

This permeation of the rational with the non-rational is to lead, then, to the deepening of our rational conception of God; it must not be the means of blurring or diminishing it. For if (as suggested at the close of the last chapter) the disregard of the numinous elements tends to impoverish religion, it is no less true that 'holiness', 'sanctity', as Christianity intends the words, cannot dispense with the rational, and especially the clear ethical elements of meaning which Protestantism more particularly emphasizes in the idea of God. To get the full meaning of the word 'holy' as we find it used in the New Testament (and religious usage has established it in the New Testament sense to the exclusion of others), we must no longer understand by 'the holy' or 'sacred' the merely numinous in general, nor even the numinous at its own highest development; we must always understand by it the numinous completely permeated and saturated with elements signifying rationality, purpose, personality, morality. It is in this combined meaning that we retain and apply the term 'holy' in our subsequent chapters. But that the course of the historical development may be clearly understood, we venture first to recapitulate our view upon this matter as explicitly as possible.

That which the primitive religious consciousness first apprehends in the form of 'daemonic dread', and which, as it further unfolds, becomes more elevated and ennobled, is in origin not something rational or moral, but something distinct, non-rational, an object to which the mind

第十三章　两种发展过程

那么，这种非理性对理性的渗透会导致对我们有关上帝的理性概念的深化，它当然不是模糊或者减少上帝概念的理性方面的手段。因为，如果（如同在上一章的结尾处所暗示的那样）对神秘因素的漠视会导致宗教的贫困，那么，同样真实的是，“神圣”、“圣洁”作为基督教所意谓的词汇不能免除理性的东西，尤其是不能免除新教在上帝观念上所特别强调的那种含义的清晰的伦理因素。要想把握到我们所发现的使用在《新约》中的“神圣”一词的全部含义（宗教的用法使它只是确立了《新约》的意义而排斥了别的意义），我们绝不能再把“神圣”或者“神圣的”仅仅理解为一般的神秘了，甚至也不能把它理解为在其最高发展阶段上的神秘；我们必须总是把“神圣”理解为渗透并且饱含着那些意味着理性、目的、人格性以及道德等因素的完全意义的神秘。在后面的章节中，我们所保留和使用的“神圣”这一术语就是处于这种复合的含义中的。但是，如果我们首先斗胆来尽可能明确地概括一下我们对这一事情的看法，那么，这一历史发展的过程就会更容易地被理解。

那些原始的宗教意识在“对魔鬼的畏惧”中最初所领会到的东西，以及随着它的进一步开显，变成为更加严肃和更加崇高的东西，在最初，并不是某种理性的或者道德的东西，而是某种独特的、非理性的东西，对于这个东西，心灵以我们已经描述过的那种

responds in a unique way with the special feeling-reflexes that have been described. And this element or 'moment' passes in itself through a process of development of its own, quite apart from the other process—which begins at an early stage—by which it is 'rationalized' and 'moralized', i. e. filled with rational and ethical meaning. Taking this non-rational process of development first, we have seen how the 'daemonic dread', after itself passing through various gradations, rises to the level of 'fear of the gods', and thence to 'fear of God'. The *δαιμόνιον* or daemonic power becomes the *θεῖον* or divine power: 'dread' becomes worship; out of a confusion of inchoate emotions and bewildered palpitations of feeling grows '*religio*', and out of 'shudder' a holy awe. The feelings of dependence upon and beatitude in the numen, from being relative, become absolute. The false analogies and fortuitous associations are gradually dispelled or frankly rejected. The numen becomes God and Deity. It is then to God and Deity, as 'numen' rendered absolute, that the attribute denoted by the terms *qādôsh*, *sanctus*, *ἅγιος*, holy, pertains, in the first and directest sense of the words. It is the culmination of a development which works itself out purely in the sphere of the non-rational. This development constitutes the first central fact of religious study, and it is the task of religious history and psychology to trace its course.

Next, secondary and subsidiary to this, is the task of tracing the course of the process of rationalization and moralization *on the basis of* the numinous consciousness. It nearly, if not quite, synchronizes and keeps pace with the stages of the purely numinous development, and, like that, it can be traced in its different gradations in the most widely different regions of religious history. Almost everywhere we find the numinous attracting and appropriating meanings derived from social

特殊感受反映的独特的方式来作出反应,而且这种因素或者“要素”在其自身中经历了自身的发展过程,这一自身的发展过程远远不同于其他的过程(发生在其早期阶段的),即通过这一过程,它被“理性化”和“道德化”了,也就是说,在它里面,充满了理性的和伦理的含义。当我们首先处理这个非理性的发展过程时,我们已经看到,那种“对魔鬼的畏惧”在它本身经过多种多样的发展阶段后,是怎样上升到“对众神的畏惧”并进而上升到“对上帝的畏惧”的。这种魔鬼般的力量(*δαιμόνιον*)变成了神性的力量(*θεί ον*):“畏惧”变成了崇拜;从早期不完善的情感与迷惘的情感波动的混合中产生出了“宗教感”(*religio*),从“战栗”的畏惧中产生了某种神圣的敬畏。那种依附于神秘的感受以及在神秘中的至福的感受,从相对之物变成了绝对之物。错误的类比与偶然的联系被逐渐地消除掉或者被公开地拒斥。神秘变成了上帝和神。这样,当“神秘”被绝对化的时候,由 *qādôsh*, *sanctus*, *ãγιος*,神圣等术语,就这些词语最初的和最直接的意义上所标示出来的那种性质,就适用于上帝和神灵了。这是那种在非理性的领域中产生出其自身的发展过程所能达到的顶峰。这一发展构成了宗教研究的最为核心的事实,而追溯这一发展的历程,则是宗教史与心理学的任务所在。

另一点,宗教史和心理学的次要的和辅助性的任务,是在神秘意识的基础上,追寻那个理性化和道德化的发展历程。即使不是完全,这一过程也几乎与纯粹神秘的发展的各个阶段保持了同步,并且,与此相同,这一过程能够在宗教史的最不相同的领域中的各个不同的发展阶段中去追溯。几乎在每一个地方,我们都可以发现神秘的具有吸引力的、适当的含义,这种含义来自社

and individual ideals of obligation, justice, and goodness. These become the 'will' of the numen, and the numen their guardian, ordainer, and author. More and more these ideas come to enter into the very essence of the numen and charge the term with ethical content. 'Holy' becomes 'good', and 'good' from that very fact in turn becomes 'holy', 'sacrosanct'; until there results a thenceforth indissoluble synthesis of the two elements, and the final outcome is thus the fuller, more complex sense of 'holy', in which it is at once *good and sacrosanct*. The greatest distinction of the religion of ancient Israel, at least from Amos onwards, is precisely the intimate coalescence of both elements. No God is like the God of Israel: for He is the absolutely Holy One (= perfectly good). And, on the other hand, no law is like Yahweh's Law, for it is not merely good, but also at the same time 'holy' (= sacrosanct).

And this process of rationalization and moralization of the numinous, as it grows ever more clear and more potent, is in fact the most essential part of what we call 'the History of Salvation' and prize as the ever-growing self-revelation of the divine. But at the same time it should be clear to us that this process of the 'moralization of the idea of God', often enough represented to us as a principal problem, setting the main line for inquiry into the history of religion, is in no wise a suppression of the numinous or its supersession by something else—which would result not in a God, but a God-substitute —but rather the completion and charging of it with a new content. That is to say, the 'moralization' process assumes the numinous and is only completed upon this as basis.

会与个人对于责任、正义以及善的理想。这些观念变成了神秘的"意志",而神秘在此是它们的守卫者、命令者和创造者。这些观念越来越多地进入到神秘的这一本质之中,并且使这一术语充满了伦理的内容。"神圣"变成了"善",而"善"正是在这一意义上反过来变成了"神圣",变成了"至圣";直到后来两种因素结合成为某种从此永远无法分解的综合体,而这最后的产物是那种更加完满、更加丰富的"神圣"的含义,这一神圣就同时既是善,又是至圣,至少是阿摩司以前的古代以色列宗教的最大的特点,正在于这两种因素的紧密联合。没有任何一个上帝像以色列人的上帝一样:因为他[1]是绝对的神圣者(=至善),并且,另一方面,没有任何法律像耶和华的法律那样,因为它不仅仅是善,而且同时也是"神圣"(=至圣)。

神秘的这个理性化和道德化的过程,当它变得更清晰和更有力时,实际上就是我们称之为"救赎的历史"的最本质的部分以及我们珍视为不断增长着的神性的自我开显。但是,与此同时,我们也必须清楚地认识到,"上帝观念的道德化"这一过程由于设定了宗教史的研究的主线,它常常被当做一个首要的问题提供给我们,它绝不是对神秘的镇压或者以别的事物对它的取代——这种取代不会产生一个上帝,而只会产生出一个上帝的替代者——而毋宁说是神秘的完成,是以新的内容对神秘的充实。也就是说,"道德化"过程接受了神秘,并且正是以之为基础道德化才得以完成。

---

[1] 以色列人的上帝。

CHAPTER XIV

The Holy As An *A Priori* Category

PART I

It follows from what has been said that the 'holy' in the fullest sense of the word is a combined, complex category, the combining elements being its rational and non-rational components. But in *both*—and the assertion must be strictly maintained against all sensationalism and naturalism—it is a *purely a priori* category.

The rational ideas of absoluteness, completion, necessity, and substantiality, and no less so those of the good as an objective value, objectively binding and valid, are not to be 'evolved' from any sort of sense-perception. And the notions of 'epigenesis', 'heterogony', or whatever other expression we may choose to denote our compromise and perplexity, only serve to conceal the problem, the tendency to take refuge in a Greek terminology being here, as so often, nothing but an avowal of one's own insufficiency. Rather, seeking to account for the ideas in question, we are referred away from all sense-experience back to an original and underivable capacity of the mind implanted in the 'pure reason' independently of all perception.

第十四章　作为一种先验范畴的神圣

第一部分

从上面已经谈论过的内容可以得出这样一个结论："神圣"在该词的最完满的意义上是一种复合的、复杂的范畴，相互结合着的因素就是它的理性成分和非理性成分。但是在两者中，神圣都是一个纯粹先验的范畴——而且这一断言必须被严格地保持，以对抗所有的感觉主义和自然主义。

绝对、完满、必然和实体等这些理性观念，以及那些具有客观约束力和客观有效性的、作为某种客观价值的善，是不能从任何形式的感知中"进化"出来的。"渐成说"与"形变说"的观点或者任何我们可以选择来用以表达我们的妥协和困惑的其他任何观念，都仅仅是隐藏了这一问题，而此处向希腊术语求助的倾向，像通常所做的那样，也仅仅是表明了引用者本人的不完善性。相反，为了寻求解决这些被讨论的观念，我们宁可撇开所有的感觉经验，回到某种原初的、非派生的心灵能力上去，这种心灵能力植根于不依赖于所有的知觉的"纯粹理性"之中。

But in the case of the non-rational elements of our category of the Holy we are referred back to something still deeper than the 'pure reason', at least as this is usually understood, namely, to that which mysticism has rightly named the *fundus animae*, the 'bottom' or 'ground of the soul' (Seelengrund). The ideas of the numinous and the feelings that correspond to them are, quite as much as the rational ideas and feelings, absolutely 'pure', and the criteria which Kant suggests for the 'pure' concept and the 'pure' feeling of respect are most precisely applicable to them. In the famous opening words of the *Critique of Pure Reason* he says:

That all our knowledge begins with experience there can be no doubt. For how is it possible that the faculty of cognition should be awakened into exercise otherwise than by means of objects which affect our senses? ... But, though all our knowledge begins *with* experience, it by no means follows that all arises *out of* experience.

And, referring to empirical knowledge, he distinguishes that part which we receive through impressions and that which our own faculty of cognition supplies from itself, *senseimpressions giving merely the occasion.*

The numinous is of the latter kind. It issues from the deepest foundation of cognitive apprehension that the soul possesses, and, though it of course comes into being in and amid the sensory data and empirical material of the natural world and cannot anticipate or dispense with those, yet it does not arise *out of* them, but only *by their means*. They are the incitement, the stimulus, and the 'occasion' for the numinous experience to become astir, and, in so doing, to begin—at first with a naïve immediacy of reaction—to be interfused and interwoven with the present world of sensuous experience, until, becoming gradually purer, it disengages itself from this and takes its stand in absolute contrast to it. The proof that in the numinous we have to deal with purely a priori cognitive elements is to be reached by introspection and a critical

但是，在我们神圣范畴的非理性因素的情形中，我们宁可回到某种比那种至少是人们通常所理解的“纯粹理性”更加深刻的东西上去，也就是说，回到神秘主义所正确地称之为“深渊之底”(*fundus animac*)或者“灵魂的地基”(Seelengrund)上去。与它们相对应的神秘的观念与感觉，完全和理性的观念与感觉一样，都是绝对“纯粹的”，而康德为“纯粹”观念与“纯粹”尊敬感所提出来的那些标准，更加适合于有关神秘的观念及其相应的感受。在《纯粹理性批判》一书的著名的开场白中，康德说道：

我们所有的只是都开始于经验，这是毋庸置疑的。如果没有对象刺激我们的感官，我们的认识能力如何能被唤醒并且进入到活动之中呢？……但是，虽说我们所有的知识都是从经验开始的，但是，并不能由此得出结论，说一切知识都来自于经验。

而在谈到经验知识时，康德区分了我们从感觉印象中所得到的知识以及我们自己的认识能力从其自身提供给我们的知识，感觉印象仅仅提供了机会。

神秘就属于后一种情形。它来自灵魂所具有的知性理解力的最深的基础，同时，尽管神秘的确是在关于自然界的感觉材料和经验材料中形成的，并且也不能没有或去除这些材料，但它却不是产生于这些材料，而只是借助于这些材料。这些感觉材料和经验材料是神秘经验得以激活的诱因、刺激与“机会”，而一旦此种经验被激发起来，它就开始——最初带有某种质朴的、直接反应的性质——与感官经验的当下世界相融合、相交汇，直到在逐渐变得更加纯粹之后，它才从这种融汇中脱离出来并绝对地与之相对立。在神秘中我们不得不与纯粹先验的认知因素打交道的证据可以通过像康德所做过的那样，即通过对理性的内省与批判

examination of reason such as Kant instituted. We find, that is, involved in the numinous experience, beliefs and feelings qualitatively different from anything that ' natural ' senseperception is capable of giving us. They are themselves not perceptions at all, but peculiar interpretations and valuations, at first of perceptual data, and then—at a higher level —of posited objects and entities, which themselves no longer belong to the perceptual world, but are thought of as supplementing and transcending it. And as they are not themselves sense-perceptions, so neither are they any sort of ' transmutation ' of sense-perceptions. The only ' transmutation ' possible in respect to sense-perception is the transformation of the intuitively given concrete percept, of whatever sort, into the corresponding concept; there is never any question of the transformation of *one* class of percepts into a class of entities qualitatively *other*. The facts of the numinous consciousness point therefore—as likewise do also the ' pure concepts of the understanding ' of Kant and the ideas and value-judgements of ethics or aesthetics—to a hidden substantive source, from which the religious ideas and feelings are formed, which lies in the mind independently of sense-experience; a ' pure reason ' in the profoundest sense, which, because of the ' surpassingness ' of its content, must be distinguished from both the pure theoretical and the pure practical reason of Kant, as something yet higher or deeper than they.

The justification of the ' evolutionist ' theory of to-day stands or falls with its claim to ' explain ' the phenomenon of religion. That is in truth the real task of the psychology of religion. But in order to explain we must have the data from which an explanation may be forthcoming; out of nothing nothing can be explained. Nature can only be explained by an investigation into the ultimate fundamental forces of nature and their laws: it is meaningless to propose to go farther and explain these laws themselves, for in terms of what are they to be explained? But in the domain of spirit the corresponding principle from which an explanation is derived is just the

性考察来得到。我们看到,那些包含在神秘经验中的信念和感受,在性质上不同于“自然的”感知所能给予我们的东西。这些信念和感受本身根本就不是感知,而是特殊的解释与评价,首先是对知觉材料的解释与评价,其次——在某种更高的水平上——对假定对象与实体的解释与评价,这些解释与评价本身不再属于这个感觉世界,而是被视为对这个感觉世界的补充和超越。由于这些信念和感受本身并不是感官知觉,所以它们也不可能是感官知觉的任何形式的“变形”。对于感官知觉来说,唯一可能的“变形”,就是把那种来自直觉的具体知觉(无论是哪一种)转变为相应的概念;这一变化并不存在把一种知觉变为性质上完全不同的另一种。因此,神秘意识的那些事实——正如康德“关于理解的纯粹概念”以及那些伦理学的或者美学的那些概念和价值判断——就指向了宗教观念和感受所由以产生的某个隐蔽而真实的源泉,这一源泉存在于心灵深处的,不依赖于感觉经验;这是一种最深意义上的“纯粹理性”,它因为内容的“非凡卓绝”,必然不同于康德的纯粹理论理性与纯粹实践理性,而是比这它们还更高或者更深的东西。

当代“进化主义”理论的合理性,取决于它是否宣称要去“解释”宗教现象。事实上,这是宗教心理学的一项真正任务。但是,为了能够解释,我们必须要有可供解释的材料;没有材料,就谈不上解释了。只有通过对大自然的最根本的力量及其自然法则的探究,大自然才可能得以解释:如果我们建议,应该更加深入地解释这些规律本身,那也是没有意义的,因为又是根据什么,这些规律才得以解释?但在精神的领域中,使一种解释得以作出的相应原则正是这种精神本身,即人的理性精神及其先天倾向、能力以

spirit itself, the reasonable spirit of man, with its predispositions, capacities, and its own inherent laws. This has to be presupposed: it cannot itself be explained. None can say how mind or spirit 'is made'—though this is in effect just what the theory of epigenesis is fain to attempt. The history of humanity begins with man, and we have to presuppose man, to take him for granted as he is, in order that from him we may understand his history. That is, we must presuppose man as a being analogous to ourselves in natural propensities and capacities. It is a hopeless business to seek to lower ourselves into the mental life of a *pithecanthropus erectus*; and, even. if it were not, we should still need to start from man as he is, since we can only interpret the psychical and emotional life of animals regressively by clumsy analogies drawn from the developed human mind. To try, on the other hand, to understand and deduce the human from the sub-human or brute mind is to try to fit the lock to the key instead of vice versa; it is to seek to illuminate light by darkness. In the first appearance of conscious life on dead unconscious matter we have a simple, irreducible, inexplicable datum. But that which here appears is already a manifold of qualities, and we can only interpret it as a seed of potentiality, out of which issue continually maturer powers and capacities, as the organization of the body increases in stability and complexity. And the only way we can throw any light upon the whole region of sub-human psychical life is by interpreting it once again as a sort of 'predisposition' at a second remove, i. e. a predisposition to form the predispositions or faculties of the actual developed mind, and standing in relation to this as an embryo to the full-grown organism. But we are not completely in the dark as to the meaning of this word 'predisposition'.① For in our own awakening and growth to mental and spiritual maturity we trace in ourselves in some

① Anlage.

及它自身固有的法则。这就不得不假设:它本身是不能被解释的。没有人能够说出思想或精神是如何“被造出来的”——尽管这正是渐成说的理论欣然力图去解释的。人性的历史是由人开始的,我们必须预设人的存在,如人所是地来看待人,以便我们能从人来理解人的历史。这就是说,我们必须把人假设为一种在自然倾向和能力上类似于我们自己的存在物。试图把我们降低到直立猿(*pithecanthropus erectus*)的精神生活的水平,这是一种无望之举。即便并非无望,我们也仍需从人之为人出发,因为只有通过取自发达的人类心灵的笨拙类比,我们才能回过头来解释动物的精神生活与情感生活。另一方面,力图从低于人的或野蛮的心灵出发来理解人、推断人,不啻是一种让锁去适应钥匙而不是以钥匙来适应锁的做法,这就像是要用黑暗来照亮光明。从奠基在死的、无意识物质之上的意识生活的最初显现中,我们获得了一种单纯的、不可还原的、无法阐明的材料,但在这里显现的那种东西早就拥有多种性质,我们只能把它解释为一种潜能的种子,从中将不断地产生出越来越成熟的力量与能力,就像人体的组织变得越来越稳定与复杂一样。我们能够对低于人的精神生活的整个领域加以说明的唯一途径,是通过重新把它解释为一种更远层次的“倾向”,也就是说,是那种构成假定的假定或者是构成实际上发展了的心灵的能力的假定,这种假定与发展了的心灵的关系就相当于胚胎与完全成熟的机体的关系一样。但是,我们对“倾向”[1]这个词的意思并非完全一无所知。因为在我们自身的心灵与精神成熟的觉醒与成长过程中,我们也能在

① 倾向

sort the evolution by which the seed develops into the treethe very opposite of 'transformation' and 'epigenesis' by successive addition. ①

We call the source of growth a hidden 'predisposition' of the human spirit, which awakens when aroused by divers excitations. That there are 'predispositions' of this sort in individuals no one can deny who has given serious study to the history of religion. They are seen as propensities, 'predestining' the individual to religion, and they may grow spontaneously to quasi-instinctive presentiments, uneasy seeking and groping, yearning and longing, and become a religious *impulsion*, that only finds peace when it has become clear to itself and attained its goal. From them arise the states of mind of 'prevenient grace', described in masterly fashion by Suso:

Loving, tender Lord! My mind has from the days of my childhood sought something with an earnest thirst of longing, Lord, and what that is have I not yet perfectly apprehended. Lord, I have now for many a year been in hot pursuit of it, and never yet have I been able to succeed, for I know not aright what it is.

---

① The physical analogue to these spiritual or mental relationships is the relation of potential to kinetic energy. The assumption of such a relation in the world of mind (i. e. a relation between potential and kinetic mind) is, of course, only to be expected from one who is prepared to accept as the final cause of all mind in the world as a whole the absolute mind as 'pure actuality' whose *ellampatio* or effulgence (in Leibniz's phrase) all other mind is. For all that is potential presupposes an actual as the ground of its possibility, as Aristotle long ago showed. But indeed how can we afford to reject such a 'pure actuality'? It is an inconsequent proceeding to postulate actuality, as is done, for a starting point for the physical world, as a system of stored-up energy, whose transference to kinetic energy constitutes the 'rush of worlds and wheel of systems', and yet to reject the analogous assumption in the world of mind and spirit.

自己身上追踪到那个种子以某种进化的方式长成大树的过程——即由于量的逐渐积累而引起的“形变”和“渐成”完全相反的过程。①

我们把这个成长的根源称做人类精神的隐蔽“倾向”，这种倾向因受到各种各样的刺激而被唤醒。凡是对宗教史作过认真研究的人，都不可能否认在个人身上存在着这种“倾向”。它们被视为倾向性，即“注定”了个人要走向宗教的倾向，这些倾向能够很自然地发展为类本能式的预兆感觉，在心神不宁地追寻着、探索着、向往着、渴盼着，并变成一种宗教冲动，这种冲动只有在它本身变得明晰并且达到了它的目的之后才会平息下来。从这些倾向中产生出“前恩典”心理状态，对此，苏索作了极为精彩的描写：

仁慈温和的主啊！从孩提时起，我的心灵就带着最真诚的渴盼在追求某种东西了，但主啊！我却不完全清楚我所追求的是什么。主啊！我热切地追求这些东西已有好些年了，但却始终未能如愿，因为我不能很好地知道它是什么。尽管如此，可它仍是

---

① 在物理世界中，类似于这些精神或心智的关系的，是势能与动能的关系。当然，只有那种准备把绝对精神作为“纯粹现实性”而当做整个世界上一切精神的根本原因接受下来的人，才可能假设精神世界中的这种关系（即心灵的势能与动能之间的关系）。此种精神的“光辉”（莱布尼茨语）是一切精神都具有的。正如亚里士多德早就已经表明的那样，因为凡是潜在的东西都预设了某种现实来当做它的可能性的根基。但是，我们如何能驳斥这种“纯粹现实性”呢？“纯粹现实性”是一种不合逻辑的东西，它为了替物质世界找一个起点而把现实性假设为一个能量储备系统，这个系统向动能的转化就形成了“世界的涌流和体系的运转”，可是，拒斥在心灵与精神世界中作这种类似的假设也是不合逻辑的。

And yet it is something that draws my heart and my soul after it, and without which I can never attain to full repose. Lord, I was fain in the earliest days of my childhood to seek it among created things, as I saw others before me do. And the more I sought, the less I found it; and the nearer I went, the further I wandered from it. . . . Now my heart rages for it, for fain would I possess it. . . . Woe is me! . . . . What is this, or how is it fashioned, that plays within me in such hidden wise?①

These are manifestations of a *predisposition* becoming a search and a driving *impulsion*. But here, if nowhere else, the 'fundamental biogenetic law' really does hold good, which uses the stages and phases in the growth of the individual to throw light upon the corresponding stages in the growth of his species. The *predisposition* which the human reason brought with it when the species Man entered history became long ago, not merely for individuals but for the species as a whole, a *religious impulsion*, to which incitements from without and pressure from within the mind both contributed. It begins in undirected, groping emotion, a seeking and shaping of representations, and goes on, by a continual onward striving, to generate ideas, till its nature is self-illumined and

① Works, ed. Denifle, p. 311.

吸引我的心和灵魂去追求的东西,而没有这种东西,我将永远不能得到完全的安息。主啊!在我童年的早期岁月中,我就乐于在被造物中去寻求这种东西的存在,就像我看见这之前的其他人也这样做一样。但我追求的越多,我对它的发现就越少;我离它靠得越近,我离它反而就越远。……现在,我的心为之而发狂,因为我渴望占有它。……我是多么不幸啊!……那个以这种隐匿的方式在我心中起作用的东西是什么,它又是怎样被形成的呢?①

这些就是那变成一种探求与驱使冲动的倾向的种种表现,但是,如果在其他地方不是如此的话,在这里,“根本的生物起源法则”完全有效,这一法则用个体成长的时期与阶段来说明他所属的种族成长的相应阶段。不仅对于个人,而且也就整个类而言,当人类产生之后,随同人的理性一道产生出来的这种倾向,很早以前就变成了一种宗教冲动,来自外界的刺激和来自心灵的内在压力,都对这种宗教冲动的形成作出了贡献。这种冲动开始于没有方向的、摸索性的情绪,即一种不断探寻和正在成形的陈述表达,接着,通过一种不断向前的努力,产生出了观念,直到通过对它自身思想的模糊的先验基础的说明,它的本质才自我被照亮,并变得清

① 苏索:《著作集》,德尼幅尔版,第331页。

made clear by an explication of the obscure *a priori* foundation of thought itself, out of which it originated.① And this emotion, this searching, this generation and explication of ideas, gives the warp of the fabric of religious evolution, whose woof we are to discuss later.②

① The reader may compare what Kant says in his Lectures on Psychology (Leipzig ed., 1889, p. 11) of 'the treasure buried in the field of obscure ideas, constituting the deep abyss of human knowledge, which we cannot sound'. This 'deep abyss' is just the fundus animcs that is aroused in Suso.

② Cf. pp. 177, 178.

晰起来，正是在这一先验思想的基础上它才得以产生。[①] 这种情绪，这种探索，这种观念的产生与说明，提供了宗教进化之网的经线，它的纬线我们要在后面讨论。[②]

① 读者可把苏索的话与康德关于心理学的讲演（1899 年莱比锡版第 11 页）中所说的“掩藏在模糊理念下面的宝藏，构成了我们无法言说的人类知识的‘深渊’”相比较。这个“深渊”正是苏索所谓的“灵魂的根基”。

② 参见本书第 177、178 页。

CHAPTER XV

Its Earliest Manifestations

Only upon the basis of the foregoing assumptions is it possible to understand the historical origin and further development of religion. It must be admitted that when religious evolution first begins sundry curious phenomena confront us, preliminary to religion proper and deeply affecting its subsequent course. Such are the notions of 'clean' and 'unclean', belief in and worship of the dead, belief in and worship of 'souls' or 'spirits', magic, fairy tale, and myth, homage to natural objects, whether frightful or extraordinary, noxious or advantageous, the strange idea of 'power' (*orenda or mana*), fetishism and totemism, worship of animal and plant, daemonism and polydaemonism. Different as these things are, they are all haunted by a common—and that a numinous—element, which is easily identifiable. They did not, perhaps, take their origin out of this common numinous element directly; they may have all exhibited a preliminary stage at which they were merely 'natural' products of the naive, rudimentary fancies of primitive times. But these things acquire a strand of a quite special kind, which alone gives them their character as forming the vestibule of religion, brings them first to clear and explicit form, and furnishes them with the prodigious power over the minds of men which history universally proves them to possess. Let us attempt to grasp this peculiar strand, common to all these modes of thought and practice which stand upon the threshold of religion.

第十五章　最初的表现

只有立足于上述的诸多假设,理解宗教的历史起源与其进一步的发展才是可能的。必须承认,当宗教进化过程最初开始时,我们遭遇到了各式各样的奇怪现象,它们既预示着宗教的出现,又深刻地影响到它后来的发展进程。诸如“洁净”与“不洁净”的观念,对死者的信仰与崇拜,对“灵魂”或“精神”以及魔法、童话与神话的信仰与崇拜,对自然对象(无论是可怕的还是特别的,有害的还是有益的)的敬畏,对于“能量”(*orenda* 或 *mana*)的奇特观念,拜物主义与图腾崇拜,对于动物和植物的崇拜,魔鬼信仰与多元魔鬼信仰等。尽管这些现象各不相同,但它们全都贯串着一个容易辨认的、共同的并且也是神秘的因素。或许,这些现象并不都是直接从这一共同的神秘的因素中产生出来的;它们或许全都展示了某种最初的阶段,在这一阶段上,它们不过是原始时期的朴素初级的幻想的“自然”产物罢了。然而,这些现象获得了某种十分特殊的成份,这种成份单独就能赋予这些现象以形成宗教前厅的特征,单独就能率先把清晰明显的形式带给这些现象,就能为这些现象提供那种影响人们心灵的巨大能量,历史已完全证明了这些现象拥有这种能量。我们要努力把握住依照宗教发端时这种为一切宗教思想和宗教实践所共有的特殊成份。

1. We will begin with magic. There has been at all times, and there still is to-day, a 'natural' magic, that is to say, modes of behaviour exhibiting some simple analogy and carried out quite unreflectively and without any basis in theory, whose object is to influence and regulate an event in accordance with the wishes of the agent. It may be noticed on any skittle-alley or bowling-green. A bowler aims and plays his bowl, wishing it to run true and hit the jack. He watches eagerly as it rolls, nodding his head, his body bent sideways, stands balancing on one leg, jerks over violently to the other side as the critical point is reached, makes as though to push the ball on with hand or foot, gives a last jerk—and the end is reached. Its hazards past, the ball rolls safely into position. What was the man doing in this case? He was not simply imitating the course of the ball; he meant to prescribe and determine it, but this obviously without any reflection on his queer behaviour, without the belief of primitive man in 'universal animism', i. e. in the animatedness of everything, in this instance, of the ball, and without a belief in some sympathetic *rapport* between his own 'soul' power and the 'soul' of the ball. His action was merely naively analogical, for the attainment of a definite wish. The proceedings of 'rain-makers' were often, perhaps at first were always, just the same sort of thing; and so were the naive charms purporting to influence the course of sun and moon, clouds, and winds. But clearly, so long as they are not more than this, these are not by any means *magic* in the proper sense. There must be in addition a new ingredient, unique in quality, the element that is usually called 'supernatural efficacy'. But this expression is a misnomer: 'supernatural' has nothing to do with the case; it is much too imposing an expression, and ascribes far too much to the naive mind. The conception of Nature as a single connected system of events united by laws

1. 我们先从魔法开始。一切时代，一直到今天，都存在着“自然的”魔法，也就是说，存在着某些行为方式，这些行为方式表现出一种简单的类比，实行起来非常草率，并且也没有任何理论上的根据，其目标是要按照实施魔法者的意愿来影响和控制事件。在任何九柱游戏或草地保龄球游戏中都可看到这种情形。滚球者瞄准目标后掷出保龄球，希望保龄球直线滚动并击中作木瓶。滚球者急切地注视着木球的滚动，他勾着头，身体弯向一边，他单腿独立并保持平衡，在紧要关头到来时会突然换成另一条腿，他的手和脚做出要去推动保龄球的样子，来给它最后一把力——而终点达到了。危险过去了，保龄球顺利地到达了它的位置。在这个例子中，滚球者在做什么呢？他不是在简单地模仿着保龄球的滚动过程，他是要控制、决定木球的滚动，但这里显然不存在对其奇怪行为的任何反思，也不存在原始人的“万物有灵”信仰，即对于万物（在这个例子中是保龄球）皆有生命的信仰，而且，在滚球者自己的“灵魂”能力与保龄球的“灵魂”之间也不存在关于什么交感关系的信仰。他的行为只是一种天真的类推，其目的就在于某种确定的愿望。“求雨者”的做法常常也是（或许最初总是）这类行为方式；那些旨在影响日、月、云、风运行的原始符咒也是如此。但是很清楚，只要这些求雨者仅仅做这些东西，那么这些行为就绝不是本来意义上的魔法。这里必然还存在着一种新的成分，这种因素性质独特，通常被称为“超自然效应”。但这个表述用词不当：“超自然”与本例没有丝毫关系，这是一种过于华丽的措辞，并且对原始心灵的关注有些过多。自然这个概念，作为被法则联合

is the final and most difficult outcome of abstraction; and this conception of nature, or at least some hint of it, must have been arrived at before there could be any place for its negation, the ' supernatural'. Again, nothing is explained, as Wundt would have it, by ' spirit-power' or ' soul-power'. For, first, it is to-day universally recognized that magic is independent of a belief in spirits or souls, and probably existed before it. And, second, the point at issue is not by means of what *class* of powers the magical effect was produced—whether ' soul-wers' or others—but by means of what *quality* or character in the powers. And this quality can be indicated solely through the ' daemonic', a character ascribed to certain definite operations of force, be they strong or weak, extraordinary or quite trivial, the work of a soul or a ' non-soul'. The quality can be only suggested through that unique element of feeling, the feeling of ' uncanniness', of which we have already spoken, whose positive content cannot be defined conceptually, and can only be indicated by that mental response to it which we called ' shuddering'.

2. The same is true of the *worship of the dead*. It does not arise out of any theory of animism, according to which the primitive man thinks of inanimate objects, and so also of the dead, as animate and operative. Even in itself this entire theory of an ostensible attribution of ' soul' or the principle of animation to everything is a mere fabrication of the study. How much more when it is clumsily spatchcocked and welded together with ' belief in spirits or souls', which is something quite different! The dead man, in point of fact, exercises a spell upon the mind only when, and only because, he is felt as a thing of horror and ' shudder'. But alike to the naive mind of the savage and to the blasé mind of modern civilized man this feeling comes about with such an immediate compelling

起来的事件的单一的联系体系，是抽象活动的最后的也是最困难的产物；而关于自然这个概念，或者至少是对它的某种暗示，一定是在它的否定方面即“超自然”产生之前就已经被抽象出来了。同样，正如冯特所说，仅靠“精神力”或“灵魂力”，是什么也说明不了的。这是因为，首先，今天人们已经普遍认识到，魔法并不依赖于对精神或灵魂的信仰，而且很可能存在于这种信仰之前。其次，争论的焦点并不在魔法作用被生产出来是凭借的哪一种力量——无论是“灵魂力”还是别的什么，而在于是凭借着这些力量的什么性质或什么特点。只有借助于“魔鬼的”，即一种被归结为某种确定的力量的运作（不管它们是强还是弱，是异乎寻常还是微不足道，是灵魂的作用还是“非灵魂”的作用）的特征，这种性质才能得到阐明。只有通过那种独特的感受因素，即那种我们早已提到过的对于“神秘”的感受——这种感受的肯定性内容不能由概念来界定，而只能通过我们称之为“战栗”的那种精神反应来加以指称——这种性质才能够被暗示出来。

2. 对于死者的崇拜也是如此。对于死者的崇拜并不是来自任何泛灵论——依此理论，原始人把无生命的对象，也把死者看做有生命的、能动的。甚至就其整个理论本身来说，它把“灵魂”或生命赋予万物这一点仅仅是一种虚构而已。更何况这个理论还被拙劣地与“信仰精神或灵魂”这种风马牛不相及的东西硬扯在了一起！事实上，死去的人对心灵产生影响，只有在并且只是因为死者被感受为一种可怕的、令人“战栗”的东西的时候才发生。但是，无论对野蛮人天真纯朴的心灵来说，还是对现代文明人倦于享乐的心灵来说，这种害怕的感受都同样带有一种直接的

force that we usually accept it as something immediately selfevident, failing altogether to remark that even the estimating something as 'horrible' or 'grisly' shows the emergence of a qualitatively separate content of feeling which the mere fact of death does not explain. Feeling-reactions to the dead, if prompted 'naturally', are pretty obviously only of two kinds: on the one hand, the experient feels disgust at the corpse's putrefaction, stench, revoltingness: on the other, he feels his own will to life disturbed and checked, the fear of death and the startled fright that directly follows on the sight of a corpse, especially if it be that of a member of one's own species. Both these sorts of feeling-response, viz. disgust and startled fright, are already found manifested among animals. I observed this in a very pronounced degree on one occasion, when, upon a lonely ride, we suddenly came upon the body of a dead horse, and Diana, my excellent mount, on recognizing her dead fellow, gave every indication of the most natural fright and disgust. But these two 'moments' of feeling do not by any means afford in themselves the materials for the 'art of making shudder' (in the words of the old folk-tale). It is something new and demands to be 'learnt' as the folktale rightly declares: that is, this is a feeling that is not simply present with the other 'natural' and normal mental functions, disgust, or fright, and cannot be got from these by analysis. It is a 'dread' (or awe), qualitatively *sui generis*; and even with regard to this rudimentary stage represented by the primitive 'worship of the dead' we cannot admit that we have to do merely with a universal feeling, that has simply to be presupposed at the outset as a regular factor of folk psychology, a collectively engendered feeling that explains itself. On the contrary, it cannot be disputed that here too there have been persons endowed with special propensities in this direction, who possessed such feelings actually, and then, by giving expression to them, aroused them in others. Even the 'awe of the dead' and from it the 'worship of the dead' have been,

强制力量,我们通常把它作为不言自明的东西接受下来,完全没有注意到,正是在把某物看做“可怕”或“可怖”时,刚好显示出了某种性质独特的感受内容的浮现,而这种感受内容是单纯的死亡事实所解释不了的。对于死人的感受-反应,如果是“自然地”产生的,那就显然只有两类:一方面,当事人对尸体的腐烂、恶臭、令人作呕感到厌恶;另一方面,当事人感受到了他自己的生命意志受到干扰和阻挠,感受到了对于死亡的恐惧与震惊,这种恐惧与震惊直接来自于他所看到的尸体,尤其是假如这一尸体是他本族成员的。这两种感受-反应,亦即厌恶与震惊,即使在动物那里也有所表现。有一次,我曾非常明显地观察到了这种现象。当时我独自骑马行走,我们突然遇见一具马尸,当黛安娜——我的出色坐骑——认出它死去的同类后,便表现出了种种最自然的害怕与厌恶。但是,这两种感受“要素”在其自身中却绝不可能为那种“引起战栗的艺术”(用古老的民间故事的话说)提供材料。这是一种新东西,正如民间故事所正确主张的那样,需要对它加以“了解”:也就是说,这样一种感受并不与别的“自然的”、正常的心理功能,如厌恶或害怕一起简单地出现,并且也不能通过分析从这些功能中得到它。这是一种在性质上自成一类的“害怕”(或畏惧),甚至在涉及这种通过原始的“对于死者的崇拜”表现出来的初级阶段时,我们也不能认为我们必须仅仅与某种普遍的感受打交道,认为我们只须从一开始就把某种能自我解释的集体性感受假设成大众心理的某一固定的因素。相反,此处同样不容争辩的是,存在着在这方面具有特殊能力的人,这些人实际上拥有这种感受,然后,通过对这些感受的表达,他们也在他人的心中唤起这些感受。甚至“对死者的畏惧”以及从中产生的“对死者的崇拜”,

as it were, 'instituted' and have had 'founders'.

3. We consider next ideas of '*souls*' and '*spirits*'. It would be possible to show, did not the subject lead us too far afield, that these were not conceived by the fanciful processes of which the animists tell us, but had a far simpler origin. But again the important point is not the origin of 'spirits' in their ideational aspect, but the qualitative element of feeling relative to them. And this does not consist in the fact that 'spirits' or 'souls' are thinner or less easily visible than the body, or quite invisible, or fashioned like air: often all this is true of them; no less often none of it is; most frequently of all it is both true and false. The essence of the 'soul' lies not in the imaginative or conceptual expression of it, but first and foremost in the fact that it is a *spectre*; that it arouses 'dread' or 'awe', as described above. But again, a 'spectre' is not to be explained from 'natural' feelings, and these are equally unable to explain the further development by which these 'somethings' (and this is the only core of conceptual meaning that can really be given them), at first always very eagerly shunned, later on become beings honoured in a positive way and loved, capable of rising into heroes, *pitris*, daemons, holy or sacred ones, and gods.

4. We turn to the idea of '*power*', the *mana* of the Pacific Islands and the *orenda* of the North American Indians. It can have its antecedents in very 'natural' phenomena. To notice power in plants, stones, and natural objects in general and to appropriate it by gaining possession of them; to eat the heart or liver of an animal or a man in order to make his power and strength one's own—this is not religion but science. Our science of medicine follows a similar prescription. If the 'power' of a calf's glands is good for goitre and imbecility, we do not know what virtue we may not hope to find in frogs

也是被“建构”起来并且有其“创建者”的。

3. 我们接着考察“灵魂”与“精神”的观念。如果这个主题没有把我们过多地引入歧途，它就有可能显示出，这两个观念并不像泛灵论者告诉我们的那样是由想象所构造出来的，而是有着更加简单的起源。但重要的并不是“精神”在其观念方面的起源，而是与这些“精神”相联系的感受的质的因素。而这种质的因素并不在于“精灵”或“魂灵”比身体更稀薄、更难以看到，或完全不可见，或是像空气那样构成这个事实：通常所有这些说法都对，或者一个也不对；而更多的时候是这些说法同时既对又不对。“灵魂”的本质并不存在于对它的想象的或概念性的表达中，而首先在于这个事实，即它是一种幽灵；正是这种幽灵引起了上述的“害怕”或“恐惧”。但是此外，“幽灵”是无法从“自然的”感受去加以解释，而且同样，“自然的”感受不能解释它的进一步发展，凭着这种发展，这些“神秘之物”（这是我们能够真正给予这些感受的概念性含义的唯一内核）最初总是被人竭力回避着，后来变成以某种肯定的方式来加以赞扬和爱戴的东西，可以升华为英雄、亡灵、魔鬼、圣物与神灵。

4. 现在我们转到“能量”的观念，即太平洋群岛的“马纳”与北美印地安人的“奥伦达”。它在“自然的”现象中有其渊源。在植物、石头以及一般的自然物中发现了能量并通过占有这些东西来获得了能量，吃动物或人的心脏或肝脏以便使它们的能量和力量为自己所拥有——这不是宗教而是科学。我们的医药科学也遵循着相同的规则。如果说一条小牛的腺所具有的“能量”对治疗甲状腺肿和低智能有好处，那么，我们就会明白我们将会希望在青蛙的大脑中或犹太人的肝

brains or Jews' livers. All depends here upon observation, and our science of medicine in this respect only differs from that of the medicine-man in being more exact and in possessing experimental methods. 'Power' does not take its place in the antechamber of religion, is not appropriated by religion in 'communion rites' and 'sacraments' (as we call them), until it too has come to include the idea of 'spell' and 'magic'.

5. Volcanoes, mountain peaks, moon, sun, and clouds are regarded by primitive man as being *alive* or *animate*, not in consequence of a naive theory of the omnipresence of 'spirit' or 'soul'—'panthelism', so called—but as a result of precisely the same criterion that we ourselves apply when we recognize anything to be alive or animate, apart from the one live thing we can observe directly, ourself; that is to say, both we and the primitive credit an object with life if, and in so far as, we think we remark in it living efficacy and agency; and whether we do so rightly or wrongly is again simply a matter of more or less exact observation. But while from this criterion the natural objects mentioned above, and of course others, may be invested with life by the naive observer, this does *not* in itself lead to myth or religion. Purely as *animate* or living beings, these entities are far from being yet 'divine' or 'gods'; nay, they do not even become so when the man turns to them with desire and petition; for petition is something less than prayer, and trust need not have a religious character. The objects in question only become 'divine'—objects of *worship*—when the category of the numinous is applied to them, and that does not come about until, first, an attempt is made to *influence* them by numinous means, viz. by magic; and, second, their special efficacy or way of working is at the same time accepted as something numinous, viz. something magical.

6. As regards *fairy-stoires*, these presuppose the 'natural'

脏中发现什么有益的东西。这里，一切都取决于观察，而且，在这个方面，我们的医学仅仅由于更加精确并且拥有不少实验手段而与巫医区别开来。直到把“魅力”和“魔法”的观念也包含到自身中来之后，“能量”的观念才在宗教中占有了一席之地，才在宗教的“圣餐仪式”和“圣餐”(我们如此称呼)中被采用。

5. 火山、山峰、月亮、太阳以及云彩被原始人当做是活的或有生命的，并不是来自那种视“精神”或“灵魂”无所不在的幼稚理论——即所谓的“泛神论”，而正好是我们自己使用的同一标准的产物，这种标准是当我们看出，除了我们能直接观察的活体——人自身以外的任何一个对象都是有生命的或活跃的时所采用的。这也就是说，只要而且只有在我们认为我们注意到某一事物有活的功能与作用时，我们和原始人都会认为这个事物是有生命的，而且无论我们这样做是对还是错，同样也只是一个观察的精确程度问题。但是，尽管按照这个标准，上述自然对象以及其他对象可被天真的观察者赋予生命，但这本身并不会导致神话或宗教。虽然这些实体被完全视为有生命的或活的东西，但它们却远非“神圣”或“神祇”；不仅如此，即便在人们带着欲望与祈求转向它们时，它们也没有变成“神圣”或“神祇”；因为祈求是一种低于祈祷的东西，而相信也不需要具有宗教的性质。只有当神秘这一范畴被用于这些对象时，这些被讨论的对象才变得“神圣”——即崇拜的对象，而且这一变化只在下述两种情况下才会发生：第一，要有用神秘的手段即通过魔法去影响对象的意图；第二，这些对象的特殊效力或运作方式同时也要被看成是一种神秘的东西即有魔力的东西。

6. 至于童话故事，它们已经给幻想、叙述、娱乐预设了“自然

impulse to fantasy, narrative, and entertainment, and its products. But the fairy-story proper only comes into being with the element of the 'wonderful', with miracle and miraculous events and consequences, i. e. by means of an infusion of the numinous. And the same holds good in an increased degree of *myth*.

7. All the factors and elements named so far in this chapter are but, as it were, the vestibule at the threshold of the real religious feeling, an earliest stirring of the numinous consciousness, which comes upon the scene blended with associated feelings in conformity to principles of analogy which it would be easy to specify for each several case. Only with the rise of the '*daemon*' do we have a really separate beginning. The most authentic form of the 'daemon' may be seen in those strange deities of ancient Arabia, which are properly nothing but wandering demonstrative pronouns, neither 'given shape and feature by means of myth', for there is in the main no mythology attached to them at all, nor 'evolved out of nature-deities', nor grown out of 'souls' or 'spirits', but none the less felt as deities of mighty efficacy, who are the objects of very living veneration. They are pure products of the religious consciousness itself. And in their case it is very evident that they do not arise as a collective product of crowd-imagination, and that they do not therefore have their origin in 'group-' or 'folk-' psychology, but were the intuitions of persons of innate prophetic powers. For there is always the *kāhin* (the primitive form of the 'prophet') belonging to these numina, and he alone experiences a numen or divine-daemonic power at first hand. Only where and when it has been 'revealed' through such a one do the forms of worship and a common cult arise. To each numen is assigned a seer and there is none without one.

8. The notions 'clean' and 'unclean', 'pure' and 'impure', are already found in a purely natural sense, prior to their religious application. The unclean is the loathsome, that which stirs

的”冲动及其结果。然而,只有伴随着“惊奇”的因素,同奇迹与奇迹般的事件和结果一道,也就是说,依靠一种神秘的灌输,童话故事才得以产生出来。这对于更高程度的神话来说也是如此。

7. 迄今在本章中所提到的所有要素与因素,都只不过是真正的宗教感受的前厅而已,即神秘意识的最初的激发,这种意识是遵循着类比原理与相关的感受混合在一起出现的,而这很容易在每一个别情形中加以指明。只是伴随着魔鬼意识的产生,我们才拥有了真正独立的开端。从古代阿拉比亚奇特的神祇中,我们可以窥到这种“魔鬼”最真实的形式,这些神祇只不过是飘忽不定的指示代词,既未“被神话赋予形貌与特征”(因为大体上来说,它们身上还根本没有附上神话的色彩),又不是“由自然神进化而来”,也不是来自于“灵魂”或“精神”,但却依然被感受为具有强大效力的神,即那种极活跃的崇拜的对象。它们是宗教意识本身的纯粹产物。就这些神祇而言,很明显,他们并不是作为大众想象的集体产物而出现的,因而他们并不是起源于“群体的”心理或“大众的”心理之中,而是起源于那些具有先天的预言能力的个人的直觉。因为这里总是存在着属于这些神秘的*kāhin*(原始形式的“先知”),他自己就能够直接体验到某种神秘或者神-魔的力量。只有在这种力量被这样一个先知“揭示”出来的地方和时候,崇拜的各种形式和共同的礼拜仪式才会出现。每一个“神秘”都有一个先知,没有先知的神秘是不存在的。

8. 我们已经在一种先于宗教含义的纯自然的含义上发现了“洁净”与“不洁净”、“纯粹”与“不纯粹”的观念。不洁净是令人生厌的,能激起自然厌恶的强烈感受。正是在人类发展

strong feelings of natural disgust. And it is just during the more primitive stages of human development that the emotion of disgust exercises such special power. Probably these emotional reactions are a part of our natural selfprotective endowment, instinctive safeguards for many important vital functions. The effect of civilization is to refine these emotions of disgust and loathing by diverting them to different objects, so that things which were loathsome to the savage cease to be so and things which were not become so. This refinement spells at the same time a weakening in the intensity of the emotion; we do not now *loathe* and feel disgust with the unbridled violence and strength of the savage. In this respect we can notice even to-day a plain distinction between our more primitive rural and our more 'refined' urban population: we townsmen feel disgust at much that is harmless to the countryman, but where the latter does feel it he is affected by the emotion more radically than we are; it is a profounder reaction in him.

We have so far been concerned with the ordinary feeling of disgust. Between this and the feeling of the 'horrible' there is a very close analogy; and from this it becomes apparent, in accordance with the law of reciprocal attraction between analogous feelings and emotions, how the 'natural' unclean or impure is bound to pass over into, and develop in, the sphere of the numinous. Once, in fact, we have in our hand the key of the problem—the analogy and the law just mentioned— we can reconstruct a *priori* the actual genetic process involved, by which the one emotion prompts the other. We indeed have ourselves a direct experience of the same thing to-day in our emotional reaction to the sight of flowing blood, in which it would be hard to say whether the element of 'disgust' or 'horror' is the stronger.

Later, then, when the more maturely developed elements of 'awe' came upon the scene and went to shape the more elevated ideas of the daemonic and the divine, sacer and sanctus, things could become 'unclean' or 'impure' in the numinous sense without

的更加原始的阶段上,厌恶的情绪才发挥出如此特殊的力量。很可能这些情绪反应是我们天生具有的自我保护天赋,即对许多重要生命功能的本能捍卫天赋的一部分。文明的作用就是要通过把这些情绪转移到不同的对象上去,使那些在野蛮人看来是令人厌恶的东西不再令人感到厌恶,同时使那些不令野蛮人感到厌恶的东西变得令人厌恶起来,来提炼这些厌恶的情绪。这一提炼同时又招致情绪强度的减弱;我们现在对野蛮人不加约束的暴力与力量并不感到恶心与厌恶。在这个方面,甚至今天我们还能看到存在于较粗鄙的乡下人与较“文雅的”都市人之间的一个显著区别:我们城里人对乡下人视为无害的很多东西感到厌恶,但一旦乡下人真的感到厌恶了某种东西,他所受到的情绪影响要比我们强烈得多;这是发生在他心中的一种更深刻的反应。

到此为止,我们所谈的都是普通的厌恶之情。这种厌恶之情与“畏惧”的感受之间存在很多类似之处,由此可以非常明显地看到:“自然的”不洁净或不纯洁是怎样依照着类似感受与情感相互吸引的规律,注定了要进入到、发展到神秘的领地。事实上,一旦我们找到开启这个问题的钥匙——即刚才谈到的类比及其规律,我们就能先验地重建那个实际发生的相关过程,通过这个过程,一种情绪会引发出另一种情绪。的确,我们今天是在我们对于看到流血的感受反应中直接体验到了相同的东西,在其中,很难说究竟是“厌恶”还是“恐惧”的成分更强烈一些。

后来,当那些更加成熟地发展了的“畏惧”因素出场并进而形成“魔鬼般的”、“神圣的”、“威严”、“神圣”等更高观念的时候,事物就变成了神秘意义上的“不洁净”或“不纯洁”而无需以“自然

any substratum of 'natural' impurity to serve as point of departure. And we can learn something of the relation of feeling-analogy involved from the fact that in the reverse direction the feeling of the *numinously* impure calls up easily by association the 'natural' emotion of disgust (i. e. the feeling of the 'naturally' impure), so that things become disgustful or loathsome which intrinsically were not objects of disgust at all, but of numinous horror. In fact such secondary and derived feelings of disgust can maintain themselves independently long after the original numinous awe which they once evoked has died away. Certain *social* feelings of loathing, such as those of caste, can be explained in this way: they had once a purely daemonic root, but long after that has died out they still survive in their secondary, acquired character as feelings of disgust.

9. If the examples numbered 1 to 8 may be termed 'prereligion', this is not in the sense that religion and the possibility of religion are explicable by their means: rather, they are themselves only made possible and can only be explained from a religious basic element, viz. the feeling of the numinous. This is a primal element of our psychical nature that needs to be grasped purely in its uniqueness and cannot itself be explained from anything else. Like all other primal psychical elements, it *emerges* in due course in the developing life of human mind and spirit and is thenceforward simply present. Of course it can only emerge if and when certain conditions are fulfilled, conditions involving a proper development of the bodily organs and the other powers of mental and emotional life in general, a due growth in suggestibility and spontaneity and responsiveness to external impressions and internal experiences. But such conditions are no more than conditions; they are not its causes or constituent elements. To recognize this is not to relegate the whole matter to the domain of mystery and supernaturalism,

的”不纯洁的基础作为出发点。我们可以从如下事实对有关感受-类比的关系有所了解,即:在相反的方向上,那种神秘意义上的不纯洁的感觉可以通过联想很容易地唤起“自然的”厌恶之情(也就是“自然意义上的”不纯洁的感觉),结果事物就变得令人厌恶或讨厌,但这些事物本质上根本就不是厌恶的对象,而只是神秘恐惧的对象。事实上,这种次要的派生的厌恶之情,能够在它们一度煽起的最初的神秘畏惧消逝很久之后独立地保持下来。某些社会厌恶感,诸如对种姓厌恶感,就能够以这种方式得到解释:这些感受曾经有着纯粹的对魔鬼畏惧的根源,但在这种畏惧消逝很久之后,它们却依然作为厌恶感存活于那个次要的、获得性特征之中。

9. 如果说 1 ~ 8 条的例证可被称为“前宗教”,这并不意味着宗教与宗教可能性可以凭借着这些方式而得到说明:恰好相反,只有通过一种宗教基本因素即神秘感,这些宗教与宗教的可能性本身才得以可能并且才能得到解释。这是我们心理本性的一种首要因素,这种因素需要完全从其独特性去加以把握,本身不能从任何别的东西加以解释。同其他主要的心理因素一样,这种神秘感出现于发展着的人类心灵和精神生活的某一适当阶段,而且从此以后就仅仅是存在着。当然,只有在某些特定的条件得到满足的情况下,它才能够出现。这些条件包括:身体器官的适当发展,以及一般的情感生活与精神生活等其他能力的适当发展,对于暗示和自发性的感受能力以及对外部印象与内部体验做出反应的能力的适当发展。但这些条件都不过是条件而已,它们并不是神秘感出现的原因或构成因素。认识到这一点并不是要把整个问题归入神秘与超自然力的领域,而只是要坚持一

but simply to maintain that the same thing holds good of this which holds good of all other primal elements of our mental or spiritual life. Pleasure or pain, love or hate, all faculties of sense-perception, such as susceptibility to light and sound, consciousness of space and time, and subsequently all higher capacities of the mind, all duly emerge, sooner or later, in the course of development. That they do so in conformity to laws and under definite conditions is indisputable, but each is none the less a new, original, underivable fact, and they are only to be 'explained' on the assumption of a rich potentiality of spirit or mind, which underlies the course of their development and realizes itself more and more abundantly in them in proportion as the conditions of organic and cerebral evolution are more fully realized. And what is true of all these other elements of our mental life is also true of the feeling of the numinous.

10. The purest case, however, of the spontaneous stirring of numinous emotion would seem to be that mentioned in No. 7 (the feeling of daemons), which is of quite special significance for the evolution of religion. This is because here the 'religious' emotion does not from the first get diverted (following the 'stimulation' of emotional associations) to earthly things, wrongly taken as numinous: but either it remains a pure feeling, as in 'panic' terror (in the literal sense of the word), or itself invents, or, better, discovers, the numinous object by rendering explicit the obscure germinal ideas latent in itself. Even this latter case is not altogether beyond the reach of introspective analysis, which, moreover, can throw some light upon the transition from mere feeling to its 'explication' and to the positing of the numinous object. At least there is none of us who has any living capacity for emotion but must have known at some time or at some place what it is to feel really 'uncanny', to have a feeling of 'eerieness'. And more exact psychological analysis will notice the following points in such a state of mind. First, there is the

点，即适用于我们心理或精神生活的所有其他主要因素的东西，也同样适用于神秘感。愉悦或痛苦，爱或恨，所有的感知能力，诸如对光与声的敏感性，时空意识，以及随之而来的所有更高的心灵能力，都迟早会在发展进程中适当地产生出来。所有这些的发生都依照着规律并在确定条件下进行，这一点是无可争辩的，但每一因素也同样是一种新的、原初的、非衍生的事实，而且只有在假设精神或心灵具有某种丰富的潜能的基础上，所有这些因素才可能得到"解释"——这种潜能蛰伏在这些因素的发展过程中，并随着机体和大脑进化诸条件的更加完满的实现而越来越充分地从这些因素中实现自己。我们精神生活的所有这些因素，包括神秘感都是这样。

10. 然而，对神秘情感的自发激起的最完美的例子，也许是第7条提到的那种（对魔鬼的感受），这种感受对于宗教的进化具有十分特殊的意义。这是因为，这里的"宗教"情绪还没有从一开始就被转移（遵循感受联想的"刺激"）到被误认为是神秘之物的尘世事物上去：但是，这种情绪要么保持为某种纯粹的感受，如同保持在"惊恐"（就该词的字面意义而言）中一样，要么通过对那种潜伏在自身之中的模糊的初生的观念加以清晰的表达，自已创造出，或者更准确地说，发现那个神秘对象。甚至这后一种情形也没有完全超出内省分析的范围，而且这种分析会帮助我们理解那种单纯的感受如何变成对它的"解释"以及将其变成到神秘对象位置。至少，我们中间没有任何一个人，拥有着活跃的情绪感受能力，却只是在某些时候某些地方，知道他所真正体验到"神秘"以及那种关于"荒诞不经"的感受是什么。更为精确的心理分析将会注意到这种心态中的下述特点：第一，

point of which we have already spoken, its separate and underivable, irreducible, qualitative character. Second, there is the very curious circumstance that the external features occasioning this state of mind are often quite slight, indeed so scanty that hardly any account can be given of them, so disproportionate are they to the strength of the emotional impression itself. Indeed the clutching force and violence of the emotion so far exceeds any impressiveness contributed by the circumstances of time and place that one can often scarcely speak of an 'impression' at all, but at most of an encounter, serving as cue or occasion for the felt experience. This experience of eerie shuddering and awe breaks out rather from depths of the soul which the circumstantial, external impression cannot sound, and the force with which it breaks out is so disproportionate to the mere external stimulation that the eruption may be termed, if not entirely, at least very nearly, spontaneous. And with this we are brought to the third point which psychological analysis of the 'uncanny' experience brings to view: meanings are aroused and awakened in it of a unique and special content, though altogether obscure, latent, and germinal, which are the real ground for the emotion of awe. For, if such meanings are not there at the start in some form or other, the mental and emotional disturbance could never take place. In the fourth place, the mental state we are discussing may, on the one hand, remain pure 'feeling', pursue its course, and pass away without its obscure thought-content being rendered explicit. If in this implicit form it is summed up in a phrase, this will be merely some such exclamation as: 'How uncanny!' or 'How eerie this place is!' On the other hand, the implicit meaning may be rendered explicit. It is already a beginning of this explicative process—though still in merely negative terms—when a man says: '*It* is not quite right here'; '*It* is uncanny.'

存在着我们已经讲过的这种心态所具有的独立的、非衍生的、不可化约的质的特性。第二,存在着一个很奇怪的条件,即产生此种心态的那些外部特征通常十分微弱,微弱到几乎无法给与它们任何说明,它们与情绪影响力本身所具有的力量相比是如此得不成比例。的确,这种情绪的钳制力与猛烈程度,远远超过了由时空条件给与的任何影响,以致通常几乎没有人把它称为一种"影响",而是更多地称为一种遭遇,用以表示对那种被感受到的经验的暗示或者机缘。这种奇异的战栗与畏惧的经验是从那种来自外部环境方面的影响力所无法探测的灵魂的深处爆发出来的,而爆发所产生的力量又与单纯的外部刺激是这么得不成比例,以致这种感受的爆发即便不能被全部地,至少也非常接近全部地被称为是自发的。由此我们就得到第三点,即对"神秘"体验的心理分析所要揭示的观点:在这种经验中被激发、被唤醒的意义具有某种独特的特殊内涵,尽管还完全是模糊的、潜在的、萌芽状的,但它们却是畏惧情绪的真正的基础。因为,如果这些意义不是从一开始就以这样或那样的形式存在于那儿,那么,心理的、情绪的骚动就一定不会发生。第四,我们讨论的这种心理状态,一方面可以保持为纯粹的"感受",继续自己的进程,而且在其模糊的思想内涵没有得到清晰表达的情况下悄然逝去。如果在这种模糊的形式中要用一句简短的话来加以概括,那就只能是这样的感叹:"多么不可思议啊!"或者是"这地方多怪异啊!"另一方面,这种模糊的意义可以得到清晰的表达。当一个人说;"这很不对劲"以及"这是不可思议的"时,就已经开始了这种解释的过程——尽管它仍然只是存在于否定性的语词中。英语"这

The English 'This place is haunted' shows a transition to a positive form of expression. Here we have the obscure basis of meaning and idea rising into greater clarity and beginning to make itself explicit as the notion, however vague and fleeting, of a transcendent Something, a real operative entity of a numinous kind, which later, as the development proceeds, assumes concrete form as a 'numen loci', a daemon, an 'El', a Baal, or the like.

In Gen. xxviii. 17 Jacob says: 'How dreadful is this place! This is none other than the house of Elohim.' This verse is very instructive for the psychology of religion; it exemplifies the point that has just been made. The first sentence gives plainly the mental impression itself in all its immediacy, before reflection has permeated it, and before the meaningcontent of the feeling itself has become clear or explicit. It connotes solely the *primal numinous awe*, which has been undoubtedly sufficient in itself in many cases to mark out 'holy' or 'sacred' places, and make of them spots of aweful veneration, centres of a cult admitting a certain development. There is no need, that is, for the experient to pass on to resolve his mere impression of the eerie and aweful into the idea of a 'numen', a divine power, dwelling in the 'aweful' place, still less need the *numen* become a *nomen*, a named power, or the '*nomen*' become something more than a mere pronoun. Worship is possible without this further explicative process. But Jacob's second statement gives this process of explication and interpretation; it is no longer simply an expression of the actual experience.

The German expression *Es spukt hier* (literally, it haunts here) is also instructive. It has properly no true subject, or at least it makes no assertion as to what the es, the 'it', is which 'haunts'; in itself it contains no suggestion of the concrete representations of 'ghost', 'phantom', 'spectre', or 'spirit' common to our popular mythology.

个地方闹鬼”,显示出向肯定的表达方式的转变。在这里,我们看到意义与观念的模糊的基础正上升为越来越清晰的东西,而且作为某个超验之物的概念,开始使自身明晰起来,尽管这种概念还是含混的、短暂易逝的。这个超验的某物是一种神秘类型的真正运作的实体,后来,随着发展的进程,它采取了诸如“神秘之处”、魔鬼、“邪神”(EI)、巴力[1]以及与之类似的具体形态。

在《创世纪》第28章第17节处,雅各说:“这地方何等可畏!这不是别的,乃是上帝的殿。”这一句话对宗教心理学很有启发性,这话正好例证了刚刚得出的观点。第一句话直截了当给出了心理感受本身,这是反思渗透进去之前的、感受的意义内涵变得清楚明晰之前的心理感受。这种感受只意味着原始的神秘的敬畏,这种畏惧在很多情形中无疑自身就足以标示出“神圣”或者“圣洁”的地方,并且使这些地方成为敬畏的场地,成为一个促成宗教的某种发展的礼拜中心。体验者不需要进一步把他对怪诞和畏惧的纯粹感受纳入到关于“神秘”,即居于“可畏”处所的神性力量的观念中,也无需把 *numen* 转变成 *nomen*,即变成一种已被命名的力量,或者把 *nomen* 变成不仅仅是一个代词的某种东西。崇拜可以不要这种进一步的解释过程,但雅各的第二句话却给出了这种说明与解释的过程;这已经不再是对实际经验的简单表达了。

德语的 *Es spukt hier*(字面意思是:这里作祟)同样富于启发性。这句话完全没有真正的主语,或者至少没有确定“作祟”的那个“东西”(es)是什么;这句话本身并没有包含任何暗示出“鬼”、“鬼魅”、“幽灵”、“精神”这类为我们大众神话所共有的具体东

〔1〕 巴力也是一种邪神,是古代迦南人信奉的。

Rather is the statement simply the pure expression of the emotion of 'eerieness' or 'uncanniness' itself, when just on the point of detaching and disengaging from itself a first vaguely intimated idea of a numinous something, an entity from beyond the borders of 'natural' experience. It is to be regretted that the German language possesses no general word less vulgar than 'spuken', no word which, instead of pointing us aside, as this word does, to the domain of superstition and the impure offshoots of the numinous consciousness, should retain its fundamental meaning in an unperverted form.① But even so we can feel by an effort of imaginative introjection how akin the debased feeling of haunting, given by this word, is to those primary numinous experiences by which long ago seers had experience of 'aweful', 'holy', numen-ssessed places, discovering thereby the starting-points for local cults and the birth-places of the 'El' worshipped there. The echo of such primeval experiences lingers in Gen. xxviii. 17 (Jacob at Bethel) and Exod. iii (the burning bush). The places here set apart by Moses and Jacob are genuine 'haunted places', at which '*es spukt*', places about which '.there is something eerie'. Only, the feeling of being haunted has in these cases not the im-

---

① The expression *es geistet hier* may serve, but it has an artificial sound. The English 'to haunt' is a nobler expression than the German *spuken*. We might legitimately translate Hab. ii. 20: 'Yahweh haunts His holy Temple.' Such a 'haunting' is frequently the meaning of the Hebrew *shākan*. And we get a fuller and truer rendering of Ps. xxvi. 8: 'the place where Thine honour dwelleth' by translating it: 'the places haunted by Thy majesty'. The *Shekinal.* is properly the *haunting presonce* of Yahweh the Temple at Jerusalem.

西。相反,这句话仅仅是对于"怪诞"或"不可思议"情绪本身的单纯表达,这种情绪正要从自身中分离出关于某个神秘事物的最初被模糊暗示的观念,这种神秘事物是超越了"自然"经验范围的某种实体。遗憾的是,德语中并没有一个比 spuken(闹鬼、幽灵作祟)这个词汇更加不粗俗的了,即没有这样的词汇,它不会像 spuken 所做的那样,把我们引入迷信与神秘意识的不纯粹的支流上去,而是在未被歪曲的形式中葆有它的根本含义。① 但是,即使在这种情形下,我们也能通过某种内在想象而感受到:由 spuken 一词所给出的那种品质低劣的"闹鬼"感受是多么类似于那些原始的神秘经验,通过这些经验,先知们很久以前就体验到那种"可怕的"、"神圣的"、"神秘的"地方了,并且因此发现了地域性崇拜的起源以及在那儿被崇拜的"邪神"(El)的诞生地。这种原始的经验在《创世纪》第 28 章第 17 节"雅各在伯特利"与《出埃及记》第 3 章"燃烧的荆棘"中不断回响。由摩西和雅各在这里所划出的地方就是真正的"作祟之地","它出没"(*es spukt*)在此,即这些地方"有某种令人胆怯的东西"。只是,在这些情形中,那种受到纠缠的感受并没有我们今天对被鬼魅困扰的

① *es geistet hier* 这个表述或许起作用,但它尚有人为的痕迹。英语的 to haunt 是一个比德语 *spuken* 更华丽的词,我们可以合理地把《哈巴谷书》第 2 章第 20 节译成:Yahweh haunts His holy Temple(即"耶和华常在他的圣殿中出没"),这个 haunting 通常就是希伯来语的 *shākan*。这样,通过把《诗篇》第 26 章第 8 节"the place where thineh honour dwelleth"("你显荣耀的居所")译为"the place haunted by thy majesty"("你常出没的居所"),我们就得到了一种更完善、更真实的表达。*Shekinah* 完全就是耶和华在耶路撒冷的圣殿中神出鬼没的在场。

poverished and debased sense of our modern eerie feeling of being haunted by ghosts and spectres; it comprises all the rich potentialities and possibilities of development inherent in the true primal numinous emotion. Nor can we doubt that even to-day the finer awe that may steal over us in the stillness and half-gloom of our own present-day sanctuaries has ultimate kinship not only with that of which Schiller writes in his verses:

Und in Poseidons Fichtenhain

Tritt er mit frommem Schauder ein①

but also with genuine ' ghostly ' emotions. The faint shiver that may accompany such states of mind is not unrelated to the feeling of ' creeping flesh ', whose numinous character we have already considered (p. 16). In its efforts to derive ' daemon ' and ' god ' forcibly from ' souls ' and ' spirits ', animism is looking the wrong way. It would be, at any rate, on the right path if it maintained that they are haunting apparitions.

This is partially proved by certain ancient, still extant terms, which long ago had reference to the original awe of the haunting spirit (in the good sense), and later grew to become designations both of the lowest and the highest forms of ' awe '. Such a term is the enigmatical word *asura* in Sanskrit. *Asura* is the ' aweful ' or ' dreadful ' in the sense in which Jacob used the word, the eerie or uncanny. Later, in

① *Schiller, Die Kraniche des Ibykus* (The Cranes of Ibykus): ' And to Poseidon' s grove of pine With awe devout he enters in.

害怕所包含的那种无力而又低下的含义；它包含了内在于真正原始神秘情感之中的所有丰富的发展潜力与可能性。我们丝毫都不怀疑，甚至直到今天，那种在我们现在的教堂的朦胧与寂静之中弥漫在我们身上的更精致的畏惧不仅与席勒在他的诗中所描写的那种东西有着密切的联系：

他怀着虔诚的畏惧

走进波塞冬的松林①

而且也与真正的“鬼魅般的”情绪有最密切的联系。那种伴随着这种心态的轻微的战栗，并非与这种“令人毛骨悚然”的感受无关，这种感受的神秘性质我们已经考察过了（第16页）。在那种强行从“灵魂”与“幽灵”中引出“魔鬼”与“神祇”的努力中，泛神论面对的却是一条错误的道路。如果泛神论坚持“魔鬼”与“神祇”是到处游荡的幽灵，那它至少还走在正确的道路上。

这一点可以通过一些非常古老但是依然没有被废弃的术语而得到部分证实，这些术语在很久以前都关涉到对于到处逡巡的精灵（在好的意义上）的最初的畏惧，而后来则逐渐变成了既是最低级的又是最高级的“畏惧”形式的指称。梵语中的“阿修罗”（*asura*）就是这样一个不可思议的古老术语。*Asura* 正是雅各所用的 eerie 或 uncanny 一词意义上的“怪诞”或“不可思议”。

① 席勒：《伊俾科的鹤》（*Die kraniche des lbykus*）。他怀着虔诚的畏惧走进波塞冬的松林。

Indian religion, it is used as the technical expression for the lower forms of the spectral, ghostly, and daemonic. But at the same time it is from primeval times a title of the sublimest of all the gods of the Rig-Veda, the weirdly exalted *Varuna*. And in the Persian expression *Ahura-mazda* it becomes the name of the one and only eternal god-head itself. The same thing is true of the term *adbhuta*. You experience an *adbhuta* when you are 'in an empty house', says an old defini-tion. ① It is the experience of our 'shuddering'. But, on the other hand, *adbhuta* is also the name for the supreme transcendent marvel and its attractive spell, the element of 'fascina-tion', even for the eternal Brahman himself and his salvation, the *Adbhutam* that passes beyond the reach of speech. ②

11. Finally, it is only upon our assumption of an a priori basis of i-deas and feelings that an explanation is forthcoming for the interesting phenomena to which Andrew Lang③ rightly drew attention. These do not, of course, support the hypothesis of a 'primitive monotheism', that off-spring of missionary apologetic, which, eager to save the second chapter

---

① *Adbhuta* means literally the inapprehensible, inexpressible. But in the first instance it is exactly our *mysterium stupendum*, whereas *asara* is the *tremendum.*

② Adbhuta (and ācarya) would be an accurate rendering in Sanskrit for our 'numinous', were it not that the word, like the German wunderbar and the English 'awful', has long ago become trite and shallow from the 'profane'—non-religious—uses to which it has been so perpetually put.

③ Myth, Ritual, and Religion, 1899; The Making of Religion, 1902; Magic and Religion, 1901. Cf. also P. W. Schmidt, Grundlinien einer Vergleichung der Religionen und Mythologien der austronesischen Völker, Vienna, 1910.

后来，在印度宗教中，asura 这个词被专门用来表达幽灵、鬼魅与魔鬼这类较低的形式。但同时，这个词从原始时代起就是梨俱吠陀（Rig-Veda）中的最高神即出离神圣的“伐楼拿”（*Varuna*）的名称。而在波斯语 *Ahura-mazda* 这个词中，它本身变成了那个唯一永恒之神的名字。对于 adbhuta 这个词也是一样的。正如一个古老的定义[①]所说的，倘若你“在一座空房子中”，你就能体验到 *adbhuta*，这就是我们的“战栗”体验。但是另一方面，*adbhuta* 所指称的，则是那种极端超验的奇迹及其吸引力，即“沉迷”因素，甚至还指称永恒的梵本身及其救赎，即那个无法用语言来表达的 *Adbhutam*。[②]

11. 最后，只有基于我们关于观念与感受的先验基础的假设之上，才能得出安德鲁·兰格[③]给与了相当注意的那些有趣现象的解释。当然，这些现象并没有支持“原始一神教”的假设，这种假设是教会辩护的产物，它在急于保全《创世纪》第二章的同时，

---

① Adbhuta 这个词的字面意思是“无法理解”、“难以形容”。但在第一例中，它正相当于我们的“令人惊奇的神秘”，而 asura 则相当于“令人恐惧的”。

② Adbhuta（与 ascarya）这个梵语就像德语的 wunderbar 与英语的 awful 一样，若不是在“世俗的”（非宗教的）反复使用中已经变得陈腐浅陋，本可成为我们的“神秘”一词的准确表达。

③ 安德鲁·兰格《神话、仪式与宗教》，1899 版；《宗教的形成》，1902 版；《魔法与亲教》，1901 版；也请参见 P. W. 施米特的《奥地利各民族的宗教与神话的比较基础》（Grundlinien einer Vergleichung der Religionen und Mythologien der austronesischen Völker，维也纳，1910 版）。

of Genesis, yet feels the shame of a modern at the walking of Yahweh 'in the garden in the cool of the day'. But they do point to facts which remain downright riddles, if we start from any naturalistic foundation of religion—whether animism, pantheism, or another—and must in that case be got out of the way by the most violent hypotheses. The essence of the matter is this, that elements and strands are to be found in numerous mythologies and the stories of savage tribes, which reach altogether beyond the point they have otherwise attained in religious rites and usages. Notions of 'high gods' are adumbrated, with whom the savage has often hardly any relations in practice, if any at all, and in whom he yet acknowledges, almost in spite of himself, a value superior to that of all other mythological images, a value which may well accord with the divine in the highest sense.

Sometimes, but by no means always, we can discern that these anticipations of a higher religious experience are the outcome of a past growth of myth. What is characteristic and at the same time so puzzling is the elevation with which they stand out from the surrounding more primitive religious life amid which they are found. Indeed, in cases where missions have introduced the preaching of Christian theism, these apprehended, exalted divinities are readily and frequently identified with God and reinforce the preaching of the missionary. And converts often come to admit that, though they had not honoured God, they had had knowledge of Him. It is, of course, true that this sort of fact can sometimes be explained as due to traditional influences, protracted from an earlier time, when the tribe in question was in contact with a higher theistic religion: the very names given to these higher beings sometimes prove as much. But even in this form the phenomenon is a very singular one. Why should 'savages', set in other respects in an utterly alien milieu or barbaric superstition, accept and, what is more, retain these

又因耶和华“在寒冷的天气里于园中”行走而感到一个现代人的羞耻。但是,假如我们从宗教的自然基础出发——无论是万物有灵论、泛神论还是别的什么——并且必然在这种情况下被那些最有力的假设引入歧途,那么,这些现象就的确指向那些谜底尚待揭示的事实。问题的实质是,这些因素和成份可以在原始部落的无数神话和故事中看到,这些因素和成份完全超出了它们在宗教仪式与宗教用法上所达到的高度。“高位神”的观念被勾勒出来了,但原始人却很少在实践中与他发生联系,即便如此,但原始人却承认——几乎无视他自己——“高位神”具有某种高于其他所有神话形象的价值,即具有某种与最高意义上的神性相一致的价值。

有些时候,但是绝对不是经常,我们可以看到,这些对于某种较高宗教经验的预期是神话在过去发展的结果。那种具有特色的,同时又使人大惑不解的东西,是在这些期望被从中发现出来的那种更原始的宗教生活背景中突现出来的上升过程。的确,在传教使命已被引入基督教一神论说教的情形下,这些被领会到的、崇高的神,就会被很容易地经常与上帝等同起来并加强教士的说教。皈依者常常倾向于承认,尽管他们过去不尊奉上帝,但他们却拥有关于上帝的知识。当然,这类事实有时也可被解释为受那些从较早时代延续下来的传统的影响,那时,我们所论及的部落正处于同一种较高的有神教相接触的过程中:正是那些被授予给这些较高存在者的名称有时很能证明一些问题,但即使在这种形式中,这一现象也是非常独特的。为什么“野蛮人”——他们从野蛮迷信的某种完全陌生的环境中出发,会接受,更有甚者,会保留这些观念,除非他们未开化的心灵是如此

notions, unless their own savage minds were so predisposed to them that, so far from being able to let them go, they were obliged to take at least an interest in them as a tradition and very frequently to acknowledge their authority by the felt witness of their own consciences? But, though the theory ot a surviving tradition is sometimes applicable, there are many of these cases in which it is impossible to apply it without doing violence to the facts. In these we have clearly to do with anticipations and presentiments rather than survivals. Assuming the continual pressure and operation of an inward reasonable disposition to form certain ideas, these anticipations are not only no matter for surprise; they are as naturally to be expected as are the achievements of gipsy musicians, who, set otherwise in a milieu of the most primitive culture, yet respond to the pressure of a strong, innate, musical disposition. Without such an assumption the facts would re-main as an insoluble puzzle.

Naturalistic psychologists, in this as in other cases, ignore a fact which might be thought at least to have a psychological interest, and which they could notice in themselves by careful introspection, namely, the self-attestation of religious ideas in one's own mind. This is, to be sure, more certain in the case of the naïve than in that of the more blasé mind; but many people would identify it in their own consciousness if they would only recall deliberately and impartially their hours of preparation for the ceremony of Confirmation. But what the mind 'attests' it can also under favourable circumstances evince and elicit from itself in premonitory stirring and felt surmise. The upholders of the theory of 'primitive monotheism', on the other hand, show no less serious disregard of this central fact than the naturalistic psychologists. For if the phenomena we have been considering were based simply

自然地倾向于这些观念，他们非但能做到不放弃这些观念，而且还感到有必要对作为传统的这些观念至少保持兴趣，同时还经常通过他们自己的良心的见证来承认这些观念的权威？但是，虽然这种关于续存传统的理论有时也是适用的，但许多情况下运用这些理论不可能不歪曲事实。而在这些情况中，我们所要明确处理的是预期和预感，而不是那些幸存下来的东西。假定有某种内在的、合理的倾向在持续地督促和作用于形成某种确定的观念，那么，这些期望就不仅仅是毫不足怪的东西；人们很自然地期待着它们，就像人们期待吉普赛音乐家的成功一样——那些吉普赛音乐家虽在别的方面进入了某种最为原始的文化之中，但却依然对有力的、内在的音乐倾向的困扰作出了反应。如果没有这样一种假设，这些事实就会一直保持为一种无法消解的困扰。

在这里，正如在别的地方一样，自然主义心理学家忽略了一个事实，这个事实至少可以被认为具有某种心理学上的价值，并且也是这些心理学家可以通过仔细反省而在其内心深处注意到的，这就是一个人在自己心灵深处的宗教观念的自证。自然，与倦于享乐的心灵相比，此种自证在纯朴的心灵中较容易产生，但是，只要人们专门地而且毫无偏见地回想一下他们准备“坚信礼”仪式的那些时刻，那么，很多人都可以在他的意识中辨认出这种自证。但心灵所“证明”的那种东西，也可能在有利的条件下，通过有预兆的激动和感受到的猜测而从其自身产生出来。另一方面，“原始一神教”理论的支持者们同自然主义心理学家一样，也同样忽视了这个核心事实。因为，如果我们一直在思考的这些现象完全并且仅仅建立在历史传统

and solely on historical traditions and dim memories of a 'primeval revelation', as on such a theory they must be, this self-attestation from within would be just as much excluded as before.[①]

① Compare with this chapter my recently published book Das Gefühl des Überweltlichen, especially Chapter VI: 'Das Werden eines Gottes'.

和对“原始启示”的模糊记忆之上——按照这种理论它们必然如此，那么，这种内心的自证将会同过去一样，同样被排斥出去。①

① 请将本章与我新近出版的《超世俗的感受》（Gefühl des Überweltlichen）一书，特别是该书的第6章“神的产生”（Das Werden eines Gottes）相比照。

CHAPTER XVI
The 'Cruder' Phases

It is not only the more developed forms of religious experience that must be counted underivable and a *priori*. The same holds good throughout and is no less true of the primnitive, 'crude', and rudimentary emotions of 'daemonic dread' which, as we have seen, stand at the threshold of religious evolution. *Religion is itself present at its commencement*: religion, nothing else, is at work in these early stages of mythic and daemonic experience. Let us consider the circumstances in which alone the primitive and crude character of these consists.

(a) First, it is due to the merely gradual emergence and successive awakening of the several 'moments' of the numinous. The numinous only unfolds its full content by slow degrees, as one by one the series of requisite stimuli or incitements becomes operative. But where any whole is as yet incompletely presented its earlier and partial constituent moments or elements, aroused in isolation, have naturally something bizarre, unintelligible, and even grotesque about them. This is especially true of that religious moment which would appear to have been in every case the first to be aroused in the human mind, viz. daemonic dread. Considered alone and *per se*, it necessarily and naturally looks more like the opposite of religion than religion itself. If it is singled out from the elements which form its context, it appears rather to resemble a dreadful form of auto-suggestion, a sort of psychological nightmare of the tribal mind, than to have anything to do with religion; and the supernatural beings

第十六章　“较粗糙的”诸阶段

不单是宗教经验的较发达各种形式应该被看做是不可派生的和先验的。“对于魔鬼的恐惧”——如我们所知，它处于宗教进化的最开端处——的种种原始的、“粗糙的”、尚未发展的情感，也完全应当如此看待。宗教在其开始时就表现为其自身：宗教，而不是别的其他任何东西，在神话的、恶魔经验的这些初期阶段，就在起作用。让我们考察一下初期阶段原始粗糙的特点唯一赖以存身的种种境况吧。

(a)首先，神秘感的一些“要素”是逐渐出现、相继觉醒的。只有在一系列必不可少的刺激或激励逐个发生作用时，神秘感才会缓缓地展示它的全部内容。但是，在整体没有完全地展现自身的地方，整体的那些被单独激发起来的早期的、部份的构成要素或因素就自然地会有些奇特和不可理解，甚至有些奇形怪状。这种情况对于那种似乎总是在人的思想中被首先激起的宗教要素，即对于恶魔的恐惧来说，尤其如此。如果人们单独考虑它并只考虑它本身，必然而且自然地，它看起来更像是宗教的对立物而不是宗教本身。如果把它从组成它前后联系的那些因素中抽取出来，它表现得更像是一种自我暗示的可怕形式，像是一种部落心灵中的心理梦魇，而和宗教没有任何关系；而且，人在这个早期阶段表

with whom men at this early stage profess relations appear as phantoms, projected by a morbid, undeveloped imagination afflicted by a sort of persecution-phobia. One can understand how it is that not a few inquirers could seriously imagine that 'religion' began with devil-worship, and that at bottom the devil is more ancient than God.

To this serial and gradual awakening of the different aspects and moments of the numinous is also to be ascribed the difficulty of classifying religions by genus and species. Every one who undertakes the task produces a different classification. For the facts to be classified are for the most part not at all related as the distinct species of one and the same genus; they are not alternative, determinate forms into which the whole—'religion'—may be analysed, but constituent elements, out of which it is to be 'synthesized' or built up. It is as though a whale should begin to show itself above the water part by part, and as though people should then attempt to classify the arched back, the end of the tail, and the head spouting water, by genus and species, instead of seeking for such a real understanding of these phenomena as would recognize each of them in its place and proper connexion with the rest as a part and member of *one* whole body, which must itself have been grasped in its entirety before its parts could be properly apprehended.

(b) In the second place, the 'primitiveness' of the cruder phases is due to the abrupt, capricious, and desultory character which marks the earliest form of numinous emotion; and, in consequence, to its indistinctness, which causes it to be merged and confounded with 'natural' feelings.

(c) It is due, next, to the fact that the valuation prompted by the moment of numinous consciousness (e.g. the 'daemonic dread' phase) is attached in the first place, and very naturally, to objects, occurrences, and entities falling within the workaday world of primitive experience, which prompt or give occasion to the stirring of numinous emotion by analogy and then divert it to themselves. This circumstance is more

示与之有关系的种种超自然之物表现为各种幻象，这些幻象是通过病态的、不发达的想象受到一种迫害恐惧症的困扰而凸现出来的。人们因此可以理解，把“宗教”想象成开始于魔鬼崇拜的研究者的确并非少数，而且从根本上来说，魔鬼比上帝更古老。

由于神秘感的各个不同方面和不同要素是相继逐渐地觉醒的，也导致了要以种以及种类来区分各种宗教类别的困难。每一个承担这项工作的人都会提出一种不同的分类。因为要被分类的事实在极大的程度上绝不像同一个或者同一种的各个截然不同的属那样相互联系着；它们不是整体——即“宗教”——中能够通过分析而得出的可选择的、确定的种种形式，而是整体可以由它们“综合”或构建而成的组成元素。这就像是鲸鱼开始一点点地露出水面时，人们便打算用种属去对它的弓形的脊背、尾巴的末端以及喷水的头部进行分类，而不是把每一个部分当做一个整体的一部份，在整体与整体其余部份的空间关系及联系中识别它，以求得对这些现象的真正理解——整体只有在其本身被全面把握的情况下，它的各个部份才能够被完全地理解.

(b)其次，这一比较粗糙阶段的“原始性”是由于形成神秘情感最初形式的那种突然的、反复无常的以及随意的特点，因此，“原始性”也归因于神秘情感的含混性。这种含混性导致它与“自然的”感情相混合、相混淆。

(c)再次，这原始性也归因于这种事实，由神秘意识(例如“对魔鬼的恐惧”的阶段)的要素所引发的估计，首先而且也很自然地是与原始经验的日常世界的各种物体、事件以及各种实体联系在一起的。这种原始经验的日常世界通过类比刺激或引起了神秘情感的骚动，然后将其转向它们自身。这种情况不是别的，正是

than anything else the root of what has been called nature-worship and the deification of natural objects. Only gradually, under pressure from the numinous feeling itself, are such connexions subsequently 'spiritualized' or ultimately altogether rejected, and not till then does the obscure content of the feeling, with its reference to absolute transcendent reality, come to light in all its integrity and self-subsistence.

(d) A fourth factor contributing to the crudity of primitive 'religion' is the uncontrolled, enthusiastic form, making for wild fanaticism, in which the numinous feeling storms the savage mind, appearing as religious mania, possession by the numen, intoxication, and frenzy.

(e) Again, a quite essential factor is the wrong schematizations it undergoes, when interpreted in terms of some experi-ence analogous, perhaps, but not really appertaining to it. Examples of this have already been given (e.g. pp. 122–4).

(f) Finally, and most important, there is the deficient rationalization and moralization of the experience, for it is only gradually that the numinous feeling becomes charged with progressively rational, moral, and cultural significance.

These considerations account for the primitive and savage character of the numinous consciousness at its outset. But it must be repeated that in its content even the first stirring of 'daemonic dread' is a purely a *priori* element. In this respect it may be compared from first to last with the aesthetic judgement and the category of the beautiful. Utterly different as my mental experiences are when I recognize an object as 'beautiful' or as 'horrible', yet both cases agree in this, that I ascribe to the object an attribute that professes to interpret it, which I do not and cannot get from sense-experience, but which I rather ascribe to it by a spontaneous judgement of my own. Intuitively I apprehend in the object only its sensuous qualities and its spatial form, nothing more. That the

所谓的自然崇拜和自然物体神格化的根源。只是逐渐地,在神秘感自身的压力之下,这些联系物才随即被“精神化”了,或者最终被完全地排斥掉,直到那时,这种感觉的模糊不清的内容,通过它与绝对超验实在的参照,才显出它全部的完整性及自我存在性。

(d)造成原始“宗教”粗糙性的第四个因素是它那未加控制的、热烈的形式,有助于造成野性的狂热,在这种形式中,神秘感席卷野蛮的头脑,表现为宗教的狂热,为神秘所占有、陶醉和疯狂。

(e)另外,一个十分重要的因素是它所经历的错误的图式化过程,在这个图式化过程中,人们用一些也许类似但事实上并不属于它的经验来解释它。本书已列举过这方面的例子。(参见122~124页)

(f)最后,也是最重要的,对这种经验的理性化和道德化都十分不足,因为神秘感觉只是逐渐地被添加上了理性的、道德的、以及文化的意义。

以上这些考察解释了神秘意识在其开端阶段的原始和野蛮特性。但是,必须要重申的是,就其内容来说,甚至“对魔鬼的恐惧”的最初的骚动都是一种纯粹的先验成份。在这一方面,它可以自始自终地与对美的审美判断和范畴相比较。当我认识到某物为“美的”或是“可怕的”时,尽管我的精神体验完全不同,但这两种情况在这一点上是一致的:我都是在赋予该物体一种属性以解释该物体,这属性我不是、也不能从感觉经验中得到的,而是通过自已的自发的判断赋予给它的。在这一对象中,我只是直觉地领悟到了它的感官品质以及它的空间形式,而没有其他的任何东

meaning I call 'beautiful' fits the object, i. e. that these sensedata *mean* 'beautiful', or even that there is any such meaning at all—these are facts which sensory elements can in no wise supply or tell me. I must have an obscure conception of 'the beautiful itself', and, in addition, a principle of subsumption, by which I attribute it to the object, else even the simplest experience of a beautiful thing is rendered impossible. And this analogy may be pursued farther. Joy in the beautiful, however analogous to mere pleasure in the agreeable, is yet distinguishable from it by a plain difference in quality, and cannot be derived from anything other than itself; and just such is the relation of the specific religious awe to mere natural fear.

The 'crude' stage is transcended as the numen reveals 'itself' (i. c. becomes manifest to mind and feeling) ever more strongly and fully. An essential factor in this is the process by which it is filled out and charged with rational elements, whereby it passes at the same time into the region of the conceivable and comprehensible. Yet all the time all the elements of non-rational 'inconceivability' are retained on the side of the numinous and intensified as the revelation proceeds. 'Revelation' does not mean a *mere* passing over into the intelligible and comprehensible. Something may be profoundly and intimately known in feeling for the bliss it brings or the agitation it produces, and yet the understanding may find no concept for it. To *know* and to *understand conceptually* are two different things, are often even mutually exclusive and contrasted. The mysterious obscurity of the numen is by no means tantamount to unknowableness. Assuredly the '*deus absconditus et incomprehensibilis*' was for Luther no '*deus ignotus*'. And so, too, St. Paul 'knows' the peace, which yet 'passeth understanding'.

西。我所称为"美"的东西,其意义符合于该物体,也就是说,这些感觉材料就意味着"美",或者甚至可以说,确实就存在着这样一种意义——这些就是感觉元素根本无法提供给我或告诉我的事实。我必须有一个关于"美本身"的模糊概念,另外,还有一个归类的原则,通过这个原则我就可以把这个概念赋予该物体,否则,即便对美的事物进行最简单的体验都是无法表达的。这个类比还可以被进一步推展。在美中所体验到的快乐,无论它与舒适造成的喜悦度多么类似,都在性质上与后者明显区别开来,这种快乐只能产生于它自身,而不能产生于任何其他事物;特定的宗教敬畏与单纯的自然恐惧之间的关系也正是如此。

当神圣更加强烈地、全面地展示"自身"(也就是说,对于思想和感觉变得明晰起来)时,神秘感的"粗糙"阶段便被超越了。在这个超越的过程中的一个基本的因素就是,在这个阶段神圣逐渐地被填充和赋予理性的因素的同时,并且通过这个过程,它也进入了可想象的、可理解的领域。然而,所有的非理性的"不可想象性"因素仍然一直保留在神秘的边缘,而且,随着启示的过程而被强化。"启示"并不意味着仅仅变得可知与可理解。由于它所带来的那种狂喜,或它所产生的那种兴奋,人们会在感觉上深刻而亲切地认识到某种东西,但是,这种理解还是找不到与之对应的概念。去认识和在概念上理解是两件不同的事情,它们二者甚至常常互相排斥,互相对立。神圣的那种神秘的模糊性绝不等同于不可知。确实,对于路德来说,所谓的"*deus abseonditus et incomprehensibilis*"(隐藏的、不可理解的上帝)并不是"*deus ignotus*"(陌生的上帝)。因此同样,圣保罗也能"认识"那"超越理解的"和平。

CHAPTER XVII

The Holy As An *A Priori* Category

PART II

We conclude, then, that not only the rational but also the non-rational elements of the complex category of ' holi-ness ' are a *priori* elements and each in the same degree. Religion is not in vassalage either to morality or teleology, *ethos* or *telos*, and does not draw its life from postulates; and its non-rational content has, no less than its rational, its own independent roots in the hidden depths of the spirit itself.

But the same a priori character belongs, in the third place, to the *connexion* of the rational and the non-rational elements in religion, their inward and necessary union. The histories of religion recount indeed, as though it were something axiomatic, the gradual interpenetration of the two, the process by which ' the divine ' is charged and filled out with ethical meaning. And this process is, in fact, *felt* as something axiomatic, something whose inner necessity we feel to be self-evident. But then this inward self-evidence is a problem in itself; we are forced to assume an obscure, a *priori* knowledge of the necessity of this synthesis, combining rational and nonrational. For it is not by any means *a logical* necessity. How should it be logically inferred from the still ' crude ', half-daemonic character of a moon-god or a sun-god or a numen attached to some locality, that he is a guardian and

第十七章　作为一种先验范畴的神圣

第二部分

因此我们得出如下的结论,“神圣”这个复杂范畴的理性的诸因素与它的非理性的诸因素都是先验的,而且各自都处于同一程度。宗教既不隶属于道德,也不隶属于目的论,它既不是伦理的(*ethos*),也不是目的的(*telos*),而且它不从假定中吸取自己的生命;它的非理性内容,同它的理性内容一样,在精神自身隐秘的深处有它自己独立的根。

但是,第三个方面,这一同样的先验特性还属于宗教中理性和非理性成份之间的联系,即它们内在的必然的结合。宗教的历史的确叙述了这二者之间逐渐相互贯通的过程,似乎它是某种具有公理性的东西,正是通过这个过程,“神圣”被赋予和填充了伦理的意义。事实上,作为被感觉为某种公理性的东西,这个过程的内在必然性是不言自明。但是,这种内在自明性本身也是一个问题;我们不得不假设对这种由理性和非理性成份结合起来的合成物的必然性有一种模糊的、先验的认识,因为它绝不是一种逻辑的必然性。怎么能够逻辑地从月神、日神或附着着某种地方性的那种尚且“粗糙”、半魔鬼的特性中得出这种推论:他便是誓言、

guarantor of the oath and of honourable dealing, of hospitality, of the sanctity of marriage, and of duties to tribe and clan? How should it be inferred that he is a god who decrees happiness and misery, participates in the concerns of the tribe, provides for its well-being, and directs the course of destiny and history? Whence comes this most surprising of all the facts in the history of religion, that beings, obviously born originally of horror and terror, become *gods*—beings to whom men pray, to whom they confide their sorrow or their happiness, in whom they behold the origin and the sanction of morality, law, and the whole canon of justice? And how does all this come about in such a way that, when once such ideas have been aroused, it is understood at once as the plainest and most evident of axioms, that so it must be?

Socrates, in Platos *Republic*, ii. 382 E, says: 'God, then, is single and true in deed and word, and neither changes himself nor deceives others. . . . ' And Adeimantos answers him: 'So too is it apparent to me, now that you say it. ' The most interesting point in this passage is not the elevation and purity of the conception of God, nor yet the lofty rationalization and moralization of it here enunciated, but, on the side of Socrates, the apparently 'dogmatic' tone of his pronouncement—for he does not spend the least pains in demonstrating it—and, on the side of Adeimantos, the ingenuous surprise and, at the same time, the confident assurance with which he admits a truth novel to him. And his assent is such as implies convincement; he does not simply believe Socrates; he sees clearly for himself the truth of his words. Now this is the criterion of all a *priori* knowledge, namely, that, so soon as an assertion has been clearly expressed and understood, knowledge of its truth comes into the mind with the certitude of first-hand insight. And what passed here between Socrates and Adeimantos has been repeated a thousand times in the history of religions. Amos, also, says something new when he proclaims Yahweh as the God of inflexible, universal, and absolute righteousness, and yet this is a novelty that he neither proves nor justifies by an appeal to authorities. He

诚实行为、好客精神、婚姻的圣洁以及部落氏族职责的保卫者和保证者呢？怎么能够推导出他就是散播幸福和苦难、关心部落、为它提供福利并且决定其命运和历史进程的神灵呢？在宗教的历史中，到底是什么时候出现了这一最惊人的事实，那些显然最初是出自恐怖和恐惧的东西变成了神灵——人们向它祈祷、向它倾诉哀痛或幸福，并将它视为道德、法律和整个正义准则的本源和尊严？而且何以这一切又是以这样的方式发生的，一旦这些观念被激起，人们立即就像对待最清晰、最明白的公理一样将它视为必然如此？

在柏拉图的《理想国》II. 382E 中，苏格拉底说道："所以神在行为和言辞上是独一无二的，真实的，他既不改变自己也不欺骗他人……"阿戴芒土斯答道："你这样一说，我也就明白了。"这一段文章中，最有趣的一点并不是神的概念的崇高性和纯粹性，也不是在这里阐明的对这个概念的崇高的理性化和道德化，而是，在苏格拉底方面，是他宣布这一看法时的那种明显的"教条的"口吻——因为他丝毫都没有费力去阐述这一看法——而在阿戴芒土斯方面，则是在他承认这种对他来说很新奇的真理时的那种坦率的惊讶和确信的保证，而他的赞同意味着他被说服了；但他并非只是相信苏格拉底，他自己清楚地理解了苏格拉底话语中的真理。现在，这成了一切先验知识的标准，也就是说，一旦一个主张被清楚地表达和理解了，关于它的真理的认识就随着直接洞见的确信进入头脑。而此处苏格拉底和阿戴芒土斯所交谈的内容在宗教史上已经被重复了上千次。同样，当阿摩司宣布耶和华是不可更变的、普遍的、绝对的正义之神时，他也说了某种新的东西，而且这也是一种他既没有证明，也没有诉诸典籍来加以确证

appeals to a *priori* judgements, viz. to the religious conscience itself, and this in truth bears witness to his message.

Luther, again, recognizes and maintains such an a priori knowledge of the divine nature. His rage against the 'whore Reason' leads him, to be sure, usually to utterances in the opposite sense, such as the following:

It is a knowledge a *posteriori*, in that we look at God from without, at His works and His government, as one looketh at a castle or house from without and thereby feeleth (*spüret*) the lord or householder thereof. But a *priori* from within hath no wisdom of men yet availed to discover what and of what manner of being is God as He is in Himself or in His inmost essence, nor can any man know nor say aught thereof, but they to whom it has been revealed by the Holy Ghost.

Here Luther overlooks the fact that a man must 'feel' or detect the 'hoùseholder' a *priori* or not at all. But in other passages he himself allows the general human reason to possess many true cognitions of what 'God is in Himself or in His inmost essence'. Compare the following:

Atque ipsamet ratio naturalis cogitur eam concedere *proprio suo iudicio convicta*, etiamsi nulla esset scriptura. Omnes enim homines inveniunt hanc sententiam in cordibus suis scriptam et *agnoscunt* eam ac probatam, licet inviti, cum *audiant* eam tractari: primo, Deum esse omnipotentem ... deinde, ipsum omnia nosse et praescire, neque errare neque falli posse.... Istis duobus corde et sensu concessis....①

① Luther, Weimar ed., xviii. 719: 'And the natural reason itself is forced even were there no holy scripture, to grant it (*sc.* this assertion),

的新东西。他诉诸先验的判断，也就是说诉诸宗教良心本身，而这事实上见证了他所传达的信息。

路德同样承认并坚持对神的本性的这样一种先验的认识。他对“卑劣的理性”的愤怒，很自然地，通常会导致他表达出相反意义的看法，如同下述这一段话：

这是一种后天认识，在这种认识中，我们从外部去查看上帝的，查看他的成果，查看他的统治，正如人们从外部去看一座城堡或房子，并由此去感受（*spüret*）里面的领主或户主。但是，上帝作为一种来自内部的先验，人的智慧并不能发现他本来是什么，或在最内在的实质上是一种什么样的存在。对于他，任何人也不能认识、不能说出任何东西来。能说出来的只有这样一些人，上帝凭圣灵曾向他们昭示过自己的本质。

这里，路德忽略了这样一个事实，即人必须去“感受”或者察觉这先验的“户主”呢，还是根本就不必。但是，在另一段文章里路德却承认普遍的人类理性可以对“上帝就是其本身，或上帝就在其最内在的实质中”的问题具有许多真实可信的认识。比较下文：

自然的理性本身，甚至在没有圣经的情况下，也不得不承认它（也就是这种断言），对它自己的判断深信不疑。因为，所有的人，一旦听到人们谈到它，就会发现这一信念铭刻在心头，于是就把它当成被证实过的东西予以承认，尽管他们不愿意也要这样做。人们认定：首先，上帝是万能的，……其次，他知道而且能预知天下的一切，既不会犯错误，也不会被欺骗……既然这两点被心灵和感情所承认……①

① 见路德作品集，魏玛版第18卷，第719页：“自然的理性本身，甚至在没有圣经的情况下，也不得不承认它（也就是这种断言），对它自己的判断

The interesting words of this statement are: *proprio suo iudicio convicta*, for they make the distinction between cognitions and mere 'innate ideas' or supernaturally instilled notions, both of which latter may produce 'thoughts', but not convictions '*ex proprio iudicio*'. Note also the words: 'cum *audiant* eam tractari', which exactly correspond to the experience of Plato's Adeimantos, already quoted. ①

---

convinced by its own judgement. For all men, *as soon as they hear it treated of*, find this belief written in their hearts, and acknowledge it as proved, even unwillingly: first, that God is omnipotent,... then, that He has knowledge and foreknowledge of all things and can neither err nor be deceived .... Since these two things are admitted by heart and feeling.... '

① The most interesting features in Luther in this connexion, however, are the passages upon 'Faith', in which Faith is described as a unique cognitive faculty for the apprehension of divine truth, and as such is contrasted with the 'natural' capacities of the Understanding, as elsewhere the 'Spirit' is contrasted. 'Faith' is here like the 'Syntesesis' in the theory of knowledge of the mystics, the 'inward teacher' (*magister internus*) of Augustine, and the 'inward light' of the Quakers, which are all of them of course 'above reason', but yet an a priori element in ourselves. A particularly striking passage is the following from Luther's *Table-Talk* (Wei. v. 5820):

'The knowledge of God is impressed upon the mind of every man by God. Under the sole guidance of nature all men know that God is-without any acquaintance with the arts or sciences; and this is divinely imprinted upon all men's minds. There has never been a people so wild and savage that it did not believe that there is some divine power that created all things. And thus it is that Paul says: "the invisible things of God from the creation of the world are clearly seen, being understood by the things that are made, even His eternal power and Godhead." Wherefore all the Gentiles knew that there is a God, however much they were Epicureans, however much they maintained that there is no God. Did they not confess God's being in that very denial of Him? For no one can deny that of which he has no knowledge. Wherefore, although men have all their lives long been occupied in the greatest sins and crimes and have lived just as though there were no God, yet they have never been able to cast forth from their minds the conscience that testifies and affirms that God is. And although that conscience has been overborne for a time by evil and perverse opinions, yet it comes back to convict them in their life's final breath.'

这段文章中,有趣的词汇是“自己的判断深信不疑”*proprio suo iudicio convicta*,因为它们区分了认识和单纯的“先天观念”或超自然地灌输的观念之间的不同,后两者或许都能产生“思想”,但不能产生根据对“自身判断”(*ex proprio iudicio*)的确信。也要注意这些词句:“一旦听到人们论及它”(cum *audiant* eam tractari),这完全符合我们上面引用的柏拉图的阿戴芒土斯的体验。[①]

深信不疑。因为,所有的人,一旦听到人们谈到它,就会发现这一信念铭刻在心头,于是就把它当成被证实过的东西予以承认,尽管他们不愿意也要这样做。人们认定:首先,上帝是万能的,……其次,他知道而且能预知天下的一切,既不会犯错误,也不会被欺骗……既然这两点被心灵和感情所承认……”

① 然而路德在这方面最有趣的特征还是他论及“信仰”的段落,在那些文章段落中,信仰被描述为一种对神性真理的顿悟能力,它与理解的“自然的”能力相对,正如在其他地方“精神”与后者相对一样。这儿,“信仰”一语与神秘主义认识论中的“悟性”、奥古斯丁的“内心导师”(*magister internus*)以及贵格教派的“内心之光”等术语相似,它们当然都是“超乎理性的”,但同时也是我们自身中的一个先验成份。路德这方面论述中特别突出的便是下面选自他《谈话录》(Table-Talk)(魏玛版卷5,第5820页)的一段话:

“对上帝的认识是由上帝铭刻在每个人的头脑中的。在天性的唯一指导下,所有的人都知道,上帝是与艺术和科学没有任何联系的,这一认识被神圣地铭刻在每个人的头脑里。从来就没有一个民族如此原始,如此野蛮,乃至于不相信存在着某种创造一切的神圣力量。所以圣保罗才作如是说:‘上帝的那些为世间万物所不能见的东西,因被造物所理解而能被清楚地看见,甚至上帝永恒的力量和神性也不例外。’所以,所有的异教徒都知道存在着上帝,不管他们如何信仰伊壁鸠鲁学说,无论他们如何坚持认为不存在上帝。难道他们不正是通过否认上帝而承认了他的存在吗?因为,没有人会否认他一无所知的东西。所以,虽然人们长期让他们的生命被最大的恶与罪所占据,而且似乎像是不存在着上帝那般地生活着,但是,他们从未能从思想中抛弃那证明和断言上帝存在的良心。虽然那良心在某个时候被邪恶和妄念所压抑,但是,在他们生命的最后一息,它却会重返他们的意识以让他们知罪。”

It is the same experience which missionaries have so often undergone. Once enunciated and understood, the ideas of the unity and goodness of the divine nature often take a surprisingly short time to become firmly fixed in the hearer's mind, if he show any susceptibility for religious feeling. Frequently, thereupon, the hearer adapts the religious tradition that has hitherto been his to the new meaning he has learned. Or, where resistance is offered to the new teaching, it is yet often noticeably in the face of pressure the other way from the man's own conscience. Such experiences have been made known to me by missionaries among the Tibetans and among African negroes, and it would be interesting to make a collection of them, both in regard to the general question of the a priori factors in religion, and especially as throwing light upon the a priori knowledge of the essential interdependence of the rational and the non-rational elements in the idea of God. For this the history of religion is itself an almost unanimous witness. Incomplete and defective as the process of moralizing the 'numina' may often have been throughout the wide regions of primitive religious life, everywhere there are traces of it to be found. And wherever religion, escaping from its first crudity of manifestation, has risen to a higher type, this process of synthesis has in all cases set in and continued more and more positively. And this is all the more remarkable when one considers at what widely different dates the imaginative creation of the figures of gods had its rise in different cases, and under what diverse conditions of race, natural endowment, and social and political structure its evolution proceeded. All this points to the existence of a priori factors universally and necessarily latent in the human spirit: those, in fact, which we can find directly in our own religious consciousness, when we, too, like Adeimantos, naÏvely and spontaneously concur with Socrates' saying, as with an axiom whose truth we have seen for ourselves: 'God is single, and true in deed and word.'

这是那种教士们常常会经历到的相同的经验。有关神的本质的统一性和善性的各种观点一旦被宣讲、被理解，只要这些听众表现出任何宗教感觉的敏感性，那么，这些观点常常在短得惊人的时间内便在听者的脑子里深深地扎下根来。因此通常，听众都会以自己迄今为止所拥有的宗教传统去适应他所学到的新的意义。或者，即使对这种新的教导有所抵制，这种抵制也常常要明显地面临来自他自己良心的另一方面的压力。在西藏人与在非洲黑人中的传教士曾经告诉过我这种经验，而且，如果从以下两个方面将这些经验收集起来，那将是十分有趣的：不仅着眼于宗教中的先验因素这个一般问题，而且尤其是这些经验能够阐明，有关上帝的观念中的理性和非理性因素之间的根本的相互独立是一种先验认识。对于这一点，宗教史本身就几乎是无异议的见证。尽管在原始宗教生活的广阔领域中，将"神圣"道德化的过程是不完整的、有缺陷的，但是，这个过程的踪迹却能够在任何地方被发现。一旦宗教从其早期表现形式的粗糙性中摆脱出来，上升为一种较高形式，这种综合的过程就开始了，而且会越来越肯定地继续下去。如果考虑到，对神的形象的想象性创造在十分不同的时期产生于不同的事件中，是在各种各样的种族、自然资质，以及社会的和政治的结构等不同的条件下进行的，那么这个综合的过程就更加引人注目了。所有这些都表明了在人的精神中普遍必然地潜藏着先验因素的存在：事实上，我们能够直接在自己的宗教意识中发现的那些东西，正是这些先验因素，如果我们像阿戴芒土斯一样，天真而自发地赞同苏格拉底的话——就像赞同某种我们已经亲眼看到了它的真理的公理似的："上帝在行为和言辞上是独一无二的、真实的。"

As the rational elements, following a priori principles, come together in the historical evolution of religions with the nonrational, they serve to 'schematize' these. This is true, not only in general of the relation of the rational aspect of 'the holy', taken as a whole, to its non-rational, taken as a whole, but also in detail of the several constituent elements of the two aspects. *The tremendum*, the daunting and repelling moment of the numinous, is schematized by means of the rational ideas of justice, moral will, and the exclusion of what is opposed to morality; and schematized thus, it becomes the holy 'wrath of God', which Scripture and Christian preaching alike proclaim. *The fascinans*, the attracting and alluring moment of the numinous, is schematized by means of the ideas of goodness, mercy, love, and, so schematized, becomes all that we mean by Grace, that term so rich in import, which unites with the holy wrath in a single 'harmony of contrasts', and like it is, from the numinous strain in it, tinged with mysticism. The 'moment' *mysteriosum* is schematized by the *absoluteness* of all rational attributes applied to the Deity. Probably the correspondence here implied—between 'the mysterious' and the *absoluteness* of all rational attributes —will not appear at first sight so immediately evident as in the two foregoing cases, wrath and grace. None the less it is a very exact correspondence. God's rational attributes can be distinguished from like attributes applied to the created spirit by being not relative, as those are, but absolute. Human love is relative, admitting of degrees, and it is the same with human knowledge and human goodness. God's love and knowledge and goodness, on the other hand, and all else that can be asserted of Him in conceptual terms, are formally absolute. The *content* of the attributes is the same; it is an *element of form* which marks them apart as attributes of God. But such an element of form is also the 'mysterious' as such: it is, as we saw on p. 31, the formal aspect of the 'wholly other'. But to this plain correspondence of the two

当理性的成份遵循着先验的原则，与非理性成份一同进入宗教的历史进化时，它们就会对这些非理性成份进行“图式化”。这不仅总体上符合作为整体的“神圣”的理性方面与作为整体的“神圣”的非理性方面之间的关系，而且在细节上也符合这两个方面的一些构成要素。神秘的那种令人畏惧的、令人畏缩和令人厌恶的要素，被关于正义、道德意志和对不道德的排除等理性观念所图式化了；而一经这样图式化后，它就变成了神圣的“上帝的忿怒”，圣经和基督教的布道都作了如此宣称。那种“*fascinans*”要素，即神秘的那种吸引人的、充满诱惑的要素，则经由善、慈悲、爱等观念被图示化了，而且，一经图式化，它就变成了我们所谓的神恩，这个术语是如此的重要，它与神圣的忿怒结合成了一个独特的“和谐的对比”，而且，由于它自身所包含的神秘性质，它便仿佛染上了神秘主义的味儿。神秘的“要素”被神所具有的一切理性特征的绝对性所图式化。也许，这儿所暗示的那种对应性——即“神秘”与所有理性特征的绝对性之间的联系——初看之下并不像前面所讲的例子中的忿怒与恩惠之间的联系那样一目了然，但是无论如何这仍然是一种精确的对应。上帝的理性特征能够与属于被创造精神的类似特征区别开来，因为上帝的理性特征不像被造精神是相对的，而是绝对的。人类的爱是相对的，因为它容许有各种各样的程度，同样，人的知识以及人的善良也是如此。另一方面，上帝的爱、知识与善良，以及所有可用概念性的术语来表达的他的一切，在形式上都是绝对的。这些特征的内容都是相同的；它是形式的一个因素，这个形式将它们作为上帝的特征区分开来。但是，这样一种形式的因素也是如此“神秘的”：正如我们在第31页上所见，它是“完全的他者”的形式外观。但是，对于

things, 'the mysterious' and the absoluteness of rational attributes, a further one must be added. Our understanding can only compass the relative. That which is in contrast absolute, though it may in a sense be *thought*, cannot be *thought home*, *thought out*; it is within the reach of our conceiving, but it is beyond the grasp of our comprehension. Now, though this does not make what is 'absolute' itself genuinely 'mysterious', as this term was expounded on pp. 27-8, it does make it a genuine *schema* of 'the mysterious'. The absolute exceeds our power to comprehend; the mysterious wholly eludes it. The absolute is that which surpasses the limits of our understanding, not through its actual qualitative character, for that is familiar to us, but through its formal character. The mysterious, on the other hand, is that which lies altogether outside what can be thought, and is, alike in form, quality, and essence, the utterly and 'wholly other'. We see, then, that in the case of the moment of 'mystery', as well as those of 'awefulness' and 'fascination', there is an exact correspondence between the non-rational element and its rational *schema*, and one that admits of development.

By the continual living activity of its non-rational elements a religion is guarded from passing into 'rationalism'. By being steeped in and saturated with rational elements it is guarded from sinking into fanaticism or mere mysticality, or at least from persisting in these, and is qualified to become a religion for all civilized humanity. The degree in which both rational and non-rational elements are jointly present, united in healthy and lovely harmony, affords a criterion to measure the relative rank of religions—and one, too, that is specifically religious. Applying this criterion, we find that Christianity, in this as in other respects, stands out in complete superiority over all its sister religions. The lucid edifice of its clear and pure conceptions, feelings, and experiences

这两者间的这种明显的对应性，即理性特征的“神秘”和绝对之间的联系，还应当再加上一点。我们的理解能力只能把握相对的东西。那种在对比中是绝对的东西，虽然在一定意义上可以被思考，但却不能被深入地思考，彻底地思考；它在我们构思的范围之内，但却超越了我们的理解力。现在，尽管这并不能使“绝对的”东西本身变成真正“神秘的”，正如这一术语在第27到28页所被详细阐述的那样，但却确实使它成为了“神秘”的真正的图式。绝对的东西超越我们的理解力，神秘的东西则完全避开了我们的理解力。所谓绝对的东西就是超越了我们理解界限的东西，但它不是通过其实际的性质特点——因为那是我们所熟悉的，而是通过其形式特点超越了我们的理解界限。另一方面，所谓神秘的东西则全然处于可被思考的东西之外，它在形式上、性质上、本质上都绝对是“完全的他者”。因此，我们看到，正如在“敬畏”和“沉迷”等要素中一样，在“神秘”这一要素中，非理性成份与其理性的图式之间存在着一种确切的对应关系，这是那种能够发展的联系。

通过非理性因素的持续的生动活动，宗教避免了沦为“理性主义”。通过理性因素的浸染与饱和，宗教又不至于堕落为一种盲信或者纯粹的神秘物，或者至少它不会固执于这两种东西，它才发展成为全体文明人类的宗教。理性因素与非理性因素共同出现的程度以及它们结合为一种健康而可喜的和谐的程度，提供了衡量各种宗教不同相关等级的标准——而这也是一种特别具有宗教性的标准。应用这个标准，我们发现，如同在其他方面一样，基督教在这一方面比它所有的姊妹宗教都要优越。它那清晰、纯净的概念、情感以及经验的明晰大厦，建立在比理性要深邃

is built up on a foundation that goes far deeper than the rational. Yet the non-rational is only the basis, the setting, the woof in the fabric, ever preserving for Christianity its mystical depth, giving religion thereby the deep undertones and heavy shadows of mysticism, without letting it develop into a mere rank growth of mysticality. And thus Christianity, in the healthily proportioned union of its elements, assumes an absolutely classical form and dignity, which is only the more vividly attested in consciousness as we proceed honestly and without prejudice to set it in its place in the comparative study of religions. Then we shall recognize that in Christianity an element of man's spiritual life, which yet has its analogies in other fields, has for the first time come to maturity in a supreme and unparalleled way.

得多的基础之上。它非理性的一面仅仅是基础,仅仅是背景,是编织物的纬线,为基督教保留了它神秘的深度,从而赋予宗教以神秘主义的深沉调式和浓重阴影,但又不使它仅仅发展成为神秘性质的一个生长阶段。于是,基督教——它的构成因素处于一种健康的、成比例的和谐中——就呈现出一种绝对正统的形式和尊严,这一点,当我们诚实而无偏见地将它与其他宗教进行比较性研究时,就在意识中得到了十分生动的验证。于是我们就将认识到,在基督教中,人类精神生活中的一种成份——在其他的领域中它也有其类似物——已经以一种至高无上的方式首次变得成熟了。

CHAPTER XVIII

The Manifestations Of The 'Holy' And The Faculty Of 'Divination'

It is one thing merely to believe in a reality beyond the senses and another to have experience of it also; it is one thing to have ideas of 'the holy' and another to become consciously aware of it as an operative reality, intervening actively in the phenomenal world. Now it is a fundamental conviction of all religions, of religion as such, we may say, that this latter is possible as well as the former. Religion is convinced not only that the holy and sacred reality is attested by the inward voice of conscience and the religious consciousness, the 'still, small voice' of the Spirit in the heart, by feeling, presentiment, and longing, but also that it may be directly encountered in particular occurrences and events, selfrevealed in persons and displayed in actions, in a word, that beside the inner revelation from the Spirit there is an outward revelation of the divine nature. Religious language gives the name of 'sign' to such demonstrative actions and manifestations, in which holiness stands palpably selfrevealed. From the time of the most primitive religions everything has counted as a sign that was able to arouse in man the sense of the holy, to excite the feeling of apprehended sanctity, and stimulate it into open activity. Of this kind

第十八章 “神圣”的诸种表现以及“直觉感受”的能力

仅仅信仰一种超越感觉的事实是一回事,除信仰之外同时还有对它的体验则是另外一回事;拥有“神圣”的观念是一回事,自觉地意识到它是一种主动地干涉现象世界的、起作用的事实,又是另一回事。对于所有的宗教来说,或许我们可以说,同样对于每一种宗教来说,都有这样一个基本的确信,即后者与前者同样可能。宗教确信,不仅神圣与圣洁的事实能够被良心内在的声音和宗教意识,即内心深处圣灵的“详和而微弱的声音”所证实,能够被感觉、预感和渴望所证实,而且神圣与圣洁的事实会直接遭遇到特别的偶然事件和事变,会在人身上自我揭示并且在各种行动中展示出来。一句话,紧随着来自内心深处的圣灵的启示,还有一种外部的神性的启示。对于神圣借以清楚地自我显现的那些说明的行为以及各种表现,宗教语言称作“神迹”。从最原始的宗教起,任何能在人的心中激发起神圣感、激起那种被领悟到的圣洁的感觉,并将这种感觉引发成公开的活动的一切事物,都被看成是一种神迹。在这类事物中,包括了我们已经谈论过的

were those factors and circumstances of which we have already spoken—the thing terrible, sublime, overpowering, or astounding, and in an especial degree the uncomprehended, mysterious thing, which become the 'portent' and 'miracle'. But, as we saw, all these were not 'signs' in the true sense, but opportunities, circumstances, prompting the religious feeling to awake of itself; and the factor promoting this result was found to lie in an element common to them all, but merely analogous with 'the holy'. The interpretation of them as actual appearances of the holy itself in its own nature meant, we saw, a confounding of the category of holiness with something only outwardly resembling it: it was not a genuine 'anamnesis', a genuine recognition of the holy in its own authentic nature, made manifest in appearance. And therefore we find that such false recognitions of the holy are later rejected and wholly or partly extruded as inadequate or simply unworthy, so soon as a higher level of development and a purer religious judgement have been reached. There is a precisely parallel process in another department of judgement, that of aesthetic taste. While the taste is still crude, a feeling or fore-feeling of the beautiful begins to stir, which must come from an obscure *a priori* conception of beauty already present, else it could not occur at all. The man of crude taste, not being capable of a clear 'recognition' of authentic beauty, falls into confusion and misapplies this obscure, dim conception of the beautiful, judging things to be beautiful which are in fact not beautiful at all. Here, as in the case of the judgement of holiness, the principle underlying the erroneous judgement of beauty is one of faint analogy. Certain elements in the thing wrongly judged to be beautiful have a closer or remoter analogy to real beauty. And later here, too, when his taste has been educated, the man rejects with strong aversion the quasibeautiful but not really beautiful thing and becomes qualified to see and to judge rightly, i. e. to recognize as beautiful the

那些因素和情况——可怕的、崇高的、无法抵抗的或惊人的事物，以及在特殊的程度上无法理解的和神秘的事物，这些事物都变成了“征兆”和“奇迹”。但是，正如我们所知，所有的这一切都不是真正意义上的“神迹”，它们不过是一些机会和环境，以促使宗教感觉自己苏醒过来；而造成这一结果的原因就隐身在它们共有的一种因素之中，只不过类似“神圣”罢了。我们看到，将它们解释成为神圣本来性质的实际表现，意味着将神圣这一范畴与某种仅仅在外表上同它相似的东西相混淆了：这不是一种真正“反思”，不是一种在其自身可信的本质上对神圣的真正认识，以使神圣的外观清晰起来。因此我们发现，一旦宗教发展到了更高的阶段，而人们获得了更加纯粹的宗教判断后，这种对神圣的错误的认识随即就会遭到拒斥，并被整个地或者部分地被看成是不完善的或者简直就是毫无价值而遭到驱逐。在判断力的另一个领域，即审美品味的领域存在着一种与之完全相似的过程。当人的审美品味还十分粗糙时，一种对美的感觉或者前感觉就开始骚动了——这种感觉或前感觉必定是来自一个已经存在的、模糊的、有关美的先验概念，否则就根本不会出现。有这种粗糙审美品味的人不能对真正的美有清楚的“辨别”，对于有关美的这个模糊含混的概念陷于混淆和误用之中，从而把那些实际上根本不美的事物判断为美。这里，就像是在神圣的判断的情形中一样，隐含在关于美的错误判断之下的原则是一种模糊的类比。事物中被误判为美的那些成份与真正的美多少有些接近。后来也是一样的，当人的审美品味因教育而提高后，他便会十分反感地拒斥那似美而非美的事物，而且他自己也就具有了正确理解和判断的能力了，也就是说，在那种他已经获得了关于“美”的内在观念

outward object in which the 'beauty' of which he has an inward notion and standard really 'appears'.

Let us call the faculty, of whatever sort it may be, of genuinely cognizing and recognizing the holy in its appearances the faculty of *divination*. Does such a faculty exist, and, if so, what is its nature?

To the 'supernaturalistic' theory the matter is simple enough. Divination consists in the fact that a man encounters an occurrence that is not 'natural', in the sense of being inexplicable by the laws of nature. Since it has actually occurred, it must have had a cause; and, since it has no 'natural' cause, it must (so it is said) have a supernatural one. This theory of divination is a genuine, solidly rationalist theory, put together with rigid concepts in a strict demonstrative form and intended as such. And it claims that the capacity or faculty of divination is the *understanding*, the faculty of reflection in concept and demonstration. The transcendent is here proved as strictly as anything can be proved, logically from given premisses.

It would be almost superfluous to adduce in detail in opposition to this view the argument that we have no possibility of establishing that an event did not arise from natural causes or was in conflict with the laws of nature. The religious consciousness itself rises against this desiccation and materialization of what in all religion is surely the most tender and living moment, the actual discovery of and encounter with very deity. Here, if anywhere, coercion by proof and demonstration and the mistaken application of logical and juridical processes should be excluded; here, if anywhere, should be liberty, the unconstrained recognition and inward acknowledgement that comes from deep within the soul, stirred spontaneously, apart from all conceptual theory. If not 'natural science' or 'metaphysics', at least the matured religious consciousness itself spurns such ponderously solid intellectualistic explanations. They are born of rationalism and engender

以及真正“表现”为“美”的标准的外在事物中，他可以认识到美的存在。

无论它可能属于哪一个类型，我们就将这种在神圣的种种表现中认识和承认神圣的能力叫作直觉感受能力吧。存在着这样一种能力吗？如果存在，那么它的本质又是什么呢？

对于“超自然主义的”理论来说，这是一个再简单不过的问题。所谓直觉感受，就存在于人遭遇到了非“自然的”事件这一事实中，这种非自然的事件不能用自然的各种法则来解释。由于事实上它已经发生，那么它肯定是有原因的；并且，由于它没有“自然的”原因，它肯定（据说）有某个超自然的原因。这种关于直觉感受的理论是一种真正的、稳定的唯理主义理论，它被有意地同各种严格的概念一起安置于一个严谨的表现形式中，而且该理论宣称，直觉感应的能力或本领就是理解，即用概念和论证来反思的能力。在这里，如同任何其他能够被证明的事物一样，超验物可以逻辑地从给定的前提中严格地被证明出来。

详细地引证与下述看法相左的论点几乎是多余的，我们没有任何可能性确认一种不是出自自然的原因或者与自然法则相悖的事件。宗教意识本身就反对把这种一切宗教中显然是最柔嫩、最生动的要素——即对神的实际发现以及与神的直接遭遇——作标本化和具体化的处理。如果在哪儿能够的话，就是在这里，证明和论证的强制性以及对逻辑和法律程序的错误应用应该排除；就是在这里，需要的应该是自由，应该是来自灵魂深处、自发地骚动着的、与一切概念理论无关的、无拘无束的认识和内心的承认。如果说成熟了的宗教意识本身不摒弃“自然科学”或“形而上学”，那么它至少要摒弃这种笨重坚实的唯理智主义的解释。这种解

it again; and, as for genuine 'divination', they not only impede it, but despise it as extravagant emotionalism, mysticality, and false romanticism. Genuine divination, in short, has nothing whatever to do with natural law and the relation or lack of relation to it of something experienced. It is not concerned at all with the way in which a phenomenon— be it event, person, or thing—came into existence, but with what it *means*, that is, with its significance as a 'sign' of the holy.

The faculty or capacity of divination appears in the language of dogma hidden beneath the fine name '*testimonium Spiritus Sancti internum*', the inner witness of the Holy Spirit —limited, in the case of dogma, to the recognition *of Scripture* as 'Holy'. And this name is the only right one, and right in a more than figurative sense, when the capacity of divination is itself grasped and appraised by divination. This is not our task here. We therefore employ a psychological rather than a religious expression as being more appropriate to the nature of our discussion.

In this sense, then, 'divination' is no new theological discovery. Schleiermacher, in his *Discourses upon Religion* (1799), Jacob Friedrich Fries, in his doctrine of *Ahndung* ('inkling', surmise, presage), and Schleiermacher's colleague and Fries's pupil, De Wette, have all in effect made use of it and given it a footing in theology, the last-named with special reference to the divination of the divine in history, under the name 'surmise of the divine government of the world'. I have discussed Schleiermacher's discovery at greater length in my edition of his *Discourses*,[1] and in my volume, *Kantisch*

---

① Schleiermacher, Über die Religion (Vandenhoeck & Ruprecht, Göttingen), PP. 17 ff.

释出自唯理主义,又反过来产生唯理主义,而对于真正的“直觉感受”,它们不仅加以阻碍,而且还轻视它,把它看成是过度的唯情论,故弄玄虚以及虚伪的浪漫主义。总之,真正的直觉感受与自然法则毫无关系,与它是否与某一经验过的事件有没有关系也毫不相干。它根本就不关心现象——无论是事件、人物或事物——进入存在的方式,而是关心该现象意味着什么,也就是说,它关心的是这种现象作为神圣者的“神迹”的意义。

直觉感受的本领或能力隐含在“神圣精神的内在见证”这一精当的名称之中,以教义的语言表现出来——在教义宣传中,这名称仅限于《圣经》所承认的范围。而且,这个名称也是唯一正确的名称,当直觉感受能力本身被直觉感受所把握、所评价时,这个名称就不只是在比喻意义上才是唯一正确的了。这一点并不是我们此处的任务,所以,我们与其使用一个宗教用语,还不如使用一个心理学用语,以便更适合我们讨论的性质。

那么,在这个意义上,“直觉感受”就不是新的神学发现了。施莱尔马赫在他的《论宗教》(1799)中,雅各布·弗里德里希·弗里斯在他的关于预兆感觉(“暗示”、猜度、预兆)的理论中,以及施莱尔马赫的同事、弗里斯的学生德韦特,实际上都有效地使用过这个术语,而且在神学中给予了它一定的地位,最后这位还特别提到对历史上的神圣的直觉感受,他称之为“对神统治的世界的猜度”。在我所编著的施莱尔马赫的《论宗教》①一书中,我对他的发现作了更详尽的讨论,另外,在我的《康德-弗里

① 见施莱尔马赫的《论宗教》,哥廷根版,Vandenhoeck 和 Ruprecht 出版社第 17 页。

Fries' sche Religionsphilosophie und ihre Anwendung auf die Theologie, I have given a more precise statement of the Ahndung theory, as it is found in Fries and De Wette. To these two works the reader is referred for a more detailed exposition of the matter, and I shall here note only very briefly the more salient features of this doctrine.

What Schleiermacher is feeling after is really the faculty or capacity of deeply absorbed *contemplation*, when confronted by the vast, living totality and reality of things as it is in nature and history. Wherever a mind is exposed ini a spirit of absorbed submission to impressions of 'the universe', it becomes capable—so he lays it down—of experiencing 'intuitions' and 'feelings' (*Anschauungen* and *Gefühle*) of something that is, as it were, a sheer overplus, in addition to empirical reality. This overplus, while it cannot be apprehended by mere theoretic cognition of the world and the cosmic system in the form it assumes for science, can nevertheless be really and truly grasped and experienced in *intuition*, and is given form in single 'intuitions'. And these, in turn, assume shape in definite statements and propositions, capable of a certain groping formulation, which are not without analogy with theoretic propositions, but are to be clearly distinguished from them by their free and merely felt, not reasoned, character. In themselves they are groping intimations of meanings figuratively apprehended. They cannot be employed as 'statements of doctrine' in the strict sense, and can neither be built into a system nor used as premisses for theoretical conclusions. But, though these intuitions are limited and inadequate, they are none the less indisputably *true*, i.e. true as far as they go; and for all Schleiermacher's aversion to the word in this connexion they must certainly be termed *cognitions*, modes of *knowing*, though, of course, not the product of reflection, but the intuitive outcome of feeling. Their import is the glimpse of an Eternal, in and beyond the temporal and penetrating it,

斯的宗教哲学及其在神学中的应用》一书中，如弗里斯及德韦特所做的那样，我对“预兆感觉”理论进行了更准确的阐述。建议读者到这两本著作中去查阅对这一问题更详尽的阐述，在这里我只是非常概括地谈谈该理论更具特色的部分。

施莱尔马赫所探索的，的确是当人们面临着事物如同它处在自然和历史上广阔而生动的全貌和真相时所表现出的那种全神贯注的沉思的本领或能力。无论在什么地方，一旦人的思想暴露于一种专注地服从于“宇宙”的各种印象的思想时，它就能够——以施莱尔马赫的话来说——体验到对某种不单是经验现实，而且纯粹是一种额外之物的某种东西的种种“直觉”和“感觉”。由于这个额外的东西不能通过表现在科学中的那种对世界与宇宙系统的纯粹理论认识来理解，它却能够在直觉中被真正地、确切地把握和体验，而且也能够被给与单纯“直觉”的形式。而反过来，这些直觉又表现为种种确定的陈述和命题的形式，能够进行摸索性的阐述，尽管与理论命题并非没有类似之外，但由于它们那种自由的、只是被感受到而不是被推理出的特点，所以它们与后者明显地区别开来。它们本身是摸索性、对于被象征性地领悟到的种种意义的暗示。在严格意义上，它们不能被用做“理论的陈述”，而且既不能被构建成为一个系统，又不能用做理论结论的前提。但是，尽管这些直觉是有限而不完善的，它们仍然不可争辩地是真实的。也就是说，就它们所达到的程度而言，它们是真实的。尽管施莱尔马赫厌恶在这个意义上使用这个词，但是，这种种直觉显然应该被称之为认识，或认识的方式，尽管，它们当然不是反思的产物，而是情感的直觉结果。它们的意义正是对一种永恒者的一瞥，这永恒者既

the apprehension of a ground and meaning of things in and beyond the empirical and transcending it. They are *surmises* or *inklings* of a Reality fraught with mystery and momentousness. And it is to be noted that Schleiermacher himself sometimes avails himself of the term ahnden (divining, surmise) instead of his principal ones, 'intuition' and 'feeling', and expressly connects together the divination of prophecy and the knowledge of 'miracle' in the religious sense of a 'sign'.

When Schleiermacher, in expounding the nature of the experience, tries to elucidate its object by giving examples, he is for the most part led to adduce impressions of a higher τέλος, an ultimate, mysterious, cosmic purposiveness, of which we have a prescient intimation. Here he is quite in agreement with the exposition of Fries, who defines the faculty of *Ahndung* as being just a faculty of divining the 'objective teleology' of the world. And De Wette says the same thing even more unreservedly. But in Schleiermacher this rational element is none the less grounded in eternal mystery, that basis of the cosmos that goes beyond reason. This is shown in the groping, hesitant, tentative manner in which the meaning of the experience always reveals itself. And it is emphasized especially forcibly when Schleiermacher shows where in his own case this experience is to be found in the world he confronts; that it is not so much in its universal conformity to law—a rational quality, interpretable by the intellect in terms of purpose—but rather by means of what appears to us as a baffling 'exception' to law, thereby hinting at a meaning that eludes our understanding. ①

① Op. cit., p. 53.

在现世之内又超越现世，并渗透在整个现世之中，是对事物的背景及意义的领悟，这些事物既在经验的范围之内又在其外，同时又超越了经验。它们是对一种充满神秘和重要性的存在的猜测或暗示。应该注意到，施莱尔马赫自己有时就使用“ahnden”（预测、猜测）这个术语，而不使用“直觉”、“感觉”这些他所使用的主要术语，而且明确地在宗教“神迹”的意义上将对预言的预测和对“奇迹”的认识联系起来。

在解释这种经验的本质时，施莱尔马赫试图通过举出例证来阐述它的对象，在很大程度上，他倾向于引证一个关于较高的 τέλos 的种种印象，即一种根本的、神秘的、广大无边的目的性，对于这个目的性，我们有着一种预先的暗示。在这里，施莱尔马赫与弗里斯的解释非常一致，弗里斯把“预兆感觉”的本领界定为一种预测世界的“客观目的论”的本领。德韦特甚至更加率直地说了同样内容的话。但是，按照施莱尔马赫的观点，这种理性的成份也同样是建立在永恒的神秘的基础上的，也就是那个超越理性的世界的基础。这一点表现在经验的意义总是以摸索的、犹豫的、尝试的方式表现自己。当施莱尔马赫表明，就他本人来说，这种经验可在他所面对的世界中被发现时，这一点得到了尤其强有力的强调；他表明：与其说这种经验可在它与规律的普遍一致性——一种理性的性质，在目的方面它可以依靠理智来解释——中去寻找，还不如说借助于那种对我们来说表现为规律的无法理解的“例外”来寻找，从而这个“例外”就暗示了一种我们的理解所不能把握的意义。[①]

---

① 引文见上书第 53 页。

No intellectual, dialectical dissection or justification of such intuition is possible, nor indeed should any be attempted, for the essence most peculiar to it would only be destroyed thereby. Rather it is once again to aesthetic judgements that we must look for the plainest analogy to it. And the faculty of judging (*Urteilsuermögen*), here presupposed by Schleiermacher, certainly belongs to that 'Judgement' (*Urteilskraft*), which Kant analyses in his Third Critique, and which he himself sets as 'aesthetic judgement' in antithesis to logical judgement. Only, we may not infer from this that the particular several judgements passed in this way need be judgements of 'taste' in their *content*. Kant's distinction between the 'aesthetic' and logical judgement did not mean to imply that the faculty of 'aesthetic' judgement was a judgement upon 'aesthetic' objects in the special narrow sense of the term 'aesthetic', as being concerned with the beautiful. His primary intention is simply and in general terms to separate the faculty of judgement based upon feeling of whatever sort from that of the understanding, from discursive, conceptual thought and inference; and his term 'aesthetic' is simply meant to mark as the peculiarity of the former that, in contrast to logical judgement, it is not worked out in accordance with a clear intellectual scheme, but in conformity to obscure, dim principles which must be felt and cannot be stated explicitly as premisses. Kant employs sometimes another expression also to denote such obscure, dim principles of judgement, based on pure feeling, viz. the phrase 'not-unfolded' or 'unexplicated concepts' (*unausgewickelte Begriffe*); and his meaning is here exactly that of the poet, when he says:

Und wecket der dunklen Gefühle Gewalt,
Die im Herzen wunderbar schliefen.①

① 'It waketh the power of feelings obscure
That in the heart wondrously slumbered.' (Schiller: Der Graf von Habsburg.)

对这种直觉作任何理智的、辩证的解析或证明都是不可能的，实际上也不应该有这种企图，因为这样做将只可能损害它那独特的本质，我们倒不如再一次用审美判断来对它进行一次最明晰的类比。施莱尔马赫在这里所提出的判断的（*Urteilsuermögen*）能力，确实属于康德在他的第三批判中所分析的那种“判断力”（*Urteilskraft*），康德把它称为“审美判断”，并把它设定为逻辑判断的对立面。只是我们不能由此推论出，这儿提到的这些特殊的判断在内容上必须是“鉴赏”判断。康德将“审美的”判断与逻辑判断相区分，这并不意味着“审美”判断力是在“审美”这一术语的特殊的、狭隘意义上，对“审美”对象做出的判断，如同只关注美。康德作出这一区分的主要目的，简要说来，就是要将建立在任何一种感觉基础上的判断力与理解的判断力区分开，与推论的、概念的思想和推断区分开；他使用的“审美的”这一术语，只是要标明，与逻辑判断相比，前者的独特之处就在于，它不是依据一种明确的理智方案产生出来的，而是与一些模糊的，朦胧的原则保持一致，这些原则是只能被感受到，而不能像前提那样被清晰地表述出来的。有时候，康德也使用另一个术语来表达那些建立在纯粹感觉基础上的模糊的、朦胧的判断原则，也就是“未展开的”或“不可解释的概念”（*unausgewickelte Begriffe*）等；此处他的意思和下面这两行诗中所表达的意思完全一样：

它唤醒了那沉睡于心灵的
模糊的感觉之力。[①]

① 见席勒《哈普斯堡的伯爵》：“它唤醒了那沉睡于心灵的模糊的感觉之力。”

Or again:

Was von Menschen nicht gewusst
Oder nicht bedacht,
Durch das Labyrinth der Brust
Wandelt bei der Nacht. ①

On the other hand, those judgements that spring from pure contemplative feeling also resemble judgements of aesthetic taste in claiming, like them, objective validity, universality, and necessity. The apparently subjective and personal character of the judgement of taste, expressed in the maxim *de gustibus non disputandum*, simply amounts to this, that tastes of different degrees of culture and maturity are first compared, then so opposed one to the other that agreement is impossible. But unanimity, even in judgements of taste, grows and strengthens in the measure in which the taste matures with exercise; so that even here, despite the proverb, there is the possibility of taste being expounded and taught, the possibility of a continually improving appreciation, of convincement and conviction. And if this is true of the judgement arising from aesthetic feeling in the narrower sense, it is at least equally true of the judgement arising from 'contemplation'. Where, on the basis of a real talent in this direction, 'contemplation' grows by careful exercise in depth and inwardness, there what one man feels *can* be 'expounded' and 'brought to consciousness' in another: one man can both educate himself to a genuine and true manner of feeling and be the means of bringing others to the same point; and that is what corresponds in the domain of 'contemplation' to the part played by argument and persuasion in that of logical conviction.

Schleiermacher's exposition of his great discovery suffers from

---

① 'What beyond our conscious knowing
Or our thought's extremest span Threads by night the labyrinthine
Pathways of the breast of man. ,(Goethe: An den Mona.)

或者与下面这几行诗所表达的意思一样：

那超越我们意识认知的，

超越我们思想最远界限的东西，

趁着幽幽的暗夜

穿行于人类胸怀的迷宫。①

另一方面，那些从纯粹冥想感觉中涌现出来的判断在宣称自身具有客观有效性、普遍性和必然性方面也相似于审美鉴赏判断。表达在格言"*de gustibus non disputandum*"（谈到趣味无争辩）中的鉴赏判断的明显的主观性质和个人性质，仅仅意味着这样一个意思，不同文明程度和成熟程度的鉴赏力首先互相比较，然后变得互相对立，以致达成一致是不可能的。但是，伴随着鉴赏力通过锻炼而成熟起来，甚至鉴赏判断之间的一致性也产生并加强了，因此，尽管有上面的格言，鉴赏力依然有可能被解释，被传授，于是不断地提高欣赏能力成为可能，说服和确信也随之成为可能。如果这种观点适合产生于较狭隘意义上的审美感觉的判断，那么它至少也同样适合产生于"冥想"的判断。在一个人确有冥思才能的基础上，通过内心深处深刻的细心的练习，"冥想"就产生出来，此时，一个人所感觉到的东西便能够被"解释"和"带入"另一个人的"意识"：一个人可以教会自己一种本真的、真实的感觉方式，也能借助自身使其他人达到同样的程度，在"冥想"的领域中，这就相当于逻辑确证领域里论点和论据所起的作用。

施莱尔马赫对他这一伟大发现的揭示存在着两个缺陷。我

① 歌德《致月亮》："那超越我们意识认知的，超越我们思想最远界限的东西，趁着幽幽的暗夜穿行于人类胸怀的迷宫。"

two defects. We will consider one of them here, leaving the other to the next chapter. Schleiermacher, then, naively and unreflectingly assumes this faculty or capacity of 'divination' to be a universal one. In point of fact it is not universal if this means that it could be presupposed necessarily in every man of religious conviction as an actual fact, though of course Schleiermacher is quite right in counting it among the general capacities of mind and spirit, and regarding it indeed as the deepest and most peculiar element in mind, and in that sense—man being defined by his intelligent mind—calling it a 'universal human' element. But what is a universal potentiality of man as such is by no means to be found in *actuality* the universal possession of every single man; very frequently it is only disclosed as a special endowment and equipment of particular gifted individuals. And Schleiermacher gives an excellent indication of how the matter rightly lies in his very interesting exposition of the nature and function of the *Mittler* (mediator) in his first Discourse. Not Man in general (as rationalism holds), but only special 'divinatory' natures possess the faculty of divination in actuality; and it is these that receive impressions of the transcendent, not the undifferentiated aggregate of homogeneous individuals in mutual interplay, as held by modern social psychology. ①

It is questionable whether Schleiermacher himself, in spite of his (re-) discovery of 'divination', was a really 'divinatory'

① And this is undoubtedly true as far back as the lowest levels of development, when the 'religious dread' first begins to stir in primitive form and to manifest itself in ideas. To derive these from an original group- and massfantasy collectively operating is itself sheer fantasy, and the results this theory helps to produce are about as queer and grotesque as any of the ideas of which it treats.

们在这儿只谈其中的一个,另一个将在下一章讨论。施氏当时天真而缺乏深思地认为,这种"直觉感受"的本领或能力是一种普遍的能力。如果所谓"普遍的"意思是指这种能力就像一种确定的事实必然预先存在于每一个有宗教信仰的人身上,那么,事实上它就不是普遍的,尽管施莱尔马赫把它看成是思想和精神的一般能力中的一种,并且的确把它看成思想中最深刻、最独特的成份,而且在那种意义上——人是通过其理智的思想被界定的——将其称之为一种"普遍的人性"成份,他当然是正确的。但是,这种人类的普遍潜能,事实上却根本无法为每一个单独的人所普遍地拥有。通常,它只是作为特别有禀赋的人的一种特殊的天资和天分被揭示出来。在他最早的《布道》中,施莱尔马赫十分精彩地指出,问题就在于他对"*Mittler*"(中介者)的性质和作用的十分有趣的阐述。并不是普遍的人类(正如理性主义所认为的那样),而是只有那些特殊的具有"直觉感受"性质的人们,才真正拥有直觉感受的能力;而且,正是这些具有直觉感受的天性的人们,而不是在相互影响中的所有相似的个体所组成的无差别的人类统一体,才接受了那种超越者的印象,就像现代社会心理学所认为的那样。①

尽管施莱尔马赫发现(或者再发现)了"直觉感受",但是,他自己是否是一个真正具有"直觉感受"天性的人,这依然值得怀

① 毫无疑问,即使是当宗教处于最低的发展水平,也就是当"宗教的恐惧"最初以原始的形式骚动,并将自身表现为种种观念时,这一点也是正确的。要从一种原初的团体幻想或者群体幻想的机体的共同作用中引申出这些观念,这本身就纯粹是个幻想,而且,这一理论所产生的结果将会和它所研究的那些观念一样离奇古怪。

nature, although in his first Discourse he maintains that he is. One of his contemporaries, to wit, Goethe, was at any rate decidedly his superior in this respect. In Goethe's life the power of divination, not latent but finding vital exercise, plays an important part, and it finds singular expression in the meaning he gives to the term 'daemonic', put with such emphasis in *Dichtung und Wahrheit*, Book 20, and in his 'talks' with Eckermann. ①Let us briefly examine these. The most characteristic feature in his notion of the 'daemonic' is that it goes beyond all 'conceiving', surpasses 'understanding' and 'reason', and consequently is 'inapprehensible' and cannot properly be put into a statement:

The Daemonic is that which cannot be accounted for by understanding and reason. It chooses for itself obscure times of darkness. ... In a plain, prosaic town like Berlin it would hardly find an opportunity to manifest itself.... In Poetry there is from first to last something daemonic, and especially in its unconscious appeal, for which all intellect and reason is insufficient, and which, therefore, has an efficacy beyond all concepts. Such is the effect in Music in the highest degree, for Music stands too high for any understanding to reach, and an all-mastering efficacy goes forth from it, of which, however, no man is able to give an account. Religious worship cannot therefore do without music. It is one of the foremost means to work upon men with an effect of *marvel*.

'Does not the daemonic (asks Eckermann) also appear in *events*?' 'Pre-eminently so,' said Goethe, 'and assuredly in all

① Cf. Goethe's *Sämtliche* Werke, ed. Cotta, vol. xxv, pp. 124 ff.; Eckermann, *Gespräche mit Gecthe*, ed. A. v. d. Linden, Part II, pp. 140 ff.

疑，虽然他在他的最早的《布道》中坚持认为他是这种人。他的一位同时代的人，即歌德，在这一方面无论如何都断然比他高明。在歌德的一生中，直觉感受的能力并不是潜在的，而是得到充分应用，发挥了重要的作用，而且，在他赋予"魔鬼的"这个术语的意义中，直觉感受的能力得到了独特的表现。同时在全集第20卷《诗与真》中，在与艾克曼的《谈话录》中，他给"魔鬼的"这一术语给与了特别的强调。① 我们来简略地考察一下这些情况。他的"魔鬼的"观念的最具特色的特征就是：它是超越一切"构想"的，是超越"理解"和"理性"的，因此是"不可理解的"，是不能被恰当地表述的：

所谓魔鬼的就是不能用理解和理性来解释的东西。它喜欢给自己选择黑暗的模糊时刻出现……在柏林这样的简单而平凡的城市中，它几乎很难找到机会表现自己……在诗歌中，自始至终都有某种魔鬼的东西，尤其是在它那无意识的感染力中。对于它，一切理智和理性都不足以说明，因此诗歌就有了一种超越一切概念的效力。音乐里也表现出最高的魔鬼性，因为音乐处于很高的层次，任何理解都达不到那样的高度，它散发出一种征服一切的效力，任何人也不能对这种效力进行解释。所以，宗教崇拜离了音乐是不行的。音乐是以奇迹般的效果作用于人的最重要的手段之一。

"（艾克曼问）一般事件中不也显现出魔鬼吗？""十分突出，"歌德说，"而且尤其出现于一切我们不能用理智或理性解释

① 参见《歌德全集》，科塔版，第25卷，第124页及其后；以及林登编著的《歌德谈话录》第2部分，第140页及其后。

which we cannot explain by intellect or reason. And in general it is manifested throughout nature, visible and invisible, in the most diverse ways. Many creatures in the animal kingdom are of a wholly daemonic kind, and in many we see some aspect of the daemonic operative.'

We notice here how the elements of the numinous we discovered plainly recur: the wholly non-rational, incomprehensible by concepts, the elements of mystery, fascination, awefulness, and energy. The note of the daemonic in the animal kingdom reminds us of Job and the leviathan. But in another respect Goethe's intuition falls far short of Job's intuition of the *mysterium*. By his ignoring of the warning of the book of Job and by applying to the *mysterium* the standards of the rational understanding and reason and conceptions of human purpose, the non-rational comes to involve for Goethe a contradiction between meaning and meaninglessness, sense and nonsense, that which promotes and that which frustrates human ends. Sometimes, however, he approximates it to *wisdom*, as when he says:

So there was something daemonic governing the circumstances of my acquaintance with Schiller all through. We might have met earlier or later. But that we should have met just at the time when I had my Italian tour behind me and Schiller had begun to weary of his philosophical speculations—that was a fact of great significance and fraught with success for both of us.

It even comes near the divine:

Such occurrences have often befallen me throughout my life. And one comes in such cases to believe in a higher influence (*Einwirkung*), something daemonic, to which one pays adoration, without presuming to try to explain it further.

Invariably the 'daemonic' has an import of 'energy' and 'overpoweringness', and sets its stamp upon men of vehement and overpowering personality.

的事件中。总的说来,它以最多样的方式表现于整个自然之中,无论是可见的自然,还是不可见的自然。动物王国中的许多生物都是全然恶魔的种类,在许多种类上面我们看到了恶魔作用的某些方面。”

在这里我们注意到,我们以前所发现的神秘的诸种因素是如何又明显地再现出来:全然非理性的,通过概念所无法理解的,神秘的各种成份,沉迷,敬畏以及活力等。对动物王国里的恶魔现象的描述,让我们回想起了约伯和“利维坦”。但是,在另一个方面,歌德的直觉远远不及约伯对神秘的那种直觉。由于歌德忽视了《约伯书》的告诫,将理性理解和推理以及人类目的的种种概念等标准应用于神秘,因此,对于歌德来说,非理性就逐渐包含了意义与无意义、感觉与非感觉之间的矛盾,它们一个激发人类目的,一个阻滞人类目的。然而,有时候他又认为魔鬼近似于智慧。他说:

所以在我与席勒相识的整个过程中,似乎有某种魔力在起作用。我们本可能会早些或迟些相识,但我们却偏偏相识于我结束了我的意大利之行,而席勒则正开始对他的哲学思考感到厌倦的时候——这是一桩有着重大意义的事实,对我们二人来说,都是充满了成就感的事。

有时,恶魔甚至接近了神性:

我一生中经常出现这类事情。在这种情况下,人往往便逐渐开始相信一种更高的影响,即某种魔力,人对它充满了崇拜,但决不会尝试着进一步去解释它。

通常,“魔鬼的”总是意味着一种“活力”和“不可抗拒性”,而且总是在那些个性强烈而且无法抵抗的人身上留下印记。

'Napoleon', said I, 'seems to have been a daemonic sort of man.'

'He was so absolutely and to such a degree', said Goethe, 'that hardly any other man can be compared with him in this respect. The late Grand Duke also was a daemonic nature, full of limitless, active force and restlessness.'

'Has not Mephistopheles also "daemonic" traits?'

'No, he is much too negative a being. The daemonic manifests itself in a downright positive and active power.'

In *Dichtung und Wahrheit* (p. 126) he delineates still better the impressions such numinous persons make, and in this passage especially sets in the foreground our *tremendum* as the element alike of 'dread' and 'overpoweringness'.

This daemonic character appears in its most *dreadful* form when it stands out dominatingly in some *man*. Such are not always the most remarkable men, either in spiritual quality or natural talents, and they seldom have any goodness of heart to recommend them. ① But an incredible force goes forth from them and they exercise an incredible power over all creatures, nay, perhaps even over the elements. And who can say how far such an influence may not extend?

But the efficacy and influence of such a 'daemonic' man, even when it is beneficent, moves to amazement rather than to admiration; it is more a tumultuous urgency than ordinary agency, and is at any rate absolutely non-rational. This is what Goethe tries to describe in the series of antitheses in *Dichtung und Wahrheit* (p. 124):

---

① i. e. they are merely '*numinous*,' not '*holy*' men.

“拿破仑”,我说,“似乎是一种魔鬼一样的人。”

“他绝对是这种人,而且还到了如此的程度,”歌德答道,“以至于在这方面很难有人能与他相比。已故的大公爵也是一个具有魔力本性的人,他浑身充满了无穷的、生动的活力并且永不停息。”

“墨菲斯托菲里斯不也具有‘魔鬼’特性吗?”

“不,他的存在过于消极了。魔鬼特征只在一种完全积极而主动的力量中表现其自身。”

在《诗与真》(第126页)中,他更好地描绘了这种神秘的人物所造成的影响,而且在这个段落中,他特意把我们的恐惧感当做是类似于“恐惧”和“不可抗拒性”的因素设置在前景中凸现出来。

当这种魔鬼特征突出地表现在某些人身上时,它表现为最可怕的形式。这类人无论是在精神品质上还是在自然才能上,并不总是最突出的人,他们极少有好的德行受人欢迎。[1] 但是,他们散发出一种令人难以置信的力量,他们对所有生物,不仅如此,他们甚至可能对所有的元素,都具有一种令人难以置信的征服力。谁能说他们的影响还有什么地方达不到呢?

但是,对于这样一个“魔鬼般的”人物的效力和影响来说,即使当它是善意的时候,它所引起的也绝非欣羡而是惊诧;它是一种躁动着的催促,而不是一种普通的作用,而且,无论如何都是绝对非理性的。这就是歌德在《诗与真》(第124页)的一连串的对比中试图要描述的东西:

① 也就是说,他们仅仅是“神秘的”人,而不是“神圣的”人。

... Something that only manifested itself in contradictions and therefore could not be comprehended under any concept, Still less under any one word. It was not divine, for it seemed unreasonable; not human, for it lacked understanding; not devilish, for it was beneficent; not angelic, for it often displayed malicious joy. It was like chance, for it pointed to no consequence; it resembled providence, for it indicated connexion and unity. All that hems us in seemed penetrable to it; it seemed to dispose at will of the inevitable elements of our being, contracting time and expanding space. Only in the impossible did it seem at home, and the possible it spurned from itself with contempt.

Although this daemonic thing can be manifested in everything corporeal and incorporeal, finding indeed most notable expression among animals, still it is pre-eminently with men that it stands in closest and most wonderful connexion, and there fashions a power which, if not opposed to the moral world order, yet intersects it in such a way that the one might be taken for the warp and the other for the woof.

There can be no clearer expression than this of the prodigiously strong impression which divination of the numinous may make upon the mind, and that obviously not on a single occasion but repeatedly, till it has become almost a matter of habit. But at the same time this 'divination' of Goethe is not one that apprehends the numinous as the prophet does. It does not rise to the elevation of the experience of Job, where the non-rational mystery is at the same time experienced and extolled as supra-rational, as of profoundest value, and as holiness in its own right. It is rather the fruit of a mind which, for all its depth, was not equal to such profundities as these, and to which, therefore, the non-rational counterpoint to the melody of life could only sound in confused consonance, not in its authentic harmony, indefinable but

……因为某种东西只是在各种矛盾中展现自己，因此就不能借助于任何概念而被理解，更谈不上借助于任何词语了。它不是神性的，因为它似乎是非理性的；它也不是人性的，因缺乏可理解性；它不是魔鬼性的，因为它是仁慈的；它不是天使性的，因为它常常显示出恶意的欢乐。它像是偶然的，因为它不指向任何结果；它类似神意，因为它暗示了联系和统一。包围着我们的一切似乎都是为它所洞悉的；它似乎可以随意处置构成我们存在的必然元素，可以压缩时间，也可以扩张空间。只有在不可能的领域，它才显得得心应手，而在可能的领域，它则满含轻蔑，唾弃而去。

虽然这种魔鬼般的东西能够在一切有形和无形的事物中表现出来，在动物中也确实找到了最明显的表现，然而，在那些与它联系得最紧密、最完美的人们身上，它却表现得最突出，而且在那些人身上形成了一种力量，这种力量与道德世界的秩序即使不是相互对抗的，也是彼此交错的，以至一方会被人们看成经线，另一方被看成纬线。

对于神秘的直觉感受在人的头脑中所留下的无比强烈的印象，没有比这个更加清楚的了，而且很显然，这种印象不是出现在某个单一的场合，而是反复出现，直到几乎形成了习惯。但同时，歌德的这种"直觉感受"并不是像先知所做的那样，是领悟神秘时的那种直觉感受。它没有达到约伯经验的高度，在约伯那儿，非理性的神秘是同时作为超理性的、具有最高价值的、以及作为真正的神圣性而被经验到和受到赞扬的。而歌德的这种直觉感受却只是一种思想的果实，尽管它有相当的深度，却也不能和以上所提到的这些相比，因此，对于它来说，生活旋律

palpable. Therefore, though it is genuine divination, it is the divination of Goethe 'the pagan', as he sometimes used to call himself. Indeed, it is a divination that functions only at the level of the 'daemonic' which, as we saw, precedes religion proper, not at the level of the divine and the holy in the truest sense; and it shows very clearly how that sort of merely 'daemonic' experience of the numinous may in a highly cultivated mind only stir emotional reactions of bewilderment and bedazzlement, without giving real light or warmth to the soul. Goethe did not understand how to adjust this divination of the 'daemonic' to his own higher conception of the divine; and, when Eckermann turned the conversation to that, his answer was hesitating and evasive:

'The operative, efficacious force (said I tentatively), which we call the "daemonic", does not seem to fit in with the idea of the divine'. 'Dear boy,' said Goethe, 'what do we know of the idea of the divine, and what can our narrow conceptions presume to tell of the Supreme Being? If I called him by a hundred names, like a Turk, I should yet fall short and have said nothing in comparison to the boundlessness of his attributes.'

But, if we leave out of account the comparatively low level of Goethe's 'divination', we have yet in it a most exact example of what Schleiermacher had in mind. These are 'intuitions and feelings', if not of something divine, still of something numinous in the natural world and in history, and intuitions brought to the higher vitality by an individual with an innate 'divinatory' gift. At the same time the principles on which this divination works cannot even be suggested, for all the examples Goethe may give. What does the 'daemonic' really consist in? How does he come to be conscious of it? How does he identify it as one and the same through all the manifold and contradictory forms in which it manifests itself?

的非理性对位声部只能发出杂乱的音响,而不能奏出那种虽不可定义但明晰可见的真正的和谐。所以,虽然它是真正的直觉感受,却是歌德这个“异教徒”(歌德有时就这样称呼自己)的直觉感受。确实,这只是一种在“魔怪的”层次上发生作用的直觉感受(如我们所知,这种层次是完全先于宗教的),而不是在真实意义上的神性与神圣层次上发生作用的直觉感受;这十分清楚地表明,对于神秘的那种仅仅是“魔怪”的体验,在具有高度教养的头脑中只能激起迷惑、茫然等情感反应,而不能给予灵魂以真正的光和热。歌德不懂得怎样把这种“魔怪”层次的直觉感受与他自己的关于神性的更高级的概念调整一致;所以当艾克曼将话题转到这里时,他的回答就变得犹豫而躲闪起来:

“这种强大而有效的力量,”(我试探着问),“即我们称之为‘魔魔般的’力量似乎不符合有关神性的概念。”“亲爱的孩子,”歌德说,“关于神性的概念我们知道些什么呢?而且我们这种狭隘的概念又能让我们对最高存在说出些什么呢?即便我像个土耳其人那样,用一百个名字来称呼它,比起它那无限的属性来,我说得还是远远不够的,而且等于什么也没说。”

但是,如果不考虑歌德“直觉感受”的相对较低的层次,我们就可以在其中发现在施莱尔马赫头脑中所设想的最确切的例子。这些东西即便不是对某种神性事物的“直觉与感受”,也是对自然世界中和历史上某种神秘物的“直觉与感受”,是被某个具有先天“预兆感觉”禀赋的人引向更加强大的生命力的那些直觉。同时,尽管歌德提出那么多例子,直觉感受据以发生作用的各种原则依然无法找到。这种“魔怪”到底存在于什么地方呢?他是怎么逐

These are the questions to which Goethe can suggest no answer. It is evident that in this experience he is being guided by 'mere feeling', that is, by an a *priori* principle that is not explicit and overt, but dim and obscure.

渐意识到它的呢？他是怎样在它表现自身于其中的纷繁而矛盾的种种形式中将它作为同一个东西识别出的呢？这些都是歌德无法回答的问题。显然，在这种经验中，歌德是被“纯粹感受”指引着，也就是说，他不是被一种清楚、明显的先验原则指引着，而是被朦胧而模糊的先验原则指引着。

CHAPTER XIX
Divination In Primitive Christianity

In the last chapter we spoke of two defects in Schleiermacher's doctrine of divination. The first of these—his misleading assumption that this is a universal human faculty —has already been considered, and we have now to turn to the second. This is that, though Schleiermacher's description of divination in relation to the world of nature and history has both warmth and insight, he gives no clear detailed account, but only the scantiest hints, of what is after all its worthiest object and the object most propitious to its development, namely, the history of *religion*, especially that of the Bible and its culmination in the person of Christ Himself. His concluding 'discourse' makes emphatic and significant mention of Christianity and Christ, but Christ is here only introduced as the supreme divining *subject*, not as the *object* of divination *par excellence*. And it is the same in Schleiermacher's *Glaubenslehre*. In this, too, the significance of Christ is, essentially, intended to be fully given in the fact that he 'admits us into the power and beatitude of his consciousness of God'. Now this is a thought of high value, but it does not attain to that supreme value which Christianity imputes to Christ, of being in His own person 'holiness made manifest', that is, a person in whose being, life, and mode of living we realize of ourselves by 'intuition and feeling' the self-revealing power and presence of the Godhead. For to the Christian it is a momentous question whether or no a real

第十九章　原始基督教中的直觉感受

上一章我们提到了施莱尔马赫直觉感受理论中的两个缺点。第一个缺点——他错误地认为直觉感受是人类普遍的本能——我们已谈过了，现在我们来谈他的第二个缺点。这就是，虽然施莱尔马赫对于与自然世界和历史有关的直觉感受的描述既有热情又有洞察力，但他却没有详细解释，而只是极其简略地暗示了究竟什么才是这种直觉感受的最有价值的对象，究竟什么才是最有利于它的发展的对象，即宗教历史，尤其是《圣经》及其在基督本人身上达到巅峰的历史。他在最后的“布道”中着重而意味深长地提到了基督教和基督，但是基督在这里仅仅是被当做最高直觉感受的主体，而不是卓越的直觉感受的客体。在施莱尔马赫的《教义》中，情况也是如此。也是在这本书中，基督的意义根本就是故意地被充分地给予在这样的事实中：他“让我们享有体会上帝的能力和至福”。这虽是一种有高度价值的思想，但它还没有达到基督教赋予基督的那种至高无上的价值，即他本人就是“神圣的清晰显现”，也就是，在这个人的存在、生命以及生活方式中，我们通过“直觉和感觉”，意识到了神性自我展示的力量和神性的存在。因为对于基督徒来说，能否从基督这个人以及他的生活中获得一种真正的直觉感受——即对表现出来的神圣的直接的、第

divination—a direct, first-hand apprehension of holiness manifested, the ‘intuition’ and ‘feeling’ of it—can be got from the person and life of Christ; whether, in short, ‘the holy’ can be independently experienced in Him, making Him a real revelation of it.

In this matter we can obviously get no help from the painful and fundamentally impossible inquiries, so often started, into ‘Jesus’s consciousness of Himself. They are impossible, if for no other reason, because the evidence at our disposal is neither sufficient in quantity nor appropriate to such a purpose. Jesus puts as the content of His message and all His utterances, not Himself, but the ‘kingdom’, its beatitude and righteousness, and, in its first and most straightforward interpretation, the ‘gospel’ is the ‘good tidings’ of the kingdom of God. What statements about Himself do occur are fragmentary and incidental. But even were this not the case, even if we could find in the gospels a detailed theory of Jesus as to His own nature, what would this prove? Religious enthusiasts have not infrequently had recourse to the most exalted modes of self-proclamation, and often enough no doubt their statements about themselves have been completely bona fide and sincere. And it is just such self-revealing statements of the prophets of all ages that are more than any others dependent for their form upon their temporal or local context, the equipment of myth or dogma with which his environment supplies the speaker. The fact that the prophet or seer or inspired teacher applies all this material to state something about himself merely demonstrates the intensity of his self-consciousness, his sense of mission, his conviction, and his claim to be believed and obeyed—all of which are to be taken for granted where a man stands forward in response to an inner call. The immediate, intuitive ‘divination’ of which we are speaking would indeed *not* come as a result of such statements by the prophet about himself, however complete; they can arouse a belief in his authority, but cannot bring about the peculiar experience of spontaneous

一手的感悟,对它的“直觉”和“感觉”,这是一个至关重要的问题。简而言之,“神圣”能否在基督身上被独立地体验到,使他成为神圣的真正启示者。

在这种事情上,我们显然不能求助于过去常常进行的对“耶稣的自我意识”的那种痛苦而又根本不可能的研究。这些研究之所以不可能,如果不是因为其他的原因,那就是因为,对于这样一个研究目的来说,我们所掌握的证据既在数量上不充分,又在性质上不适合。耶稣在他的教导和所有的言论中所谈的内容都不是他自己,而是“天国”,它的至福和它的正义,而且在对天国进行最初的也是最直接的解释时,“福音”就是上帝的天国里的“好消息”。关于他自己的陈述确实出现过,但只是零星的、偶然的。但是,情况即使不是这样,即使我们能在《福音书》里发现了有关耶稣,比如他的本性等的详细论述,这又能证明什么呢?宗教狂热者采用最崇高的方式进行自我声明,这并非罕见的事,而且,毫无疑问,他的那些有关自己的声明也常常是真诚而诚挚的。正是所有时代的先知们的这类自我展示的声明,比起其他声明来,在方式上更依赖于它们的时间和空间的背景,即环境提供给说话人的神话或教义的装备。先知,或预言家,或富有灵感的导师,都应用所有的这些材料来陈述有关自己的某种东西,这仅仅表明他强烈的自我意识,他的使命感,他的确信以及他对信仰及顺从的要求——当一个人面临着来自内心的召而做出的反应时,所有这一切都会被看成是理所当然的事情。不管先知们的自我声明怎样完整,我们现在所讨论的作为这种声明结果的直接的、直觉的“直觉感受”实际上也不会出现。这类声明可以引发对他自己的权威的信仰,但却不能带来自发的洞察力这种独特的体验,在这里

insight that here is something holy made manifest. 'We have heard him ourselves and know that this is indeed the Christ' (John iv. 42).

It cannot now be doubted that such an avowal was made to him as a result of a spontaneous, original divination. This must at any rate be true of Christ's own first disciples. Otherwise it would be unintelligible how the Church could have come into existence at all. Mere proclamation, mere authoritative statement, cannot bring about these massive certainties and that impelling strength, that power to maintain and assert itself, which were necessary if the Christian community was to come into being and which can be recognized in it as its unmistakable characteristics.

Misapprehension of this is only possible if, attempting a one-sided approach to the phenomenon of the origin of the Christian Church, we try to reconstruct the facts solely by the methods of scholarship and out of the material afforded by the staled feelings and blunted sensibility of our presentday artificial civilization and complex mentality. It would be an advantage if, in addition to these methods, an attempt were made to frame a less abstract intuition of the genesis of original and genuine religious communities with the aid of living instances of the thing as it may still be found to-day. It would be necessary for this to seek places and moments at which even to-day religion shows itself alive as a naïve emotional force, with all its primal quality of impulse and instinct. This can still be studied in remote corners of the Mohammedan and Indian world. Even to-day one may come upon scenes in the streets of Mogador or Marrakesh, which have the strangest outward resemblance to those recorded by the Synoptic Gospels: 'holy men' (and very queer specimens they generally are!) now and then make their appearance, each the centre of a group of disciples, and about them the people come and go, listening to their sayings, looking at their miracles, observing how they live and what they do.

这种自发的洞察力指的是神圣显露出来某种东西。"我们自己已经听见他了,而且知道这的确就是基督。"(《约翰福音》第 4 章 42 节)

毫无疑问,正是作为一种本能的、原初的直觉感受的结果,他才作出了这样的声明。对于基督自己的首批门徒来说,情况肯定也是这个样子,否则就无法理解,教会究竟是怎样才得以形成的。仅有宣告,仅有权威的声明不可能带来众人的确信和强大的力量,以及那种维护自身、表现自身的力量,而这些正是基督教团体得以形成所必不可少的条件,也是人们可以从基督教团体中辨认的它的准确无误的特征。

如果我们试图以一种片面的方法来看待基督教教会的起源这一现象,打算仅仅通过学究的方法和我们现代人造文明与复杂心理所具有的陈腐感情及迟钝感觉所提供的材料,来重构这些事实的话,误解就是不可避免的。如果除了这些方法之外,我们借助于就像在今天依然可以找到的事物的活生生的例子的帮助,努力构筑一种对原初的、真正的宗教团体的产生的不那么抽象的直觉,情况就好得多了。这就必须要为它探寻这样的地点和时刻,在那里,即便是今天,宗教也依然如同一种天真的情感力量将自身表现得生机勃勃,具有它所有的冲动和本能的原始性质。这一点仍然可以在偏远的穆斯林和印度地区被发现。甚至在今天,人们还能在墨卡多或马拉喀什的街道上突然遭遇到一些外表酷似对观福音书[1]中所记载的独特场景:"圣人"(他们一般都是非常奇特的人!)不时地出现,每人都是一组门徒的中心,人们在他们周围走来走去,倾听着他们的言论,观看着他们的奇迹,观察着他们怎样生活、干些什么。成群的信徒聚集在

[1] 指马太、马可及路加三福音书。

Bands of adherents gather round them, more loosely or more closely united as the case may be. '*Logia*', tales, and legends form and accumulate;[①] new brotherhoods arise or, if already arisen, extend in widening circles. But the centre of it all is always the man himself, a 'holy man' in his lifetime, and what sustains the movement is always the peculiar power of his personality, the special impression he makes on the bystander. Those who should know assure us that *ninety-eight* per cent. of these 'holy men' are impostors; but, even so, we are left with two per cent. who are not, a surprisingly high percentage in the case of a matter that invites and facilitates imposture as much as this does. The consideration of this remaining two per cent. should continue to throw much light on the actual fact of the genesis of a religious community. The point is that the 'holy man' or the 'prophet' is from the outset, as regards the experience of the circle of his devotees, something more than a 'mere man' (ψιλὸs ἀνθρωπος). He is the being of wonder and mystery, who somehow or other is felt to belong to the higher order of things, to the side of the numen itself. It is not that he himself teaches that he is such, but that he is experienced as such. And it is only such experiences, which, while they may be crude enough and result often enough in self-deception, must at least be profoundly and strongly felt, that can give rise to religious communities.

Such cases of contemporary religious movements afford after all a very inadequate analogy, far removed from that which occurred long ago

① It is astonishing that the main problem of Gospel criticism, viz. how the collection of '*Logia*' arose, is not studied in this still-living milieu. It is even more astonishing that the *logia*-series were not long ago elucidated from the closely corresponding milieu of the 'Sayings of the Fathers' ('Αποφθ έγματα τ ών Πατ έρων), from the Hadith of Muhammed, or from the Franciscan legends. And a particular striking case of the same thing is the collection of the *Logia* of Rāma-Krishna, which has grown to completion in our own day and under our very eyes.

他们周围,依情况不同而或松散或紧密地联系在一起。“语录”(Logia)、故事和传说形成并积累起来;[①]新的兄弟会出现了,或者,如果已经出现,那就会扩大到更大的范围。但是,它的中心却总是那么一个人,一位在世的“圣人”,维持着这一运动的往往是他人格的独特力量,以及他给旁观者所留下的特殊的印象。那些了解内情的人向我们担保说,这些“圣人”中有百分之九十八都是冒名顶替的,但是尽管如此,我们面临着百分之二的人。在这样一个拥有如此惊人的高百分比的易于引起并且易于滋生欺骗的情况下,那没有骗人的是谁呢。我们应考虑一下这剩下的百分之二,以继续说明宗教团体的产生这一当下的事实。问题的关键在于,从一开始,这种“圣人”或“先知”在其信徒们的经验范围内,就是某种远远高于“一般人”(ψιλὸs ἀνθρωποs)的人。他是一种奇妙的、神秘的存在,不知怎么的,人们总觉得他属于事物的更高级别,属于神秘本身那一边。他自己并没有做这样的教导,而是被人们体验成这样的。而且仅仅就是这些体验,尽管它们是相当粗陋的,也常常被证明是一种自欺,但是,它们至少必须被深刻而强烈地感受到,才可能产生宗教团体。

当代宗教运动中的这种情况,毕竟与当初的不完全类似,远远不同于很久以前发生在巴勒斯坦的那种情况。但是,如果连这

---

① 令人吃惊的是,福音书批判中的主要问题,即“耶稣语录”的收集是如何开始的,在目前这依然起作用的环境里还没有得到研究。甚至更令人吃惊的是,,耶稣语录辑在不久前根据与“教父语录”(‘Αποφθ έγματα τ ών Πατ έρων)密切相关的环境,根据穆罕默德的“言行录”,或者根据芳济各会的传说,得到了解释。同样特别引人注目的事例是关于罗摩克里希纳语录的收集,这件工作就是在今天,在我们的眼皮下完成的。

in Palestine. Yet, if even these movements are only made possible by the fact that men actually experience, or presume that they experience, veritable holiness in the personalities of individuals, how far more true must this not be of the early Chrisitan community! That this was so is attested directly by the whole spirit and the universal conviction of the early communities as a whole, so far as we can discern it in their modest records. And certain of the slighter touches in the Synoptic portrait of Jesus confirm the fact expressly in particular cases. We may in-stance here the narratives already referred to of Peter's haul of fishes (Luke v. 8), and of the centurion of Capernaum (Matt. viii. 8; Luke vii. 6), which point to spontaneous responses of feeling when the holy is directly encountered in experience. Especially apt in this connexion is the passage in Mark x. 32: *καὶἦν πρὸαγων ἀντὸυsὁἸησοὺs · ὀ' Ἰησουσκα ὶἐθαμβουντο, οὶ δὲ ἀ κολουθοῦντε ἐ φοβοῦντο* ('and Jesus went before them: and they were amazed; and as they followed, they were afraid'). This passage renders with supreme simplicity and force the immediate impression of the numinous that issued from the man Jesus, and no artistry of characterization could do it so powerfully as these few masterly and pregnant words. The later saying in John xx. 28 (the confession of Thomas, 'My Lord and my God') may perhaps appear to us by contrast the utterance of a time too far-reaching in its formulations, and very far removed from the simplicity of the original experience of the disciples. And this passage in Mark may appeal to us all the more just because the living emotion here disdains any precise formulation at all; none the less does it contain the real roots of all later developments of Christology.

Such intimations of the numinous impression made by Jesus upon those who knew Him occur in the Gospel narrative only, as it were, incidentally to the main purpose of the narrator, who is scarcely interested in

些运动都只有当人们在一些个人的人格中实际上体验到(或者假设他们体验到了)确切的神圣后才能成为可能,那么,早期的基督教团体又怎么会不是这样呢！只要我们能从这些团体的朴素记载中将其识别出来,这种情形就能够被作为一个整体的早期宗教团体的全部精神和普遍确信所证明。对观福音书中对耶稣的一些不经意的描绘,就以一些特殊例子清楚地证实了这一事实。我们可以在这里举出前面已经提到过的有关彼得捕鱼的故事(《路加福音》,第5章第8节),迦百农百夫长的故事(《马太福音》第8章第8节;《路加福音》第7章第6节),这些故事都指出了当人们在体验中直接遭遇到神圣时所做出的情感上的自发的反应。在这方面特别合适的例子是《马可福音》第10章第32节:*καὶἦν πρὸαγων ἀντὸνsδΙησοὺs · ὁ’ Ιησουσκαὶ ἐθαμβουντο, οἱ δὲ ἀκολονθοῦντε ἐφοβοῦντο*(“耶稣领他们到耶路撒冷去;门徒们很吃惊,跟从的人也害怕。”)这段话极其简洁有力地表现了耶稣这个人所散发出来的神秘的直接印象,没有任何艺术描述能够像这短短的几句高明而含义丰富的话那样更加有力。后来在《约翰福音》第20章第28节(即多马的忏悔:“我的主！我的神！”)中的话语也许比较起我们一时的言词,显得简洁而意义深远,但远不同于众门徒原初经验的简单性。而且《马可福音》中的这段话之所以吸引我们,只是因为在这里活生生的情感完全鄙视任何精确的简述,同样,这段话也包含了基督学后来全部发展的真正根源。

耶稣给认识他的人们所留下的神秘的印象的暗示在《福音书》的叙事里,好像只是偶然地出现在叙述者的主要目的中,而叙述者对这些神圣印象丝毫都不感兴趣,他只是全神贯注于有关奇迹

them, but absorbed rather in the record of the miraculous. In our eyes their interest is all the greater, and we can fancy how numerous similar experiences must have been of which no trace survives in the records, just because there was no miracle to be told of in connexion with them and they were simply taken for granted by the narrator as a matter of course.

To this place belong further the belief in Jesus's supremacy over the demonic world and the tendency to legend that began to take effect from the start; the fact that His own relatives take Him for a man 'possessed', an involuntary acknow-ledgement of the 'numinous' impression He made upon them; and in an especial degree the conviction that breaks spontaneously upon the minds of His disciples as by a sudden impact, won not from His teaching but from the very experience of Him, that He is the 'Messiah', the being who stood for the circle in which He moved as the numinous being *par excellence*. The experiential character of this belief in His Messiahship stands out clearly in Peter's first confession and Jesus's answer to it (Matt. xvi. 15-17), 'Flesh and blood have not revealed it unto thee, but my Father, which is in heaven.' Jesus himself is astonished at Peter's confession, which shows that this was not learnt on authority, but found out by Peter himself, a genuine *discovery*, arising from the impression Jesus made upon him and the testimony borne to it in the depth of the mind, where no teaching of flesh and blood, or even of 'the word', can avail, but only 'my Father in heaven' Himself and without any intermediary.

For this factor—the mind's own witness to the impression—is, it need hardly be said, an indispensable one. Without it all 'impression' is without effect, or rather no impression could occur at all. Therefore, all doctrines of the 'impression made by Christ' are inadequate if they do not pay regard to this second element, which indeed is

的记载中。在我们眼中,他们的兴趣更加重要,我们可以想象在这些记录中没有踪迹保留下来的类似的体验将会变得多么得神秘,正是因为没有关于它们的奇迹可讲,正是因为叙述者照例将它们当做是理所当然的事。

正是在这个地方,人们对耶稣对魔鬼世界的支配力的信仰以及从起初就开始产生影响的传说的趋势进一步加强了,耶稣自己的亲戚把他看成是一个"着魔的人"这样的事实,就是不知不觉地承认他给他们带来的"神秘的"印象。而在一个独特程度上的信念,即他就是"弥赛亚",代表那个他与神秘存在者同等卓越(*Par excellence*)的神性存在活动于其中的王国的信念,是通过突如其来的影响,自发地涌现在他的门徒们的头脑中的,不是来自他本人的教导,而是来自对他深切的体验。信徒对于耶稣弥赛亚身份的信仰所带有的经验的特征明显地表现在彼得首次认出耶稣就是基督时所说的话,以及耶稣的回答(见《马太福音》第 16 章第 15 ~17 节)"凡人不能将这一真理昭示予你,只有我那天上的父亲才能。"耶稣自己也对彼得认出自己大为吃惊,这表明它不是得自权威的教导,而是彼得自己的发现,一个真正的发现,它来自耶稣留给他的印象以及在思想深处对此印象的证实,在那里,不存在凡人的教导,甚至也没有"圣言"的教导可以借助的,而只能求助于"我那天上的父亲"本身,并无需任何中介。

因为这一因素——即心灵本身对这种印象的自身见证——是必不可少的,这一点毋须多说。没有它,所有的"印象"都不会有效果,或者说,根本不就会出现什么印象。所以,有关"由基督所留下的印象"的所有的理论如果不留心这个第二成份,就是不充分的。这个第二成份的确不过是对神圣的体验所必需的精神

nothing but the mental predisposition necessary for the experience of holiness, to wit, the category of the holy, potentially present in the spirit as a dim or obscure *a priori* cognition. 'Impress' or 'impression', that is, presupposes something capable of receiving impressions, and that is just what the mind is not, if in itself it is only a 'tabula rasa'. In that richer sense in which we use the word here, we do not in fact mean by 'impression' merely the 'impression' which, in the theory of the Sensationalist school, is the psychical result of sense-perception and is left behind as a psychical trace or vestige of the percept. To be 'impressed' by some one, in the sense we use the term here, means rather to cognize or recognize in him a peculiar significance and to humble oneself before it. And we maintain that this is only possible by an element of cognition, comprehension, and valuation in one's own inner consciousness, that goes out to meet the outward presented fact, i. e. by the 'spirit within'. In Schleiermacher's language the 'presentiment' goes out to meet the 'revelation' to which it belongs. Music can only be understood by the musical person; none but he receives an 'impression' of it. And to every unique kind of real impression corresponds in the same way a unique and special sort of 'congeniality', if the word maybe used in this special sense of a particular disposition or aptitude, akin to the object arousing the impression. 'Nemo audit verbum, nisi spiritu intus docente.'[①] Once again let us recall the example of the beautiful. A beautiful thing can only make an impression as such, i. e. as signifying beauty, if and in so far as a man possesses in himself *a priori* the potentiality of framing a special standard of valuation, viz. aesthetic valuation. Such a disposition can only be understood as an original, obscure awareness and appreciation of the value of 'beauty' itself.

Because a man has this in him, or better, because he is capable

---

① Cf. Luther's remark that only he who is *verbo conformis* understands the Word, and cf. Augustine, *Confessions*, x. 6. 20.

的先天倾向，它作为一种幽暗的或模糊的认识潜藏在精神之中，去见证神圣的范畴。“留下印象”或者“留下的印象”，也就是说，预见到某种东西能够接收到印象，而这正是头脑所做不到的，假如它本身仅仅是一块“白板”。在我们这里所使用的“印象”一词的较丰富的意义中，通过该词，我们事实上并不仅仅指感觉论所说的那种“印象”，即感性知觉的精神结果，只是作为知觉的某种精神踪迹或残余而存留下来的东西。在这个意义上，当我们说被某人“打上印象”时，不如说是意味着在某人身上认识了或认出了某种奇特的意义，同时在这种意义面前自感卑下。我们认为，只有当人们以其内在意识中的一种认识、领悟和评价的成份，也就是说，利用那种“内在精神”，从内心走出去迎接外在的事实时，以上所说的才会成为可能。用施莱尔马赫的话来说就是，“预知感觉”走出去迎接它所属于的“启示”。音乐只能被有乐感的人理解，只有他才能接受它的“印象”。对于每一种独特的真正“印象”来说，都有一种与之相对应的独特而特殊的“亲和力”，如果这个词可以用做某种特殊的秉赋或倾向的独特意义，类似于引起印象的物体的话。“唯颖悟者可以悟道”。[1] 我们再来回想一下关于美的例子吧。当而且只有当一个人自身具有构想某种特殊的评价标准（即审美评价）的先验潜力时，一件美的事物才能形成美的印象，也就是说，表现为美丽。人们只能把这种秉赋理解成一种对“美”本身的价值的原初而模糊的认识和欣赏。由于人本身具有这种秉赋，或者通过训练后意

---

① 参见路德的话：唯颖悟者可以悟道。也见于圣·奥古斯丁《忏悔录》第10卷第6章第20节。

of realizing it by training, he is able to recognize beauty in the particular given beautiful object that he encounters, to feel the correspondence of this object with the hidden 'standard of value' within him. And so, and only so, will he get an 'impression'.

识到了这种秉赋,他就能够在他所遇见的某个特殊的美的物体中识别出美来,感受这个物体与潜藏在他内心深处的"价值标准"之间的一致。于是就这样,也只有这样,他才会获得一种"印象"。

CHAPTER XX

Divination In Christianity To-Day

The question whether the primitive Church did or could experience holiness in the person of Christ, which we can but answer in the affirmative, is not so important to us as the question whether we too to-day can still do so. Has the portrayal of Christ's life, His actions and achievement, as preserved and handed down by the Christian Church, the value and power of a revelation for us to-day, or do we in this matter but live upon the inheritance bequeathed us by the first community of Christians and base our faith on the authority and testimony of others? There would be no hope of answering this question, were it not that in us too that inner divining power of apprehension and interpretation which has already been considered may find a place—that witness of the spirit, only possible on the basis of a mental predisposition to recognize 'the holy' and to respond to it. If without this no understanding and no 'impression' of Christ was possible even to the first disciples, of what avail should any tradition be that requires the mediation of generations of Christian men? But if we may make this assumption of a predisposing inner 'witness of the Spirit'—as we must—the matter is very different. In that case there is no harm even in the fact that the records of Christ's life are fragmentary, that they contain manifold uncertainties, that they are intermingled with legendary and overlaid with Hellenistic elements. For the Spirit knows and recognizes what is of the Spirit.

第二十章　今日基督教中的直觉感受

原始基督教会是否确实经验过或能够经验存在于基督这个人身上的神圣性这个问题(对此我们能够作出肯定的回答),对于我们来说,没有下一个问题重要,即我们今天是否还能够经验这种神圣性。基督教会保留并留传下来的关于基督的生活、行为以及成就的描述,对于今天的我们还有启示的价值和力量吗?或者在这个方面,我们只能靠基督徒的第一个团体遗留给我们的遗产为生,并将我们的信仰建立在其他的典籍和陈述上吗?如果我们没有已经讨论过的那种领悟和诠释的内在直觉感受的能力——即对圣灵的见证,它只有在具备了辨认"神圣"并对它作出反应的先天精神禀赋的前提下才成为可能——对这个问题的回答是没有任何希望的。如果没有这种能力,即使第一批门徒都不可能理解基督,也不可能获得对他的"印象",那么,那些需要一代又一代的基督徒们加以调整的传统还有什么用处呢?但是,如果我们能够假设一种先天的内在的"对神灵的见证"——这是我们必须做的——事情就大不相同了。在那种情形下,即便实际上有关基督生活的记载是零碎的,包含了各种各样的不确定性,而且与传奇故事混合在一起,被各种希腊风格的元素所覆盖,也没有什么害处,因为灵性知道并且辨认出了什么是灵性。

As evidence of the way in which this inward principle—this co-witnessing spirit within us—works, prompting, inter-preting, and sending out intimation and surmise, I have found the information of a keenly observant missionary from a remote field very instructive. He told me that he had found it a constant matter for fresh astonishment to see how a presentment of the Word so inadequate—which could only hint at its meaning in a difficult foreign tongue and had to work with alien conceptions—could yet at times win so surprisingly deep and inward an acceptance. And he said that here, too, the best results always were due to the responsive apprehension that came out of the hearer's heart half-way to meet the presented truth. Certainly it is only in this fact that we have a clue to the understanding of the problem of St. Paul. Persecutor of the Church as he was, the intimations he had of the being and meaning of Christ and his Gospel must have come to him piecemeal, in fragmentary hints and caricature. But the spirit from within forced upon him the acknowledgement to which he succumbed on the way to Damascus. It taught him that infinitely profound understanding of the Christ made manifest which has led a critic like Wellhausen to confess that, when all is said, no man has understood Christ himself so deeply and thoroughly as Paul.

If, now, the experience of holiness and 'the holy' in Christ is still to be possible and so afford support to our faith, one thing is evidently to be presupposed at the outset, namely, that his own most immediate and primary achievement and intention can be directly understood and appraised in our experience, so that out of this may grow the 'impression' of his holiness with a like directness. And here a difficulty seems to confront us, which has to be removed if the entire problem is not to be barred from the start. It is this: is that which we to-day think we find in the person of Christ and in Christianity at bottom at all the same as that which He really intended to achieve and that which the first community

就在这种方式的证据（在其中，内在的原则——即我们内心的这种相互印证的灵性——发生着作用）激起、解释并且发出暗示和猜度时，我从一个很有启发意义的偏僻领域发现了一位具有敏锐观察力的传教士的信息。他告诉我说，经常使他感到震惊的是，无论一段话的表达是多么得词不达意——这种布道只能以一种艰涩的外语来暗示出它的意义来，而且还不得不使用陌生的概念——但是它却常常令人惊奇地赢得听众深深的、由衷的接受。而且他说，在这儿，同样，最好的结果总是由于那种发自倾听者的内心的响应的悟性，它在半路上就迎着了被宣讲的真理。确实，正是在这一事实中，我们发现了理解有关圣保罗问题的线索。作为教会的迫害者，他所得到的有关基督及其福音的存在和意义的种种暗示肯定都是零碎的，是零星的暗示，是经过歪曲了的，但是内在的灵性在他去往大马士革的路上迫使他接受这些。它教导他对显灵的基督进行无限深广的理解，这使得像韦尔豪森这样的批评家都承认，结果，没有任何人对基督本人的理解像保罗那样深刻和透彻。

如果现在基督中的神性与“神圣”的体验仍是可能的，并且足以支撑我们的信仰，那么，显然，有件事我们从一开始就要假设出来，即他自己最直接的、最根本的成就和企图可以在我们的经验中被直接理解和评估，因此同样直接地，从这个假设中就可生长出关于他的神圣性的“印象”来。在这里，我们似乎遇上了一个困难，如果不想让整个问题从一开始就被阻拦，这个困难就必须加以排除。这个困难就是：我们今天认为我们在基督这个人身上以及在基督教中所发现的东西到底是不是基督当初真正想达到的同一个东西，是不是他的首批门徒在他身上所发现的同一个东西

of Hisdisciples found in Him? In other words, has Christianity really a 'principle' of its own, which, however capable of historical evolution, yet remains unchanged in essence, so that the Christianity of today may be measured against the faith of the first disciples and awarded a rank essentially the same?

Is Christianity at all and in a strict sense Jesus's religion? That is, is the religion we know to-day as Christianity, with its peculiar and unique content of belief and feeling, standing in all its historical greatness and supremacy when measured against other religions, with all its power to-day over the hearts and consciences of men to elevate or to excite, to launch accusation or confer benediction, to attract or to repel —is this religion still in its essence and inner meaning the same thing as the simple, unpretentious religion and form of piety which Jesus Himself had, which He Himself aroused and 'founded' in the circle of those little, heartstirred bands of men in that out-ofthe-way corner of the world, Galilee? It must be generally agreed that it has at least changed its form and its colour very significantly since those days, and that it has been exposed to violent alterations and metamorphoses. But is there any abiding essence, any enduring 'principle' at all behind the sequence of its manifestations, susceptible of evolution and development, but remaining one and the same thoughout? Is it a case of development and evolution, or rather merely of continual transmutation, the influx of something quite different, which one man laments as a perversion, a second admires as a welcome substitution, and a third merely records as a simple historical fact?

Christianity, as it stands before us today in present actuality as a great 'world religion', is indubitably, so far as its claim and promise go, in the first and truest sense a religion of Redemption. Its characteristic ideas today are Salvation —overabounding salvation, deliverance from and conquest of the 'world' and from existence in bondage to the world,

呢？换句话说，基督教是不是真的有一个自身的“原则”，能够经历无论怎样的历史演化，依然能够在实质上保持不变，因而今天的基督教依然可以参照首批门徒的信仰而被衡量，并被授予本质上相同的级别呢？

基督教根本就是并且在严格的意义上是耶稣的宗教吗？也就是说，我们今天当做基督教来认识的这种宗教，具有信仰和情感上的特殊而且独有的内容，与其他宗教相比，显示出自身的伟大历史意义和极高的地位，现在还以其全部的力量振奋或激励人们的心灵和良心，惩恶扬善，聚善弃恶——这个宗教在其实质上、在其内在意义上还是耶稣本人当初在世界的僻远角落加利利，在一群卑微的、内心骚动的人们中间所唤起和“建立”的那个朴素、不矫揉造作的宗教和虔诚的形式吗？人们一定普遍同意，从那些日子以来，基督教的形式和色彩都发生了非常重大的改变，并且经受了剧烈的改造和变形。但是，在它一系列的易于进化发展的表现形式后面，是否根本上还存在着某些不变的实质，持续的“原则”，在整个过程中始终固定不变？它是否是一种发展和进化的场合，或者毋宁说只是一种持续的变形，某种绝不相同的事物的注入，对此有人视为曲解而为之悲伤，有人视为一种可喜的替换而大加赞扬，还有人则仅仅把它当做一种简单的历史事实而加以记载？

基督教，作为伫立在我们面前的当今现实中的一种伟大的“世界宗教”，从其要求及许诺来看，毫无疑问，在首要意义和确实的意义上是一种救赎宗教。今天，它的富有特色的理念就是救赎——即永远充沛的救赎，从“尘世”中脱离出来并且征服“尘世”，从尘世的奴役的存在中挣脱出来，甚至从这种被造物身份中

and even from creaturehood as such, the overcoming of the remoteness of and enmity to God, redemption from servitude to sin and the guilt of sin, reconciliation and atonement, and, in consequence, grace and all the doctrine of grace, the Spirit and the bestowal of the Spirit, the new birth and the new creature. These conceptions are common to Christendom, despite the manifold cleavages that divide it into different confessions, churches, and sects, and they characterize it sharply and definitely as a 'religion of redemption' par excellence, setting it in this respect on a level with the great reli-gions of the East, with their sharp, dualistic antithesis of the state of liberation and bondage, nay, justifying its claim not to fall short of these in regard to the necessity of redemption and the grant of salvation, but to surpass them, both in the importance it gives to these conceptions and in the richness of meaning it finds in them. It cannot be doubted that here, in these elements, is to be found the inner 'principle' and essence of contemporary Christianity to-day, and what we have to ask is whether the wealth of mental and emotional content was in very truth the 'principle' of that plain 'religion of Jesus' long ago, whose establishment must be termed the first and most immediate achievement of Christ.

In answering this question in the affirmative, we would point to a parable which, intended to have reference to the kingdom of God, fits the principle of Christianity equally well: the parable of the grain of mustard seed and the tree that grew therefrom. This parable hints at a change and alteration, for the grown tree is something different from the seed, but an alteration that is no transformation, no transmutation or 'epigenesis', but genuine 'evolution' or develop-ment, the transition from potentiality to actuality.

The 'religion of Jesus' does not change gradually into a religion of redemption; it is in its whole design and tendency a religion of redemption from its earliest commencement, and that in the most uncompromising sense. Though it lacks the theological terms which the Church later possessed, its 'redemptive' character is manifest and unambiguous. If we try to determine as simply and concisely as possible what really characterized the message of Jesus, ignoring what was

挣脱出来，克服与上帝的距离和对上帝的敌意，把人从原罪及原罪的罪恶感的奴役中救赎出来，恢复圣洁，神人和解，随之而来的就是宽恕以及有关宽恕的一切理论，圣灵与圣灵的赠与，新生与再造等。对于基督教界来说，这些都是普遍的概念，尽管由于种种的分歧，它分裂出不同的团体、教会及教派，并且它们都将基督教刻化成为具有一种卓越的“救赎宗教”的明显而确定的特色，使基督教在这方面与东方的伟大宗教处于同一水平，都具有解脱与束缚这种尖锐的二元对立的状态，不仅如此，还确证了基督教的救赎的宣称在救赎的必要性与拯救的许可上不是不如东方宗教，而是超越了东方宗教，不仅在它给予这些概念的重要性上，而且在它们从这些感念中发现丰富的意义上。毫无疑问，正是在这儿，在这些元素中，人们将发现当今基督教的内在“原则”和实质，而我们必须要问的是，这些精神和情感内容的财富是否的确就是很久以前那个朴素的“耶稣的宗教”的真实的“原则”，这种“耶稣的宗教”的建立应当被看成是基督的首要和最直接的成就。

要肯定地回答这个问题，我们需要提到一个寓言，它本来指的是上帝的天国，却也同样很好地适用于基督教的原则：这个寓言就是一粒芥菜种籽以及由此长成的大树。这个寓言暗示了一种变化和变更，因为长成的树虽然是不同于原先种子的某种东西，但它却只是一种变化而不是转变，不是变质或“渐成”，而是真正的“演化”或发展，是一种从潜在到实在的过渡。

“耶稣的宗教”并不是逐渐变化成一种救赎的宗教的，从一开始并在丝毫都不妥协的意义上，它在整个设计和倾向上就是一种救赎的宗教。尽管它缺少后来的教会所拥有的神学术语，但它的“救赎的”特点是清晰而明显的。如果我们忽略那些在历史意义

historically inessential, we are left with two central elements: (I) First, there is the proclamation of the kingdom of God, as no mere accessory, but the foundation of the whole Gospel. This is characteristic of His ministry from the beginning and throughout its course. (2) Second, there is the reaction against Pharisaism, and, in connexion with this, Jesus' s ideal of godliness as the attitude and mind of a child when its fault has been forgiven. But both points comprise in principle everything which later became separately formulated in the specifically 'redemptive' doctrines of Christianity: Grace, Election, the Holy Ghost, and Renewal by the Spirit. These were possessed by and experienced by that first group of disciples as truly as by any later Christians, though in an implicit form. A closer consideration may make this more plain.

To speak of a 'religion of redemption' is, one may say, to be guilty of a redundancy, at any rate if we are considering the more highly developed forms of religion. For every such religion, when once it has won its autonomy and freed itself from dependent references to an ideal of merely worldly 'welfare' (εὐδαιμονία), whether private or public, develops in itself unique and overabounding ideals of beatitude which may be designated by the general term 'salvation'. Such a 'salvation' is the goal to which the evolution of Indian religions has tended ever more markedly and consciously, from their beginning with the notion of deification of the Upanishad-pantheism on to the blissstate of the Buddhist Nirvāna, which, as we have seen (pp. 38—9), is negative only in appearance. It is also the goal of the 'religions of redemption', specifi-cally so called, which spread with such vigour over the civilized world from Egypt, Syria, and Asia Minor about the beginning of our era. Further, it is obvious to an examination

上无关紧要的东西,尽可能简单明了地确定耶稣的预言所真正赋予的特色,那么留给我们的就是下面两个核心因素:(1)首先,在耶稣的预言中有关于上帝的天国的宣告,它不是仅仅作为一种附属,而是整个《福音书》的基础。这就是耶稣的使命从一开始及整个过程中都具有的特色。(2)其次,在耶稣的预言中有对法利赛教派的教义的反对,还有与之相联系的耶稣的虔信理念,就像是一个缺点过错被宽恕了的小孩的态度及思想。但是这两点都原则上构成了后来基督教特别的"救赎性"教义所分别解说的一切中:宽恕、圣选、圣灵以及通过圣灵的复活。这些都是首批门徒所拥有和经验到的东西,与后来的任何基督徒经验到的完全一样,尽管后者的方式经验是无形的。更进一步的考察会使这一问题更加清晰。

也许有人会说,要说某种宗教是一种"救赎的宗教"简直是同义反复,至少当我们考察一种宗教的较高级发展形式时就是如此。因为,每一种这样的宗教,当它赢得了自主并将自身从依赖于对纯粹俗世"幸福"(εὐδαιμονία)——无论是个人的还是公众的——的理想中解脱出来时,都会在自身中生成独特而丰沛的至福的理想,这些理想可以用"救赎"这个一般术语来指称。这样一种"救赎"是印度各种宗教的演进的特别明显而有意追寻的目标,它们从最开始表现在《奥义书》泛神论的神格化的概念中,后来又表现为佛教涅槃(Nirvāna)的那种极乐状态,如同我们在第38~39页所看到的那样,这种涅槃只是在表面上才是否定的。这也是"救赎的宗教"所追求的目标,人们特意这样称呼那类宗教,它大约在我们这个纪元的开始就伴以强大的气势从埃及、叙利亚和小亚细亚流铺展到文明世界。更进一步地说,很显然通

sharpened by the comparative study of religions that the same tendency to 'salvation' is operative also in the vesture of eschatology that gives form to the religion of Persia. Islam, too, embodies the longing for and the experience of salvation. In this case 'salvation' is not simply in the 'hope' of the joys of Paradise: rather the most vital element in Islam is 'Islam' itself, i. e. that surrender to Allah which is not merely the dedication of the will to him, but also at the same time the entering upon the 'Allah' state of mind here and now, the object of longing and striving, a frame of mind which is already 'salvation', and which may possess and enrapture the man like an intoxication and can give rise to a mystic transport of bliss.

But if the idea of 'salvation' thus lies at the base of all higher religion everywhere, it is manifested quite unmistakably and in supreme fashion, both in intensity and intrinsic purity, in the 'Kingdom of Heaven' of Christianity, which is at once a tenet of faith, an object of desire, and a present experience. It is quite immaterial whether this thought in ancient Israel issued from purely political considerations, only gradually rising above the ground of mere fact, till it finally was exalted to a transcendent meaning, or whether there were from the first authentic religious motives at work to shape and develop it. All this is beside the point, inasmuch as the materials by which the religious impulse works are very frequently at first of an unspiritual, earthly nature. It is just the unresting activity and continual urgency of this impulsion, enabling it to attain to freedom and press onward and upward to ever higher levels of development—it is just this that manifests it most characteristically, and reveals best its inner essential being. And this is nothing else than the pure impulsion to redemption, and the pre-intimation and anticipation of a boded 'good', transcendent and 'wholly other', a 'salvation' comparable to those 'salvations' striven after in other religions, but supreme above them in the measure in which the Lord of the Kingdom found and possessed in the

过对各种宗教的比较研究能使考查工作更加敏锐,这种考察会发现,同样的"救赎"倾向,在赋予波斯宗教以形式的末世学的笼罩下也依然发生作用。伊斯兰教也包含了对救赎的渴求与体验。在这种例子中,"救赎"不仅仅存在于对天堂快乐的"希望":倒不如说,伊斯兰教中最重要的因素就是"伊斯兰"本身,即向真主顺服,这并不单单是指把意志奉献给他,同时也指立刻进入"真主"的精神状态,这正是人们渴望而努力追求的目标,一种本身就是"拯救"的精神状态,它会支配着人,使人如同陶醉一般地狂喜,并且给人带来一种神秘的福佑的激动。

但是,如果这种"拯救"的观念隐伏在各地所有较高级的宗教的基础之上,它会被毫无错误地以高级的形式,不仅在强烈性上,而且在内在的纯洁性上,显现在基督教的"天国"中,而"天国"立刻就成为一种信仰的原则,一种渴求的对象,以及一种当下的经验。无论这种思想在古代以色列是出自纯粹的政治考虑,仅仅是逐渐超越了单纯事实的基础,从而最后升华为一种超验的意义,还是从一开始便有确定的宗教动机来构成它、发展它,这个问题毫不重要。所有这些都是离题的,因为宗教冲动由之产生的那些材料,最初常常都是非宗教性的,是俗世性质的。正是这种宗教冲动的不停息的行动和持续的催促使得有关"救赎"的思想获得了自由,不仅向前,而且向上地发展到了较高水平——正是这一点将这一思想最具特色地表达了出来,最好地揭示了它的内在的本质存在。而这不是别的,正是纯粹的救赎的冲动,是对一种被预示的"善"的暗示和预知,这种"善"是超验的,是"完全的他者",是一种可以和其他宗教所追求的"救赎"相比拟的"救赎",但是以在基督徒经验中所发现和葆有的天父来衡量,这种"救赎"

Christian experience is supreme above Brahmā, Vishnu, Ormuzd, Allah, as also above the Absolute in the form of Nirvana, Kaivalyam, Tao, or whatever other name it may be given. So redemption is throughout the purport of the gospel even in its first and simplest form, a redemption which is both to be fulfilled by God hereafter and yet at the same time already experienced here and now. In the former aspect it comes as the assured promise of the Kingdom of God; in the latter, by the present experience of His fatherhood, instilled by the Gospel into the soul of the disciple as his most intimate possession. That the early Christians were conscious of this as something entirely novel and unheard of and exceeding all measure (a good news), is seen in the saying of Jesus that 'the Law and the Prophets were until John: since that time the gospel of the kingdom of God is preached' (Luke xvi. 16), in which John the Baptist, who also preached a 'Kingdom of God', is yet classed with 'the Law and the Prophets'.

But to describe this novelty most truly and concisely it would be necessary to invent the saying of Paul (Rom. viii. 15), did it not already stand written:

For ye have not received the spirit of bondage again to fear; but ye have received the spirit of adoption, whereby we cry, Abba, Father.

Here Paul has penetrated to the heart of the matter, breaking definitely with the older religion and seizing unerringly upon the very principle and essence of the new. And this 'principle and essence' was the same for the first fishermen by the Lake of Galilee and has remained one and the same throughout the whole history of Christianity. With it is given the new attitude to sin and guilt, to law and to freedom, and, in principle, 'justification', 'second birth', 'renewal', the bestowal of the Spirit, new creation, and the blissful freedom of God's children. It was inevitable that these or similar expressions and doctrines and the profound speculation to

高于其他一切的"救赎"的形式,即高于印度教中的梵天(Brahmā),毗湿奴(Vishnu),祆教中的善之神(Ormuxd),伊斯兰教中的真主安拉,而且也高于以涅槃、耆那教中的皈依终极状态(Kaivalyam)、道或者其他被给予任何名字的东西。所以,即使在最初的、最简单的形式中,救赎始终都是福音的主旨,这种救赎既是将来会被上帝所实现的,同时又是人们当下就已经体验到的。从前一个方面来看,它是天国的明确的承诺;从后一个方面来看,通过对上帝父性的现世体验,《福音书》将它灌输进了门徒的灵魂中,作为他最珍贵的财产。早期的基督徒把它看成是某种全然新奇的、闻所未闻的并且是无法衡量的东西(这是个好消息),这一点可从耶稣的这句话中看出:"先知和法律到约翰为止:从此天国的福音便流布开来。"(《路加福音》第16章第16节)在这句话中,同样宣扬"天国"的施洗者约翰是与"律法与先知"被归入一类的。

但是,要很准确、很简洁地描述这福音的新奇性,有必要发明出保罗的一句话(见《罗马人书》第8章第15节),尽管《圣经》上并没有这样写:

"因为你们所接受的不是反抗恐惧的束缚的灵魂,而是收养的灵魂,据此我们呼喊,神父,天父。"

在这儿,保罗已经洞察了事情的核心,干脆地与旧宗教绝裂,正确地抓住了新宗教的原则和实质。这个"原则和实质"就是在加利利湖畔的首批渔民所发现并且在整个基督教的历史中一直保持不变的同一个。伴随着这种"原则和实质",人们以新的态度来对待原罪与罪恶,律法与自由,而且在原则上还有"辩护"、"再生"、"复活",圣灵的赠与,新的造物,以及作为上帝儿女的极乐的自由。当"圣言"向对它作出响应的圣灵呼唤时,以上

which they would give rise should make their appearance when the Word called to the Spirit responsive to it. ①

And so Christ's first and direct work and achievement, as we can clearly understand it to-day, is the effectual bestowal of 'salvation' as future hope and present possession by arousing a faith in his God and in the Kingdom of God.

And now how can Divination, in respect to such work of Christ, awake in us also, in us who stand so remote in time from Him? How can we, too, come to experience in Him 'holiness made manifest'?

Obviously not through demonstration and proof, by applying some conceptual rule. We cannot suggest any conceptual criterion in the form: 'When the elements x and y are brought together, a revelation results.' It is just this impossibility which makes us speak of 'divination', 'intuitive apprehension'. The experience must come, not by demonstration, but by pure contemplation, through the mind submitting itself unreservedly to a pure 'impression' of the object. For this purpose all that was given and contained in the message and work of Jesus must be combined with the picture of His Person and life and viewed as a whole and in its context with the long and wonderful advance in the religious history of Israel and Judah that was the preparation for it, and with the interplay of diverse tributary lines of development which, even where apparently divergent, ultimately converged upon this as their single culmination. Account must be taken of the elements of 'fulfilment' which the Gospel contains, and due heed given to the attraction and impelling force which it

---

① We can even comprehend thereby the later influx of 'dualistic' or 'gnostic' currents, or at least see how they became possible. A man like Marcion is an extreme 'Jesu-ist' as well as an extreme 'Paul-ist'.

这些,或者相似的术语和教义,以及由它们引发的深刻的反思,就必然会出现。①

所以,就像我们今天所能清楚地理解的,基督的最初的、直接的工作和成就,就是通过唤起人们对他的上帝和天国的信仰,将“救赎”作为将来的希望及当下的财产有效地赠给人们。

那么,就基督的这个工作而言,对神的直觉感受又怎么能在我们的身上苏醒呢?我们这些人在时间上与他相距得如此遥远,我们又怎么能在他身上去逐渐体会到“显露的神圣性”呢?

显然,这不是通过运用某种概念性的规则来论证和证明的。我们无法以这种方式提出概念性的标准:“当X和Y两种因素被放在一起时,就产生了一种启示。”正是这种不可能性,才使得我们谈及了“直觉感受”和“直觉领悟”。这种经验必定不是通过论证,而是通过纯粹的沉思,从心灵本身完全顺从与对对象的纯粹“印象”中得来的。为了这一目的,所有那些在耶稣的教导和工作中所给予和所包含的东西都必须与关于他个人及其生活的图像联系起来,被视为一个整体,并且必须将其前后发展与以色列及犹太的宗教史上漫长而精彩的进步联系起来,这段宗教史就是它的准备,还要把它与发展的各种不同支线之间的相互作用联系起来,即使这些支线明显地互相分歧,最终还是要汇聚到它们唯一的顶点。我们必须考虑《福音书》所包含的有关“完成”的各种因素,也应注意到,由于它与它的犹太的环境的对比或者由于它给这个

① 因此,我们甚至可以理解后来的“二元论”或“诺斯替”潮流的流行,或者至少可以了解它们何以成为可能。像马西昂这样一个人,既是极端的“保罗信徒”,也是极端的“耶稣信徒”。

owed to its contrast with its Judaic environment or to parallels which it bore to this. And all the while, for the full impression to be received, regard is to be paid to the non-rational, the woof of the web, the strange setting of the whole experience, which can nowhere be felt so palpably as in the case of Jesus Christ—how His effect upon the men of his own day rises and ebbs, revealing his spiritual content, on which the salvation of the world depends, ever more and more manifestly, and revealing at the same time that mysteriously growing opposition of powers in which the problem of Job recurs a thousand-fold more urgently—where we have the suffering and the defeat not merely of a righteous person, but of all that is most vitally important for the highest interests of humanity. In fine there is that burden of non-rational, mystical significance, which hangs like a cloud over Golgotha. Whoever can thus immerse himself in contemplation and open his whole mind resolutely to a pure impression of all this combined will surely find growing in him, obedient to an inward standard that defies expression, the pure feeling of 'recognition of holiness', the 'intuition of the eternal in the temporal'. If something eternal, something holy, ever results from the blending and interpenetration of rational and non-rational, purposive and indefinable elements in the way we tried to describe, in the person of Jesus this stands as nowhere else potently and palpably apparent.

And in a very real sense we of the later day are not worse but more fortunately placed for grasping it than Jesus's own contemporaries. Realization of Him through 'surmise (*Ahndung*) of the divine government of the world'① depends essen-tially upon two factors. On the one hand there

① An expression of De Wette. (V. p. 147.)

环境提供的各种类似物，它被赋予了吸引力和魅力。而且，为了接受完整的印象，我们始终都要留意非理性的因素，即这张网的纬线，整个体验的奇异的背景，没有任何地方能够像在耶稣基督那儿被如此清楚地感觉到——他对他的同时代人的影响是怎样起起落落的，越来越清晰地揭示着他的宗教内容，而这宗教内容正是世界得以拯救的依据，与此同时，也揭示了各种力量之间神秘地增长着的对立，在其中，约伯的问题万分紧急地重现出来——在这里，我们不仅为一个正直的人，而且也是为了人类最高利益至关重要的一切东西而遭受苦难和失败。总之，存在着非理性的、神秘意义的负担，它就像乌云一样笼罩在耶稣殉难地(Golgotha)的上空。无论是谁，只要他能将自身沉浸在这样的沉思之中，而且坚定地将自己的心灵对着那种联合起来的所有东西的纯粹印象敞开，就一定能够发现在他内心深处不断生长着的、服从某种蔑视经验的内在标准的、关于"对神圣的辨识"的纯粹感觉，即"对暂时之中的永恒的直觉"。如果某种永恒的东西、某种神圣的东西竟然来自于理性因素与非理性因素、目的性因素和不确定性因素的以我们试图描述的方式的相互混和与相互渗透，那么这种情况没有在什么地方比在耶稣的身上表现得更为强烈，也更为明显。

而且，从真正意义上来看，我们这些后来时代的人，比起耶稣同时代的人，在理解这一点上确实处于更加有利的位置。通过"猜测神对世界的统治"①来认识上帝，根本上取决于两个因素。一方面，要对以色列那种作为联合为一个整体的绝妙的精神史有

① 德韦特语(第五卷，第147页)。

is the general view of the marvellous spiritual history of Israel as a connected whole, with its prophetic and religious development, and with Christ appearing as its culmination. And on the other hand there is the complete life-work and achievement of Christ himself in its entirety. Now in both cases a general comprehensive view is more perfectly to be attained by us to-day than in the time of Christ; for, not only is our historical insight more keen, but we can also see the whole in better perspective at our greater distance. Whoever sinks in contemplation of that great connected development of the Judaic religion which we speak of as the 'Old Covenant up to Christ' must feel the stirrings of an intimation that something Eternal is there, directing and sustaining it and urging it to its consummation. The impression is simply irresistible. And who-ever then goes on to consider how greatly the scene is set for the completion of the whole story and the mighty stature of the personality that is its fulfilment, His firm, unfaltering hold upon God, His unwavering, unfailing righteousness, His certitude of conviction and assurance in action so mysterious and profound, His spiritual fervour and beatitude, the struggles and trustfulness, self-surrender and suffering, and finally the conqueror's death that were His—whoever goes on to consider all this must inevitably conclude: 'That is godlike and divine; that is verily Holiness. If there is a God and if He chose to reveal Himself, He could do it no otherwise than thus.'

Such a conclusion is not the result of logical compulsion; it does not follow from clearly conceived premisses; it is an immediate, underivable judgement of pure recognition, and it follows a premiss that defies exposition and springs directly from an irreducible feeling of the truth. But that, as we have seen, is just the manner in which genuine divination, in the sense of an intuition of religious significance, takes place.

一个普遍的认识，这一精神史伴随着它的预言的、宗教的发展，并且伴随着作为它的发展顶点的基督的出现。另一方面，就是在完整意义上的基督本人的整个毕生的事业和全部的成就。现在，比起基督的时代来，在这两种情形中，一个普遍全面的观点被今天的我们更加完美地把握到了；这不仅仅是因为我们的历史洞察力更加敏锐，而且也因为我们隔着长长的时间距离，可以更好地透视它的整体。无论是谁，只要他沉浸到对犹太宗教的那种相互联系的伟大发展的沉思中去——犹太宗教即我们称之为“到基督为止的旧契约”——都一定会感觉到一种暗示（某种永恒存在的东西）的骚动，指导着、支持着并且催促着它达到完善的极致。这种印象简直就是不可抗拒的。而且，无论是谁，只要他继续想一想，为了其整个故事的完满而设立的背景是多么好，只要想一想作为该故事的完成的基督的人格的重要地位，以及他对上帝的坚定而专注的支持，他的毫不动摇的无穷无尽的正义，他的信仰的明确性以及他在其如此神秘而深奥的行动中所表现出的自信，他精神上的热情与祝福，他的斗争及信赖，忍让与受难，以及最终的征服者（即他）的死亡——任何人，只要他继续去想到以上这些，不可避免地会总结道：“那是与上帝相称的，是神圣的；那肯定就是神圣性。如果真有一个上帝，而且如果他愿意展现自身，那么，没有比他这样去做更好的了。”

这样的结论并不是逻辑上强行得出的结果，它并不遵循于被清楚地构想出来的前提；它是纯粹认识的一种直接的、不可推导的判断，它遵循着一种不可解说的前提，并且直接从一种对真理的无法削减的感觉中涌现出来。但是，诚如我们已看到的，正是在这种方式中，真正的直觉感受即宗教意义上的直觉发生了。

Such an intuition, once granted, issues, for us no less than for the first disciples, necessarily and independently of exegesis or the authority of the early Church, in a series of further intuitions respecting the Person, the Work, and the Words of Christ, and it is the task of theology to render these explicit. Such are the intuitions gained of 'sacred history' in general, of its preparation in prophecy, and of its fulfilment in Jesus's 'Messiahship'—the Being in whom all the religious potentialities of prophet and psalmist and all the anticipatory movements and currents in the old covenant became actualized, in whom all previous development found its culmina-tion, and the evolution of a people at once its real significance and its goal, the completion of its course and the consummation of its allotted historical task. And there are further intuitions which have the same origin: the intuition by which we recognize in Christ the portrayal and presentment of God, divining in His agony and victory, His redemptive search and love, the very stamp and signature of God; the intuition of his 'Sonship', by which we recognize Christ as the 'only begotten', the called, the fully empowered with deity, as one whose being, only made possible and intelligible of God, repeats and reveals the divine nature in human fashion; or the intuition of the 'new covenant', of adoption and reconciliation through Christ, of His lifework and self-surrender to God as sacrifice and as a warrant of divine grace. And last, not least, the intuition of the 'covering' and 'propitiating' Mediator. For the abyss between creature and Creator, '*profanum*' and '*sanctum*', sin and holiness, is not diminished

这种直觉一旦被承认,就会必然而且独立地生发出在一系列的与基督本人、他的工作、他的圣言有关的进一步的直觉中,关于早期教会的注解与典籍,这一点对于首批门徒和对于我们是一样,而且,把这一系列的直觉说清楚正是神学的任务。这些直觉总体上是从关于它在预言中的准备的"神圣的历史"中和它在耶稣的"弥赛亚身份"身份中的实现的"神圣的历史"中得到的——耶稣的"弥赛亚身份"就是上帝,在他的身上,先知与赞美诗作者的所有宗教潜能以及《旧约》中的一切预期的运动和潮流都变成了实在,在他的身上,先前所有的发展都达到极致,一个民族的进化立刻就找到了它的真正意义和目标、它发展进程的终点以及它被分派的历史任务的圆满完成。而且还有更多的直觉,它们有着共同的起源:有这种直觉,通过它,我们在基督身上认出了对上帝的描绘与陈述,在他的痛苦和胜利中,在他的救赎的探求和仁爱中,猜测出了上帝的标记和信号;还有那种关于基督的"圣子身份"的直觉,通过它,我们认出基督是"唯一的圣子",受神召唤,充满了神力,只有他的存在才能使上帝成为可能并且能够被认识,在人类的形式中不断重复和揭示神性的本质;还有那种对"新约"的直觉,对通过基督被神接纳并且人神和解的直觉,以及对基督的毕生事业,以及作为牺牲、作为对神的恩赐的一种证明而自动服从于上帝的直觉。还有最后的但绝非最不重要的一种直觉,即对那个"庇护的"、"抚慰的"中保[1]的直觉。因为,随着对基督福音的更深的认识,被造物与造物主之间、罪恶与神圣之间

〔1〕 中保,指耶稣,《圣经·新约》称他是上帝和人之间的中保。

but increased by that deeper knowledge that comes from the Gospel of Christ: and, as a result of the emotion spontaneously stirred in the recognition of it, that in which 'the holy' stands self-revealed is taken here, as in other cases, both as the refuge from, and the means by which to approach, Holiness. And this impulsion of the mind to see in Christ mediator and propitiator may be roused to seek expression spontaneously, even in cases where it is not—as in Hebrew and primitive religion—prepared for and sustained by a traditional cult and mysticism of 'sacrifice'. That is, it is a natural religious instinct, due to the pressure of the numinous experience and to nothing else.

We are not, then, to deplore the fact that intuitions of this kind find a place in the doctrines of the Christian faith: they do so of necessity. What we must deplore is, that their free character, as springing from 'divination', is so generally misinterpreted; that too commonly we dogmatize and theorize about them, deducing them from 'necessary truths' of exegesis or dogma (which are in fact always dubious), and so failing to recognize them for what they are, free-floating utterances and trial flights at expression of the numinous feeling; and that too often we give them an emphasis which puts them unwarrantably at the centre of our religious interest, a place which nothing but the experience itself of God ought to occupy.

In this connexion we may draw attention to what are commonly called the 'miracles' of Christ, but which we may perhaps more aptly call, in the words of Mark xvi. 20, 'signs following' (έ πακολουθοûντα σημεῖα). It is not upon them primarily that the experience of 'holiness made manifest' is based; but, where there has been real 'divination', there certain traits in the portrait of Christ come to acquire a fresh significance, as confirmation of the divination rather than its ground. I refer to the signs of exalted spiritual power over

的鸿沟不是被缩小,而是被扩大了:而且,作为在对这种直觉的认知中所自发引起的情感的结果,在这儿就像在其他情况中一样,这种在其中,“神圣”得以自我揭示的东西,既被当做来自神圣的庇护,又被当做接近神圣的手段。想在耶稣基督身上发现人与神之间的中介者与抚慰者的这种心灵的冲动,或许自发地要表现出来,即使在有些情况中,它没有被传统仪式和关于“牺牲”神秘主义所准备好并且保持下来——在希伯来与原始宗教中就是如此。也就是说,这是一种自然的宗教本能,它来自于神秘体验的压力,而不是来自任何别的东西。

不过,我们并不去痛惜这类直觉在基督教信仰的教义中有了一席之地:它们这样做是必然的。我们应该痛惜的是,这些直觉的丰富特征——当它们从“直觉感受”中涌现出来的时候——普遍遭到歪曲;我们常常将这些直觉加以教条化和理论化,从《圣经》注释或教义的“必然真理”的角度(它们实际上往往是值得怀疑的)来推断这些直觉,因而未能认识出它们究竟是什么——它们在对神秘感受的表达上的自由随意的言说和大胆的尝试。我们也常常过于强调这些直觉,这种强调毫无根据地把它们置于我们宗教兴趣的中心,而本来应该占据这个中心的不是别的,只应该是对上帝的经验本身。

关于这一点,我们应当留意通常所谓的基督的“神迹”,不过我们或许更应该用《马可福音》第16章第20节的用语,称之为伴随着“道”的“神迹”(ἐπακολουθοῦντα σημεῖα)。对于“神性显明”的体验,并不是主要建立在这些“神迹”的基础之上;但是,哪里有真正“直觉感受”,在那里,在基督肖像中的确定特性就会获得新的意义,它们与其说是直觉感受的基础,不如说是对直觉感受的肯定。我指的是在耶稣

nature to be detected in the portrait of Jesus. These have their parallels elsewhere in the history of religion: in the great prophets of Israel, for instance, they are shown in the form of that visionary intuition and boding foreknowledge with which the prophet was endowed for his calling. In the life of Christ they recur unmistakably as 'gifts of the Spirit', raised to a supreme power. These things are not 'miracles', for they are powers of the spirit, and so are as 'natural' as our will itself is, with its control over our body. But they clearly only come upon the scene where the spirit is itself exalted to its fullest stature and in its fullest vitality, and are most of all to be expected where the spirit is in closest and most intimate union with its eternal cause and foundation, and is thereby set free to the highest it can itself achieve.

It is, in the last place, clear that it is in the Passion and death of Christ that the objects of the strongest religious intuition must be sought. If His Incarnation, His mission, and the manner of His life come to be considered as a piece of selfrevelation, in which an eternal Will of Love is mirrored, before all else is this Love and Faith seen accomplished in the Passion. The Cross becomes in an absolute sense the 'mirror of the eternal Father' (*speculum aeterni Patris*); and not of the 'Father' alone—the highest rational interpretation of the holy—but of Holiness as such. For what makes Christ in a special sense the summary and climax of the course of antecedent religious evolution is pre-eminently this—that in His life, suffering, and death is repeated in classic and absolute form that most mystical of all the problems of the Old Covenant, the problem of the guiltless suffering of the righteous, which re-echoes again and again so mysteriously from Jeremiah and deutero-Isaiah on through Job and the Psalms. The 38th chapter of Job is a prophecy of Golgotha. And on Golgotha the solution of the problem, already adumbrated in

的肖像中可以分辨出来的那种超越自然的昂扬的精神力量的神迹。在宗教史上,别的地方也有这种类似物:比方说,在以色列的那些伟大的先知身上,它们以一种梦幻直觉和先兆预见的形式表现出来,这些都是先知为了他的召唤而被赋予的。在基督的生涯中,这些作为"圣灵的天赋"而明确无误地不断重现,并上升为最高的力量。这些东西并不是"奇迹",因为它们是精神的力量,而且就像我们的意志本身那样"自然"地控制着我们的身体。但是,只有当精神上升到它的最高地位并且处于最有生机的地方,它们才会清楚地出现,而且,只有当精神与它的永恒的起因与基础处于最亲密无间的联合中,并因此可以被释放到它所能达到的最大高度时,人们才有可能见到这些神迹。

最后,很显然,人们必须在基督的受难与死亡中去追寻最强烈的宗教直觉的对象。如果他的道成肉身、他的使命以及他的生活方式被看成是一种自我启示,其中反映了一种永恒的爱的意志,那么这种爱和信仰被看做在基督受难中实现是先于其他任何东西。在某种绝对的意义上,那个钉死基督的十字架就成了"永恒之父的写照"(*speculum aeterni Patris*);这不是单纯对"天父"的写照——对神圣的最高的理性解释——而是神圣性本身的写照。因为,使基督在某种特殊意义上成为先前宗教演化进程的总结和顶峰的,主要正是这一点——在他的生命、受难与死亡中,总是以传统而绝对的形式重复着《旧约》所有问题中最神秘的那一个,这个问题就是好人无辜受难,这个问题从《耶利米书》、《申命记》和《以赛亚书》起,一次又一次神秘地回响,一直持续到《约伯记》和《诗篇》。《约伯记》的第 38 章是对耶稣受难地的预言。而在耶稣受难地,这个已经在《约伯记》中预示过的问题

Job, is repeated and surpassed. It lay, as we saw, entirely in the non-rational aspect of deity, and yet was none the less a solution. In Job the suffering of the righteous found its significance as the classic and crucial case of the revelation, more immediately actual and in more palpable proximity than any other, of the transcendent mysteriousness and 'beyondness' of God. The Cross of Christ, that monogram of the eternal mystery, is its completion. Here rational are enfolded with non-rational elements, the revealed commingled with the unrevealed, the most exalted love with the most aweinspiring 'wrath' of the numen, and therefore, in applying to the Cross of Christ the category 'holy', Christian religious feeling has given birth to a religious intuition profounder and more vital than any to be found in the whole history of religion.

This is what must be borne in mind in the comparison of religions, when we seek to decide which of them is the most perfect. The criterion of the value of a religion as religion cannot ultimately be found in what it has done for culture, nor in its relation to the 'limits of the reason' or the 'limits of humanity' (which, forsooth, are presumed capable of being drawn in advance apart from reference to religion itself!), nor in any of its external features. It can only be found in what is the innermost essence of religion, the idea of holiness as such, and in the degree of perfection with which any given religion realizes this.

There can naturally be no defence of the worth and validity of such religious intuitions of pure feeling that will convince a person who is not prepared to take the religious consciousness itself for granted. Mere general argument, even moral demonstrations, are in this case useless, are indeed for obvious reasons impossible from the outset. On the other hand the criticisms and confutations attempted by such a person are unsound from the start. His weapons are far too short to touch his adversary, for the assailant is always standing right outside the arena! But if these intuitions, these separate

的解决被重复和超越了。正如我们所见,它完全存在于神性的非理性方面,而且不过是一种解决方案罢了。在《约伯记》中,好人受难是作为一种传统的、至关重要的启示而获得意义的,在超验的神秘性和上帝的“不可及性”方面,比其他任何启示都更加直接实在,也更触手可及。基督的十字架,那个永恒神秘的字母组合,就是它的极致。在这里,理性的因素与非理性的因素缠绕在一起,已被揭示的与未被揭示的混合在一起,对神圣者最崇高的爱意与神圣者的最令人敬畏的“忿怒”交织在一起,因此,在把“神圣”范畴应用于基督的十字架方面,基督教的宗教情感中就产生出一种宗教直觉,它比整个宗教史中所发现的任何东西都更加意义深远、更加富有活力。

当我们比较各种宗教、试图从中确定它们谁是最完善的时,有一点必须牢记于心。一种宗教,作为宗教的价值标准不能在它为文化所做的事情中最终发现,也不能在它与“理性极限”或“人性极限”的关系中找到(的确,有人认为不参考宗教本身就假定能够预先描绘出人性的极限!),还不能在它的任何外部特征中找到。宗教的价值只能在它最内在的本质中找到,例如在关于神圣的观念中以及在任何宗教对神圣观念的认识的完善程度中找到。

很自然地,人们无法对这种纯粹感受的宗教直觉的价值的有效性进行辩护,来说服那种不打算将宗教意识本身视为当然的人。纯粹一般的辩论,甚至是道德的论证,在这种情形下都是无用的,而且,因为明显的理由,从一开始就是不可能的。另一方面,这种人试图进行的批判和诘难从一开始就是不健全的。因为这位攻击者总是站在决斗场之外,他的武器太短了,根本触不到他的对手!但是,如果这些直觉,这些对福音故事及其核心人物

responses to the impress upon the spirit of the Gospel story and the central Person of it—if these intuitions are immune from rational criticism, they are equally unaffected by the fluctuating results of biblical exegesis and the laboured justifications of historical apologetics. For they are possible with-out these, springing, as they do, from first-hand personal divination. [①]

① Compare with this chapter my book Reich Gottes und Menschensohn (The Kingdom of God and the Son of Man).

的精神上的印象所作出的各不相同的反应——如果这些直觉免于理性的批判，那么它同样也不应受到圣经解释的变动结果的影响，不应受到历史上护教学的吃力辩护的影响。正是因为没有这些东西，直觉才成为可能，就像它们本来所是，直觉是从直接的个人直觉感受中涌现出来的。[①]

① 将这一章与我的《神国与人子》（Reich Grottes und Menschsohn）一书相互参看。

CHAPTER XXI

History And The *A Priori* In Religion: Summary And Conclusion

We have considered 'the holy' on the one hand as an *a priori* category of mind, and on the other as manifesting itself in outward appearance. The contrast here intended is exactly the same as the common contrast of inner and outer, general and special revelation. And if we take 'reason' (*ratio*) as an inclusive term for all cognition which arises in the mind from principles native to it, in contrast to those based upon facts of history, then we may say that the distinction between holiness as an *a priori* category and holiness as revealed in outward appearance is much the same as that between 'reason' (in this wide sense) and history.

Every religion which, so far from being a mere faith in traditional authority, springs from personal assurance and inward convincement (i. e. from an inward first-hand cognition of its truth)—as Christianity does in a unique degree—must presuppose principles in the mind enabling it to be independently recognized as true. ① But these principles

---

① The attestation of such principles is the '*testimonium Spiritus Sancti internum*' of which we have already spoken. And this must clearly be itself immediate and self-warranted, else there would be need of another 'witness of the Holy Spirit' to attest the truth of the first, and so on *ad infinitum*.

第二十一章　历史与宗教中的先验：总结与结论

一方面，我们把"神圣"看做精神的一个先验范畴，另一方面又把它看做把自身展现在外表中的东西。此处有意作出的这种对比，完全等同于内在与外在、一般与特殊的启示的之间的一般对比。而且，如果我们把"理性"(*ratio*)看成是包含了从心灵内在的准则中产生出来的所有认识的一个术语，与之相对照的是那些建立在历史事实基础上的东西，那么我们就可以说，作为一种先验范畴的神圣与作为从外在表象中揭示出来的神圣之间的区别，同"理性"(在广义上)与历史的区别没有什么两样。

任何一种宗教，只要不是对传统典籍的一种纯粹信仰，而是来自个人的确信和内在的信服(也就是来自对它的真理的一种内在的直接认识)——基督教尤其如此——就必须在思想中预设一些原则，从而使该宗教能够被独立地承认为是正确的①。但是这

① 对这些原则的证明就是我们已经谈过的内在的神圣精神的验证。这个证据本身就必须清楚地表现为是直接的和自我确证的，否则就需要另一个"关于圣灵的证据"来证明第一个证据的真理性，如此下去，以至无穷(*ad infinitum*)。

must be a priori ones, not to be derived from 'experience' or 'history'. It has little meaning, however edifying it may sound, to say that they are inscribed upon the heart by the pencil of the Holy Spirit 'in history'. For whence comes the assurance that it was the pencil of the 'Holy Spirit' that wrote, and not that of a deceiving spirit of imposture, or of the 'tribal fantasy' of anthropology? Such an assertion is itself a presumption that it is possible to distinguish the signature of the Spirit from others, and thus that we have an *a priori* notion of what is of the Spirit independently of history.

And there is a further consideration. There is something presupposed by history as such—not only the history of mind or spirit, with which we are here concerned—which alone makes it history, and that is the existence of a *quale*, something with a potentiality of its own, capable of *becoming*, in the special sense of coming to be that to which it was predisposed and predetermined. An oak-tree can become, and thus have a sort of 'history'; whereas a heap of stones cannot. The random addition and subtraction, displacement and rearrangement, of elements in a mere aggregation can certainly be followed in narrative form, but this is not in the deeper sense an historical narrative. We only have the history of a people in proportion as it enters upon its course equipped with an endowment of talents and tendencies; it must already *be something* if it is really to *become* anything. And biography is a lamentable and unreal business in the case of a man who has no real unique potentiality of his own, no special idiosyncrasy, and is therefore a mere point of intersection for various fortuitous causal series, acted upon, as it were, from without. Biography is only a real narration of a real life where, by the interplay of stimulus and experience on the one side and predisposition and natural endowment on the other, something individual and unique comes into being, which is therefore neither the result of a 'mere self-unfolding' nor yet the sum of mere traces and impressions, written from without from

些原则必须是先验的，而不能源自“经验”与“历史”。无论听起来是多么的有益，说这些原则是由“历史上的”圣灵之笔刻写到心灵上去的，都没有什么意义。因为，说它们是由“圣灵”之笔所写的，而不是欺诈之灵的欺诈之笔或人类学所谓的“部落的幻想”之笔所写的，这种确信从何来？这样的一个断言本身就是一个假设，它认为人们可以把圣灵的笔迹与其他的笔迹区别开来，由此我们就拥有了一个关于什么是独立于历史的圣灵的先验的概念。

此外，还存在着更进一步的考察。存在着某种被历史预料到了的东西——不仅仅是我们在这里所谈论的心灵或精神的历史——这个东西自己就能够成为历史，而且那就是某种特质的存在，即某种具有自身潜力的东西，它能够成长——这个成长，在这儿的特殊意义是指它能逐渐变成为被预先安排和预先确定好了的那种东西。一棵橡树可以成长，因而也就具有某种“历史”，而一堆石头就不行。在叙事的方式中，对一些纯粹堆积起来的素材当然可以作随意的增删、替换和重组，但在更深的意义上，这并不是一种历史的叙事。只有当一个由各种才能和倾向的资质装备起来的民族进入了自己的发展历程，我们才依其程度得到这个民族的历史；如果它真的想要成长为任何东西，它必须已经是某种东西。对于一个没有自己真正独特的潜能，没有特殊素质的人来说，他的传记将是一件可悲而且失实的东西，它只不过是各种各样的偶然因果序列的交叉点，遵照着宛如来自外部的影响行事。只有通过两个方面，一方面是刺激和经验的相互影响，另一方面是先天倾向和自然禀赋的相互作用，某种个人的、独特的东西逐渐形成了，因而这个东西既不是“单纯的自我展现”的结果，也不是从外部一点一滴地书写到某块白板

moment to moment upon a *tabula rasa*. In short, to propose a history of mind is to presuppose a mind or spirit determinately qualified; to profess to give a history of religion is to presuppose a spirit specifically qualified for religion.

There are, then, three factors in the process by which religion comes into being in history. First, the interplay of pre-disposition and stimulus, which in the historical development of man's mind actualizes the potentiality in the former, and at the same time helps to determine its form. Second, the groping recognition, by virtue of this very disposition, of specific portions of history as the manifestation of 'the holy', with consequent modification of the religious experience already attained both in its quality and degree. And third, on the basis of the other two, the achieved fellowship with 'the holy' in knowing, feeling, and willing. Plainly, then, religion is only the offspring of history in so far as history on the one hand develops our disposition for knowing the holy, and on the other is itself repeatedly the manifestation of the holy. 'Natural' religion, in contrast to historical, does not exist, and still less does 'innate' religion. ①

A priori cognitions are not such as every one does have— such would be *innate* cognitions—but such as every one is capable of having. The loftier *a priori* cognitions are such as —while every one is indeed capable of having them—do not, as experience teaches us, occur spontaneously, but rather are 'awakened' through the instrumentality of other more highly endowed natures. In relation to these the universal 'predisposition' is merely a faculty of *receptivity* and a *principle of judgement and acknowledgement*, not a capacity to produce the cognitions in question for oneself independently. This latter capacity is confined to those specially 'endowed'. And this 'endowment' is the universal disposition on a higher level

① For the distinction between 'innate' and a priori cf. R. Otto, *Religions-philosophie*, p. 42.

上的各种纯粹痕迹和印象的总和，传记才能成为对真正生活的真正叙述。简而言之，要想写一部思想史就要预先假定一种确实合格的思想或精神；声称要写一部宗教史就要预先假定一种对于宗教来说特别够格的精神。

于是，就存在着三种要素，通过它们，宗教在历史的进程中得以形成。首先是先天倾向和刺激的相互作用，它在人类思想的历史发展过程中实现了前者的可能性，同时还帮助它确定了自己的形式。其次，正是依靠这种倾向，作为"神圣"的表现，人们对于历史的某些特殊部份的不断探索的认识，随着人们已经获得的宗教经验在性质和程度上都作了相应修正。第三，在前两者的基础上，在认识、感受和意愿方面，与"神圣"达成了伙伴关系。因此，坦白地说，宗教只是历史的产物，因为一方面，历史发展了我们认识神圣的倾向性，另一方面，它本身就是不断重复的对神圣的表现。与历史宗教相对的"自然"宗教是不存在的，"先天的"宗教更不可能存在。①

先验认识并不是那种人人都有的认识——这应当是先天认识——而是那种人人都能够拥有的认识。正如经验所教导我们的，更高级的先验认识——尽管每个人确实都能够拥有它们——并不是自发地出现的，倒更应说是借助于其他更高级的先天性质而被"唤醒"的。与这些认识比较起来，普遍的"先天倾向"仅仅是一种感受的能力，一种判断和确认的原则，而不是为自身独立地产生出被讨论的认识的一种能力。后者这种能力只局限于那些有特殊"先天禀赋"的人身上。这种"先天禀赋"就是在更高层次、

① 关于"先天"和先验的区别，请参见 R·奥托《宗教哲学》第 42 页。

and at a higher power, differing from it in quality as well as in degree. The same thing is very evident in the sphere of art: what appears in the multitude as mere receptiveness, the capacity of response and judgement by trained aesthetic taste, reappears at the level of the *artist* as invention, creation, composition, the original production of genius. This difference of level and power, e. g. in musical composition, seen in the contrast between what is a mere capacity for musical experience and the actual production and revelation of music, is obviously something more than a difference of degree. It is very similar in the domain of the religious consciousness, religious production, and revelation. Here, too, most men have only the 'predisposition', in the sense of a receptiveness and susceptibility to religion and a capacity for freely recognizing and judging religious truth at first hand. The 'Spirit' is only 'universal' in the form of the '*testimonium Spiritus internum*' (and this again only '*ubi ipsi visum fuit*'). The higher stage, not to be derived from the first stage of mere receptivity, is in the sphere of religion *the prophet*. The prophet corresponds in the religious sphere to the creative artist in that of art: he is the man in whom the Spirit shows itself alike as the power to hear the 'voice within' and the power of divination, and in each case appears as a creative force. Yet the prophet does not represent the highest stage. We can think of a third, yet higher, beyond him, a stage of revelation as underivable from that of the prophet as was his from that of common men. We can look, bevond the prophet, to one in whom is found the Spirit in all its plenitude, and who at the same time in His person and in His performance is become most completely the object of divination, in whom Holiness is recognized apparent.

Such a one is more than Prophet. He is the Son.

更大能量上的那种普遍的倾向,它在程度上和性质上都不同于上述的那种能力。在艺术领域里也存在着同样十分明显的情况:那种在大众身上仅仅表现为感受性的东西,也就是通过训练过的审美鉴赏所作出的反应和判断的那种能力,到了艺术家的层次,就以发明、创造、作品以及天才的原创物等形式再现出来。这种在层次上和能量上的区别,显然不仅仅是程度上的区别,例如在音乐创作中,就是音乐体验与音乐的实际创作以及音乐表现之间的区别。在宗教意识、宗教生产和宗教启示的领域中,情况非常相似。在这里,大多数人也只具有"先天倾向",也就是对宗教的感受性和敏感性,以及一种自由地直接认识和判断宗教真理的能力。仅仅在"内在精神验证"的形式中,"圣灵"才是"普遍的"。更高的阶段在宗教领域中表现为先知,它不是从单纯感受的初级阶段中发展出来的。宗教领域里的先知相当于艺术领域里有创造性的艺术家:他是这样的一个人,在他身上,"圣灵"把它自身既展现为倾听"内在声音"的力量,又展现为直觉感受的力量,而在每一种情况中,它都表现为一种创造的力量,但是,先知并没有表现最高的阶段。我们可以设想一种比先知阶段更高的、超越了先知阶段的第三个阶段,它是一个启示的阶段,正如先知不能从普通人的阶段发展而来一样,它不能从先知阶段发展而来。超越先知,我们能够看到这样一个人,在他的身上人们可以发现完完全全的圣灵,而且与此同时,他本人以及他的行为都最完整地变成了直觉感受的对象,在他身上,神圣性能够被清晰地认出来。

这样的一个人决不仅仅是先知。他就是圣子。

译者后记

翻译工作的繁累只有做过此项工作的人才能够理解。

由于这套书要做成中英文对照的方式,我个人认为行文的简易是至关重要的,如果还像西方语言一样,一个句子套着一个句子,恐怕中文本就没有办法与英文本对照了。但是,如果把所有的复合句都打散,势必会导致原作本义的流失。长句与短句如何取舍,这是我在翻译中最头痛的事情,好在这本书不是太长,而且我把后面的附录也去掉了,这样,精简的文本就有可能获得相对好的对照效果。

对于原著作者鲁道夫·奥托(1869～1937年)以及这本书本身,我再多说两句。奥托本人是德国路德宗信徒,曾经在格丁根大学受业于著名的神学家阿尔布雷希特·里茨尔,后来在马堡大学神学系做教授,直到去世。奥托本人不仅是一个卓越的思想家,而且还是一位大胆的旅行家,甚至在格丁根大学读书期间,他就到巴勒斯坦和埃及去亲自见识科普特教会和穆斯林的宗教仪式。后来两次到印度,其间还到过缅甸、日本和中国,亲自观察了各种宗教的形式与仪式。在奥托的这本名著中,他认为在宗教经验中存在着西方的社会理论或者心理学理论所解释不清的东西,他将其以 numinous 命名,这个词来源于拉丁文 *numen*,含义是

“神”、“鬼”、“令人敬畏的东西”等，因此，the numinous 的含义就是“神秘者”。这种神秘者既是理性的，又是非理性的，而且非理性的成分居多，而奥托的任务就在于将这一概念中的理性成分析出，留下真正的非理性的原初含义。至于这本名著，我想借用加里·特朗普的一句话来作一简单的总结：“奥托在理性上的奋斗是勇敢的，《神圣者的观念》一书对认识到宗教现象之独特性和不可还原性的宗教研究者而言仍不失为敏锐的哲学分析的典范。”

丁建波

2006 年 9 月 18 日

《西方学术经典文库》(第一辑)

功利主义	[英]约翰·斯图亚特·穆勒
诗学·诗艺	[古希腊]亚里士多德 [古罗马]贺拉斯
经济发展理论	[美]约瑟夫·阿洛伊斯·熊彼特
经济学原理	[英]阿尔弗雷德·马歇尔
国民财富的性质与原理	[英]亚当·斯密
联邦党人文集	[美]亚历山大·汉密尔顿
就业、利息和货币通论	[英]约翰·梅纳德·凯恩斯
尼各马可伦理学	[古希腊]亚里士多德
道德情操论	[英]亚当·斯密
君主论	[意]尼科洛·马基雅弗利
新教伦理与资本主义精神	[德]马克斯·韦伯
古代法	[英]亨利·萨姆奈·梅因
第一哲学沉思集	[法]勒内·笛卡儿
查拉图斯特拉如是说	[德]弗里德里希·威廉·尼采
哲学研究	[英]路德维希·维特根斯坦
实践理性批判	[德]伊曼努尔·康德
社会契约论	[法]让·雅克·卢梭
理想国	[古希腊]柏拉图
心理学原理	[美]威廉·詹姆斯
精神现象学	[德]威廉·弗里德里希·黑格尔
神圣者的观念	[德]鲁道夫·奥托
小逻辑	[德]威廉·弗里德里希·黑格尔

论人类不平等的起源	[法]让·雅克·卢梭
道德形而上学基础	[德]伊曼努尔·康德
人性论	[英]戴维·休谟
政府论	[英]约翰·洛克
论法的精神	[法]查尔斯·路易斯·孟德斯鸠
代议制政府	[英]约翰·斯图亚特·穆勒
英国法与文艺复兴	[英]弗雷德里克·威廉·梅特兰
法律社会学基本原理	[奥]尤根·埃利希
论美国民主	[法]夏尔·阿列克西·德·托克维尔
原始社会结构与功能	[英]A. R. 拉德克利夫-布朗
政治学	[古希腊]亚里士多德
罗马帝国编年史	[古罗马]科尔涅里乌斯·塔西佗
普通语言学教程	[瑞士]费尔迪南·德·索绪尔
货币哲学	[德]格奥尔格·西梅尔
法理学讲演录	[英]约翰·奥斯丁
思想录	[法]布莱兹·帕斯卡
利维坦	[英]托马斯·霍布斯
意识形态与乌托邦	[德]卡尔·曼海姆
忏悔录	[古罗马]圣·奥古斯丁
西太平洋上的航海者	[英]布罗尼斯拉夫·马林诺夫斯基
历史学:理论和实际	[意]贝内德托·克罗齐
逻辑哲学论	[英]路得维希·维特根斯坦